The
Professional
Secretary's
Handbook

Revised Edition

The Professional Secretary's Handbook

Revised Edition

Houghton Mifflin Company

Boston / New York

Material in Chapter 14 having to do with the accounting process and bank reconciliation is based on information found in *Introduction to Financial Accounting* by Kirkland A. Wilcox and Joseph G. San Miguel. Copyright © 1984 by Harper & Row, Publishers, Inc. Reprinted by permission of HarperCollins Publishers Inc.

Library of Congress Cataloging in Publication Data
The Professional secretary's handbook. — Rev. ed.
    p.   cm.
  Includes index.
  ISBN 0-395-66979-0
  1. Office practice — Automation.   2. Secretaries.
HF5547.5.P7   1993   93-5055
651.3′ 741—dc20   CIP

Manufactured in the United States of America

MP   10   9   8   7   6   5

Contents

Preface

The Professional Secretary's Handbook, Revised Edition, is a detailed and highly useful guide to the modern office. The original edition of *The Professional Secretary's Handbook* broke new ground in addressing the needs of the modern office. It was the first book of its kind to cover many aspects of the newly emerging electronic office. Our new edition expands that coverage, updating the information to reflect a decade's worth of progress in office technology.

The first edition discussed recent innovations that may have been at the time unavailable to the secretary or of peripheral importance to the more traditional concerns of office operation. Word processors, fax machines, and electronic mail, now commonplace in most offices, were either brand-new and rather rare or still over the horizon. In the past ten years these technologies have evolved to the point where they have become essential to a secretary's job. Knowledge of their operation is now a critical prerequisite to professional performance. The newly written sections on these vital subjects are a response to technology's higher profile in today's workplace.

While taking into account the importance of technology, this revision also acknowledges the important role that traditional office procedures continue to play in the secretary's job. Conventional mail, telephone usage, scheduling of meetings and appointments, accounting, travel planning, and similar standardized matters still form an integral part of secretarial responsibilities and are accordingly dealt with in detail in this book.

Indeed, certain aspects of the secretary's job remain unchanged no matter how much technology alters its overall contours. The ability to communicate in a clear, literate, and effective manner is still of the first importance, regardless of whether the information is communicated by memo, letter, or electronic mail. In the pages of *The Professional Secretary's Handbook, Revised Edition,* you will find a Business Style Guide and a chapter on Business English that can help you achieve this professional level of communication. Documents that are well written and skillfully produced are a credit to the persons who create them and to the company from which they emanate.

The Professional Secretary's Handbook, Revised Edition, not only provides information and guidance that can sharpen secretarial skills for improved work performance, but it also looks to the future, providing help in furthering the opportunities for career development. This Handbook offers a special career advancement section with information on education, professional examinations, and job search.

This edition has been newly designed to make the information it contains even more accessible. The text is enhanced by numerous tables, sample documents, drawings, and photographs. Updated in both content and design, *The Professional Secretary's Handbook, Revised Edition,* is an ideal office resource.

The Editors

The Professional Secretary's Handbook

Revised Edition

1

The Secretarial Profession

THE ROLE OF THE SECRETARY in today's office environment has changed dramatically with the introduction of high technology and with changing attitudes toward the office worker's function. There is no standardization within the secretarial field nor is there a clear list of responsibilities for a particular job title. In addition to having office proficiency, secretaries now must be able to work independently and make more decisions within the scope of their individual responsibilities. Instead of merely "taking care of" their supervisors, today's secretaries are taking on aspects of their supervisors' jobs. Secretaries make an important contribution to business, academia, human services, and government. The secretarial profession is unique in that its scope is as diversified as the number of businesses and agencies that require office workers.

A job description of general secretarial duties might well include the following:

- Answer customer correspondence
- Gather research data for reports
- Prepare statistical reports involving sales figures or budgetary information
- Attend meetings in place of supervisor and report activities that took place
- Set up conferences and meetings
- Purchase office equipment and participate in the evaluation and selection of some automated office systems
- Write a company newsletter
- Keep department expenditure records in accordance with a budget
- Transcribe documents from dictated media
- Make travel arrangements and plan itineraries

- Read and sort incoming mail and answer it when necessary
- Maintain and organize filing systems
- Take minutes at company meetings
- Make appointments
- Acquaint new employees with company systems and equipment
- Supervise one or more employees

Thus the duties required of today's secretary are far different from those of the stenographer who, in the past, was neither expected nor advised to use independent judgment and initiative in making substantive decisions. Nowhere is this difference more apparent than in the definition of *secretary* written by Professional Secretaries International:

> an executive assistant who possesses a mastery of office skills, who demonstrates the ability to assume responsibility without direct supervision, who exercises initiative and judgment and who makes decisions within the scope of assigned authority.

Office automation has permanently affected the role of the secretary. With the continued development of new telecommunications equipment, secretaries now must be prepared to learn new and more technologically oriented procedures. The secretary who has a fear of computers will not survive long in today's office. The widespread introduction of this new office technology has created many new career paths for the secretary. Many companies have established word processing centers that handle standardized contracts, reports, and proposals. As a result, the position of word processing supervisor and trainer has become common in large organizations. Depending on the sophistication of the equipment itself, word processing can be highly technical and can require some data processing knowledge. Equipment like the laser printer and graphics terminal is part of the word processing center. If the word processing equipment is connected to the company's mainframe computer, access to confidential information and password-protected documents may be the responsibility of the word processing supervisor.

How can you keep up with office automation? Many courses are available for those interested in word processing and data processing. Or, when your company installs word processing equipment, appropriate training will usually be provided by the vendor. Make sure you are trained on the new equipment and that you keep up with the ever-changing, ever-improving software. Computer technology is an integral part of most offices.

PROFESSIONAL SECRETARIAL COMPETENCY

Education has become an important factor for today's secretary. Many secretarial jobs require a college background as well as technical skills. For that reason, continuing education is a must for the secretary aspiring to advance to a higher professional level. More and more companies have made tuition assistance available for employees at the secretarial level to encourage career advancement. The abilities discussed in the next paragraphs are basic requirements for most secretarial jobs.

Business Writing

You have to be able to write effectively, clearly, and correctly. Since most business communications are read by a number of people inside and outside the organization, the content of any outgoing document must be grammatically correct, concise, and easy to understand. Many guides designed to help you enhance your writing ability are available. Along with a basic writing guide, you should also have a dictionary, a style manual, and a thesaurus at hand. In many ways, business writing is like newspaper reporting. If you follow the "who," "what," "when," "where," and "why" formula used by reporters, you will be able to cover every essential angle of your communication.

If you have trouble with writing, many courses are open to you—some of which are geared specifically to the needs of the administrative assistant or secretary. A course in business writing is a sound investment for your career. It will open up other career opportunities and make you more efficient and effective in your current position.

Knowledge of Business Math and Accounting

Knowing basic math is a necessity in a business environment. Many executives depend on the capability of administrative personnel to compile reports involving percentages of increase and decrease in sales, to perform departmental bookkeeping, or to write budget variance reports. In many cases, a knowledge of simple accounting techniques can mean the difference in job status between a secretary and an administrative or executive assistant. Chapter 14, "Accounting and Data Processing," has been written to assist you with basic, on-the-job accounting procedures.

Organization and Planning

Time management and organizational skills are solid ingredients for success in any secretarial position. The ability to set priorities and juggle several different tasks at once is necessary to command an efficient workflow. People have different ways of organizing their tasks. Some choose what they like to do first or what they don't like to do; others choose what is easiest; still others what is complicated. A common way to organize one's time is to make a list of things to do and set the order of priority for each item on the list. Some workers plan their time in blocks with different activities scheduled for certain times of the day. Whatever method you choose, it is important that you complete your tasks on time.

Since your time is valuable, it is necessary that other people in the office understand it and realize that you must complete your own scheduled activities on target. If you are in the middle of a detailed, high-priority project and someone else wants to speak with you, schedule a time later on when you can meet with that person. While interruptions are part of your job, you nevertheless need to determine the importance of each interruption. Otherwise, you will never get anything done. If your workload is too heavy and help is at hand, take advantage of it. And don't be afraid to delegate tasks that can make your own job easier. If you try to do everything yourself in a short time, you may not produce the kind of quality work you can be proud of.

Keyboarding and Shorthand

Keyboarding speed is still a prerequisite for many secretarial jobs. Top-level administrative positions often require a speed of 60 words per minute or above. Although considered by many passé, shorthand also is used as a benchmark to measure the skill level of applicants for secretarial positions. These two skills are of potential value in almost any profession. Shorthand is particularly useful when taking notes or gathering information for research, making you more effective and efficient.

INTERPERSONAL RELATIONS

Communication

The American Heritage Dictionary of the English Language, Third Edition, defines communication as ". . . exchange of thoughts, messages, or information as by speech, signals, writing, or behavior." Communication skills are needed in any profession, but they are especially crucial to the secretary, a major function of whose job is handling communications, whether they be verbal or written. We have already discussed written communications and the need to be clearly understood when executing a well-written document. But two other communication skills must be addressed.

Oral skills

You may have good ideas to contribute to your business environment, but if you can't articulate them effectively, they will be lost. Speaking well requires a command of the English language, good diction, and the self-confidence to speak. If you are shy and have little experience speaking in front of a group, take a continuing-education course in public speaking. Such a course can help you overcome your fear of addressing a group. Most of the other students in the class will be there for the same reason you are and will understand your own difficulties. If you are to take on a career role as a supervisor or trainer, chances are you will have to speak in front of one or more persons on a regular basis. And the more you speak publicly, the easier it gets.

Remember that, no matter how easy it becomes for you to speak in public, if you don't have anything to say, it is best to be silent. Some guidelines that will help you become a more confident speaker are as follows:

- Prepare what you are going to say.
- Gather the information carefully.
- Understand the issues thoroughly.
- State what you are going to say with confidence.
- Make sure statements are not defensive or aggressive.

Body language

The signals we use to communicate are often called *body language*. Your posture and gestures convey a number of attitudes and emotions including pride, anger, hostility, fear, self-esteem (or lack of it), and defensiveness. If you are nervous or jittery, you can appear uncertain or insecure about your abilities. Try to be aware of your appearance without becoming self-conscious. If you want to send a self-assured, confident signal, look directly into the eyes of the person who is talking with you. A smile or nod will assure the person with whom you are speaking that you agree with or understand what they are trying to convey. Analyze some of the gestures and nuances of your nonverbal communication style and try to determine what kind of message you are conveying. It is easy to develop bad habits in conversation and in the gestures we use to support our speech. If you become more aware of what you are doing, it will be easy to correct any bad habits.

Effective Listening

It has been said that we hear 20 percent of what is being said and we only listen to 10 percent of what we hear. In order to take direction and do many of the tasks a secretary must perform, listening ability must be markedly improved above the norm. The first step is learning how to listen actively. Try to clear your head of all other thoughts and concentrate only on what is actually being said. Take notes and avoid interrupting the speaker until his or her thought has been completed. Try not to analyze what you are listening to until you have heard the complete message. If you don't take the time to listen carefully, you may end up having to do projects over several times. Sometimes the speaker does not convey a thought as clearly as you may need to follow directions. But if you have taken notes, you may be able to ask the right questions to clarify the instructions. Remember that it is very irritating to a busy executive when a secretary continually returns with numerous questions, the answers to which were already given in previous instructions.

Table 1   Body Language and the Messages It Conveys

Negative action/mannerism/gesture/posture	Negative message/impression thus conveyed
arms tightly folded across chest	insecurity; defensiveness
clasped/unclasped hands; fiddling with rings, necktie, lapels	nervousness; stress
biting of fingernails	unreliability; nervousness and general insecurity
sitting with crossed legs, skirt hitched up; fiddling with hair (used of a woman)	flirtatiousness
lack of eye contact with the person to whom you speak	lack of interest in the other party, the conversation, or instructions being conveyed to you
slouching, either while standing or while sitting	boredom; laziness; lack of interest in job or conversation
holding hand over mouth while talking, especially during a meeting	fear; insecurity
typing, filing, etc., while wearing a transistorized headset	tuned completely out of the job and its responsibilities

Positive action/mannerism/gesture/posture	Positive message/impression thus conveyed
hands held loosely at sides, in jacket pockets, or behind back	ease; confidence; relaxation; openness with others
steady eye contact with the person to whom you speak	interest in the other party, the conversation, or instructions being conveyed to you; straightforwardness, candor, and honesty
erect yet relaxed posture while standing, walking, or sitting	energy; control; self-confidence

Your Image

In the 1960s it became acceptable to wear dungarees and long hair to public school. Offices then reflected the trend of more casual dress, and as a result women began to wear slacks, jeans, and pantsuits to work. Although casual dress for professionals became commonplace, it never became the preferred mode. Many competent secretaries have been passed over for promotions because their appearance did not fit the corporate image. Employers still ask employment agencies and recruiters for so-called "front office types" when they look for executive secretaries and administrative assis-

Table 2   Dressing for Success: Questions and Answers

Question	Answer
Do many companies have dress codes?	No, but they do have unwritten rules or standards of attire.
Please characterize a typical business environment in which corporate style is considered important.	A typical conservative, or traditional, business environment might be that of a bank, or a law or accounting firm, or a government office where the general public or outside clients are often received. In such an environment, the importance of a positive public image is keenly felt.
Who is most influential with respect to dress and general style in a company?	The chief executive and operating officers set the overall style and tone of the business environment. This style is often reflected in the dress and manner of the employees at all levels. But in some companies, studied informality in itself is an indicator of the desired image.
What attire is generally acceptable in a relatively conservative business environment?	In such workplaces, we recommend suits, although separates and sweaters are also acceptable as long as they are conservative and professional in appearance. Women have an additional option in dresses. Whether or not a man chooses to wear a suit, in a conservative work environment he should wear a tie. Jewelry, shoes, and hairstyles ought to convey an image of businesslike self-confidence. In short, the employee—not the clothes—should stand out.

tants. Since you want to make a positive impression on an employer, you should project a professional image by the way you are dressed.

HUMAN RELATIONS

Getting along with other people is an essential part of your job. You don't have to like someone personally to foster a good working relationship. If you present an even-tempered, positive image to all of your coworkers, they will more than likely respond to you in the same fashion. Your ability to get along with many different personalities will play a major role in your ultimate career development. It's a challenge to deal with a difficult person successfully—one that you will encounter many times over.

To survive in a business environment, you must be objective and aware of the ways in which you interact with other people. Everyone has prejudices or predetermined ideas about others affecting their communication ability. Avoid stereotyping people or putting them into set categories. To deal with people effectively you yourself must be perceptive and understanding. Stereotyping builds an immediate barrier against open communication—a barrier that will hold you back from effective, sensitive interactions with others. Learn to evaluate your reactions to other people as well as their reactions to you. If you have an innate understanding of why people project certain images, it will be easier for you to interact positively with people from all walks of life.

Personal contact with visitors, service people, and customers should always be pleasant and businesslike. People associate a business with the person from that organization with whom they have had direct contact. Keep in mind that you are The Company to anyone from the outside, and the corporate image projected by you should be above reproach at all times.

You and Your Supervisor

Getting along with your supervisor is of major consequence to you. To a great extent, your supervisor will have a marked effect on your future. Many qualified secretaries have lost chances to advance because of personality conflicts with supervisors, situations that have resulted in poor recommendations. Learning to control your temper and emotions in business is therefore essential to your professional development. If you take criticism from your supervisor personally and harbor resentment about it, you will probably not be able to handle your job well.

Learn to control your temper and evaluate a situation before you take any oral or written action. Sometimes the criticism is warranted and is meant to help you improve rather than to hurt your feelings. Of course, there will be times when you are called upon to deal with an extremely difficult person. Even though you may make every effort to get along with that person, it just won't work. In a case like that, the first step might be to ask for a meeting with your supervisor. During this meeting, ask for input about your performance and listen to the response. If appropriate, you might also state that you are concerned about the relationship. If all the avenues you pursue do not change the situation, ask to meet with Personnel to discuss a transfer or look for another job.

Trust is another factor in a successful relationship with your supervisor. Many executives are under a great deal of pressure and will use you as a sounding board for confidential matters, particularly if you display good judgment. Never divulge any confidential information to your coworkers.

Juicy secrets have a way of getting around a company fast. If word of this should get back to your supervisor, it could ruin your working relationship and eventually result in the loss of your job. Thus, absolute loyalty to your supervisor is essential. It can mean the difference between working with instead of for someone. Keep in mind also that the image you project is associated with that of your supervisor. If you are able to look upon your working relationship as a team effort, you will be considered capable of assuming as much responsibility as your supervisor is willing to delegate.

Good Human Relations

Certain qualities make a good secretary stand out from the crowd and progress quickly. You should try to develop the qualities discussed below in order to become exceptional at your job.

Responsibility and teamwork with the supervisor. Your ability to accept responsibility and be accountable for your tasks will be judged on a daily basis. If you are conscientious and well organized, you should be able to perform those tasks well. Your willingness to assume additional responsibility will also be looked upon as an asset when your superior evaluates your performance. Acceptance of increasing responsibility by the secretary results in closer teamwork with the executive.

One way of increasing your worth in the eyes of your supervisor is to assist him or her actively in managing the flow of on-line projects in the office. To effect true executive/secretarial teamwork, you should meet with the executive at least once a day, preferably early in the day, to set priorities for the day's activities—including appointments, anticipated telephone calls, dictation, correspondence keyboarding, and incoming/outgoing mail. Try to bypass crises by knowing your executive's daily plans in advance. In this way you can at least attempt to expedite the influx and outflow of people and paper. Ensure that the executive's appointment book and the entries in your copy of it match. Take the initiative to call expected visitors if you know that the executive is running behind schedule. Try to remember what took place the day before. Consult your calendar, diary, or appointment book so that you can, if possible, anticipate tomorrow's events to some extent. If your supervisor travels a lot, know where he or she can be reached at all times, and find out what is required of you in your supervisor's absence.

Understand the goals of your executive within the corporation and familiarize yourself with the goods, services, and products of the corporation. Only by exercise of initiative, use of common sense, and acceptance of responsibility can you work as a real team player with the executive.

Flexibility. Business environments change rapidly due to growth, change in management, the fluctuating economy, and many other factors. In order to maintain a position in a business that is going through such changes, you must be able to adapt easily to new situations and be flexible enough to accept change. Changes can be upsetting if you are not forward-thinking.

A good disposition. It is necessary to be even-tempered and good-natured to maintain a pleasant working atmosphere. A moody or irritable employee can adversely affect the morale of the entire office. A good sense of humor can help you through stressful situations. Many times you will be asked to do a rush job that will keep you overtime or you will be requested to perform a task in an unreasonably short time. If you allow the situation to upset you emotionally or make you lose your temper, you could be displaying an immaturity that will haunt you when you want to make a career move later. People remember unpleasant situations.

Courtesy. Since most offices are fairly formal, courtesy should be an integral part of your work habits. If you share an open space with others, care should be taken not to disturb your coworkers. If you smoke and your coworkers don't, find a place where you can have a cigarette break or ask to be moved to a spot where you will not irritate anyone else when you smoke. More and more offices are now providing specific smoking areas instead of allowing smoking in the entire office area.

Stability. A well-integrated personality stands out in a crowd. If you are able to keep calm when an upsetting situation develops, you will become known as a very stable employee. Problem-solving is also part of the secretary's job. A clear and logical approach to a problem would be to identify it, break it down into components, and then determine a workable solution. Much valuable time and energy can be wasted by overreacting to a situation instead of trying to devise a sensible way to change the situation for the better. The more responsibility you assume, the more problems you will encounter. If you learn to deal with problematic situations as they occur in a step-by-step fashion, your self-confidence to assume more and more responsibility will be enhanced.

Assertiveness. You can stand up for your own rights without being hostile. You also need to be able to deal with those who may be rude or who try to take advantage of you without becoming emotionally upset, intimidated, or overly aggressive in response. Assertiveness training teaches us to express our opinions and feelings freely and candidly without playing a power game. A few mannerisms, particularly in conversations with superiors and coworkers, serve as assertive (but not hostile) signals. For example, when you and your superior have a crisis situation, say *we*, as in "*We* have a big problem today. What should *we* do about it?" as opposed to "*I* just can't deal with this. Whatever am *I* going to do?'' When talking with your co-workers, use *you* as much as possible in all situations. Reserve the trump card *I* for instances in which you sense an impending conflict. If you use *I-I-I* and *me-me-me* constantly you will be (and sound) aggressive, thus generating hostility from those around you.

Firm repetition of your position in a conflict is another signal of healthy assertiveness. This technique is especially useful when you are attempting to get a reluctant employee to perform a task that you've been authorized to delegate. The key to effective use of this technique is sticking to the issue at hand, keeping calm, and not allowing yourself to be sidetracked into ancillary discussions by the other party. A number of excellent books and courses in assertiveness training are available and are well worth the time spent on them. In the highly competitive business environment of today, a sensitivity to the well-documented profiles of the assertive personality, the nonassertive personality, and the aggressive/hostile personality is essential to job survival and enjoyment.

Office Politics

The term *office politics* almost always has a negative connotation. It's true that getting involved in office politics in terms of gossip and deceitful behavior is negative. But in order to get your job done, you will find it necessary to understand the overall political structure of your office and your place within that structure. Whether the office is large or small, there is a political structure based on power and decision-making.

People striving for advancement in business constantly develop and apply new strategies to enhance their positions within the corporate political structure. The secretary lacking keen political savvy can easily be caught in the middle. You must be observant and aware of other people's positions within the organization. Determine who gets certain jobs done and who makes the important decisions. Read the company's organizational chart and determine the structure of your own office first and then that of the corporation in general. This kind of knowledge will help you when dealing with other departments and disseminating information outside your own office.

PROFESSIONAL DEVELOPMENT AND GROWTH

To advance in your career, it is important to continue your education in some form. One of the easiest ways to grow professionally is to read. Business and industry newsletters and publications, current professional and news magazines, and trade publications can keep you abreast of events, new procedures, and trends in your area.

Another way to learn new skills is through teaching yourself. You can do this on your own, on your own time, or you can organize a group of people with the same interest and hold class together after hours.

You also may wish to continue your education formally by attending a local college or enrolling in continuing education courses. There may also be company-sponsored workshops and seminars available to you. You can also encourage your company to offer certain workshops that may be needed by the staff. Professional organizations such as Professional Secretaries International (PSI) also offer seminars. These organizations provide a wealth of information, and most have publications to keep you informed.

PROFESSIONAL EXAMINATIONS AND CERTIFICATION PROGRAMS

Your professional development should involve the constant learning of new skills and the sharpening of those already acquired. This is the only way to survive and advance in today's business place. One way to enhance your professional status is by achieving certification through some of the examinations administered for professional secretaries. Certification is a valid goal for the career-minded secretary.

The Professional Secretaries International® (PSI®) Certifications

Currently Professional Secretaries International (PSI) administers two business-oriented certification programs in the office professional field.

PSI has an entry-level certification assessment program. The Office Proficiency Assessment and Certification™ (OPAC™) Program is a PC-based program administered by educational institutions and corporations and is scheduled for three and one-half hours. The areas covered include keyboarding and word processing, handling mail, telephone usage, appointments, technical and financial records management, and communication.

The second certification program is the Certified Professional Secretary® Rating (CPS®). To obtain this rating, you must complete and verify the required educational and secretarial employment experience and pass a six-part, two-day examination administered each May and November by a department of PSI, the Institute for Certifying Secretaries.

In addition to working secretaries, students and business educators are eligible to take the examinations. The examination is divided into six parts:

- *Office Technology* covers data processing, communications media, office management, technological applications, records management, and office systems.
- *Office Administration and Communication* measures proficiency in those areas specific to the secretary's position, such as office management, reprographics, preparing documents, editing, and record management.
- *Economics and Management* consists of 35 percent economics and 65 per-

cent management; the emphasis is on understanding the basic concepts underlying business operations.

- *Accounting* measures knowledge of the basic elements of accounting, including the accounting cycle, financial statements, math associated with accounting, and the ability to summarize and interpret financial information.
- *Business Law* measures knowledge of the principles of business law and the effect of governmental controls on business.
- *Behavioral Science in Business* measures the knowledge of the principles of human relations and organizational dynamics in the workplace, such as conflict, motivation, problem-solving techniques, supervision and communication, leadership styles, and understanding of an informal organization.

For more information, call or write Professional Secretaries International, 10520 NW Ambassador Drive, P.O. Box 20404, Kansas City, MO 64195; (816) 891-6600.

Professional Legal Secretary (PLS) Rating

The PLS examination offers the legal secretary the opportunity to acquire career-enhancing professional credentials. The National Association of Legal Secretaries offers this seven-part exam nationally. The candidate must have three years of legal secretarial experience to qualify for the exam. Part of the experience will be waived if the applicant has a bachelor's or associate's degree. This is the only certification program for legal secretaries. The seven areas tested include: legal secretarial procedures; legal secretarial accounting, written communication, ethics, legal terminology, judgment, and legal terminology, techniques, and procedures. For more information, call or write National Association of Legal Secretaries, 2250 East 73 Street, Suite 550, Tulsa, OK 74136; (918) 493-3540.

Certified Medical Assistant (CMA)

Medical assistants are eligible to join the American Association of Medical Assistants (AAMA). The AAMA offers a certifying examination that leads to a certification as a Certified Medical Assistant (CMA). The three and one-half hour exam is given twice a year on the last Friday in January and June at designated sites. Recertification is mandatory every five years. For more information call or write American Association of Medical Assistants, 20 North Wacker Drive, Suite 1575, Chicago, IL 60606; (312) 899-1500 and (800) 228-2262.

Certified Medical Transcriptionist (CMT)

Certification as a medical transcriptionist can be obtained from the American Association for Medical Transcription (AAMT). Certification is valid for three years. It can be renewed by paying the annual certification administration fee and earning a minimum of 30 continuing education credits in each three-year period or by passing another certification examination every three years. For more information, call or write American Association for Medical Transcription, P.O. Box 6187, Modesto, CA 95355; (800) 982-2182.

2
Opportunities and Advancement

D ECIDING WHAT CAREER PATH to take is often determined by what you do best. When thinking about pursuing another position within your company or in another company, it is important to take certain steps before you make a move. First you must determine if you are qualified for the position you aspire to. If you are not so qualified, are you willing to upgrade your capabilities by taking courses and participating in seminars that will assist you in advancing to a higher level?

As we have indicated, certain basic competencies are required for any position labeled *secretarial*. Although shorthand may not be required, Dictaphone skills will usually substitute for it in an average position. Keyboarding speed and accuracy are a must, as well as a good command of English. The specific level of the position may be defined by the number of tasks the secretary must perform without supervision. Entry-level secretarial positions include such duties as:

- Typing or composing letters for the executive
- Ordering office supplies
- Making travel arrangements
- Writing a company newsletter
- Screening callers and visitors
- Sorting the executive's mail according to priority.

SPECIALIZED CAREER OPPORTUNITIES

Medical secretary. This highly specialized position requires training in medical terminology, medical office ethics and practice, and medical dictation/transcription procedures. The medical secretary is often required to manage an entire office, taking responsibility for its billing, records management, medical and office supply organization, and appoint-

15

ments. The position also requires good knowledge of accounting procedures and financial record-keeping. The medical secretary—usually called a *medical assistant/administrative* or a *medical assistant/clinical*—must be able to understand and process many kinds of complex health insurance forms. This position also requires excellent human relations skills, as well as the ability to deal with sick people, often in emergency situations. Colleges and some business schools offer certificate programs lasting from six months to two years. Medical secretarial positions can be obtained in hospitals, medical schools, private doctors' offices (single-physician or group practices), health maintenance organizations, and clinics.

Legal secretary. The job opportunities for one seeking this position are abundant. There are positions for legal secretaries in private law offices, courts, and corporate law departments. The training is also highly specialized and requires knowledge of legal and court procedures and familiarity with a myriad of forms and legal documents. There are all types of law practices. Many jobs are available in single-attorney offices where the legal secretary may serve really as an office manager, performing duties such as appointment scheduling, court appearance scheduling, preparing documents, billing, bookkeeping, and record-keeping. If the lawyer is a generalist, the legal secretary has to be proficient in a broad spectrum of procedures and documentation such as handling subpoenas, mortgages, deeds, closings, pleadings, briefs, wills, proxies, and abstracts. Working for a generalist is good experience for the neophyte legal secretary who would like to sharpen basic skills and gain wide experience. Positions are also available with lawyers specializing in real estate, criminal law, insurance, taxation, divorce, estate planning, government contract law, and bankruptcy. Large corporations often have their own in-house law departments specializing in labor law, insurance law, and taxation law. Opportunities to work in corporate law departments are available to those interested and qualified. The court systems—federal, state, and local—have legal secretaries working for district attorneys, for judges, and for clerks of a court. Community colleges and secretarial schools offer career courses for legal secretaries. And if a secretary wants to achieve a higher level of specialization in the legal field, he or she may decide to become a paralegal aide—a position demanding further education.

Technical secretary. Engineering, aerospace, environmental protection, sciences, mathematics, and agriculture are a few of the career areas available to a technical secretary. Knowledge of electronic office equipment is essential. Technical reports require proper formatting, and a technical assistant must be able to keyboard technical data accurately and quickly. Expertise in science or mathematics and a knowledge of technical terminology will be to your benefit.

Before deciding on any area of concentration, you may want to work in a temporary capacity in a law office, a medical office, or a business office to see if the atmosphere and job responsibilities suit your needs. Working for a temporary agency affords you the opportunity to try out different types of professions and companies. It also may help you avoid making a serious, often expensive, career mistake.

Although the required training for medical and legal secretarial positions is very specific, many other positions rely just as much on experience in the field as they do on specialization. For example, if you look in the business section of your newspaper, you will see that most of the secretarial jobs advertised have specific titles like "marketing secretary," "sales secretary," "publishing secretary," "personnel secretary," and "advertising secretary." Some of these jobs require experience in a particular field and employers equate such experience with a certain number of years in a secretarial school or college. A personnel secretary should have prior experience with personnel record-keeping systems and should be able to work under rules of strict confidentiality. A marketing secretary should be familiar with different aspects of advertising, production, copywriting, and publicity. Good research skills are extremely desirable. The ability to speak with many people on the telephone is an essential attribute. A sales secretary should be familiar with following up active leads and keeping sales records as well as with customer files and correspondence. The ability to use a computer and to perform basic business mathematical operations is important. The sales secretary also must interact with various members of the company's sales force in a positive, organized manner. Planning sales meetings and covering for the executive(s) when absent are also important tasks. A publishing secretary should have an excellent command of the English language as well as some proofreading and copyediting experience, for the paperwork load in such a position is often quite heavy. An advertising secretary should be able to work under intense pressure and meet close deadlines. Excellence in communication is essential, for such a secretary is often called upon to assist in the preparation of ad copy or press releases. In addition, the ability to project a highly professional image through person-to-person contact and by way of manners and attire is requisite. These are just a few examples of the way you can specialize in a specific field. As you can see, each field of specialization demands particular abilities that you can fine-tune as you gain more and more experience in the workplace.

ADVANCED-LEVEL OPPORTUNITIES

Executive secretary. This position is a big step up from a general secretarial position and usually involves a high degree of confidentiality and formality. Working for a high-level executive often involves scheduling meetings, taking minutes at board meetings, and then transcribing or typing them, doing public relations work, composing letters and instructions on your own initiative, and performing many other tasks such as screening calls and visitors and reading and evaluating mail with little or no supervision. Interpersonal skills are of great importance in an executive secretarial position since this position is a highly visible and very political one. You must be mature, honest, sophisticated, and diplomatic at all times.

Administrative assistant. Every company seems to have a different definition for administrative assistant. In many cases it refers to an administrative support job performed with little or no supervision, and one that is a step higher than executive secretary. For example, an administrative assistant may handle dissemination of contract information or work with the chief financial officer of a company in preparing corporate reports. This position usually involves supervision of others and may require a college degree. A secretary is often promoted to administrative assistant when the manager decides to delegate additional responsibilities requiring more intensive effort than a strictly executive secretarial position does. Since so many companies differ in their definitions of administrative support positions, you should clearly understand the job description and the opportunities for advancement in the particular company offering such employment.

THE ORGANIZED JOB SEARCH

The first step before setting out on an active job search is determining your own marketability and your position in the job market itself. The succeeding steps in career advancement include:

- Preparing a resume
- Writing cover letters
- Interviewing successfully
- Writing follow-up letters

Researching the Job Market

The U.S. Department of Labor publishes annually the *Occupational Outlook Handbook*. The *Handbook* describes major industries, including information such as growth potential and general business trends. Occupations, along with information on salaries and working conditions, are covered in it. This is a good place to start when trying to determine your value in the marketplace.

Another publication that will provide you with valuable job classification information is *The Dictionary of Occupational Titles*, which may be obtained by writing the Superintendent of Public Documents, U.S. Government

Printing Office, Washington, DC 20402. Over 20,000 job titles are listed in this book, together with descriptions of each one. These publications and many others dealing with the job market are available in your public library. The U.S. Department of Labor publishes newsletters and labor statistics reports that you can also use in your research efforts. Before you apply for any job, however, you should assess your overall proficiency so that you can match your skill level with the various jobs you may apply for. A realistic, objective assessment of your own qualifications will help you capitalize on the skills you possess and learn more about the skills you need to acquire.

Your First Job

If you have recently graduated from secretarial school or have achieved a certificate in business training, you should have an accurate idea of your performance level in the most basic areas of typing, shorthand, filing, transcription, word processing, and office machine technology. But since you may have little or no job experience, it is often difficult to decide what kind of job suits your abilities and personality the first time. You might ask yourself some of the following questions at the outset:

1. Am I a people-oriented person? If so, would I enjoy a job dealing with the public on a regular basis, as in sales or customer service?
2. Would I rather work in a large, mid-size, or small company?
3. Is there a profession or business that I find particularly fascinating? If so, what is it?
4. What are my salary requirements? (NOTE: If you are a recent graduate of a secretarial school, your placement office may provide you with information on salary levels that you should pursue. Many employment agencies can provide current salary surveys and job classifications useful to you in assessing your own marketability.)
5. Where do I want to work?

If you have no idea of the kind of job you are looking for or where to start, a temporary employment agency may be the answer. With basic secretarial training, you can find work easily in a temporary agency. This is an excellent way to try out different types of jobs without making a commitment until you are ready to decide where you want to work permanently. You can work in almost any type of company and have the advantage of being able to observe the diverse jobs open in different businesses.

Companies require temporary help when there is an overload of work or when someone has left the company unexpectedly or is on vacation. Temporary agencies usually charge a fee to an employer who hires a temporary worker on a permanent basis. Since the fee is usually less than the ones charged by most permanent placement agencies, more and more companies are hiring temporaries with permanent jobs in mind if the people fill the jobs well. Use of temporary employment services gives the employer a chance to observe a candidate in action and to see if that person fits in well with the company.

Returning to the Workforce

For those secretaries returning to the workforce after a considerable amount of time has passed, the first step is to brush up on your skills. A good investment is a keyboarding course and/or a course in basic word processing. Although you may have a good idea of the kind of job you want from previous work experience, you may want to try temporary work. In addition to familiarizing you with the business world once again, temporary work will provide you with some recent work history to be included on your résumé. Temporary employment is a means of building up the self-confidence that may be lacking after a long absence from the workforce.

The Job Change

If you are presently working at a job and feel it is time for a change, you should consider several things before looking elsewhere:

1. What conditions do I expect to improve or change by looking for another job?
2. Have I been at my present job long enough to have exhausted all possibilities of increased responsibilities or promotion?
3. Have I considered seeking employment in another part of my company?
4. Does my company encourage planning out a career with them? If so, have I talked with my supervisor or with Personnel to determine what my next step for advancement would be?

If you have done all of these things and truly feel that you need a change, then you need to set some goals for yourself to achieve the kind of change that will be beneficial to your career. When you already have a job, you have the security affording you time to search out another position that meets all of your needs and standards.

Before preparing your résumé, take an inventory of your present abilities and all of the responsibilities you have had in your present job and any previous jobs. After completing the inventory, decide which tasks you like the most and which ones you like the least. By doing this you will have a basis for comparing what you want to do with what is available to you when looking for your new job. It will also help you to avoid getting into a situation similar to the one causing you to want to leave your present job. When you have completed an accurate ability and task analysis, you will then be ready to prepare your work history.

Locating Job Opportunities

Having done some research and having determined your job target, you are now ready to begin the actual search. Several avenues can be taken in looking for a job.

The newspaper. This is probably the first place that people look when they are trying to get information on available jobs. The classified section usually divides job opportunities by the general headings of professional help, medical help, business help, and sales. Most secretarial jobs are advertised in the business section of the classifieds, but specialized positions like medical secretarial jobs would probably appear under the medical section of the classifieds. Look through all the jobs. One suiting all of your qualifications might be listed in any section of the classifieds.

Be sure to keep a file on all of the ads that you have answered so that you do not answer the same ad twice and also so that you remember what positions you have applied for. This may sound odd, but if you have ever been involved in an active job search during which you might have answered twenty-five or more ads, you know that mix-ups can happen. You also can confuse the contact names in the ads if you are not careful. Do not call the company unless a telephone call is requested. If the ad requests a résumé, send one with a cover letter.

Try to stay away from blind ads using newspaper box numbers instead of company names. Companies placing blind ads usually want to avoid sending out reply letters to the applicants. If the ad sounds like just what you've been looking for, apply; but don't get your hopes up for a quick answer. If you answer an ad placed by an employment agency, be sure to call first to see whether or not the job is still available. Agencies often run tantalizing ads to draw clients into the agency, or they run ads for jobs that have already been filled.

Trade journals and specialty publications. If you are looking for a job in a specialized industry, you may want to check out the classifieds in professional trade journals. For example, if you are looking for a job in advertising, you may want to look through *Advertising Age* or *New England Advertising Week*. Your local library will have trade journals and specialty publications available for you to browse through.

Employment agencies. The goal of an employment agency is to match the talents and interests of the prospective employee with the company and the job. Agencies usually specialize in specific fields. If you are going to use an employment agency to find a job, be sure to find one specializing in secretarial jobs. You will be able to tell from the newspaper ads and from the listings in the Yellow Pages which agencies are best suited to your needs and qualifications. Agencies screen and test job candidates before sending them on interviews. Hence, an agency interview should be treated exactly like an interview with a prospective employer.

Companies requiring confidentiality and desiring prescreened candidates usually use employment agencies. If the hiring company has experienced success with employee placements from a particular agency, the employment counselor at that agency may be your ticket to a good job. Try to stay away from high-pressure agencies. You'll know which ones to avoid next time when you sit in a counselor's office whose walls are adorned with high-performance plaques for best placement records. Agencies like these are more interested in the fee paid by the hiring company than in putting you into a job that fits your abilities.

Most agencies give skill tests to applicants for secretarial jobs. Typing and shorthand will be tested as well as transcription skills. If you are unfamiliar with the equipment on which you will be tested, ask to practice for a while before taking the test. If you do poorly on the test, ask to take it again. Most employment counselors are understanding in testing situations since people are usually nervous.

When the agency sends you on an interview, they will do all of the communicating and negotiating with your prospective employer before and after the interview. Do not call the company where you have been interviewed until you hear from your employment counselor. If a job has been advertised as "fee paid," the hiring company will pay for the placement services. If the job has not been so advertised, you should ask what the fees are before signing any employment contracts.

School placement services. If you are a recent business school graduate, you should register with the school's placement office. Companies will often list job openings with these offices.

Opportunities abroad. The United States Department of State offers positions in over 300 countries around the world to secretaries who meet criteria for foreign service. When applying for the Foreign Service, you must be willing to work anywhere in the world. You also must meet the following criteria:

1. You must be in excellent health and must be able to pass a physical examination.
2. You must have a high school diploma or G.E.D. certificate.
3. You must be a U.S. citizen as must your spouse if you are married.
4. You must be able to pass the U.S. Civil Service Examination requiring a shorthand speed of 80 words per minute and typing speed of 40 words per minute.

If you successfully meet the requirements, the Department of State conducts a security check including an interview with the Central Intelligence Agency. If you pass the investigation, you are then assigned to the Foreign Service Institute for orientation and further training before receiving a posting. For further information on opportunities in the U.S. Foreign Service, write to the Recruitment Branch, Employment Division, U.S. Department of State, Washington, DC 20520.

The government is not the only overseas employer. Large multinational corporations often recruit personnel in the United States for foreign assignments. Foreign job opportunities are advertised in major newspapers such as *The New York Times, The Christian Science Monitor,* and *The Washington Post.* If you enjoy travel and variety, you should consider applying for such a position.

The Résumé

Your personal vita or résumé is a marketing tool for selling yourself to a prospective employer. Since you will have limited page space on which to present everything relevant about your work history, you should go back to the "who," "what," "where," "when," "why" formula and be concise and clear in your presentation and format. A lot of people out there are looking for jobs—all of them with résumés in one form or another. An employer may have to look through many résumés for one position before deciding which people to interview. Therefore, your résumé must be eye-catching and brief so that a person scanning a page can immediately pick out your best assets and work experience.

Heading. The heading includes your name, complete address, and home and/or work telephone numbers, including area code. If you have an answering machine at home, make sure the message is professional. Before using your work number, make sure you can speak freely about a new position at work.

Career objective. The career objective immediately follows the heading and states a job title or particular field. Some possible job objectives are:

• Administrative assistant to marketing director
• Medical secretary in a hospital
• Legal secretary for a small law firm

It is possible that you may not want to state a career objective. If you state your job objective, i.e., executive secretary, you may be limiting your opportunities by categorizing yourself. There may be a job out there that can combine all of your skills with a title that does not even resemble that of executive secretary. On the other hand, you may have determined in your research that you definitely want the job atmosphere associated with the title *executive secretary*.

Work experience. In this section of your résumé, you should list and describe the jobs you have held over the years. In presenting your work history, keep in mind that employers want to know what you have accomplished on the job, not just what your job description was. It is important to use verbs that help create an image of your contributions and accomplishments. Listed below are some examples of action verbs:

Assist	Evaluate	Present
Budget	Maintain	Purchase
Compose	Manage	Research
Coordinate	Negotiate	Schedule
Design	Organize	Supervise
Develop	Plan	Train
Edit	Prepare	Write

The following are additional suggestions for writing about your work experience:

- Avoid long sentences.
- Use years instead of months and days.
- Omit jobs that go back 10 or 15 years.
- Omit company addresses; the name and location are adequate.

The format. You may put identical information into several different formats and thereby present totally different images with each. The choice of format will depend on the way you want to focus attention on your proficiencies.

Guidelines for résumé presentation. The appearance of your résumé is almost as important as its content, for your résumé is a reflection of your professionalism. As such, it should project a businesslike image. Here are a few general guidelines for résumé preparation that will help you:

1. Paper should be $8\frac{1}{2}''$ × $11''$ and white or off-white. If you are going to use colored paper, it should be conservative in tone or shade.
2. Use a high-quality copying process such as offset printing or laser printing.
3. Don't include personal information other than your name, address, and telephone number. Do not include information such as your age, marital status, height, weight, or sex.
4. Use the active voice throughout and be careful not to change tenses in the body of the résumé.

5. Try to keep the format pleasing to the eye. Avoid overuse of underlining and capitalization.
6. Spell out names of organizations and agencies. Titles also should be spelled out.
7. Proofread your résumé carefully. In fact, have someone else proofread it for you a final time before you have it printed. There is nothing more embarrassing than finding a mistake on your résumé after having given it to a prospective employer!

The chronological résumé. Over the years, the chronological format has been one of the most commonly used. It starts with your latest job experience and works backward. It focuses on your career development and is easy to follow. Since tasks for each position are detailed separately in the chronological format, try not to repeat elements of job descriptions. Only the inclusive years should be used to designate employment dates; there is no need to specify the months. If you want to highlight skills instead of chronological work history, the functional résumé may better suit your needs.

The functional résumé. If you want to highlight your skills, you may want to use the functional format for your résumé. This format details your skills under the specific function areas that you choose to highlight. This format may also give you an opportunity to cover each of your positions in more detail at your interview. A disadvantage in using this format is the possibility that your interviewer might want to relate your duties to each previously held job. If you have had more than three or four jobs or if your experience looks scattered, this is an excellent format to use. Because the functional résumé focuses on your marketable skills rather than on your job history, it also can be used advantageously if you are worried that a prospective employer will be concerned with too many moves.

The Application Cover Letter

When you answer an ad through the mail, you should always send a descriptive cover letter with your résumé. The letter should be brief and formal while at the same time sparking the interest of the prospective employer. Try to give a reason why you should be interviewed for the advertised position. Never prepare a cover form letter for photocopying and submission to numerous firms. Such letters indicate that the sender is lazy and not interested in taking the time to write personally to a prospective employer.

Preparing for the Interview

An interview provides a wonderful chance to learn about yourself and about the opportunities in your field. Think of the interview as an opportunity to emphasize all of your positive professional qualities. At the same time, you

Chronological Résumé Format

LINDA LEE WEB
19 Monroe Drive
Cambridge, MA 02140
(617) 354-8261

Career Objective To secure a position as an executive secretary.

Experience
1992 - Present   DATRONICS, INC.
                                    Burlington, MA

                                    Executive Secretary to Vice President/Personnel

                                    • Schedule Executive Committee meetings and
                                      record minutes for distribution.
                                    • Act as liaison between employees filing grievance
                                      procedures and Executive Committee.
                                    • Maintain calendar of social functions.
                                    • Compose letters of reply to applicants for
                                      executive positions.

1990 - 1992   DUNN AND TAYLOR ADVERTISING, INC.
                                    Medford, MA

                                    Account Secretary

                                    • Organized and maintained client files for
                                      three account executives.
                                    • Scheduled layout and design meetings with
                                      freelance designers.
                                    • Made travel arrangements and planned itineraries.
                                    • Took minutes of meetings with clients.

Education
1986 - 1990   B.A.--Liberal Arts
                                    University of Massachusetts
                                    Amherst, MA

References furnished upon request.

Functional Résumé Format

GENEVIEVE F. WARD
119 Oakley Boulevard
Chicago, IL 60606
(312) 753-1324

Experience
ADMINISTRATION

- Standardize contract filing systems for sales department.
- Prepare schedules and agendas.
- Plan exhibits and trade shows.

COMMUNICATION

- Correspond with customers regarding product information and schedules.
- Handle customer complaints.
- Communicate operational procedures to field sales managers.

PUBLIC RELATIONS

- Write sales department newsletter.
- Represent company at trade shows.
- Act as department liaison with all levels of personnel.

TECHNICAL SKILLS

- Proficient in WordPerfect and Lotus 1-2-3 computer software.
- Working knowledge of office machines.

Work History
1990 - Present

Administrative Assistant to National Sales Manager
Parker-Hill Chemical Company
Chicago, IL

Education
1990

Bachelor of Arts--English
University of Chicago

References furnished upon request.

Job Application Cover Letter

> 100 School Street
> Framingham, MA 01701
> March 22, 1993
>
> Ms. Valerie Kaishian
> Human Resources Director
> Trademark Books
> 50 Broad Street
> Boston, MA 02110
>
> Dear Ms. Kaishian:
>
> I am interested in applying for the position of Editorial Assistant that you advertised in The Boston Globe of March 19, 1993.
>
> As I indicate in the enclosed résumé, I have worked in the acquisitions departments of two publishing houses. My duties have included the coordination of the manuscript review process and the maintenance of communication with authors. This work has been interesting and challenging to me, and I am eager to expand my knowledge and experience. I hope that my background qualifies me as a serious candidate for the Editorial Assistant position with your firm.
>
> I would very much appreciate the opportunity for a personal interview. My telephone number during business hours is 295-8326, extension 451.
>
> It would be an honor and a challenge to work with the staff at Trademark Books. I have long admired the quality and seriousness of Trademark's publications.
>
> Thank you for your consideration.
>
> > Sincerely yours,
>
> Enclosure

must be aware of your weaknesses and know how to defend them or put them in a more positive perspective. In any case, being positive and enthusiastic is the real key to a successful interview.

On the day of the interview, dress conservatively and professionally in an outfit that you are comfortable with. Women should avoid using heavy makeup or trying a new hairstyle for the interview. Don't do anything that will make you uncomfortable before the interview. Give yourself plenty of time to get there. If you are unsure of the directions, call and confirm them with the receptionist. Find out as much about the company as you can before you go to the interview. If you are dealing with an employment agency, you should be able to glean some of this information from the employment counselor. If you are leaving your present job for a negative reason, do not discuss it with the interviewer. Do not discuss former jobs in any context other than your work experience. Speak confidently and appear calm when answering questions.

If the salary range has not been stated in the advertisement, wait for the interviewer to introduce the topic. If you have been sent to the interview by an agency, the employment counselor should have given you an idea of the salary range. Salary negotiations are always handled by the employment agency. If you are asked what your salary requirements are, ask what the salary range for the position is (if you don't know) *before* you answer the question. Keep in mind that you should aim for an increase in salary when you make a job change. Ask questions about the benefits packages and the salary and performance review process. If you are going to be reviewed within six months for a salary increase, you may be willing to start at a lower rate than if you will not be reviewed for a year from your starting date with the company.

Dealing with difficult interview questions. Try to prepare yourself in advance for some of the more difficult questions an interviewer might ask. For example:

> **Interviewer:** Why are you leaving your present job?
> **Applicant:** I've been at my present job for three years now, and although I have had two promotions, I feel that I need to make a move for my professional growth.

You may be asked about your weaknesses, and you should be prepared to answer that question. Try to focus on a weakness that can also be a positive quality in your profession. A conversation about your weaknesses might go as follows:

> **Interviewer:** We have discussed your strengths, Ms. Clark. What about your weaknesses?

Applicant: I think my biggest weakness is being a perfectionist. Sometimes I take my work too seriously and strive too hard for perfection. I take pride in my work, and it bothers me if it isn't perfect.

Open questions are always difficult and most of the questions a good interviewer asks require answers that reveal a lot about the job candidate. Another dialogue may go as follows:

Interviewer: Why do you think you want this job?
Applicant: I think this job would give me the opportunity to put the skills I have to their full use. I also think I could learn a great deal from working in a successful, established company.

Another open question with a twist is shown in the next hypothetical example. You should answer this question assertively and truthfully without sounding conceited.

Interviewer: Why should we hire you?
Applicant: From what you have told me about the job specifications, you require a person with (*specify the kind*) educational background, state-of-the-art skills such as (*specify the skills*), and dependability (*or whatever else*). I think that I can bring you those attributes.

Try to anticipate as many difficult questions as you can and prepare yourself for them. The key to a good interview is being able to answer questions with intelligent, confident, honest answers.

After the interview. Always send a follow-up letter to your interviewer. It may be the touch that gets you the job over another equally qualified applicant.

Professional Support and Assistance

If you wish to advance professionally, it is important to establish the right connections with people who can aid you in furthering your career.

Mentors. If you have been lucky enough to establish a relationship with a professional person whom you consider to be a role model, you might refer to that person as a *mentor*. A mentor has the kind of professional wisdom gained through experience that is invaluable to another person who wants to improve his or her job status. For instance, when you want to make a career move, your mentor can advise you about the viability of the prospective move, explain its positive aspects, and counsel you about its negative aspects. Having made a connection with a person whom you respect and admire, you should nurture the relationship. Counseling and guidance from an experienced person based on trust and mutual admiration is one

Interview Follow-up Letter

---

100 School Street
Framingham, MA 01701
April 17, 1993

Mr. Lee C. Costa
Senior Editor
Trademark Books
50 Broad Street
Boston, MA 02110

Dear Mr. Costa:

Thank you for inviting me to your offices to discuss the opening for an Editorial Assistant position at Trademark Books. The job as you described it is one that I know I would find interesting and challenging, and I believe I could assume its responsibilities successfully.

I would like to reaffirm my interest in this position. I also want to thank you for taking the time to show me around the company and to explain in detail the nature of the publications you produce. I hope that we will have an occasion for further discussions.

Sincerely,

of the most valuable elements for success in business. Connections often make the difference between a mediocre career and success in reaching your professional goals.

Associations and networks. Professional networks and associations are also valuable vehicles for career development. Attending meetings with other people in the same profession can do a great deal to expand your professional horizons. Many networks and associations exist today for the professional secretary. Professional Secretaries International, sponsors of the Certified Professional Secretary exam, has long been considered a particularly effective network. As we have said earlier, PSI offers courses and seminars to assist you in career advancement. PSI also publishes a journal entitled *The Secretary* which is published nine times a year.

It is sometimes difficult to stay interested in your professional development once you have found a comfortable niche in a company. People often settle for job situations that are less than satisfactory because comfort has become a habit. Involvement in associations and networks helps you to keep your eyes open to continuing educational opportunities and the need for ongoing career development.

3

Word Processing

I N THE 1960s data processing significantly altered the way information was processed in the office. Word processing became a substitute for repetitive typing in the 1970s. Information processing quickly became a reality in the 1980s. What will technology bring to the office throughout the 1990s?

Information technology has increased productivity, improved quality, expedited work flow, and monitored the ever-increasing volume of business documents and correspondence. Technology has changed forever the way offices operate and the way information is processed. Within the next few years, it is predicted that computers will take voice dictation, transcribe and type letters, correct vocabulary and syntax, and do filing.

Because of the technology boom, the role of the secretary and administrative assistant has changed dramatically. The basic skills of language arts, keyboarding, and human relations continue to be important, but the secretary also needs to integrate these skills with the new office technology. It is important for all office workers to acquire skills in office technology as part of their education and to continue to seek out opportunities to learn new skills as they are needed by business and industry.

EQUIPMENT

Word processing is the automated production of documents and correspondence using electronic equipment. It includes inputting the data (keyboarding), processing (editing), outputting (printing), and storage and retrieval (filing). Two categories of word processing equipment exist—computerized word processing and electronic typewriters.

Computerized Word Processing

The first category consists of mainframe computers, minicomputers, and microcomputers, also known as personal computers. Mainframes, devel-

Computer

Courtesy of Apple Computer, Inc. Photograph by
John Greenleigh.

oped in the late 1940s, were the earliest computers. They process information at extremely fast speeds and are used to manipulate a large volume of information. Minicomputers, developed in the 1960s, are smaller
than mainframes and usually have much more memory than microcomputers. They are used at the department level to perform functions such as
word processing, filing, and accounting. Microcomputers, developed in the
1970s, are also known as personal computers (PCs). These computers are
usually meant for one user and have less powerful central processing units
(CPUs) than minicomputers do.

Electronic Typewriters

Electronic typewriters are used for a limited volume of documents. Forms,
labels, index cards, and envelopes are ideally suited for the electronic typewriter, especially since they are difficult to use with computer printers.

PARTS OF A WORD PROCESSOR

Input Devices

An input device is a means by which a user can enter data into the computer. The *keyboard* is the primary input device for the word processor. It
allows the user to type commands, to create and edit text, and to control
the other devices attached to the word processor.

Each manufacturer's keyboard may be of a different design, but the industry standard has become the QWERTY keyboard. The QWERTY, meaning the first six alphabet keys in the upper left-hand corner, is very similar to the keyboard on a typewriter. Some additional keys not required by a typewriter have been added to the word processor keyboard:

Cursor key. A cursor is a spot of light, which may blink, that identifies the position in the text where you are working.

Directional keys. There are four directional keys with arrows usually imprinted on the key. A directional key is used to move the cursor up, down, left, and right.

Function keys. A function key instructs the processor to perform a particular function, such as *insert* or *delete*. Function keys are programmable, changeable, keys, switches, or buttons that initiate predetermined instructions when depressed. These keys eliminate some of the repetitive, time-consuming tasks performed on a typewriter.

Operation keys. Operation keys send keyboarded information to the storage unit for saving or retrieve saved information for viewing on the screen. An operation key is also used to instruct the printer to print a hard copy.

Format keys. Format keys direct the overall placement or layout of the information within a document. Format keys can be used for several functions, such as spacing, centering, underscoring, indenting, boldface, italics, and automatic hyphenation.

Mouse. A mouse is a handheld input device. When moved across a surface, it moves the cursor to a location on the display.

Scanner. This device captures a graphic image and transforms it into signals that can be accepted for processing by the computer.

Touchscreen. The user of a touchscreen simply touches the screen with a finger or an object to select available options.

Optical character reader (OCR). This device can read printed or typed characters and convert them to text or numeric data.

Light pen. Shaped like a pen, this device is light sensitive, and when placed in contact with the display screen, it can create or change images on the display.

Mouse

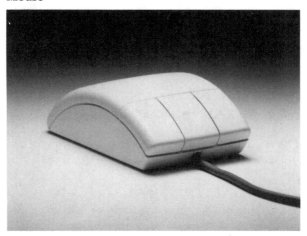

The Image Bank. Photograph by Ken Cooper.

Display Monitors

A monitor is an output device that provides an image of information on a screen. A visual display terminal consists of a cathode ray tube (CRT) that displays anywhere from a few lines of text to a full page. A display screen can be a flat panel or it can resemble a television screen. Monitors vary in size, type, and quality of resolution. The CRT typically comes in sizes 12, 13, 14, and 19 inches. They can be monochrome—one background color and one foreground color—or multicolor.

The image of a single on-screen character is made up of a group of tiny illuminated dots. These dots form a matrix arranged in such a fashion as to represent a particular character, such as a number or a letter, when illuminated on the screen.

Central Processing Unit

The central processing unit (CPU) controls all the operations of the system and executes the instructions given to the processor by the software.

Storage Devices

A variety of materials are used for data and program storage. The type of storage is usually chosen on the basis of what best suits the office needs.

Floppy disk. The most popular storage medium for word processing is the *floppy disk* or *diskette*. This is a magnetically encoded disk that comes in two sizes—$5\frac{1}{4}''$ and $3\frac{1}{2}''$. The $5\frac{1}{4}''$ version is flexible and comes in a protective envelope. The 3½″ version is encased in hard plastic. A backup copy of the diskette must be kept in case a diskette is damaged or lost.

Hard disk. A hard disk is a rigid magnetic disk fixed permanently within a computer drive unit and used for storing data. Hard disks generally offer more storage and quicker access to data than floppy disks do. If this medium is used, it is important to keep a backup copy, preferably on a diskette.

Output Devices

Output usually takes the form of a printed copy. After a document has been keyboarded, formatted, and processed, it is ready for printing.

Before printing a document using a dedicated word processor or using a particular software program, you may need to indicate the number of originals and make certain decisions, such as the typeface and type of justification. Other software may have required you to provide this information during the initial keyboarding or you may use the defaults in the standard printing summary.

Printers provide the output—hard copy—from a computer. They vary in speed, quality of output, fonts, features, and price. There are two types of printers—*impact* and *nonimpact*.

Impact printers strike a ribbon and are of two types—*letter-quality* and *dot matrix*. A letter-quality printer produces a document that has the same quality as an original typed on an electric typewriter. A dot matrix printer strikes the ribbon with a series of dots that form a character. It is used when the

Laser Printer

Courtesy of Apple Computer, Inc. Photograph by John Greenleigh.

quality of the output is not important. Dot matrix printers also print at a higher speed than letter quality printers and are relatively inexpensive.

Nonimpact printers are nearly noiseless and cannot make carbons. There are four types of nonimpact printers, *laser* and *ink jet* being the two most common. Ink jet printers are similar to dot matrix printers in that the character images are formed from a matrix of ink dots, in this case sprayed onto the paper from the print head. The ink jet printer is comparable to a dot matrix printer in speed, but the ink jet produces much higher print quality than the dot matrix printer. Laser printers use a laser beam to form images. These images are then transferred to the paper one page at a time. Laser printers usually have a variety of fonts and can produce graphics. The quality and speed are very good, and the machine is extremely quiet. Although the cost of this technology is high, it has come down over the last few years.

WORD PROCESSING SOFTWARE

Computer software contains programmed instructions that direct and control a computer's operation. Software falls into two categories:

- *System software* governs the operation of the computer.
- *Application software* includes programs that perform specific applications, such as word processing.

Word processing is the most common computer application. With a word processing program, the user can enter, edit, and print documents and correspondence, such as letters, reports, and memos. The available word processing functions vary, depending on the brand. The needs of the office, the budget, and the size of the machine's memory will influence the software selected.

Basic Word Processing Functions

Vertical scrolling. Vertical scrolling is the automatic upward movement of text or graphics on a screen as additional text is entered. The text or graphics can scroll up the screen one line at a time or it can move up only when the screen becomes full.

Word wrap. As text is entered, this feature automatically determines if a word can fit at the end of a line and if not will move it to the start of the next line.

Create. The create capability refers to the creation of a new document on the word processing system. The create function will automatically place an index entry in the system's document index file and will allow the user to assign information to it such as name, author, operator, date, special instructions, and so forth.

Automatic indentation. The indent function allows the operator to indent an entire block of text at once. It can be used to alter an existing document or it can be used during text input to create an indented block. The indent function is usually terminated during input by typing a return.

Centering. By using the word processor's centering function, a user can type in text that will be automatically placed on the center of the line. The center function also can be used to edit existing text automatically.

Decimal alignment. A word processor's decimal alignment capability will automatically line up numbers in a column so that each number has its decimal point positioned below the one above it.

Column layout. This feature automatically sets the placement of columns.

Mail merge. This feature prints multiple copies of a letter or memo and merges it with a list of names and addresses or locations.

Correcting Features

There are several special features to help in correcting and editing a document.

Delete. To operate the delete key, move the cursor to the first character of any text that is to be deleted and depress one or a combination of delete keys.

Backspace. The backspace key also functions as a delete key. To operate, move the cursor to the last character created and depress.

Insert. To operate, place the cursor under the character where the insertion is to be made and keyboard the new data.

Global search and replace. A word or group of words in the text may be automatically located and replaced throughout the document in all places or in select places. The procedure varies depending on the word processing software.

Block: move/copy/delete/print. The block function allows one to mark the beginning and end of a block of text. Once text has been blocked, the move function allows one to move it from one place in a document to another. Similarly, the copy function is used to copy a block of text in another location within a document or in another document without erasing the original. The delete function can be used to delete a block of text. The print function can be used to print only text that has been blocked.

Text Formatting

Justification.   Text justification is the alignment of text along a margin. If you choose left justification, the margin on the left will be straight and the right margin ragged. If you choose right justification, the right margin will be straight and the left margin ragged. If you choose full justification, both right and left margins will be straight.

Line spacing.   The system's line spacing feature allows the operator a wide range of spacing possibilities. The operator specifies the desired spacing in a format line or ruler.

Margins.   Document margins can be specified by the user at the time of creation or before the document is printed.

Page Management

Creating pages.   On many word processors, the operator can define the end of a page by positioning the cursor at the point where the page break is desired and then typing the page key or code. The system will create the page break, marking the end of the page with a special indicator that appears only on the screen.

Page numbering.   To number the pages of a document, the user is required to indicate the desired numbering sequence, the points at which this sequence is to begin and end, and the location of the numbers on the pages. Depending on the system being used, this information may be required at the time of printout on a print menu, or as part of a footer command—discussed in a forthcoming section.

Pagination.   Pagination, the act of placing page breaks in an unpaginated document, can be a manual or an automatic process. In the manual mode the user scans through the document by viewing screen after screen and inserts page breaks in locations where deemed most appropriate. In the automatic mode, the user specifies the number of lines desired on each page and the system scans through the document, placing page breaks at the designated page length. When a page break lands in the middle of a block of text, the system will stop and prompt the user to place the page break manually.

Repagination. Repagination is conducted just like original page number-ing. It can be either manual or automatic. Numbering during repagination will override the original numbering scheme, thereby creating a new sequence.

Headers and footers. A header is a text entry to be repeated automatically in the top margin of all pages in a document. This text entry can be any-thing from a single character or number to a more detailed document de-scription with date and reading instructions. A page number in a document is often referred to as a header when placed at the top of each page. A footer is similar to the page header described above except that it is posi-tioned at the bottom of the page instead of the top.

Special Features

Dictionary/spell check. This feature flags misspelled words either during keying or before printing. The user can create a user dictionary to prevent the system from flagging words, for example, that are missing from the dictionary.

Grammar check. This feature identifies such things as grammatical errors or overused phrases.

Thesaurus. This feature provides synonyms for words.

4
Business Correspondence

THE APPEARANCE OF YOUR outgoing documents has a direct impact on the recipients' perception of your company's product quality and reliability, not to mention the caliber of its personnel. How can one presume that a company's products are excellent and its employees competent if its routine business communications are improperly formatted, error-filled, or sloppily corrected? In short, an unacceptable written communication reflects adversely on you, the executive for whom you work, and the corporation. The forthcoming sections of this chapter are intended to assist you in translating dictated or handwritten material into a keyboarded format that will convey a visual, as well as a written message to the reader. The visual message — indicated by correct format, neatness, absence of errors, and irreproachable grammar — is this: our company and all of its employees from the chief executive officer to the lowest-ranking worker are quality-conscious, and our concern for quality ranges from our most sophisticated product to our most routine piece of outgoing business mail.

LETTERS

Style
The four letter styles that are most often used in modern corporate correspondence are the Full Block Letter, the Block Letter, the Modified Block Letter, and the Simplified Letter. All of these are illustrated in full-page facsimile form within this chapter.

Full Block Letter. In the Full Block Letter, all elements are positioned flush with the left margin. Nothing is indented except for tables or displayed quotations.

Block Letter. In the Block Letter, all elements are positioned flush left except for the date and the closing lines, which are at or near the center.

Modified Block Letter. In the Modified Block Letter, all elements are positioned the same as in the Block Letter and paragraphs are indented.

Simplified Letter. In the Simplified Letter, there is no salutation and no complimentary close. The salutation is replaced by a subject line in all capital letters. The writer's identification is also given in all capital letters on one line. All elements are flush left.

Major Parts

The major parts of most business letters are the date line, the inside or letter address, the salutation, the message, the complimentary close, and the signature block. Ancillary elements included when needed or according to corporate policy include a reference line, special mailing instructions, personal notations, an attention line, a subject line, reference initials, an enclosure notation, a copy notation, and a postscript.

Date line. The date line includes the month written out in full, the day in Arabic numerals, a comma, and the full year also in numerals: January 15, 1993. You may position the date two to six lines beneath the last line of the printed corporate letterhead, depending on the estimated length of the letter or on the guidelines in your company's correspondence manual. The date is positioned flush to the left in the Full Block and Simplified Letters; about five spaces to the right of center or in the exact center in the Block and the Modified Block Letters.

Inside address. The inside address includes the recipient's personal title (such as *Ms., Dr.,* or *Mr.*) or honorific (such as *Esq.*) and his or her full name on line one; the recipient's corporate title (such as *Vice President, Marketing*) on the next line; the recipient's official corporate affiliation (such as *National Broadcasting Corporation*) on the next line; the street address on another line; and the city, state, and ZIP code on the last line. Include suite, apartment, or room numbers on the street address line if necessary. If the address includes an intracompany mail stop number such as MS 2B 31A, put it after the company name with at least two spaces intervening. If the letter is addressed to a corporation rather than to an individual, the full corporate name appears on line one followed by a departmental designation (if required) on the next line, and the full address on subsequent lines. In all letter styles, the inside address is positioned flush left in blocked, single-spaced format. You may position the inside address from 4 to 12 lines beneath the line on which the date appears, except in the Simplified Letter

Table 1   **Inside Addresses: Questions and Answers**

Question	Answer
How do I style the addressee's name and business title?	Check the letterhead or the signature block of previous correspondence for correct spelling, or check with the writer. If all else fails, call the recipient's secretary for spelling verification.

Question	Answer
When may I use abbreviations in an inside address?	You may use abbreviated personal titles and honorifics such as *Mr., Ms., Mrs., Dr.,* and *Esq.* Do not abbreviate company names, departmental designations, or corporate titles. You may, however, use abbreviations such as *Co., Inc.,* or *Ltd.* if they have been so used on the printed letterhead and form part of the official company name. Words such as *Street* may be abbreviated to *St.* If you are addressing large numbers of letters for automated sorting, use the capitalized, unpunctuated abbreviations recommended by the U.S. Postal Service. See the section on addressing envelopes for automated mail sorting in this chapter. In all cases, however, use the capitalized, unpunctutated two-letter state abbreviations recommended by the Postal Service.

Question	Answer
How do I handle overlong lines in an inside address?	When an addressee's title (such as *Vice President, Research and Development*) overruns the center of the page, carry over part of the title to another line and indent it by two spaces, as: Vice President Research and Development

Question	Answer
How many lines should an inside address have?	The inside address should not exceed 5 full lines (runovers excepted).

Question	Answer
How do I style addresses involving street numbers?	Write out full numbers up to ten: One Court Street; Ten Park Street. Use Arabic numerals for 11 and above: 12 Marlborough Street; 18 Carson Terrace.

Question	Answer
How do I style numbered streets such as *42nd Street?*	You may use ordinals or you may write out the number in full: 500 42nd Street *or* 500 Forty-second Street; 200 5th Ave. *or* 200 Fifth Avenue; 1234 19th St., NW *or* 1234 Nineteenth Street, NW.

Table 1 (*continued*)

Question	Answer
Where do I position suite numbers, mail stops, and so forth?	Put suite, room, and apartment numbers on the street address line, two spaces after the last word on the line, as:

500 Fifth Avenue   Suite 44V

Mail stop indictors, however, appear two spaces after the last word on the corporate name line:

CCC Corporation   MS 12Z 451

in which you must place the inside address exactly 3 lines below the date. Examples of the wording of typical inside addresses are:

Ms. Joan Goodwin
Vice President, Sales
CCC Corporation   MS 2A 341C
1234 Matthews Street   Suite 34
City, US 98765

Dr. Joan Goodwin
Chief, Emergency Department
City Hospital
44 Hospital Drive
City, US 98765

Joan Goodwin, Esq.
Goodwin, Talbot & Kendall
One Court Street
City, US 98765

Ms. Joan Goodwin
Vice President, Research
 and Development
CCC Chemicals
One Industrial Drive
City, US 98765

Salutation. The salutation, used with all letter styles except the Simplified, appears two lines below the last line of the inside address, flush with the left margin. The first word of the salutation as well as the first word of a proper name or title is capitalized:

Dear Dr. Lee:
My dear Dr. Lee:
Dear Professional Women:

Dear Sir or Madam:
Dear John:
Ladies and Gentlemen:

The message in a business letter is always given normal punctuation. The letter parts, however, may be punctuated according to mixed punctuation or open punctuation. In mixed punctuation a colon is used after the salutation, and a comma is used after the complimentary close. If you are using open punctuation in order to reduce keystrokes, the salutation is unpunctuated. Remember that when you leave the salutation unpunctuated, you

Table 2   **Salutations: Questions and Answers**

Question	Answer
What's the current usage status of *Dear Sir* and *Dear Madam?*	*Dear Sir* is out of fashion in general business correspondence: it is now used only in form letters and in letters to important personages such as a president-elect of the United States. The same goes for *Dear Madam* (in addition, some women find its use offensive). See the forms of address section in this chapter for detailed guidelines regarding the use of these two salutations.
Question	**Answer**
What do I do when I can't determine the sex of the recipient from the written or typed signature on previous correspondence?	You can simply omit the personal title *Mr., Ms., Mrs.* or *Miss* and say: Dear Lee Lawson. Or you can use the neuter abbreviation *M.* before the person's surname: Dear M. Lawson.
Question	**Answer**
How do I address a mixed-gender group?	Style the salutation collectively, as: Dear Engineers, Dear Professionals, Dear Management, Dear Chemists, Ladies and Gentlemen, and so on.
Question	**Answer**
Are people really using the non-sexist alternatives to *Gentlemen?*	Yes, and some of them (aside from the patterns shown above) are: Dear People, Dear Roth Corporation (or whatever the company name is), Dear Salespeople, and so on.

also must leave the complimentary close and any copy notations unpunctuated. Note the difference between the two punctuation systems:

Dear Mr. Jenkins: Dear Mr. Jenkins
Yours very truly,   Yours very truly
cc: cc

Message. The message begins two lines below the salutation in all letter styles except the Simplified, in which it begins three lines below the subject line. Paragraphs in conventional business letters are usually single-spaced themselves, with double spacing separating them one from another. Only in very short letters on half-sheet stationery is double spacing used today. If the message of a very short letter is double-spaced, you must indent the first line of each paragraph by five spaces. Paragraphs in the Full Block, Block, and Simplified Letters are typed flush with the left margin. In the Modified Block Letter, the first line of a paragraph is indented five spaces.

If the message contains an enumerated list you should block and center the listed matter by five more spaces, right and left. Single-space the individual units in the list but allow two spaces between each unit. Tables also should be centered on the page. Long quoted matter (i.e., a quotation exceeding six typed lines) must be centered on the page and single-spaced internally. No quotation marks are used unless there is a quotation within a quotation. Use double spacing above and below lists, tables, and long quotations to set the material off from the rest of the message.

If the message exceeds one page, use a blank continuation sheet matching the letterhead sheet in size, color, texture, and weight. At least two lines of the message must be carried over to the continuation sheet. At no time should the complimentary close and signature block stand alone there. The margin settings used on subsequent sheets should match those chosen for the letterhead sheet. Allow at least six blank lines from the top edge of the sheet before typing the heading which includes the name of the recipient (personal title + first name and surname or personal title + surname only), page number, and date. The continuation sheet heading may be single-spaced and blocked flush with the left margin:

Page 2
Ms. Jean McGhee
June 24, 19—

or, it may be spread across the top of the page, beginning flush left, and ending flush right:

Ms. Jean McGhee   -2-   June 24, 19—

The flush left block style is required with the Full Block and Simplified Letters. The spread is used with the Block and Modified Block. With the spread, the page number is centered and enclosed with two hyphens, either set tight with the numeral as shown above or spaced: - 2 -. Never abbreviate the date on a continuation sheet.

Complimentary close. The complimentary close is used in all letters except the Simplified. The complimentary close is typewritten two lines beneath the last message line. The first word of the complimentary close is capitalized:

Yours very truly,   Sincerely yours,   Best regards,

In mixed punctuation a comma punctuates a complimentary close. If, however, you are using open punctuation, the comma is omitted. Remember, though, that when the comma is omitted here, the colon also must be dropped in the salutation and copy notations. Placement of the complimentary close varies with the style of letter chosen. Table 3 lists choices of letter styles and complimentary close page placement for each style.

You should use the complimentary close indicated by the writer because

Table 3   **Complimentary Close Positions**

Letter Style	Complimentary Close Position
Full Block	flush left
Simplified	none
Block	aligned with date
Modified Block	

the chosen wording often reflects the nature of the relationship between writer and recipient. For instance, "Yours very truly" is rather neutral though somewhat formal in tone, while "Respectfully yours" indicates the high degree of formality often required in letters to heads of state or high-ranking clerics. "Sincerely" is more informal, and wording such as "Best regards" indicates particularly friendly close relations between the writer and the recipient. Table 4 lists and discusses a number of frequently used complimentary closes.

Table 4   **Complimentary Close Wording**

Tone	Example
most informal: indicates close personal relationship between writer and recipient	Regards Best regards Kindest regards Kindest wishes
informal and friendly: indicates personal relationship between writer and recipient who may or may not be on a first-name basis	Yours Cordially Cordially yours
friendly but rather neutral: appropriate to all but the most formal letters	Sincerely Sincerely yours Very sincerely Very sincerely yours Yours sincerely
polite, neutral, and somewhat formal: often used in law office correspondence as well as in general business correspondence	Very truly yours Yours very truly Yours truly
highly formal: indicates that the recipient outranks the writer; often used in high-level diplomatic, governmental, or ecclesiastical correspondence	Respectfully Respectfully yours Very respectfully

Signature block. The signature block indicates the writer's name and possibly his or her corporate title, if the title does not already appear in the printed letterhead. With the Full Block, Block, and Modified Block Letters, this matter is aligned vertically with at least four or five blank spaces intervening between the complimentary close and the first line of the typed signature block to allow for the written signature. Leave even more space here if your executive's signature tends toward the flamboyant. The Simplified Letter features a typed signature block positioned flush with the left margin, at least four to six lines below the last line of the message. The writer signs in the space allotted. The executive's name and corporate title are typed in capital letters with a spaced hyphen separating them.

A rather infrequently used signature block is the one in which the company name appears after the complimentary close, with the writer's name and title appearing after the written signature. This style is used primarily with small business direct-mail advertising and in some contracts. Skip two lines between the complimentary close and the company name. Type the company name in capital letters. Skip five lines for the written signature and then type the writer's name in capital and lowercase letters followed on the last line by the writer's title:

Very truly yours,

HOWARD PLUMBING CONTRACTORS, INC.

John R. Howard
President

Table 5 explains the page placement of typed signature blocks. The letter facsimiles on pages 59–63 illustrate various letter styles and the placement of the complimentary close and signature block in them.

Table 5   **Signature Block Spacing and Position According to Letter Style**

Letter Style	Vertical Spacing from Last Message Line	Page Placement	Placement of Name and Title within Signature Block
Full Block	2 lines	flush left	name (line 1) title (line 2)
Simplified	at least 4 lines	flush left	name and title all on line 1
Block, Modified Block	2 lines	aligned with date and complimentary close: center, right of center	name (line 1) title (line 2)

Ancillary Elements

The following elements are optional in a business letter: a reference line, special mailing instructions, personal notations, an attention line, a subject line, reference initials, an enclosure notation, a copy notation, and a postscript.

Reference line. This notation, including data such as a file, policy, invoice, or order number, may be included if the recipient has requested it or if the writer knows that its inclusion will facilitate the filing of correspondence. The reference line may be centered on the page between one and four lines under the date line. However, with the Full Block and Simplified Letters the reference line is always aligned flush left, one line below the date. (See the facsimile.) If you include a reference line on the letterhead sheet you also must insert it on every continuation sheet. When using the Full Block style, place the reference line on line four of the continuation sheet heading:

Page 2
Ms. Laura LaValle
March 15, 19—
Z-123-456-7

When using the Block or the Modified Block Letters, include the reference line one space below the date:

Ms. Laura LaValle   -2-   March 15, 19—
                                                    Z-123-456-7

Avoid using the Simplified Letter with material requiring the inclusion of reference lines.

Special mailing instructions. Indicate on the letter itself as well as on the envelope any special mailing instructions designated by the writer. These include certification, registration, special delivery, or overseas air mail. Such instructions may be typed in capital letters or in capital and lowercase letters and underlined, flush left, about four line spaces below the line on which the date appears and about two lines above the first line of the inside address. Vertical line spacing between the date and the special mailing instructions may vary slightly, depending on the length of the message and page space available.

Personal notations. Sometimes a letter requires either a PERSONAL or a CONFIDENTIAL indicator. The designation PERSONAL means that the letter is a communication for the recipient only. CONFIDENTIAL means

Reference Line: Block or Modified Block Letters

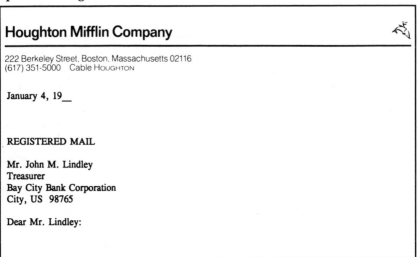

Houghton Mifflin Company

222 Berkeley Street, Boston, Massachusetts 02116
(617) 351-5000   Cable Houghton

> September 20, 19__
> Reference 12A 90C 17D

Ms. Linda Martinez
Production Manager
E-Z Typesetters Inc.
1200 Simpson Street
City, US 98765

Dear Ms. Martinez:

Special Mailing Instructions

Houghton Mifflin Company

222 Berkeley Street, Boston, Massachusetts 02116
(617) 351-5000   Cable Houghton

January 4, 19__

REGISTERED MAIL

Mr. John M. Lindley
Treasurer
Bay City Bank Corporation
City, US 98765

Dear Mr. Lindley:

that the recipient and any other persons so authorized may open and read the letter. Personal notations are placed about four lines below the date and from two to four lines above the first line of the inside address. If the message is quite brief, you may place the notation as many as six lines below the date. PERSONAL and CONFIDENTIAL notations are always posi-

Personal Notations

Houghton Mifflin Company

222 Berkeley Street, Boston, Massachusetts 02116
(617) 351-5000   Cable HOUGHTON

November 14, 19__

CERTIFIED MAIL
CONFIDENTIAL

Ms. Anne D. Raymond
Vice President
Deever Corporation
P.O. Box 4459
City, US 98765

Dear Ms. Raymond:

---

tioned flush with the left margin. If a special mailing instruction such as CERTIFIED MAIL has been included too, put the personal notation below it and block both of them flush with the left margin as shown in the above facsimile. These instructions are typewritten in capital letters on the envelope and on the letter itself.

Attention line. Letters addressed to a corporation or an organization collectively but at the same time routed to the attention of a specific department or group require insertion of an attention line. Use the following guidelines for all four letter styles:

- Block flush left.
- Position the attention line two lines below the inside address and two lines above the salutation.
- Never underscore an attention line.
- Capitalize the first letter of *Attention* and the first letters of the name of the department or group.
- Never abbreviate *Attention.*
- Put a colon after *Attention* if you are using mixed punctuation. If you are using open punctuation, do not put any punctuation after *Attention.*
- Never insert a period after an attention line.

Examples:

Attention: Advertising Department

Attention Line: Full Block Letter with Mixed-gender Salutation

---

Houghton Mifflin Company

222 Berkeley Street, Boston, Massachusetts 02116
(617) 351-5000   Cable Houghton

August 13, 19__

E-Z Typesetters Inc.
1200 Simpson Street
City, US 98765

Attention Sales Department

Ladies and Gentlemen

---

or with open punctuation:

Attention Advertising Department

The salutation that follows must be a collective one, for the letter is directed to a collective readership. Use a salutation such as *Ladies and Gentlemen, Dear Sir or Madam,* or *Dear CCC Company.*

Subject line. The subject line is an ancillary element in all letter stylings except the Simplified in which it is required. It presents the main thrust of the message in as few words as possible. In the Simplified Letter it is type-written in capital letters and appears three lines below the last line of the inside address and three lines above the first line of the message. In all other letter styles the subject line appears two lines below the salutation and two lines above the first line of the message. The subject line in all styles except the Simplified may be introduced by the word *Subject* styled in any one of the following ways, or the word may be omitted:

Subject: Pretrial Conference with Judge Baxter
SUBJECT: Pretrial Conference with Judge Baxter
SUBJECT: PRETRIAL CONFERENCE WITH JUDGE BAXTER

In the Simplified Letter, do not use the word *Subject.* Simply state the subject in capital letters:

PRETRIAL CONFERENCE WITH JUDGE BAXTER

Subject Line: Full Block Letter

Houghton Mifflin Company

222 Berkeley Street, Boston, Massachusetts 02116
(617) 351-5000   Cable HOUGHTON

March 15, 19__

Mr. Alexander I. Dalgish
Senior Product Manager
Kaycee Systems, Incorporated
4590 Sixteenth Street
City, US 98765

Dear Mr. Dalgish:

Subject: Research & Development of Product X -- Progress Reports

At our meeting on February 20, 19__, we agreed that a joint effort in producing progress reports
regarding Product X is called for. With this in mind we have established a committee to study

---

Subject lines are introduced by the terms *In re:* or *Re:* in some law office correspondence. These terms, however, are not used in modern general correspondence.

Reference initials. In modern practice the initials of the writer and/or typist are usually omitted. However, if someone other than the writer signs the letter, or if it is deemed necessary for filing purposes, the initials of the writer and/or typist are positioned flush with the left margin two lines below the last line of the signature block in all letter styles. Most companies use two or three capitalized letters for the writer's name and two or three lowercase letters for the typist's name. In the Simplified Letter only the typist's initials appear. Examples:

MAR:ahs	MAR/as	MAR:AS
MAR:as	MAR/ahs	MAR:AHS
mar:ahs	MR/as	AS

A letter to be signed by one person (such as a chief executive) but written or dictated by another (such as an executive assistant) and typed by the secretary bears three sets of initials styled as follows:

HTM:PTK:lc

Subject Line: Simplified Letter

Houghton Mifflin Company

222 Berkeley Street, Boston, Massachusetts 02116
(617) 351-5000   Cable HOUGHTON

March 13, 19__

Softsell, Incorporated
34 State Street Suite 34
City, US 98765

NEW SOFTWARE PRODUCT ANNOUNCEMENT

Senior Buyers of Softsell, we are proud to announce the forthcoming launch of a new series of personal computer software that is expected to revolutionize on-line spelling and dictionary

Here, HTM stands for the chief executive, PTK stands for the executive assistant, and lc stands for the typist/secretary.

Enclosure notation. If a letter contains an enclosure or enclosures, type a notation to this effect flush with the left margin two lines below the writer/ typist initials or two lines below the signature block if no such initials have been included. Use any one of these styles:

mixed punctuation	**open punctuation**
Enclosures: 3	3 Enclosures
Enclosures (3)	Enclosure
3 encs.	3 encs
encl. 3	encl 3

Particularly important enclosures ought to be listed numerically and described. Block and single-space such material:

Enclosures: 1. Proxy Statement
              2. P & L Statement, 1992–1993

If the enclosures themselves have not been clearly labeled as to subject and content, affix to the material a self-adhesive sticker identifying each one. To avoid confusion, use on the stickers the same descriptors used in the typed enclosure notation. If materials referred to in the letter are to be mailed under separate cover, indicate this fact:

56 Business Correspondence

Separate Mailing: Press Kit
Media Reception Schedule

Copy notation. Since photocopiers have all but replaced carbons, the abbreviation *cc* is now referred to as a *copy notation* or a *courtesy copy*. If included in a letter, this notation should be typed flush with the left margin, two lines below the signature block or two lines below any other notation preceding it. If used with reference initials or enclosure notations, the copy notation appears last. Use any one of these styles:

mixed punctuation	open punctuation
cc: Harold T. Martin	cc Harold T. Martin
CC: Harold T. Martin	CC Harold T. Martin
cc: Mr. Martin Mr. Peters Mr. Smith	cc Mr. Martin Mr. Peters Mr. Smith
CC: Ms. Taylor Ms. Uhlander Ms. Vest	CC Ms. Taylor Ms. Uhlander Ms. Vest

Signature Block, Reference Initials, and Enclosure and Copy Indicators: Modified Block Letter

and so we will expect to receive the final page proofs on January 15, 19__. Many thanks for your adherence to our schedules.

Sincerely yours,

Christopher I. Kendall
Production Manager

CIK:ahs

enclosures: 4

cc: Janet T. Booker
Mary Y. Miller

Atlanta / Dallas / Geneva, Illinois / Lawrenceville, New Jersey / Palo Alto / London

Multiple recipients are listed in alphabetical order according to full name or initials as shown above. If the writer so desires, give the copy recipient's full name and address:

single copy recipient
cc: Gene D. Dawson, Esq. (1 copy, Medical Claim)

several copy recipients
cc: Gene D. Dawson, Esq. (1 copy, Medical Claim)
One Court Street Suite 14
City, US 98765

Albert T. Goldberg, MD (1 copy, Discovery)
Two Hospital Drive
City, US 98765

Notice that double spacing separates each unit from the other, although the units are themselves single-spaced. If the writer wishes to send enclosures to the copy recipients, the enclosures are listed next to the names of the recipients.

A writer may wish that copies of a letter be distributed to others without that fact being revealed on the original. In this case, use *bcc* or *bcc:* before the names or initials of the recipients. The notation stands for *blind copy* or *blind courtesy copy* and appears only on the copies, not on the original, either in the same position as the regular copy notation or in the top left corner of the letterhead sheet.

Postscript. If a postscript is appended to a letter, it is typed from two to four lines below the last notation. In the Full Block and Block Letters the postscript is set flush left. In the Modified Block Letter, the postscript is indented exactly as the body paragraphs are. All postscripts are single-spaced, with margins matching those in the rest of the letter. In modern practice, it is now customary to omit the heading *P.S.* Have the writer initial all postscripts.

The Look of the Letter

Margins and letter symmetry. To achieve maximum balance and symmetry on the page, follow these rules:

1. Try to estimate the length of the letter before touching the keyboard. Read through the executive's handwritten notes, reread your shorthand notes, or listen to the electronically stored dictation to get a ballpark estimate of the word count.
2. Consider the inclusion of any long quotations, tables, or lists to be displayed within the running text. Inclusion of such material will af-

fect your total format and will add to the amount of tabbing you must do.

3. Determine if any special characters such as Greek letters or scientific symbols and mathematical/chemical formulas are to be included.
4. Be sure to take into account the fact that the closing section of a letter usually encompasses 2″ of vertical page space or 10–12 lines plus the bottom margin.
5. Be sure that the marginal settings on the continuation sheet match those on the letterhead.

Paper. Top quality stationery is an indicator of the company's concern about its public image. Factors to consider when purchasing business papers include weight, texture, and color. The paper ought to be heavy enough to withstand the pressure of keystrokes without pitting. At the same time it should be readily foldable without cracking. The ink from the printed letterhead must not bleed through onto the obverse side. The texture should be such that the typed characters are clear and undistorted and the written signatures and any handwritten symbols or signs appear smooth and even without blotching. If colored stationery is selected, its dye should be fast so that the paper will remain in good condition over time without fading.

The letterhead is printed on the felt side of the paper — i.e., the side from which you can read the watermark. In this connection, remember that you should type on the felt side of the continuation sheet. As we have said before, all continuation sheets and envelopes should match the letterhead in color, texture, and weight. Paper weight equals the weight in pounds of one ream cut to standard size. The heaviest paper weight is 24 for business correspondence, and the lightest is 9. Weights differ according to application in the office as shown in Table 6 on page 64.

Store your stationery in the original boxes with the tops on. Store only a small supply in your desk stationery drawer; otherwise, you can expect deterioration and soiling over time.

Model Formats

The following subsection of the chapter contains full-page facsimiles of the traditionally used business letters. The illustrations are shown in this sequence: the Simplified Letter, the Full Block Letter, the Block Letter, the Modified Block Letter. Within each illustration you will find detailed guidelines regarding the proper margin settings, the type of spacing used within and between paragraphs, and the positioning of the essential and ancillary elements of the letters.

The Simplified Letter

Houghton Mifflin Company

222 Berkeley Street, Boston, Massachusetts 02116-3764   Trade & Reference Division
(617) 351-5000   Fax: (617) 351-1108

January 4, 19__

Ms. Barbara C. Mackie
HCI Corporation MS 34A 78N
One State Street
City, US 98765

ADMINISTRATIVE MANAGEMENT SOCIETY'S SIMPLIFIED LETTER

Ms. Mackie, this is a facsimile of the Simplified Letter recommended for many years by the Administrative Management Society. It is a lean, clean format that saves you time through fewer keystrokes and less typewriter movement and enhances the look of the outgoing product.

The date is flush with the left margin from three to six lines beneath the letterhead. The inside address, also flush left, is typed three lines below the date to facilitate the use of window envelopes. There is no salutation; this solves the gender question in letters to correspondents who have signed previous letters with their initials and a surname only. (In the inside address of a letter to such a correspondent, you may also omit the courtesy title and type the person's initials plus the surname.)

Type a capitalized subject line three vertical line spaces below the last line of the inside address. Position the subject line flush with the left margin and omit the words Subject or Re. The subject line encapsulates the main topic of the message and should be brief and to the point. It is also a convenient filing tool.

The message begins three lines below the subject line. All paragraphs are set flush left. Paragraphs are single-spaced internally. Double spacing separates one paragraph from another. The first paragraph opens with use of the recipient's name in direct address as shown here--a polite way of engaging the recipient's interest at the outset.

Enumerated lists and tabular data, if included, are set flush left with double spacing separating one item from another. Items are single-spaced internally. Long quotations are block indented by five character spaces. Such quoted matter is single-spaced internally, with double spacing separating it top and bottom from the rest of the message.

If the letter exceeds one page, use a continuation sheet matching the letterhead sheet in size, color, texture, and weight. Begin the heading at least seven vertical lines below the top left edge of the page. The flush-left heading includes the recipient's name on line one, the page number

The Simplified Letter (*continued*)

Ms. Mackie
Page 2
January 4, 19__

on line two, and the full date on line three. Maintain continuation sheet margins and paragraph style as described for the first sheet. At least two message lines must be carried over to the continuation sheet. At no time should the signature block stand alone there.

The Simplified Letter has no complimentary close. Type the writer's name and corporate title in capital letters at least four to six lines below the last line of the message and flush with the left margin. A spaced hyphen separates the writer's name and title. The writer then signs the letter in the space allowed.

Skip two spaces and typewrite your own initials flush with the left margin. There is no need to include the writer's initials in this notation. If a courtesy copy or enclosure notation is required, enter the material two lines beneath your initials.

We recommend the Simplified Letter, especially to those who produce high volumes of correspondence.

JANE M. DOE - SENIOR EDITOR

ahs

enclosures (7)

cc Marietta K. Lowe
    Roberta Y. Peterson
    Candice S. Taylor

Full Block Letter

Houghton Mifflin Company

222 Berkeley Street, Boston, Massachusetts 02116
(617) 351-5000   Cable HOUGHTON

January 4, 19__

Mr. Peter C. Cunningham
Vice President, Operations
CCC Chemicals, Ltd.
321 Park Avenue
City, US 98765

Dear Mr. Cunningham:

Subject: Full Block Letter Style

This is the Full Block Letter--a format featuring elements aligned with the left margin. The date is typed from two to six (or more) lines below the letterhead, depending on the length of the message. The inside address may be typed from 4 to 12 lines below the date line, also depending on message length. Double-space between the inside address and the salutation. A subject line, if used, appears two lines below the salutation and two lines above the first message line.

The paragraphs are single-spaced internally with double spacing separating them from each other. Displayed matter such as enumerations and long quotations are indented by six character spaces. Units within enumerations and any quoted matter are single-spaced internally with double spacing setting them off from the rest of the text.

Skip two lines from the last line of the message to the complimentary close. Allow at least four blank lines for the written signature. Block the typed signature and corporate title under the complimentary close. Insert ancillary notations such as the typist's initials two spaces below the last line of the signature block.

Sincerely yours,

John M. Swanson
Executive Vice President

JMS:ahs

Enclosures: 4

The Block Letter

Houghton Mifflin Company

222 Berkeley Street, Boston, Massachusetts 02116
(617) 351-5000   Cable HOUGHTON

                                                January 14, 19__

CERTIFIED MAIL
CONFIDENTIAL

Sarah H. O'Day, Esq.
O'Day, Ryan & Sweeney
One Court Street
City, US 98765

Dear Ms. O'Day:

SUBJECT: BLOCK LETTER

This is the Block Letter, the features of which are similar to those of the Full Block Letter with the exception of the positioning of the date line, the complimentary close, and the typewritten signature block. The positioning of the date line determines the placement of the complimentary close and the signature block, both of which must be vertically aligned with the date. The date itself may be typed at center or placed about five spaces to the right of center.

The subject line, typed here in capital letters, is set flush left. Note that the special mailing and handling notations appear flush left, two lines above the first line of the inside address.

The complimentary close--aligned with the date--appears two lines below the last message line. At least four blank lines have been allowed for the written signature. The typed signature block is then aligned with the complimentary close.

Ancillary notations such as typist's initials, enclosure notations, and lists of copy recipients are placed two lines below the signature block, flush with the left margin.

                                                Very truly yours,

                                                Kathleen N. Lear
                                                Permissions Editor

KNL:ahs

The Modified Block Letter

Houghton Mifflin Company

222 Berkeley Street, Boston, Massachusetts 02116
(617) 351-5000   Cable HOUGHTON

February 14, 19__
Policy Number 34E 123W 9U

Dr. David J. Peters
State Insurance Corporation
4556 Hightower Boulevard
City, US 98765

Dear Dr. Peters:

SUBJECT: MODIFIED BLOCK LETTER

This is the Modified Block Letter. The date appears about five spaces to the right of center or at center. The reference line (the policy number) is aligned with the date line. The subject line must be centered on the page in this letter style.

The first line of each new paragraph is indented; subsequent lines are set flush left. Displayed data and long quotations are block indented further:

1. A continuation sheet heading is spaced across the top of the page six lines below the edge.

2. The complimentary close appears two lines below the last message line. The typed signature block includes the writer's name and title on separate lines. Both align with the date. At least four blank lines are allowed for the signature.

Ancillary notations position flush left two lines below the signature block. A postscript positions last, indented like message paragraphs.

Sincerely yours,

Donna W. Reardon
Personnel Manager

ahs

Table 6   **Business Papers and Their Weights**

Business Paper	Application	Weight
standard	correspondence	24 or 20
bill	invoices, billings	24 or 20
manifold or onionskin	overseas air	13 or 9
memorandum	interoffice communications	20 or 16
continuation sheets	communications exceeding one page	match that of the first sheet

Table 7   **Envelopes**

Type of Envelope	Number	Measurements
Commercial		
	$6\frac{1}{4}$	$3\frac{1}{2}'' \times 6''$
	$6\frac{3}{4}$	$3\frac{5}{8}'' \times 6\frac{1}{2}''$
	7	$3\frac{3}{4}'' \times 6\frac{3}{4}''$
	$7\frac{3}{4}$	$3\frac{7}{8}'' \times 7\frac{1}{2}''$
	Monarch	$3\frac{7}{8}'' \times 7\frac{1}{2}''$
	Check $8\frac{5}{8}$	$3\frac{5}{8}'' \times 8\frac{5}{8}''$
	9	$3\frac{7}{8}'' \times 8\frac{7}{8}''$
	10	$4\frac{1}{8}'' \times 9\frac{1}{2}''$
	11	$4\frac{1}{2}'' \times 10\frac{3}{8}''$
	12	$4\frac{3}{4}'' \times 11''$
	14	$5'' \times 11\frac{1}{2}''$

Window
Standard window size and position is
$1\frac{1}{8}'' \times 4\frac{1}{2}''$, $\frac{7}{8}''$ left, $\frac{1}{2}''$ bottom.

Type of Envelope	Number	Measurements
	$6\frac{1}{4}$*	$3\frac{1}{2}'' \times 6''$
	$6\frac{3}{4}$	$3\frac{5}{8}'' \times 6\frac{1}{2}''$
	7	$3\frac{3}{4}'' \times 6\frac{3}{4}''$
	$7\frac{3}{4}$	$3\frac{7}{8}'' \times 7\frac{1}{2}''$
	Monarch	$3\frac{7}{8}'' \times 8\frac{5}{8}''$
	Check $8\frac{5}{8}$**	$3\frac{5}{8}'' \times 8\frac{7}{8}''$
	9	$3\frac{7}{8}'' \times 8\frac{7}{8}''$
	10	$4\frac{1}{8}'' \times 9\frac{1}{2}''$
	11	$4\frac{1}{2}'' \times 10\frac{3}{8}''$
	12	$4\frac{3}{4}'' \times 11''$
	14	$5'' \times 11\frac{1}{2}''$

*Window position is $\frac{3}{4}''$ left, $\frac{1}{2}''$ bottom.
**Window size is $1\frac{1}{4}'' \times 3\frac{3}{4}''$; three positions, including $\frac{3}{4}''$ left, $\frac{13}{16}''$ bottom.

Table 7   *(continued)*

Monarch Window

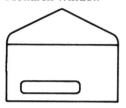

| Monarch | $3\frac{7}{8}'' \times 7\frac{1}{2}''$ |

Standard with Special Window Positions

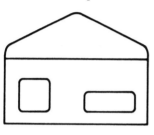

$6\frac{1}{4}$	$3\frac{1}{2}'' \times 6''$
$6\frac{3}{4}$	$3\frac{5}{8}'' \times 6\frac{1}{2}''$
7	$3\frac{3}{4}'' \times 6\frac{3}{4}''$
$7\frac{3}{4}$	$3\frac{7}{8}'' \times 7\frac{1}{2}''$
Monarch	$3\frac{7}{8}'' \times 7\frac{1}{2}''$
Check $8\frac{5}{8}$	$3\frac{5}{8}'' \times 8\frac{5}{8}''$
9	$3\frac{7}{8}'' \times 8\frac{7}{8}''$
10	$4\frac{1}{8}'' \times 9\frac{1}{2}''$
11	$4\frac{1}{2}'' \times 10\frac{3}{8}''$
12	$4\frac{3}{4}'' \times 11''$
14	$5'' \times 11\frac{1}{2}''$

Continuous

Mounted on computer carrier strip. Available in many styles and sizes. Plain or printed.

Courtesy of Boston Envelope, 150 Royall St., Canton, MA 02021.

Envelopes

Envelopes must match the letterhead and continuation sheets in color, texture, and weight. The standard $8\frac{1}{2}'' \times 11''$ stationery will fit the Numbers $6\frac{3}{4}$, 9, and 10 commercial, window, or overseas air envelopes. Table 7 provides standard envelope configurations and sizes.

Standard Envelope

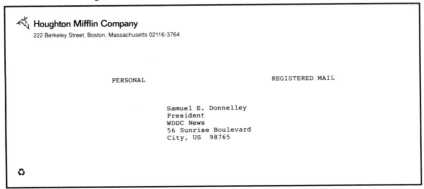

Envelope addresses must include these data:

addressee	**sender**
full name	full name
street address	street address
city, state, ZIP code	city, state, ZIP code

Optional data, included as required by the circumstances, are suite/room/ apartment numbers, special mailing instructions (such as certification, registration, special delivery, or overseas air mail), personal notations (such as CONFIDENTIAL or PERSONAL), and attention indicators (such as Attention: Advertising Department).

Guidelines for Addressing Envelopes

Follow these suggestions based on the latest United States Postal Service regulations when addressing envelopes:

Envelope Size and Color
1. Use rectangular envelopes measuring no smaller than $3\frac{1}{2}'' \times 5''$ and no larger than $6\frac{1}{8}'' \times 11\frac{1}{2}''$.
2. Ensure that color contrast between paper and typescript is sharp.

Styling of the Address Block
1. Single-space the address block; do not use double or triple spacing and never use a slanted format.
2. Type the address block at center or about 5 spaces to the left of center.
3. The address block should fill no more than $1\frac{1}{2}'' \times 3\frac{3}{4}''$ of line space. At least $\frac{5}{8}''$ of blank space should be allowed from the last line of the address to the bottom of the envelope.
4. With window envelopes, ensure that the letter has been properly

Table 8   **Two-letter Abbreviations for U.S. States and Dependencies**

State	Abbreviation	State	Abbreviation
Alabama	AL	Montana	MT
Alaska	AK	Nebraska	NE
Arizona	AZ	Nevada	NV
Arkansas	AR	New Hampshire	NH
California	CA	New Jersey	NJ
Canal Zone	CZ	New Mexico	NM
Colorado	CO	New York	NY
Connecticut	CT	North Carolina	NC
Delaware	DE	North Dakota	ND
District of Columbia	DC	Ohio	OH
Florida	FL	Oklahoma	OK
Georgia	GA	Oregon	OR
Guam	GU	Pennsylvania	PA
Hawaii	HI	Puerto Rico	PR
Idaho	ID	Rhode Island	RI
Illinois	IL	South Carolina	SC
Indiana	IN	South Dakota	SD
Iowa	IA	Tennessee	TN
Kansas	KS	Texas	TX
Kentucky	KY	Utah	UT
Louisiana	LA	Vermont	VT
Maine	ME	Virginia	VA
Maryland	MD	Virgin Islands	VI
Massachusetts	MA	Washington	WA
Michigan	MI	West Virginia	WV
Minnesota	MN	Wisconsin	WI
Mississippi	MS	Wyoming	WY
Missouri	MO		

folded and that the inside address on the letterhead has been positioned so that all elements are clearly visible through the window. You should have maintained margins of at least $\frac{1}{4}''$ between the top, bottom, left, and right edges of the inside address block and the top, bottom, left, and right edges of the window space.

5. Nothing should be printed or typed in the space extending from the right and left bottom edges of the address block to the right and left bottom edges of the envelope. Likewise, the space extending below the center of the address block to the bottom center edge of the envelope should be blank.

Table 9   **Abbreviations for Words Often Appearing in Place Names**

Street/Place Name	Abbreviation	Street/Place Name	Abbreviation
Academy	ACAD	Corners	CORS
Agency	AGNCY	Course	CRSE
Air Force Base	AFB	Court	CT
Airport	ARPRT	Courts	CTS
Alley	ALY	Cove	CV
Annex	ANX	Creek	CRK
Arcade	ARC	Crescent	CRES
Arsenal	ARSL	Crossing	XING
Avenue	AVE	Dale	DL
Bayou	BYU	Dam	DM
Beach	BCH	Depot	DPO
Bend	BND	Divide	DV
Big	BG	Drive	DR
Black	BLK	East	E
Bluff	BLF	Estates	EST
Bottom	BTM	Expressway	EXPY
Boulevard	BLVD	Extended	EXT
Branch	BR	Extension	EXT
Bridge	BRG	Fall	FL
Brook	BRK	Falls	FLS
Burg	BG	Farms	FRMS
Bypass	BYP	Ferry	FRY
Camp	CP	Field	FLD
Canyon	CYN	Fields	FLDS
Cape	CPE	Flats	FLT
Causeway	CSWY	Ford	FRD
Center	CTR	Forest	FRST
Central	CTL	Forge	FRG
Church	CHR	Fork	FRK
Churches	CHRS	Forks	FRKS
Circle	CIR	Fort	FT
City	CY	Fountain	FTN
Clear	CLR	Freeway	FWY
Cliffs	CLFS	Furnace	FURN
Club	CLB	Gardens	GDNS
College	CLG	Gateway	GTWY
Common	CMM	Glen	GLN
Corner	COR	Grand	GRND

Table 9   (*continued*)

Street/Place Name	Abbreviation	Street/Place Name	Abbreviation
Great	GR	Meeting	MTG
Green	GRN	Memorial	MEM
Ground	GRD	Middle	MDL
Grove	GRV	Mile	MLE
Harbor	HBR	Mill	ML
Haven	HVN	Mills	MLS
Heights	HTS	Mines	MNS
High	HI	Mission	MSN
Highlands	HGLDS	Mound	MND
Highway	HWY	Mount	MT
Hill	HL	Mountain	MTN
Hills	HLS	National	NAT
Hollow	HOLW	Naval Air Station	NAS
Hospital	HOSP	Neck	NCK
Hot	H	New	NW
House	HSE	North	N
Inlet	INLT	Orchard	ORCH
Institute	INST	Oval	OVAL
Island	IS	Palms	PLMS
Islands	IS	Park	PARK
Isle	IS	Parkway	PKY
Junction	JCT	Pass	PASS
Key	KY	Path	PATH
Knolls	KNLS	Pike	PIKE
Lake	LK	Pillar	PLR
Lakes	LKS	Pines	PNES
Landing	LNDG	Place	PL
Lane	LN	Plain	PLN
Light	LGT	Plains	PLNS
Little	LTL	Plaza	PLZ
Loaf	LF	Point	PT
Locks	LCKS	Port	PRT
Lodge	LDG	Prairie	PR
Loop	LOOP	Radial	RADL
Lower	LWR	Ranch	RNCH
Mall	MALL	Ranches	RNCHS
Manor	MNR	Rapids	RPDS
Meadows	MDWS	Resort	RESRT

(*continued*)

Table 9 (*continued*)

Street/Place Name	Abbreviation	Street/Place Name	Abbreviation
Rest	RST	Sulphur	SLPHR
Ridge	RDG	Summit	SMT
River	RIV	Switch	SWCH
Road	RD	Tannery	TNRY
Rock	RK	Tavern	TVRN
Row	ROW	Terminal	TERM
Run	RUN	Terrace	TER
Rural	R	Ton	TN
Saint	ST	Tower	TWR
Sainte	ST	Town	TWN
San	SN	Trace	TRCE
Santa	SN	Track	TRAK
Santo	SN	Trail	TRL
School	SCH	Trailer	TRLR
Seminary	SMNRY	Tunnel	TUNL
Shoal	SHL	Turnpike	TPKE
Shoals	SHLS	Union	UN
Shode	SDHD	University	UNIV
Shore	SHR	Valley	VLY
Shores	SHRS	Viaduct	VIA
Siding	SDG	View	VW
South	S	Village	VLG
Space Flight Center	SFC	Ville	VL
		Vista	VIS
Speedway	SPDWY	Walk	WALK
Spring	SPG	Water	WTR
Springs	SPGS	Way	WAY
Spur	SPUR	Wells	WLS
Square	SQ	West	W
State	ST	White	WHT
Station	STA	Works	WKS
Stream	STRM	Yards	YDS
Street	ST		

Conventional Address Block Styles

If addressing a letter to an individual, follow the patterns shown earlier in this chapter. If addressing a letter to a corporation, follow this pattern:

CCC Corporation
987 Industrial Drive
P.O. Box 444
Keystone, US 12345

Remember, though, that if both a street and a box number are used, the location on the line just above the line on which the city, state, and ZIP code appear is the destination of the letter. Therefore, if you wish the letter to go to the street address and not to the post office box (which may involve another ZIP code), put the street address last before the city, state, and ZIP code. If using an attention line, follow this pattern:

CCC CORPORATION
Attention Marketing Manager
987 Industrial Drive
Keystone, US 12345

Special mailing instructions are typed in capital letters below the space for the postage (i.e., approximately nine vertical line spaces from the right top edge of the envelope and not overrunning a $\frac{1}{2}''$ margin). Personal notations are also typed in capital letters and are positioned to the upper left of the address block about nine vertical line spaces below the left top edge of the envelope. Any other such notations should be styled in underscored capital and lowercase letters, as <u>Please Forward</u> or <u>Please Hold for Arrival</u>, and should be typed about nine vertical line spaces from the left top edge of the envelope.

Addressing Envelopes for Computerized Sorting

Large-volume mailers are urged to address their envelopes in such a way as to expedite and not obstruct the Postal Service's electronic mail sorting system. (This topic is also discussed in Chapter Nine.) The Postal Service recommends that you use any of seven basic address formats, all employing capital letters, abbreviations, and minimal punctuation. These formats —designed to facilitate automated mail handling— also save you unnecessary keystrokes and thereby increase your own output. The seven formats are: (1) Post Office Box, (2) Rural Route, (3) Building/Business/Personal Name, (4) Standard Street Address/Numeric, (5) Standard Street Address/Alphabetic, (6) Community Identity, and (7) Dual Address. Examples:

Post Office Box
MS SARAH SMITH
PO BOX 123
CITY, US 98765

Rural Route
MR JG LOUGHRY
RR 5 BOX 94-C
RURAL LOCALE, US 12345

Building/Business/Personal Name
EZ CREDIT CORP
ATTN Sales Department
CITY INDUSTRIAL PK
123 E INDUSTRIAL DR
CITY, US 98765

Standard Street Address/Numeric
MS JANE DOE
123 E 53RD ST APT 221
CITY, US 98765

Standard Street Address/ Alphabetic
MS JANE DOE
603 FIRST ST APT 80
CITY, US 98765

Community Identity
MR JOHN T WATSON
HILLENDALE
13 FRANKLIN ST
CITY, US 98765

Dual Address
RRR CORP
123 E PARK AVE
PO BOX 100
CITY, US 98765

or

RRR CORP
PO BOX 100
123 E PARK AVE
CITY, US 98765

Remember that the address to which you want delivery to be made must appear on the last line above the city, state, and ZIP code. In the first example under Dual Address, delivery will be made to the post office box, but in the second example, delivery will be made to the street address.

ZIP + 4. The Postal Service currently offers a voluntary ZIP + 4 coding program for extra high-speed automated sorts. This program is particularly useful to high-volume business mailers. Rate incentives have been proposed to make the program even more attractive to commercial mailers. With ZIP + 4, optical character readers (OCRs) in the originating post office can read the city, state, and ZIP code. Special printers apply a bar code on letter-size mail. The bar code — a series of vertical bars and half-bars — corresponds to ZIP + 4 and allows all subsequent sorts to be done on low-cost, high-speed bar code readers (BCRs). The equipment reads ZIP + 4 and then sorts the mail according to sector or segment. This process, in effect, separates the mail and routes it to a box number, a firm, a building, or the carrier assigned to a particular locale. ZIP + 4 looks like this: 01075–1234 where the traditional five-digit ZIP code 01075 is followed by a hyphen and four more figures: 1234, in this hypothetical example. The digits 01075 represent the major geographic location (in this case, a town in Massachusetts). The numbers 1 and 2 in 1234 represent a sector within the major geographic location. The sector might include several selected blocks, a group of streets, a large building, or another smaller geographic location within the major one. The numbers 3 and 4 represent a segment within the "12" sector. The segment might be one side of a block, two sides of a street, one floor in a large building, a cluster of mailboxes, or one post office box in a cluster. Eventually, ZIP + 4 will eliminate all hand sorting.

Address formats for military mail. The Postal Service recommends that you use the format shown in this section for mail addressed to United States military personnel using Air Force, Army, and Fleet Post Offices. For Army and Air Force addressees, enter the addressee's name on line one, followed on line two by the addressee's unit and PSC number, followed on line three by the organization to which the addressee is assigned, followed on the last line by the APO:

PVT GG DOE
COMPANY F, PSC 3250
167TH INFANTRY REGT
APO, NY 09801

With mail addressed to members of the United States Navy and Marine Corps, type the addressee's name on line one, followed on line two by the name of the addressee's shore-based organization, mobile unit, or the name of the addressee's ship. On the last line type the Fleet Post Office and its number:

JOHN M DOE QMSN USN
USS SEA SQUIRT (DD 729)
FPO SAN FRANCISCO 96601

Addressing mail to Canada. Follow the format recommended by Canada Post to expedite automated handling: use capital and lowercase letters with the addressee's name (line one), the firm name if included (line two), and the street address (lines two or three). On a subsequent line, enter the city name in capital letters followed on the same line by the name of the province styled either in written-out or abbreviated form as shown in Table 10. The six-character Canadian Postal Code is typed on another line. Remember that one character space separates the first three numbers and letters from the last three in the Postal Code. Conclude the address block with the capitalized word CANADA if you are mailing the letter from outside Canada. Example:

Ms. Ann FitzGerald
FitzGerald and McHenry
123 Queen Street
OTTAWA ON
K1A 0B3
CANADA

Table 10   **Abbreviations for Canadian Provinces**

Province	Abbreviation
Alberta	AB
British Columbia	BC
Labrador	LB
Manitoba	MB
New Brunswick	NB
Newfoundland	NF
Northwest Territories	NT
Nova Scotia	NS
Ontario	ON
Prince Edward Island	PE
Quebec	PQ
Saskatchewan	SK
Yukon	YT

FORMS OF ADDRESS

Business etiquette requires the proper use of forms of address in correspondence. Use of the right form of address applies to the inside address, the salutation, and the envelope address block. Forms of address include personal titles such as *Ms.* or *Dr.*, honorifics such as *Esq.* or *The Honorable*, military rank designations such as *Lt.* or *GySgt*, and titles such as *His Holiness, Senator,* or *The Right Reverend* for high-ranking personages. The next few subsections discuss particularly problematic usages of honorifics and personal titles. A table giving the proper forms of address for various academic, clerical, consular, diplomatic, governmental, military, and professional title holders concludes this section.

Esq.

This abbreviation stands for *Esquire,* which often follows the surnames of men and women in the American bar and in the consular corps. It is used in the inside address, on the envelope, and in the typed signature block. It is never used in the salutation or in conjunction with personal or professional titles such as *Ms.* or *Dr.* preceding a name. Likewise, it is never used in conjunction with another honorific such as *The Honorable.* Its plural form is *Esqs.*, used when referring to multiple addressees holding the title. In highly formal diplomatic correspondence, *Esquire* may be written out in full. Most recent evidence indicates, however, that the United States

Department of State is discouraging use of the term altogether. In Great Britain, *Esq.* is routinely used with the names of chief executive officers, prominent professionals in law and medicine, and high-ranking diplomats. Examples of the proper use of *Esq.* in American business correspondence are:

Janet L. Wills, Esq.   Dear Ms. Wills:
Attorney-at-Law

John L. Wills, Esq.   Dear Mr. Wills:
American Consul

Norton L. Levin, Esq.   Dear Mr. Levin and Mr. Gold:
Samuel I. Gold, Esq.   Dear Messrs. Levin and Gold:
Attorneys-at-Law

Honorable

The Honorable is used in the United States with the names of most high-ranking appointed or elected officials, as judges, clerks of courts, representatives, senators, governors, and the president and vice president. It may be used in the inside address and on the envelope of a letter destined for the holder of the title, but it is never used by the holder in written or typed signatures, on letterhead or business cards, or in invitations.

Never use *The Honorable* with a surname only (i.e., "The Honorable Smith" is incorrect); a first name, an initial or initials, or a personal title must intervene (as in *The Honorable John Sweeney; The Honorable J. M. Sweeney; The Honorable Mr. Sweeney*). As with *Esq.*, *The Honorable* may be used with the name of a high-ranking woman official. Examples:

The Honorable Lee Whalen

The Honorable L. B. Whalen

The Honorable L. Brantley Whalen

The Honorable Mr./Ms. Whalen

The Honorable Dr. Whalen

In addressing correspondence to a married couple, one of whom is the title holder, follow these patterns:

if husband holds the title

The Honorable John M. Sweeney   Dear Mr./Judge, etc., and Mrs.
and Mrs. Sweeney   Sweeney:

The Honorable and Mrs. John M.
Sweeney

The Hon. and Mrs. J. M. Sweeney

if wife holds the title/business correspondence

The Honorable Elizabeth Lee and   Dear Judge, Senator, etc., Lee and
Mr. Lee   Mr. Lee:

The Hon. Elizabeth Lee and
Mr. Lee

if wife holds the title/social correspondence

Mr. and Mrs. Albert A. Lee   Dear Mr. and Mrs. Lee:

if wife holds the title and has retained maiden name/business correspondence

The Honorable Ann Stone and   Dear Judge, Senator, etc., Stone
Mr. Allen Wheeler   and Mr. Wheeler:

The Hon. Ann Stone and Mr. Allen Wheeler

if wife holds the title and has retained maiden name/social correspondence

Ms. Ann Stone and Mr. Allen   Dear Ms. Stone and Mr. Wheeler:
Wheeler

In limited address space *The Honorable* may appear by itself on line one with the addressee's name on line two.

Madam/Madame

Use *Madam* only in letters to high-level women diplomats or government officials, such as the United States Ambassador to the United Nations or a woman justice of the Supreme Court. The term is used only in salutations:

Dear Madam:

Dear Madam Justice:

Madame, on the other hand, is used in salutations of letters destined for foreign heads of state and diplomats:

if woman holds the office

Dear Madame Ambassador:

Dear Madame Prime Minister:

Madame is also used with the names of the wives of high-ranking foreign diplomats and with the names of the wives of foreign heads of state:

if husband holds the title

Excellency and Madame Cortez:

Mesdames

This word is the plural of *Mrs., Madam,* and *Madame.* It is the equivalent to *Messrs.* in business usage and may appear before the names of two or more women (married or single) associated together in a firm. It is used in the inside address, on the envelope, and in the salutation:

Mesdames Sarah Walker and Laura Phelps	Dear Mesdames Walker and Phelps:
Mesdames Walker and Phelps	Mesdames:

If the two women share the same surname, follow these patterns:

Mesdames A. L. and L. T. Phelps	Dear Mesdames Phelps:
The Mesdames Phelps	Mesdames:

Never pluralize the surname in instances like this.

Messrs.

This term is the plural abbreviated form of *Mr.,* and, like *Mesdames,* it is used with the names of two or more men associated together in a firm. *Messrs.* is used in the inside address, on the envelope, and in the salutation:

Messrs. Dabney, Langhorne, and Lee	Dear Messrs. Dabney, Langhorne, and Lee:

If two men share the same surname, follow these patterns:

Messrs. C. D. and R. R. Langhorne	Dear Messrs. Langhorne:
	Gentlemen:

Never pluralize the surname in an instance like this.

Misses

This is the plural of *Miss* and its use parallels that of *Messrs.:*

Misses Carleton and East	Dear Misses Carleton and East:
	Ladies:
Misses A. Y. Carleton and D. C. East	Dear Miss Carleton and Miss East:
Misses Maureen and Mary O'Day	Dear Misses O'Day:
The Misses O'Day	Ladies:

Ms.

Ms., like *Mr.,* indicates nothing with regard to a person's marital status. *Ms.* may be used in the inside address, on the envelope, in the salutation, and in the typed signature block of a letter. Never use *Ms.* with a woman's married name (i.e., "Ms. Robert A. Keith" is incorrect). The plural form is either *Mses.* or *Mss.* and its use parallels that of *Misses.* Examples:

Mses. (*or* Mss.) Grey and Holt

Mses. (*or* Mss.) C. C. Grey and D. D. Holt

Mses. (*or* Mss.) Nan and Pam Lee

The Mses. (*or* Mss.) Lee

Dear Mses. (*or* Mss.) Grey and Holt:

Dear Ms. Grey and Ms. Holt:

Dear Mses. (*or* Mss.) Lee:

Dear Nan and Pam Lee:

Professor

Avoid abbreviating *Professor* to *Prof.* in instances where it appears only with a surname (i.e., "Dear Prof. Webber" is incorrect). Avoid wording salutations to professors as just "Dear Professor" and never say "Dear Prof. Smith." Correct patterns are given below:

Professor (*or* Prof.) Lee O'Brien

Dear Professor O'Brien:

Dear Dr. O'Brien:

Dear Ms./Mr./Miss/Mrs. O'Brien:

In addressing correspondence to a married couple, one spouse of which is a professor and the other is not, follow these patterns:

if husband is a professor

Professor and Mrs. Lee O'Brien

Dear Professor and Mrs. O'Brien:

Dear Dr. and Mrs. O'Brien:

Dear Mr. and Mrs. O'Brien:

if wife is a professor/business correspondence

Professor Diana O'Brien and Mr. O'Brien

Dear Professor O'Brien and Mr. O'Brien:

Dear Dr. O'Brien and Mr. O'Brien:

if wife is a professor/social correspondence

Mr. and Mrs. Lee O'Brien

Dear Mr. and Mrs. O'Brien:

If the woman has retained her maiden name, follow these patterns in social and business correspondence:

Professor Diana Quirk

Mr. Lee O'Brien

Dear Professor Quirk and Mr. O'Brien:

Dear Dr. Quirk and Mr. O'Brien:

Dear Ms. Quirk and Mr. O'Brien:

Letters addressed to multiple recipients, all of whom are professors, are styled as follows:

Professors B. B. Doe and C. C. Roe	Dear Professors Doe and Roe:
	Dear Drs. Doe and Roe:
	Dear Mr. Doe and Mr. Roe:
	Dear Messrs. Doe and Roe:
	Gentlemen:
Professors C. L. Jones and D. C. Lawton	Dear Professors Jones and Lawton:
	Dear Ms. Jones and Mr. Lawton:
	Dear Drs. Jones and Lawton:
Professors T. A. and A. Y. Lee	Dear Professors Lee:
The Professors Lee	Dear Drs. Lee:
	or if men
	Gentlemen:
	or if women
	Mesdames:
	or if wed
	Dear Professors Lee:
	Dear Drs. Lee:
	Dear Mr. and Ms. (*or* Mrs.) Lee:

Reverend

This title is the one most misused in business correspondence: few people seem able to remember that it ought to be preceded by *The*. Never use *The Reverend* or its abbreviated form *The Rev.* with a surname only (i.e., "The Reverend Smith" is incorrect). *The Reverend* or *The Rev.* is used on the envelope, in the inside address, and in the signature block but never in the salutation (i.e., "Dear Reverend Smith" is incorrect). Follow these patterns:

The Reverend John M. Mills

The Rev. John M. Mills

The Reverend Dr. John M. Mills

The Rev. Dr. John M. Mills

The Reverend, like *The Honorable,* may be used with a surname only if a courtesy title such as *Mr., Dr.,* or *Ms.* intervenes:

The Reverend Ms. Kendall

The Rev. Dr. King

The Reverend Professor O'Neill

When addressing a letter to a minister and the minister's spouse, follow these patterns:

if husband is a minister

The Reverend and Mrs. A. A. Lee   Dear Mr./Dr. and Mrs. Lee:

The Rev. and Mrs. A. A. Lee   *or, depending on denomination*

Dear Father Lee and Mrs. Lee:

Dear Father Andrew and Mrs. Lee:

if wife is a minister

The Reverend Ann T. Lee and Mr.   Dear Mrs./Dr. Lee and Mr. Lee:
Lee

The Rev. Ann T. Lee and Mr. Lee

Two or more ministers may be addressed as *The Reverends, The Revs., The Reverend* (or *The Rev.*) *Messrs.,* and *The Reverend* (or *The Rev.*) *Drs.* plus their names. You also might wish to repeat *The Reverend* or *The Rev.* before each name instead of pluralizing the title:

The Reverends P. X. and F. I.   Gentlemen:
Connon   *or, depending on denomination*

The Revs. P. X. and F. I. Connon   Dear Father Patrick and Father

The Rev. Messrs. P. X. and F. I.   Francis:
Connon   Dear Fathers:

The Rev. Messrs. Connon

The Reverend Messrs. Connon

The Rev. P. X. Connon and The
Rev. F. I. Connon

If the clerics have different surnames, these patterns are appropriate:

The Rev. Messrs. P. X. Connon   Gentlemen:
and F. I. O'Brien   Dear Mr./Dr. Connon and

The Reverend P. X. Connon   O'Brien:

The Reverend F. I. O'Brien   *or, depending on denomination*

The Revs. Connon and O'Brien   Dear Father Patrick and Father
Francis:

Dear Fathers:

Titles and Honorifics in Signature Blocks

The only personal titles used before a writer's name in the typed signature block are *Ms., Miss,* and *Mrs.* With a single exception (i.e., *Mrs.* plus the writer's husband's name), these personal titles, if used, must be enclosed in parentheses. They are never used in the written signature. Remember that *Mr.* is never used in the typed or written signature.

Typewritten signature	**Written signature**
(Ms.) Jane Doe	Jane Doe
(Miss) Jane Doe	Jane Doe
(Mrs.) Jane Doe	Jane Doe
Mrs. John M. Doe	Jane Doe

If the writer holds an advanced degree such as *M.D., Ph.D.,* or *D.D.S.,* the abbreviated form of the degree may be used in the typed and written signatures following the surname. The writer never uses *Professor* or *Doctor/Dr.* preceding the name.

Typewritten signature	**Written signature**
J. Robinson Smith, M.D.	J. Robinson Smith, M.D.
Chief of Surgery	
Nancy Y. Hanks, Ph.D.	Nancy Y. Hanks, Ph.D.
Professor of Molecular Physics	

Holders of *Esq.* may use it in the typewritten signature block but not in the written signature:

Typewritten signature	**Written signature**
Jane L. Smith, Esq.	Jane L. Smith

Holders of *The Honorable* never use the term themselves:

Typewritten signature	**Written signature**
John M. Sweeney	John M. Sweeney
Associate Justice	

Ministers may choose to use *The Reverend/The Rev.* before their names in the typewritten signature block; however, they never use it in the written signature:

Typewritten signature	**Written signature**
Francis S. O'Leary, S.J.	Francis S. O'Leary, S.J.
Jonathan K. Stein, D. D.	Jonathan K. Stein, D. D.
Eric C. Swenson	Eric C. Swenson
Pastor	
The Very Rev. Alexis I. Ivanov	Alexis I. Ivanov
Rector	

Government officials and military personnel never put their titles or rank designations before their full names in typed or written signatures. Titles and indicators of rank appear only in the typed portion of the block, one line below the writer's name:

Typewritten signature	**Written signature**
Edward M. Keene	Edward M. Keene
United States Senator	
Elizabeth A. Meaney	Elizabeth A. Meaney
United States Ambassador	
Lee A. Lawson	Lee A. Lawson
Captain, USA	

Table 11 **Forms of Address**

Academics	**Form of Address**	**Salutation**
assistant professor	Professor Joseph/Jane Stone Mr./Ms./Dr. Joseph/Jane Stone	Dear Professor Stone: Dear Mr./Ms. Stone: Dear Dr. Stone:
associate professor	Professor Joseph/Jane Stone Mr./Ms./Dr. Joseph/Jane Stone	Dear Professor Stone: Dear Mr./Ms. Stone: Dear Dr. Stone:
chancellor, university	Dr./Mr./Ms. Joseph/Jane Stone	Dear Chancellor Stone:
chaplain	The Reverend Joseph/Jane Stone	Dear Chaplain Stone: Dear/Mr./Ms. Stone: Dear Father Stone:
dean, college or university	Dean Joseph/Jane Stone *or* Dr./Mr./Ms. Joseph/Jane Stone Dean, School of _____	Dear Dean Stone: Dear Dr./Mr./Ms. Stone:
instructor	Mr./Ms./Dr. Joseph/Jane Stone	Dear Mr./Ms./Dr. Stone:
president	President Joseph/Jane Stone *or* Dr./Mr./Ms. Joseph/Jane Stone	Dear President Stone: *or* Dear Dr./Mr./Ms. Stone:
president/priest	The Reverend Joseph Stone President of _____	Sir: Dear Father Stone:
professor, college or university	Professor Joseph/Jane Stone *or* Dr./Mr./Ms. Joseph/Jane Stone	Dear Professor Stone *or* Dear Dr./Mr./Ms. Stone

Clerical and Religious Orders

abbot, Roman Catholic	The Right Reverend Joseph Stone Abbot of _____	Right Reverend Abbott: Dear Father Abbott:

Table 11   (*continued*)

Clerical and Religious Orders	Form of Address	Salutation
apostolic delegate	His Excellency The Most Reverend Joseph Stone Archbishop of _____ The Apostolic Delegate	Your Excellency: My dear Archbishop:
archbishop, Armenian Church	His Eminence the Archbishop of _____	Your Eminence: Your Excellency:
archbishop, Greek Orthodox	The Most Reverend Joseph Archbishop of _____	Your Eminence:
archbishop, Roman Catholic	The Most Reverend Joseph Stone Archbishop of _____	Your Excellency:
archbishop, Russian Orthodox	The Most Reverend Joseph Archbishop of _____	Your Eminence:
archdeacon, Episcopal	The Venerable Joseph Stone Archdeacon of _____	Venerable Sir: Dear Archdeacon Stone:
archimandrite, Greek Orthodox	The Very Reverend Joseph Stone	Reverend Sir: Dear Father Joseph:
archimandrite, Russian Orthodox	The Right Reverend Joseph Stone	Reverend Sir: Dear Father Joseph:
archpriest, Greek Orthodox	The Reverend Joseph Stone	Dear Father Joseph:
archpriest, Russian Orthodox	The Very Reverend Joseph Stone	Dear Father Joseph:
bishop, Episcopal	The Right Reverend Joseph Stone Bishop of _____	Right Reverend Sir: Dear Bishop Stone:
bishop, Greek Orthodox	The Right Reverend Joseph Bishop of _____	Your Grace:
bishop, Methodist	The Reverend Joseph Stone Methodist Bishop	Dear Bishop Stone:
bishop, Roman Catholic	The Most Reverend Joseph Stone Bishop of _____	Your Excellency: Dear Bishop Stone:
bishop, Russian Orthodox	The Most Reverend Joseph Bishop of _____	Your Grace:
brotherhood, Roman Catholic, member of	Brother Joseph Stone	Dear Brother: Dear Brother Joseph:
brotherhood, Roman Catholic, superior of	Brother Joseph Superior	Dear Brother Joseph:
canon, Episcopal	The Reverend Canon Joseph Stone	Dear Canon Stone:

(*continued*)

Table 11 (*continued*)

Clerical and Religious Orders	Form of Address	Salutation
cantor (man)	Cantor Joseph Stone	Dear Cantor Stone:
cantor (woman)	Cantor Jane Stone	Dear Cantor Stone:
cardinal	His Eminence Joseph Cardinal Stone	Your Eminence:
clergyman, Protestant	The Reverend Joseph Stone *or* The Reverend Joseph Stone, D.D.	Dear Mr. Stone: *or* Dear Dr. Stone:
clergywoman, Protestant	The Reverend Jane Stone *or* The Reverend Jane Stone, D.D.	Dear Ms. Stone: *or* Dear Dr. Stone:
elder, Presbyterian	Elder Joseph/Jane Stone	Dear Elder Stone:
dean of a cathedral, Episcopal	The Very Reverend Joseph Stone Dean of ____	Dear Dean Stone:
metropolitan, Russian Orthodox	His Beatitude Joseph Metropolitan of ____	Your Beatitude:
moderator, Presbyterian	The Moderator of ____ *or* The Reverend Joseph Stone *or* Dr. Joseph Stone	Reverend Sir: My dear Sir: Dear Mr. Moderator: *or* My dear Dr. Stone:
monsignor, Roman Catholic (domestic prelate)	The Right Reverend Monsignor Joseph Stone	Right Reverend Monsignor: Dear Monsignor: Dear Monsignor Stone:
papal chamberlain	The Very Reverend Monsignor Joseph Stone	Very Reverend and Dear Monsignor Stone: Dear Monsignor Stone:
patriarch, Armenian Church	His Beatitude Patriarch of ____	Your Beatitude:
patriarch, Greek Orthodox	His All Holiness Patriarch Joseph	Your All Holiness:
patriarch, Russian Orthodox	His Holiness the Patriarch of ____	Your Holiness:
pope	His Holiness The Pope	Your Holiness: Most Holy Father:
president, Mormon Church	President Joseph Stone Church of Jesus Christ of Latter-Day Saints	Dear President Stone:

Table 11   (*continued*)

Clerical and Religious Orders	Form of Address	Salutation
priest, Episcopal	The Reverend Joseph/Jane Stone	Dear Mr./Ms. Stone:
	The Rev. Dr. Joseph/Jane Stone	Dear Dr. Stone:
priest, Greek Orthodox	The Reverend Joseph Stone	Dear Father Joseph:
priest, Roman Catholic	The Reverend Joseph Stone	Dear Father: Dear Father Stone:
priest, Russian Orthodox	The Reverend Joseph Stone	Dear Father Joseph:
rabbi (man)	Rabbi Joseph Stone *or* Joseph Stone, D.D.	Dear Rabbi Stone: *or* Dear Dr. Stone:
rabbi (woman)	Rabbi Jane Stone *or* Jane Stone, D.D.	Dear Rabbi Stone: *or* Dear Dr. Stone:
sisterhood, Roman Catholic, member of	Sister Mary Viventia	Dear Sister: Dear Sister Viventia: Dear Sister Mary:
sisterhood, Roman Catholic, superior of	The Reverend Mother Superior	Reverend Mother: Dear Reverend Mother:
supreme patriarch, Armenian Church	His Holiness the Supreme Patriarch and Catholicos of All Armenians	Your Holiness:

Diplomats

ambassador, U.S.	The Honorable Joseph/Jane Stone The Ambassador of the United States	Sir:/Madam: Dear Mr./Madam Ambassador:
ambassador to the U.S.	His/Her Excellency Joseph/Jane Stone The Ambassador of _____	Excellency: Dear Mr./Madame Ambassador:
chargé d'affaires, U.S.	The Honorable Joseph/Jane Stone United States Chargé d'Affaires	Dear Mr./Ms. Stone:
chargé d'affaires to the U.S.	Joseph/Jane Stone, Esq. Chargé d'Affaires of _____	Dear Sir/Madame:
consul, U.S.	Joseph/Jane Stone, Esq. United States Consul	Dear Mr./Ms. Stone:

(continued)

Table 11   (*continued*)

Diplomats	Form of Address	Salutation
consul, to the U.S.	The Honorable Joseph/Jane Stone Consul of _____	Dear Mr./Ms. Stone:
minister, U.S.	The Honorable Joseph/Jane Stone The Minister of the United States	Sir:/Madam: Dear Mr./Madam Minister:
minister to the U.S.	The Honorable Joseph/Jane Stone The Minister of _____	Sir/Madame: Dear Mr./Madame Minister:
representative (foreign), to the United Nations (with rank of ambassador)	His/Her Excellency Joseph/Jane Stone Representative of _____ to the United Nations	Excellency: My dear Mr./Madame Stone: Dear Mr./Madame Ambassador:
secretary general, United Nations	His/Her Excellency Joseph/Jane Stone Secretary General of the United Nations	Dear Mr./Madam/Madame Secretary General:
undersecretary to the United Nations	The Honorable Joseph/Jane Stone Undersecretary of the United Nations	Sir:/Madam: (if American) Sir:/Madame: (if foreign) My dear Mr./Ms. Stone: Dear Mr./Ms. Stone:
U.S. representative to the United Nations	The Honorable Joseph/Jane Stone United States Representative to the United Nations	Sir:/Madam: Dear Mr./Ms. Stone:

Federal, State, and Local Government Officials		
alderman	The Honorable Joseph/Jane Stone	Dear Mr./Ms. Stone:
assistant to the president	Mr./Ms. Joseph/Jane Stone	Dear Mr./Ms. Stone:
attorney general, U.S.	The Honorable Joseph/Jane Stone Attorney General of the United States	Dear Mr./Madam Attorney General:
attorney general, state	The Honorable Joseph/Jane Stone Attorney General State of _____	Dear Mr./Madam Attorney General:
assemblyman/assemblywoman, state	The Honorable Joseph/Jane Stone	Dear Mr./Ms. Stone:

Table 11   (*continued*)

Federal, State, and Local Government Officials	Form of Address	Salutation
cabinet member	The Honorable Joseph/Jane Stone Secretary of _____	Sir:/Madam: Dear Mr./Madam Secretary:
cabinet member, former	The Honorable Joseph/Jane Stone	Dear Mr./Ms. Stone:
chairman, congressional committee	The Honorable Joseph/Jane Stone Chairman, Committee on ___	Dear Mr./Madam Chairman:
chief justice, U.S. Supreme Court	The Chief Justice of the United States	Dear Mr. Chief Justice: Sir:
associate justice, U.S. Supreme Court	Mr./Madam Justice Stone	Dear Mr./Madam Justice: Sir:/Madam:
associate/chief justice, Supreme Court, former	The Honorable Joseph/Jane Stone	Dear Mr./Ms. Stone: Dear Mr./Madam Justice Stone:
clerk, county	The Honorable Joseph/Jane Stone	Dear Mr./Ms. Stone:
clerk, of a court	Joseph/Jane Stone, Esq. Clerk of the Court of _____	Dear Mr./Ms. Stone:
commissioner (federal, state, local)	The Honorable Joseph/Jane Stone	Dear Mr./Ms. Stone:
delegate, state	**—See assemblyman, state**	
director, federal agency	The Honorable Joseph/Jane Stone Director _____Agency	Dear Mr./Ms. Stone:
district attorney	The Honorable Joseph/Jane Stone District Attorney	Dear Mr./Ms. Stone:
governor	The Honorable Joseph/Jane Stone Governor of _____	Dear Governor Stone:
governor-elect	The Honorable Joseph/Jane Stone Governor-elect of _____	Dear Mr./Ms. Stone:
governor, former	The Honorable Joseph/Jane Stone	Dear Governor Stone: Dear Mr./Ms. Stone:
judge, federal	The Honorable Joseph/Jane Stone Judge of the United States District Court for the _____ District of _____	Sir:/Madam: Dear Judge Stone:

(*continued*)

Table 11   (*continued*)

Federal, State, and Local Government Officials	Form of Address	Salutation
judge, state or local	The Honorable Joseph/Jane Stone Judge of the Court of _____	Dear Judge Stone:
justice, Supreme Court, associate, chief, and former	**—See chief justice, supreme court** and subentries thereto	
librarian of congress	The Honorable Joseph/Jane Stone The Librarian of Congress	Sir:/Madam: Dear Mr./Ms./Dr. Stone:
lieutenant governor	The Honorable Joseph/Jane Stone Lieutenant Governor of _____	Dear Mr./Ms. Stone:
mayor	The Honorable Joseph/Jane Stone Mayor of _____	Dear Mayor Stone:
postmaster general	The Honorable Joseph/Jane Stone Postmaster General United States Postal Service	Dear Mr./Madam Postmaster General:
president, U.S.	The President The White House	Dear Mr. President:
president-elect, U.S.	The Honorable Joseph Stone The President-elect of the United States	Dear Sir: Dear Mr. Stone:
president, U.S., former	The Honorable Joseph Stone	Dear Mr. Stone: Dear Mr. President: Dear President Stone:
press secretary, to the president	Mr./Ms. Joseph/Jane Stone Press Secretary to the President	Dear Mr./Ms. Stone:
representative, state	**—See assemblyman, state**	
representative, U.S.	The Honorable Joseph/Jane Stone United States House of Representatives	Dear Mr./Ms. Stone:
secretary of state, for a state	The Honorable Joseph/Jane Stone Secretary of State State Capitol	Dear Mr./Madam Secretary:
senator, former (state or U.S.)	The Honorable Joseph/Jane Stone	Dear Senator Stone: Dear Mr./Ms. Stone:

Table 11 (*continued*)

Federal, State, and Local Government Officials	Form of Address	Salutation
senator, state	The Honorable Joseph/Jane Stone The State Senate State Capitol	Dear Senator Stone:
senator, U.S.	The Honorable Joseph/Jane Stone United States Senate	Dear Senator Stone:
speaker, U.S. House of Representatives	The Honorable Joseph/Jane Stone Speaker of the House of Representatives	Dear Mr./Madam Speaker:
territorial delegate to the U.S. House of Representatives	The Honorable Joseph/Jane Stone Delegate of _____ United States House of Representatives	Dear Mr./Ms. Stone:
undersecretary, of cabinet department (also for deputy and assistant secretaries)	The Honorable Joseph/Jane Stone Undersecretary of the Department of _____	Dear Mr./Ms. Stone:
vice president, U.S.	The Vice President of the United States *or* The Honorable Joseph Stone Vice President of the United States	Sir: My dear Mr. Vice President: Dear Mr. Vice President: *or* Dear Mr. Vice President:

Military Ranks*	Branch of Service	Form of Address	Salutation
admiral	USCG/USN	ADM Lee Stone, USCG/USN	Dear Admiral Stone:
brigadier general	USAF	Brig Gen Lee Stone, USAF	Dear General Stone:
	USA	BG Lee Stone, USA	Dear General Stone:
	USMC	BGen Lee Stone, USMC	Dear General Stone:
captain	USAF/USMC	Capt Lee Stone, USAF/USMC	Dear Captain Stone:
	USA	CPT Lee Stone, USA	Dear Captain Stone:
	USCG/USN	CAPT Lee Stone, USCG/USN	Dear Captain Stone:

(*continued*)

*These military ranks and their abbreviations are used with the names of military officers. The abbreviated rank is followed by the full name, a comma, and the appropriate abbreviation of the person's branch of service (USAF for United States Air Force, USA for United States Army, USCG for United States Coast Guard, USMC for United States Marine Corps, or USN for United States Navy). Example: ADM Lee Stone, USN. These forms of address apply to men and women, and the first name *Lee* is meant to cover both sexes. Subsequent pages give cadet/midshipman and enlisted ranks.

Table 11   (*continued*)

Military Ranks	Branch of Service	Form of Address	Salutation
chief warrant officer	USAF/USA	CWO Lee Stone, USAF/USA	Dear Mr./Ms. Stone:
colonel	USAF/USMC USA	Col Lee Stone, USAF/USMC COL Lee Stone, USA	Dear Colonel Stone: Dear Colonel Stone:
commander	USCG/USN	CDR Lee Stone, USCG/USN	Dear Commander Stone:
ensign	USCG/USN	ENS Lee Stone, USCG/USN	Dear Ensign Stone: Dear Mr./Ms. Stone:
first lieutenant	USAF USA USMC	1st Lt Lee Stone, USAF 1LT Lee Stone, USA 1stLt Lee Stone, USMC	Dear Lt. Stone: Dear Lt. Stone: Dear Lt. Stone:
general	USAF/USMC USA	Gen Lee Stone, USAF/USMC GEN Lee Stone, USA	Dear General Stone: Dear General Stone:
lieutenant	USCG/USN	LT Lee Stone, USCG/USN	Dear Lt. Stone: Dear Mr./Ms. Stone:
lieutenant colonel	USAF USA USMC	Lt Col Lee Stone, USAF LTC Lee Stone, USA LtCol Lee Stone,USMC	Dear Colonel Stone: Dear Colonel Stone: Dear Colonel Stone:
lieutenant commander	USCG/USN	LCDR Lee Stone, USCG/USN	Dear Commander Stone:
lieutenant general	USAF USA USMC	Lt Gen Lee Stone, USAF LTG Lee Stone, USA LtGen Lee Stone, USMC	Dear General Stone: Dear General Stone: Dear General Stone:
lieutenant (junior grade)	USCG/USN	LTJG Lee Stone, USCG/USN	Dear Lt. Stone: Dear Mr./Ms. Stone:
major	USAF/USMC USA	Maj Lee Stone, USAF/USMC MAJ Lee Stone, USA	Dear Major Stone: Dear Major Stone:
major general	USAF USA USMC	Maj Gen Lee Stone, USAF MG Lee Stone, USA MajGen Lee Stone, USMC	Dear General Stone: Dear General Stone: Dear General Stone:
rear admiral	USCG/USN	RADM Lee Stone, USCG/USN	Dear Admiral Stone:
second lieutenant	USAF USA USMC	2d Lt Lee Stone, USAF 2LT Lee Stone, USA 2dLt Lee Stone, USMC	Dear Lt. Stone: Dear Lt. Stone: Dear Lt. Stone:
vice admiral	USCG/USN	VADM Lee Stone, USCG/USN	Dear Admiral Stone:
warrant officer	USAF/USA	WO Lee Stone, USAF/USA	Dear Mr./Ms. Stone:

Table 11   (*continued*)

Military Ranks	Branch of Service	Form of Address	Salutation
Cadets and Midshipmen			
cadet		Cadet Lee Stone	Dear Cadet Lee Stone: Dear Mr./Ms. Stone:
midshipman		Midshipman Lee Stone	Dear Midshipman Stone: Dear Mr./Ms. Stone:
Enlisted Personnel: A Representative Listing			
airman	USAF	AMN Lee Stone, USAF	Dear Airman Stone:
airman basic	USAF	AB Lee Stone, USAF	Dear Airman Stone:
airman first class	USAF	A1C Lee Stone, USAF	Dear Airman Stone:
chief petty officer	USCG/USN	CPO Lee Stone, USCG/USN	Dear Mr./Ms. Stone:
corporal	USA	CPL Lee Stone, USA	Dear Corporal Stone:
gunnery sergeant	USMC	GySgt Lee Stone, USMC	Dear Sergeant Stone:
lance corporal	USMC	L/Cpl Lee Stone, USMC	Dear Corporal Stone:
master sergeant	USAF USA	MSGT Lee Stone, USAF MSG Lee Stone, USA	Dear Sergeant Stone: Dear Sergeant Stone:
petty officer	USCG/USN	PO Lee Stone,USCG/USN	Dear Mr./Ms. Stone:
private	USA USMC	PVT Lee Stone, USA Pvt Lee Stone, USMC	Dear Private Stone: Dear Private Stone:
private first class	USA	PFC Lee Stone, USA	Dear Private Stone:
seaman	USCG/USN	SMN Lee Stone, USCG/USN	Dear Seaman Stone:
seaman first class	USCG/USN	S1C Lee Stone, USCG/USN	Dear Seaman Stone:
senior master sergeant	USAF	SMSGT Lee Stone, USAF	Dear Sergeant Stone:
sergeant	USAF USA	SGT Lee Stone, USAF SG Lee Stone, USA	Dear Sergeant Stone: Dear Sergeant Stone:
sergeant major (a title not a rank)	USA/USMC	SGM/Sgt. Maj. Lee Stone, USA/USMC	Dear Sergeant Major Stone:

(*continued*)

Table 11   (*continued*)

Military Ranks	Branch of Service	Form of Address	Salutation
specialist (as specialist 4th class)	USA	S4 Lee Stone, USA	Dear Specialist Stone:
staff sergeant	USAF USA	SSGT Lee Stone, USAF SSG Lee Stone, USA	Dear Sergeant Stone: Dear Sergeant Stone:
technical sergeant	USAF	TSGT Lee Stone, USAF	Dear Sergeant Stone:

Professions	Form of Address	Salutation
attorney	Mr./Ms. Joseph/Jane Stone Attorney-at-Law *or* Joseph/Jane Stone, Esq.	Dear Mr./Ms. Stone:
dentist	Joseph/Jane Stone, D.D.S.	Dear Dr. Stone:
physician	Joseph/Jane Stone, M.D.	Dear Dr. Stone:
veterinarian	Joseph/Jane Stone, D.V.M.	Dear Dr. Stone:

5
Business Documents

THIS CHAPTER WILL FOCUS on the preparation of business documents other than letters, including memorandums, press releases, corporate reports, agendas, itineraries, and minutes of a meeting.

MEMORANDUM FORMAT

An interoffice memorandum, like a business letter, is a means of transmitting written information from one person, group, or office to another or others. Unlike a letter, however, a memorandum lacks an inside address, a salutation, and a complimentary close. Instead, a memorandum has the following headingss: a "To" line on which you type the recipient's name, a "From" line on which you type the writer's name, a date line, and a subject line. These headings are printed at the top of the memorandum sheet. Ancillary data such as a telephone extension, a department name, or a "Copies to" indicator also may be included in the printed headings, depending on the policy of your company. The rest of the page is designated for the message. The typist's initials, lists of courtesy copy recipients, distribution lists, or attachment notations appear at the end of the message, if necessary. Should the memorandum contain sensitive material, the notation CONFIDENTIAL is typed in capital letters at the very top of the sheet above the main printed heading *Memorandum*.

Paper size and the appearance of the memorandum. The most usual paper size is $8\frac{1}{2}'' \times 11''$; however, the half size measuring $8\frac{1}{2}'' \times 5\frac{1}{2}''$ may be used for very brief messages. Memos also may be typed on plain bond paper, but if this method is used you must head the sheet with the capitalized term MEMORANDUM followed on subsequent lines by capitalized

TO, FROM, DATE, and SUBJECT headings punctuated by colons. Some companies use colored memo paper especially for interoffice communications generated by chief executive and chief operating officers. Color choice, weight, size, and design of memorandum paper vary according to company policy.

Maintain appropriate margins so that the memorandum is balanced attractively on the page. Align your heading fill-ins so that they look neat and consistent. Some printed headings are themselves aligned to the right in order to facilitate typing the fill-ins:

> TO: Marketing Division
> FROM: Office of the President
> DATE: 12/13/93
> SUBJECT: Dictionary Advertising Campaign

If the printed headings have been so aligned, skip two spaces before typing the fill-ins. If the headings are aligned to the left instead, begin typing the fill-ins two spaces to the right of the longest heading (usually the subject heading) and block all other fill-ins with it:

> TO: Marketing Division
> FROM: Office of the President
> DATE: 12/13/93
> SUBJECT: Dictionary Advertising Campaign

Regardless of the positioning of the printed heads, however, you must skip two spaces before beginning the fill-ins. Ensure that your fill-ins are aligned with the printed headings: they should appear neither above nor below the headings. Use your variable line spacer or ratchet release to achieve proper horizontal alignment.

Remember also to store your memo paper in its original container. Keep only a small quantity in your desk drawer; otherwise, the paper will deteriorate from exposure to dust and also may become crumpled along the edges.

The "To" line: content and styling. The "To" line may contain a single name or several names. It also might include a departmental name or the collective designation "All Desks" with material to be distributed company-wide. A personal title such as *Mr., Ms.,* or *Dr.* is generally omitted unless the recipient outranks the writer. If the memo has been addressed to several recipients one of whom requires use of a personal title, similar titles must be used with the names of the other recipients. You may use full names or initials and surnames in the "To" block. For instance, you might say *Jane C. King* or *J.C. King.* Follow the style dictated by the writer. The recipient's departmental affiliation may be included on a line under the name, depending on the size of the company and its policy:

TO: Frank R. Richardson
       Polymer Research Division

With a memorandum directed to many individuals, type the asterisked word "Distribution*" in the "To" line space. At the end of the message, skip two lines, repeat the word "Distribution*," skip two more lines, and list the recipients in a single-spaced flush left block, one name to a line, in alphabetical order by surname or in order of corporate rank. Use the latter order only when the memorandum has been directed to a group of high corporate officers. In a case like this, the chief executive officer's name would appear first on the list followed by the names of various vice presidents in order of rank within the company.

The "From" line: content and styling. The "From" line may contain a single name or multiple names. It may indicate that the memo is from a particular office or department. The "From" line is styled just like the "To" line, except for the omission of a personal title with the writer's name: the writer's name may appear as a full form (John L. Lee) or in abbreviated form (J.L. Lee), but a personal title (such as "Mr. John L. Lee") is never used.

The date line. You may abbreviate dates in memos to the all-numeric form such as 12/13/93 where 12 means December, 13 means the thirteenth day of the month, and 93 means 1993. The full form — December 13, 1993 — is also correct. Use the style that the writer prefers.

The subject line. The gist of the letter is encapsulated in the subject line, which should be short (one-liners are preferable from the reader's standpoint and for subsequent filing purposes). The writer should dictate the subject line. Key words within the subject line may be capitalized initially or the entire line may be capitalized. Do not underscore the subject matter and do not punctuate the line with a period.

The message. Skip three vertical line spaces from the last heading and its fill-in before beginning the message. Paragraphs may be blocked flush with the left margin or indented to the right by five spaces. Single-space the paragraphs internally, and use double spacing to separate the paragraphs from each other. Maintain adequate margins to the right, left, and bottom of the page. Some writers prefer to enumerate their paragraphs with Arabic or Roman numerals or with letters. Follow the style indicated by the writer. Displayed data such as long quotations, numerical lists within paragraphs, and tables should be set off from the body of the message by block indentations and double spacing at the top and the bottom of the displayed matter. Displayed quotations and lists should be single-spaced internally. Skip two lines between each unit of an enumeration.

With a message exceeding one page, use a plain continuation sheet matching the printed memorandum page in color, texture, weight, and size. Margin settings and paragraph alignment must match the format on the first page. Skip at least seven vertical line spaces from the top edge of the sheet before typing the heading. Either block the heading flush with the left margin or spread it across the page. If the heading on the first sheet reads "Distribution*" use the flush left format, and include only the page number and the date on the continuation sheet. If you have styled the date in numerals on the first sheet, use that styling on the continuation sheet. If you have written out the date on the first sheet, write it out on the continuation sheet.

Typist's initials. Typist's initials, if included, are positioned two vertical line spaces beneath the last message line, flush with the left margin. Inclusion of these initials depends on company policy, the writer's wishes, and/or the typist's own preferences.

Copy recipients and distribution lists. Copy recipients' names appear two vertical line spaces below the typist's initials (if included) or two lines below the last line of the message:

> cc: Kathryn K. Overton
>   Michael I. Simms
>   Theodore R. Thomas
>   Laverne T. Udall

A distribution list for many recipients of copies is set up in much the same manner, with two spaces separating the distribution notation from the list itself:

> Distribution*
>
> Mary A. Brown
> Alice V. Collins
> Franklin B. Fields
> James W. Hay
> Leo V. Isaacson
> Mary W. Kay

With a memo destined for a single recipient, the writer usually retains a copy and sends the original to the intended recipient. With memos to mul-

Full-page Memorandum

Memorandum

TO   Janis Wilcox   FROM   Arthur R. Lee   DATE   12/13/9-

SUBJECT   Memorandum Format

This is an example of a full-page company memorandum featuring printed headings. Notice that the fill-ins have been horizontally aligned and that two spaces have been left between each head and the typewritten fill-in.

For this long memo, the margins are set at one inch. For a short memo use 1½-inch or 2-inch margins with double-spaced, indented paragraphs. Skip at least three lines from the last heading to the first line of the message. This space may be increased with extremely short memos.

Handle displayed enumerations like this:

1. Skip two lines between the text and the first line in the enumeration.

2. Block and indent the entire enumeration as shown here.

3. Skip two lines between each item in the list, but single-space within each unit.

4. Skip two lines between the last line of the last enumerated item and the first line of the continuing text.

Paragraphs in memorandums may be indented by five spaces or they may be set flush with the left margin as shown here.

Include your initials at the end of the message, two lines below the last line of text, if you wish. Copy recipients should be listed two lines below your initials or two lines below the last line of the message if no initials appear on the page. Attachments are listed separately below the other notations or two lines below the last message line if no other notations appear on the page.

cc: Mary Allen
     Sandra Kendall

Attachment: Style Manual

Half-sheet Memorandum

Memorandum

TO   Editors   FROM   Mary Roe   DATE   12/13/9_

SUBJECT   Editorial Department Meeting - New Product Development

There will be a meeting of all editors in my office on Monday, December 19, at

10:30 a.m. for the purpose of proposing and discussing new publications for the Reference

Division in the coming year. Please come prepared to discuss your ideas in detail and

defend them if necessary.

A detailed agenda will be issued to you before the meeting.

Memorandum on Blank Sheet

MEMORANDUM

TO: All Desks - All Locations   FROM: John R. Doe

SUBJECT: Jean Roe   DATE: December 13, 19__

I am pleased to announce the appointment of Jean D. Roe as Assistant Business Manager for our division. She will be responsible for many of the budget-related financial systems in place and for the development of new systems for project and quality control in print and electronic media. She will provide assistance in coordinating data processing projects and other administrative services.

Jean has been an auditor with the Internal Audit Department since June 1992. Jean is a Certified Public Accountant in the Commonwealth of Massachusetts. She earned her B.A. in economics from Boston College and her M.B.A. from Harvard. She and her family reside in Wellesley.

I am sure that all of you will welcome Jean as she joins our division at this time.

tiple recipients, the writer usually retains the original and sends copies to all of the recipients. Put a check by the name of each recipient before putting the memo in the envelope.

Attachment notations. If attachments accompany the memo, put a notation to this effect two lines below the last notation on the page or, if there are no other notations, put the attachment notation two lines below the last message line. Don't forget to staple or clip the attachments to the memorandum.

Attachments: P & L Statement 1984
                OP Sales Estimates 1985

Envelopes. Memorandums are generally routed to their recipients via unsealed, string-tied interoffice mailers. These envelopes have lines on which you write the recipient's name and intracompany location. With confidential memos, use a sealable manila envelope or a regular letterhead envelope with the word CONFIDENTIAL typed or hand-lettered in the top left corner, the recipient's name in the center, and the notation "Company Mail" or "Interoffice Mail" lettered or typed in the space where the postage ordinarily would have been affixed. Another way of indicating that the envelope is for interoffice delivery is to place an inked-in "X" mark where the postage ordinarily goes.

PRESS RELEASES

Companies issue press releases chiefly to help maintain a high public profile and thereby increase sales. For example, a press release might be issued to promote the launch of a new product or to announce markedly increased revenues, stock splits, or bigger dividends. Other stories might announce the appointment of a new chief executive officer or the installation of new members of the board of directors. The press release — just one component of a comprehensive public relations, advertising, and sales campaign — is a highly visible indicator of corporate style and substance. When you are called upon to type and proofread press releases, your role in maintaining your company's public image is quite important.

Since a press release is really a news story, the writer constructs it with a view to immediate newsworthiness. That is, the writer follows journalistic style by putting the most important data in the first paragraph: Who did What? When was it done and Where? And Why was it done? Supporting data are then included in subsequent paragraphs arranged in order from the most important to the least important. In this way, the writer makes the news editor's life much easier, for the story can be pruned from the bottom depending on the space available in the publication in which it will appear,

Press Release

from
 Houghton Mifflin Company 222 Berkeley Street, Boston, Massachusetts 02116-3764

Contact: Stephen O. Jaeger   September 18, 1992
        Executive Vice President   For Immediate Release
        Chief Financial Officer
        (617) 725-5017

HOUGHTON MIFFLIN COMPANY
ANNOUNCES PURCHASE OF ASSESSMENT DIVISION
OF DLM, INC.

BOSTON -- Houghton Mifflin Company announced today that it has reached agreement to

purchase the assets of the Assessment Division of DLM, Inc. of Allen, Texas. Terms were

not disclosed, other than that Houghton Mifflin will finance the cost of purchase out of

operating cash flow.

Through this purchase, Houghton Mifflin acquires the publishing rights and the

inventory of DLM's entire line of assessment instruments and related products. Best known

among these is the widely used and highly respected Woodcock-Johnson Psycho-Educational

Battery, authored by Dr. Richard W. Woodcock. The Riverside Publishing Company, a

subsidiary of Houghton Mifflin which specializes in test publishing, will utilize the expertise

and resources that have made it one of the nation's largest test publishers to publish and

market these newly acquired tests.

-more-

-2-

Nader F. Darehshori, Chairman, President, and Chief Executive Officer of Houghton Mifflin said, "The acquisition of this outstanding list of clinical/special needs assessments from DLM fulfill our long-term strategy to increase our presence in the clinical/special needs testing field. Becoming a major force in the clinical/special needs segment has been an integral part of our planning and now will become an important part of our company's future growth.

"As publishers of such well-known assessment instruments as the Iowa Test of Basic Skills, the Stanford-Binet Intelligence Scale, and others, we are very familiar with both group-administered and clinical/special needs tests, but the larger part of our business was in the group-administered category. With the acquisition of these new tests, we become a major player in the category of clinical/special needs testing as well and can benefit from the synergy that an outstanding full line of assessment instruments will produce in a market with a very strong potential for growth."

Houghton Mifflin is a leading publisher of textbooks, software, assessments, and other educational materials for the elementary and secondary school and college markets, as well as an extensive line of reference publications, business software, and fiction and nonfiction for adult and young readers.

###

without inadvertent deletion of crucial facts. Similarly, a broadcast editor can cut all but the most salient facts for inclusion in a television or radio newscast.

Paper and format. A press release is usually typewritten on a special printed form headed *Press Release, News Release,* or *News from* (company). The company's full name, address, and telephone/fax number(s) are usually printed on the form as part of the heading along with memorandum-style subheadings such as

> From: Sandee Martin
> Contact: Laura Mason

in which the writer's name appears first followed by the public affairs person whom the editor might wish to contact for further information should a major story develop. These subheadings may be positioned in the top right or left corners of the first page. If the material is to be published or broadcast immediately, the phrase For Immediate Release should be typed near the top edge of the first page in a conspicuous position relative to the heading and subheads.

The paper itself may be $8\frac{1}{2}'' \times 11''$ or it may be $8\frac{1}{2}'' \times 14''$ (legal). Double-space the text for easier editing later on. Allow right and left margins measuring $1''$ and a bottom margin of about $1\frac{1}{2}''$ to accommodate insertion of the continuation indicator *more*. Leave at least four lines of white space from the bottom of the printed heading to the typewritten headline of the first page.

The headline. The headline — a sentence or phrase focusing on the most important point of the story — is typed in capital letters centered on the page below the printed heading. Skip at least three and possibly four vertical line spaces from the headline to the first line of the story itself.

The story. Begin the story with a flush left or indented date line (such as BOSTON, December 13 —) in which the city name appears in capital letters followed by a comma, the month and the day, followed by a dash set tight or spaced with the day. The date can also be given above the phrase For Immediate Release. Do not give the state's name unless your city's name is the same as those of several other cities. Begin typing the story right after the dash, on the same line, with no space or one space intervening between the dash and the first word of the running text:

> BOSTON, December 13 — John N. Kennedy, Chairman and
> President of FFF Air Lines, has announced a new super-saver fare
> structure, effective immediately. Passengers will realize savings of
> up to 30 percent on tickets. . . .

Indent each subsequent paragraph by at least five or six spaces to set it off from the next one. If the story exceeds one page, type the word *more* in lowercase letters at the bottom of the page, centered within the bottom margin space. Style this continuation indicator as -more- or (more), using hyphens or parentheses. Use blank continuation sheets matching the first sheet in size, color, texture, and weight. Maintain margins on the continuation sheet that match those on the first sheet, except at the top of the page. The heading of the continuation sheet should begin from four to six lines below the top edge. Number and caption the continuation sheet(s) as directed by the writer. The capitalized caption will contain a key word or words derived from the substance of the headline, followed by a dash and the page number set tight on one line, as FFF SUPER-SAVER — 2.

The end. Signal the end of the story by typing one of the following devices in the center of the last page about two or three vertical line spaces from the last line:

or #### *or* ### *or* –30– *or* –end– *or* (END)

Proofreading. Proofread the entire document line-for-line against the original. Check for typographical, grammatical, and factual errors. Query the executive if a fact appears to be inconsistent with other data or if you think it might be wrong. Then read the document again from beginning to end without looking at the original. For one last check have a colleague read the original aloud while you read the final document.

CORPORATE REPORTS

Several kinds of reports are generated in business: memorandum reports, letter reports, and megareports (i.e., long complex documents sometimes encompassing hundreds of pages). These documents serve many needs and are directed to various readership levels inside and outside the company. A report might introduce and then analyze in detail a given market; discuss a particular business problem in depth and then offer a solution; lay out an annual or multiyear strategic plan; delve into a highly complicated legal or financial question; provide impetus for the research, development, and launch of a new product; or offer a stock/investment prospectus. Your task is to organize and keyboard the draft materials into a logically ordered, consistently and neatly typed final product devoid of typographical and factual errors. You also may be requested to assist in producing tabular and graphic exhibits called *visual aids*. And of course the responsibility for proofreading, fact checking, duplication/printing, collation, binding, and distribution to the designated readership probably will be yours.

Table 1   **Corporate Report Typewriting Guide**

Margins

location	machine setting: unbound & top-bound
top/p. 1	12 lines
top/p. 2 ff.	6 lines
bottom/all pp.	6 lines
left & right/all pp.	one inch
	machine setting: sidebound
left/all pp.	$1\frac{1}{2}$ inches

Spacing

element of report	machine setting: unbound, top-bound, & sidebound
body of report	single or double
between paragraphs	if single-spaced paragraphs, double spacing to separate them; if double-spaced paragraphs, triple spacing to separate them
long quoted matter, displayed	single
enumerations, tables	single within units; double between units
footnotes	single
bibliography	single

Indention

element of report	machine setting: unbound, top-bound, sidebound
paragraphs	indented format: 5 spaces block format: no indents
long quoted matter, tables, lists	blocked 5 spaces right and left
footnotes	2–5 spaces, first line only
bibliography	no indent on first line; 2–5 spaces, runover lines

Pagination: unbound & top-bound — numerals 3–6 lines from bottom center, each page; sidebound — numerals 3–6 lines from top of page or 3–6 lines from bottom and $\frac{1}{2}''$ to the right of center

element of report	kind of number
flyleaves	no pagination
title fly	lowercase Roman numeral i

Table 1   (*continued*)

title page	lowercase Roman numeral ii
front matter (i.e., letters of authorization, acknowledgments, table of contents, lists of tables and graphics, preface, foreword, executive summary)	lowercase Roman numeral iii
first text page	Arabic numeral 1
subsequent text pages (i.e., body of report, appendix, footnotes listed separately, bibliography, index)	Arabic numeral 2 ff.

In many cases a long report represents the input of a number of other executives besides yours. For instance, the summary in a new product report might have been written by your executive while the sales forecast might have been prepared by the sales director. The manufacturing cost estimates and production schedule might have been worked out by a manufacturing manager. The financials might have been prepared by a business manager or an accountant, with the advertising/promotion strategy having been developed by an advertising manager or an outside agency. Assuming that your executive is in charge of the entire document, you should be aware of some common pitfalls. Multiauthor reports usually abound in stylistic, spelling, and factual inconsistencies. Therefore, it is important to read the entire document from beginning to end and note all inconsistencies, errors, and unclear points before touching the keyboard. Query the writer or writers responsible for the problematic points or sections. Check all major and subsidiary headings in the text to ensure consistency of style. Find out if the displayed tables and graphics are to be scattered throughout the text or clustered together in an appendix.

The Memorandum Report

For a short report (one to three pages) intended for in-house distribution, use the company's printed memo paper and continuation sheets. Put the report title in the subject block and then follow the guidelines in this chapter regarding memorandum format. A typical memorandum report might be a monthly sales analysis for a product line in a given region or territory or a monthly departmental progress report with respect to on-line projects.

The Letter Report

A letter report might be used to convey information to various off-site managers or to the members of a board of directors. A letter report is just what the designation indicates: a letter to the recipient(s) that has been modified stylistically to include various headings and subheadings. The letter report is typed on corporate letterhead and continuation sheets matching the letterhead. We recommend the Full Block or the Block Letter styles for such a report. These two styles lend themselves readily to graceful, balanced presentation of information, whether it be running text or displayed matter. In most cases the letter will be duplicated for many recipients. We therefore recommend that you save extra white space in the inside address block to accommodate inclusion of names and addresses varying markedly in length.

REPORT TITLE STYLED AS SUBJECT LINE

position: 2 vertical line spaces below salutation
            2 vertical line spaces above text or first main heading
            flush left

styling: capitalized
            underscored

MAIN HEADING

position: 2 vertical line spaces below what has gone before (i.e., title or text)
            2 vertical line spaces above what follows (i.e., text or another head)
            flush left

styling: capitalized

First-level Subhead

position: 2 vertical line spaces below what has gone before (i.e., text)
            2 vertical line spaces above what follows (i.e., text or another head)
            flush left

styling: capital and lowercased letters
            underscored

Sideheads. position: flush left, run in with the text

            styling: initially capitalized and then lowercased
                        underscored
                        punctuated with period (optional)

The guidelines shown above have been developed to assist you in typing the typically occurring heads and subheads in letter reports. Read the guidelines and then refer to the two-page Full Block facsimile of a letter report at the end of this subsection (pages 108–109).

If the Block Letter style is used, the secretary positions the title/subject line, the main headings, and the first-level subheads in the center of the page while maintaining the same vertical spacing as that shown with the Block Letter. The sideheads are run in with the text.

The Megareport

The *megareport* is a lengthy, complex, formal document on a given subject or subjects intended for internal distribution or for an outside client. Its essential elements include a title page, an executive summary (also called an abstract), and pages of running text. Ancillary elements included or omitted depending on the content and purpose of the document, the writer's wishes, and/or company policy are: a cover, a flyleaf or flyleaves, a title fly, letters of authorization/transmittal, a foreword, a preface, acknowledgments, a table of contents, a list of graphics and tables, a list of conclusions or recommendations, an appendix, footnotes, and a bibliography. Sometimes an index is included.

The report is typewritten on $8\frac{1}{2}'' \times 11''$ white bond paper that will withstand repeated handling. The pages should be typed with a view toward the planned method of binding: will it be stapled at the top left (a good method for shorter reports), or will it be sidebound (preferrable for extremely long reports)? The prefatory sections (i.e., the letters of authorization/transmittal, the acknowledgments, the table of contents, the list of graphics and/or tables, the foreword and/or preface, and the executive summary) are paginated sequentially in lowercase Roman numerals (e.g., i, ii, iii, iv, v, and so on) centered on the page about three to six vertical line spaces from the bottom edge of the sheet. The body of the report and all appended materials are paginated sequentially in Arabic numerals positioned at the top right margin about one inch from the top edge of the sheet or about one inch from the bottom edge of the sheet flush with the right margin. The first page of the body of the report is unpaginated.

Select a cover for the report that will protect it over the long term and one that is appropriate for the overall length of it. A ring binder, for example, is particularly appropriate for a five-year plan running hundreds of pages in length. The cover ought to contain a gummed label bearing the title and perhaps the writer's name or the name of the company. The label should be neatly and clearly typed.

The flyleaf and title fly. Formal reports often have a flyleaf — a blank page appearing at the very beginning. Sometimes a report may have two of

Letter Report Format

Houghton Mifflin Company

222 Berkeley Street, Boston, Massachusetts 02116
(617) 351-5000   Cable HOUGHTON

December 13, 19__

Mr. Arthur R. Lacey
Lacey, Middleton & White
123 Beacon Street
City, US 98765

Dear Mr. Lacey:

THE TITLE OF THE LETTER REPORT STYLED AS A SUBJECT LINE

This is a facsimile of a letter report in which the title is styled in underscored capital letters, flush left and two vertical line spaces from the salutation and the first line of running text. Although it is not good form to underscore the subject line in conventional business correspondence, it is entirely correct to do so in the letter report in order to set off the title clearly.

THE FIRST MAIN HEADING

The first main subject heading is also typed flush with the left margin but it is not underscored. Use this format for all of the major headings in the writer's text.

The First-level Subhead

The first-level subhead, typewritten in capital and lowercase letters, is underscored and positioned two lines below the previous text and two lines above the running text applicable to it. While main headings correspond to the Roman numerals I, II, III, and so on, in outlines, first-level subheads correspond to the capital letters A, B, C, and so on, also used therein.

The first sidehead. The sidehead, run in with the paragraph text to which it relates, is initially capitalized and underscored as shown here. It may be punctuated by a period but it is not required. The sidehead in a letter report corresponds to the numerals 1, 2, 3, and so on, as used in outlines.

Note that the spacing between paragraphs within major categories is double. If you decide to use the Block Letter style instead of the Full Block Style illustrated here, you may center the subject line, the first main heading, and the first-level subhead on the page.

Page 2
Mr. Arthur R. Lacey
December 13, 19__

Since most letter reports will exceed one page, you should plan on using continuation sheets matching the letterhead in size, color, texture, and weight. Of course, your margins on all subsequent sheets must match the ones you have maintained on the letterhead.

THE SECOND MAIN HEADING

Many reports contain an Executive Summary (also called an Abstract) and lists of conclusions and recommendations. Consider these sections important enough to rate main headings as shown just above. The Executive Summary may appear at the very beginning or at the end. The conclusions and recommendations almost always come at the end.

Another First-level Subhead

Displayed data such as tables or lists may be set within the running text or grouped together in an Appendix. If the material is to be incorporated within the text, follow the guidelines given in the business correspondence section of this chapter for block indention of displayed data.

A second sidehead. The letter report concludes with a complimentary close and a typewritten signature block, just as a conventional business letter does. Follow the guidelines given in the business correspondence section of this chapter.

If enclosures are to be included along with the report, annotate the report as shown below.

Very truly yours,

Robin N. Brown
Corporate Counsel

RNB:ahs

Enclosures: Proxy Statement
             Agenda, Stockholders' Meeting
             Board of Directors' Meeting Schedule
             Agenda, Board of Directors' Meeting

these, one at the beginning and another at the end. Flyleaves protect the rest of the document and allow space for readers' comments. The title fly contains the capitalized title of the report, centered neatly on the page.

The title page. The title page contains the title plus the subtitle if there is one, the writer's name and corporate title, the writer's departmental affiliation, and the name of the firm. In a multiauthor report, the names of all the writers together with their corporate titles and departmental affiliations may be included on this page. If the report has been prepared for an outside client, the client's name and address also appear on the title page. Job numbers, purchase orders, or contract numbers are included as required by the individual company. The date on which the report was prepared must appear on the title page. If the report is a revision of an older work, that fact should be noted too, as "Revision A — 1993" or whatever. Sometimes key words reflecting the main topics discussed in the body of the report are appended to the title page for use in subject-coded computerized information retrieval systems. Type and spell the key words exactly as the author has written them.

Type the title in capital letters and the subtitle (if any) in capital and lowercase letters. Double-space the title and center it in the top third of the page. Add the writer's name and/or the name of the client plus any other necessary data in the bottom third of the page, positioned in such a way as to be attractively balanced. Use capital and lowercase letters for this material.

Letters of authorization and/or transmittal. If official written authorization has been given to do a study (such as a market research survey or an engineering proposal for an outside client), the writer often includes a photocopy of that document in the front matter of the study. The photocopy should be clean with sharp contrast between typescript and paper. A letter of transmittal encapsulating the purpose, scope, and content of the study may be included if the report has been commissioned by an outside source. This letter should be typed on company letterhead and signed by the writer or the person having overall responsibility for the project. Ensure that the left margin of the letter is wide enough to accommodate side binding (i.e., allow a margin of $2\frac{1}{2}''$ on the left side in documents to be sidebound).

Acknowledgments page. When other people have assisted the writer in preparing the report, a brief notation acknowledging their help, support, and work is the right way of showing one's appreciation and crediting their efforts. Acknowledgments of this type are included on a separate page, usually styled in one or two short, single-spaced paragraphs. The word ACKNOWLEDGMENTS is typed in capital letters three lines above the text. The text paragraphs are separated by double spacing. All of this material should be centered and balanced on the page.

Table of contents. The table of contents presents at a glance an outline of the major and subsidiary topics covered in the report together with appropriate pagination. When compiling the table of contents, you should use the major and subsidiary headings found in the body of the report. If the writer has used Roman numerals and letters to introduce the headings, include them in the table of contents. If the writer has used an all-numeric system of signaling heads in the text, use these numbers in the table of contents. Word the headings in the table of contents exactly as they are worded in the text.

The table of contents is centered on the page with ample margins all around. Double-space between headings and subheads; single-space runover lines within these headings. Headings and page numbers must be horizontally and vertically aligned. Numbers, letters, or other devices introducing heads also must be so aligned. Use a continuation sheet for a table of contents exceeding one page, and head the continuation sheet "Table of Contents — Continued", or a variation thereof. This heading should be centered and typed in capital and lowercase letters near the top of the page. Remember, however, that the title for the first contents page must be styled in capital letters, as: TABLE OF CONTENTS. The use of leaders (horizontally typed periods) to link headings with their page numbers is optional. Leaders may be set tight (i.e., typed consecutively in a line with no intervening spaces) or spaced (i.e., typed consecutively in a line with one space between each period). Leaders must align vertically as illustrated in the table of contents facsimile within this chapter.

Don't try to type the table of contents until the body of the report has been typed in final form and approved by the writer or writers; last-minute changes in the text affecting pagination may render your earlier efforts fruitless. Before typing the contents page you should check and recheck pagination, heading titles, and numerals. After the contents page has been typed, you should repeat this procedure. Have the writer check the material at least once before you release the document for duplication, printing, binding, and distribution.

Lists of graphics and tables. The table of contents of a report containing few graphics and tables can be augmented with a short list of these features appearing at the end of the contents section. List the graphics in one section and the tables in another. Head the lists: LIST OF GRAPHICS and

Table of Contents

(i)

(ii)

TABLE OF CONTENTS--Continued

LIST OF TABLES. Include figure and table numbers, titles, and pagination. Reports incorporating many graphics and tables must include complete lists that are typed on separate pages and styled as above for both of these features. The format of these lists should match that of the contents page.

Foreword and/or preface. A foreword or a preface or both may be included in a report. The foreword — written by someone other than the writer of the report itself — tells why the report was written. The preface — written by the author of the report itself — is a short statement regarding the scope and content of the study. These sections should be single-spaced on one page apiece, headed FOREWORD and PREFACE, respectively.

Executive summary. An executive summary, sometimes called an abstract, appears on one page in the front matter. Composed of about 150 words, the executive summary encapsulates for busy readers the major issues, conclusions, and recommendations contained in the body of the report. It is also a useful device in constructing computerized report files. Type the heading EXECUTIVE SUMMARY near the top of the page. Skip three lines and begin the summary. Single-space the paragraphs of the summary, but leave two spaces between each paragraph.

The text. The text of the report may be double- or single-spaced. Follow the writer's instructions, or, if none are forthcoming, follow your company's typing guidelines. (Many companies prefer that reports be double-spaced so that readers can add comments more easily.) Maintain even, ample margins all around. For sidebound reports maintain a left margin of 1". (See Table 1, Corporate Report Typewriting Guide, on page 104 of this subsection.) Ensure that the heads and subheads in the text have been typed exactly as the writer has indicated. Three heading systems are in common use today: freestanding headings, all-numeric headings, and Roman numeral/ alphabet headings. Freestanding headings are those recommended for inclusion in the letter report:

MAIN HEADING IN CAPITAL LETTERS

First-level Subhead in Underscored Capitals and Lowercase

Run-in subhead underscored and initially capitalized.

Freestanding headings may be aligned flush with the left margin or centered on the page as explained in the section on letter reports. (Run-in tertiary heads are always set flush left.)

The all-numeric system, often employed in technical reports and proposals, features the use of decimals to signal the levels of the headings. Follow the company guidelines with regard to use of all-numeric headings.

The First Text Page of a Lengthy Report

AVAILABLE INFORMATION

The Corporation is subject to the informational requirements of the Securities Exchange Act of 1934 and in accordance therewith files reports, proxy statements, and other information with the Securities and Exchange Commission (the "Commission"). Such reports, proxy statements, and other information filed by the Company can be inspected and copied at the public reference facilities maintained by the Commission at Room 1024, 450 Fifth Street, N.W., Washington, D.C. 20549, and at the Commission's regional offices at the following locations: Room 1028, 26 Federal Plaza, New York, New York 10278; Room 1228, Everett McKinley Dirkson Building, 219 South Dearborn Street, Chicago, Illinois 60604; and Suite 500, 5757 Wilshire Boulevard, Los Angeles, California 90036. Certain information filed by the Corporation with the Commission can be inspected at the Commission's regional office located at 150 Causeway Street, Boston, Massachusetts 02114. Copies of all the above-mentioned material can be obtained from the Public Reference Section of the Commission, Washington, D.C. 20549, at prescribed rates. In addition, such reports, proxy statements, and other information concerning the Corporation are available at the offices of the New York Stock Exchange, 1 Wall Street, New York, New York 10005. Additional updating information with respect to the securities covered hereby may be provided in the future to members of the Plan by means of appendices to the Prospectus.

INCORPORATION OF CERTAIN DOCUMENTS BY REFERENCE

Each of the following documents is incorporated by reference into this Prospectus:

(a) The Corporation's Annual Report on Form 10-K for the year ended December 13, 19--, filed pursuant to Section 13 or 15(d) of the Securities Exchange Act of 1934.

(b) The Plan's Annual Report on Form 11-K for the year ended December 13, 19--, filed pursuant to Section 13 or 15(d) of the Securities Exchange Act of 1934.

(c) All other reports filed pursuant to Section 13 or 15(d) of the Securities Exchange Act of 1934 with respect to the Corporation and the Plan since the end of the fiscal year covered by the annual reports referred to in (a) and (b) above.

(d) The Corporation's definitive Proxy Statement filed pursuant to Section 14 of the Securites and Exchange Act of 1934 in connection with the latest Annual Meeting of Stockholders of the Corporation and any definitive proxy statement so filed in connection with any subsequent Special Meeting of Stockholders.

1

1.0 FIRST MAIN SECTION
   1.1 FIRST MAIN SUBSECTION
   1.2 SECOND MAIN SUBSECTION
   1.3 THIRD MAIN SUBSECTION
      1.3.1 FIRST SUBUNIT
      1.3.2 SECOND SUBUNIT
      1.3.3 THIRD SUBUNIT
   1.4 FOURTH MAIN SUBSECTION
2.0 SECOND MAIN SECTION

The combined Roman numeral/alphabet system is basically the same as the general outline system followed by students when writing term papers:

I. MAIN HEADING
   A. Subheading
      1. Sub-subheading
      2. Sub-subheading
   B. Subheading
      1. Sub-subheading
         (a.) Most limited subcategory
         (b.) Most limited subcategory
      2. Sub-subheading
II. MAIN HEADING

Follow carefully the writer's directions when using this format. Remember that if you have a heading labeled A., 1., or (a.), you must have at least one other heading in the same set, as B., 2., or (b.). A heading in one set should never stand alone.

Some reports are really technical job proposals for outside clients. The body of a proposal usually includes some headings and subheadings excluded from non-technical business studies. They deserve brief mention here. The proposal begins with an introductory section in which the problem to be solved is defined, the objectives of the study are set forth, the proposed solution to the problem is described in steps or work phases, the resultant benefits to the client are given, and the capabilities of the contracting company are delineated. The introduction is followed by a technical operations plan — a detailed section explaining how the goals and objectives will be met and how the total program will be implemented step-by-step. Next comes the management plan detailing the project's organization — i.e., the number of personnel required, the on-going documentation to be generated (e.g., progress reports), and the quality control procedures to be maintained throughout the program. The report often concludes with the financials, a section outlining the forecast costs and fees.

The First Main Section of a Lengthy Report with Flush-left Paragraphs

SECTION I

XYZ CORPORATION
EMPLOYEES' SAVINGS AND THRIFT PLAN

1. General

The "XYZ Corporation Employees' Savings and Thrift Plan" (the "Plan") has been established to encourage retirement savings by participating employees ("Members") of the Corporation and of designated subsidiaries and affiliates of the Corporation. Commencing January 1, 1992, such savings shall be effected by means of pre-tax salary adjustment arrangements. The Corporation will also make matching contributions to the Plan in an amount based upon certain savings by Members. The Corporation also expects to make an additional contribution to the Plan on behalf of each eligible Member based upon its employee stock ownership tax credit. The amount of this additional ESOP contribution is based upon the total combined compensation of all eligible Members in the year. All of the Corporation's matching and ESOP contributions will be invested in Common Stock of the Corporation, and all or part of Members' savings may be so invested. All contributions and savings will be held in trust and invested by Bank of New England, N.A., Trustee of the Plan. An "Employees' Savings and Thrift Plan Committee" (the "Committee"), appointed by the Board of Directors of the Corporation, will supervise and administer the Plan.

The Plan will form part of the Corporation's program for providing competitive benefits for its employees. The operation of the Plan is expected to encourage employees to make added provision, through savings on a pre-tax basis, for their retirement income. It will also encourage employees to participate in ownership of the Corporation's Common Stock. The Board of Directors believes that the Plan will provide an additional incentive to employees to contribute to the continued success of the Corporation and will be in the best interest of the Corporation and its stockholders.

The Plan is subject to the provisions of the Employee Retirement Income Security Act of 1974, as amended ("ERISA"), including reporting and disclosure obligations to Plan participants, fiduciary obligations of Plan administrators, and minimum participation and vesting requirements. The benefit insurance coverage established by Title IV of ERISA does not provide protection for benefits payable under the Plan, and the funding requirement under Title I or ERISA are also inapplicable.

A summary of the Plan's provisions follows. This summary is qualified in its entirety by reference to the text of the Plan which is appended as Exhibit A hereto.

3

Headings and Subheadings in a Lengthy Report

15. <u>Tax Consequences</u>

The Internal Revenue Service has ruled that the Plan qualifies as a profit sharing plan under Section 401(a) of the Code. The Corporation will submit the Plan, as amended, to the Internal Revenue Service to obtain a determination as to whether the Plan, as amended, continues to qualify under Section 401(a) of the Code, whether the provisions of the Plan relating to salary adjustment contributions qualify under Section 401(k) of the Code, and whether the provisions of the Plan relating to the employee stock ownership credit qualify under Section 409A of the Code. So long as the Plan so qualifies under the Code, the Federal tax consequences to Members under present laws as understood by the Corporation may be summarized as follows:

(a) Contributions made to the Plan by the Corporation on your behalf pursuant to your salary adjustment election, and any earnings on such amounts, are not includable in your taxable income until such amounts are returned to you either as a withdrawal or distribution. At that time, the entire amount of your distribution in excess of your pre-19-- after-tax contributions to the Plan is subject to Federal income tax because none of this money was previously taxed.

(b) Any earnings on your pre-19-- after-tax contributions to the Plan are not taxable to you until returned to you either as a withdrawal or distribution. Since your after-tax contributions were subject to Federal income tax when made, such contributions are not subject to Federal income tax when distributed or withdrawn.

(c) Corporation matching contributions and Corporation ESOP contributions, and any earnings on such amounts, are not taxable to you until distributed or withdrawn.

The tax deferral aspect of the Plan can result in some important tax advantages for you.

(1) If you wait until you retire to receive funds out of the Plan, your tax rate may be lower. Retired persons generally--though not always-- have lower incomes than they had while working, so their tax rates tend to be lower.

(2) If, upon retirement or other termination of employment, you (or your beneficiary) receive a lump sum distribution from the Plan and part or all of such distribution is in the form of shares of Common Stock instead of cash, a portion of the tax (on net unrealized appreciation)

11

This basic format is augmented when necessary by other sections and subsections.

Many reports — technical and general — end with a list of conclusions and/or recommendations. These items should be listed in enumerated format. They should be block indented, single-spaced internally, and double-spaced between each other.

Appendix. An appendix containing ancillary charts, graphs, illustrations and tables may be included in the report. The appendix appears before any other back matter sections such as footnotes, a bibliography, a glossary, or an index. Introduce the appendix in capital letters; for example, a centered format:

APPENDIX

TRADE DIVISION FORECAST

VOLUME BY TITLE

1994–1995

The material appears on a separate page as shown above. Multiple appendices should be separately listed on a page as APPENDIX A, APPENDIX B, and so on. Some companies call this section a LIST OF EXHIBITS instead.

Footnotes. Keep in mind these general points when preparing footnotes to a long report:

1. Footnotes may appear at the bottom of the pages on which the quoted passages occur or they may be listed separately at the end of the report. Separate listing is the easiest from the typist's standpoint.
2. Footnotes are signaled within the running text by raised Arabic numerals positioned just after the quoted passage with no space intervening. Type the raised numeral after the final quotation mark:

   ". . . indicates an instability in an otherwise static market." [10]

3. Number the footnotes consecutively throughout the report if they are to be listed together at the end. If the report is particularly long with many major sections in which the notes have been listed on the pages where the quoted matter is found, renumber them with the start of each new section. Be sure to check and recheck the numerals for proper sequence.
4. The first line of a footnote is indented from three to six lines and runover lines are aligned flush with the left margin. The footnote is introduced by a raised numeral keyed to the appropriate quoted text passage with one space intervening, or it may be introduced by the numeral and a period all aligned on the same line as the note itself.

Appendix Format

SECTION IV

APPENDIX

The information in this Appendix will be updated from time to time. Be sure to refer to the most current Appendix.

1. Current Administrative Information

The present members of the Employees' Savings and Thrift Plan Committee are John M. Roe, Jane T. Smith, Martin I. Miller, Joseph L. Edge, and Sally A. Harris.

2. Members of the Plan

As of December 31, 19--, there were 999 employees participating in the Plan, out of a total number of approximately 1,600 employees eligible to participate.

3. Fund A Minimum Rates

The present minimum rates of interest for contributions to Fund A during the following years are set forth below. These rates are in each case guaranteed for five years:

19--	11.5%
19--	10.75%
19--	10%

4. Investment Performance

(a) The table below shows values for shares of the Corporation's Common Stock in Fund B as of the indicated dates.

Valuation Date	Fund B Price per Share of Common Stock of the Corporation*
December 31, 19--	$11.750
December 31, 19--	$19.375

---

*Adjusted for 2-for-1 split on July 3, 19--

18

Footnotes may be single-spaced internally, with double spacing separating them from one another. They should be double-spaced internally with triple spacing separating them from one another if the report is to be published in typset form. Examples:

[10]Thomas J. Peters and Robert H. Waterman, Jr., *In Search of Excellence: Lessons from America's Best-Run Companies* (New York: Harper & Row, 1982), p. 8.

or with aligned numerals:

10. Thomas J. Peters and Robert H. Waterman, Jr., *In Search of Excellence: Lessons from America's Best-Run Companies* (New York: Harper & Row, 1982), p. 8.

Bibliography. The bibliography lists alphabetically the sources used by the writer. The forthcoming paragraphs focus on points of formatting. Remember these points when typing a bibliography (note that the entries are ordered alphabetically by author surname):

1. The bibliography, entitled WORKS CITED or BIBLIOGRAPHY, appears on a separate page in the back matter.
2. The bibliography is hanging-indented: the first line of each entry is set flush left with runovers indented by five or six spaces.
3. Bibliography entries, unlike footnotes, are unnumbered.
4. Bibliography entries, like footnotes, may be single-spaced internally with double spacing separating them from one another, or they may be double-spaced internally with triple spacing separating them from one another. Use the latter approach if the report is to be typeset for outside publication. Examples:

Katzan, Harry Jr. *Office Automation: A Manager's Guide.* New York: AMACOM, 1982.
Peters, Thomas J. and Robert H. Waterman, Jr. *In Search of Excellence: Lessons from America's Best-Run Companies.* New York: Harper & Row, 1982.

Index. You may be asked to type an index for a very long, detailed study. The index lists alphabetically all major and subsidiary topics covered in the report along with applicable page numbers. An index is developed by reading through the text and circling all major and subsidiary headings plus all key words in the report. Each circled item is written on a 3″ × 5″ card together with the page number. The cards are ordered alphabetically and the page numbers and subjects rechecked. The writer then constructs from the cards a draft index.

The main components of an index are main entries, subentries, subsubentries, and cross-entries. A main entry is a prime subject category usually corresponding to a main heading in the text. A main entry includes a heading and often (but not always) a page number. It is typed flush with the left margin:

Input systems
　for computers, 22, 53–63
　optical character recognition
　　for, 16
Input/output units, 53–63

In the example, *Input systems* and *Input/output units* are main entries. Note that the first word of the main entry is initially capitalized, while the other words are lowercased unless they are proper nouns, proper adjectives, or trademarks. Main entries are alphabetically ordered by the first key word.

A subentry represents a topic of secondary importance. It appears under the main entry with which it is associated. Subentries, ordered alphabetically by the first key word, are indented by three spaces. Subentries, like main entries, are composed of headings and page numbers. Subentries are lowercased throughout unless they contain proper nouns, proper adjectives, or trademarks. In the previously shown example, *for computers* and *optical character recognition for* are subentries.

A sub-subentry is a topic of tertiary importance. It appears under the subentry with which it is associated:

Communications, 80–108
　electronic mail systems for, 80–90,
　　100–101
　　Telex in, 91–92

In the example, *Telex* (a proper noun) is the sub-subentry under *electronic mail systems*. The alphabetically ordered sub-subentries, indented by three spaces, are usually lowercased unless they contain proper nouns, proper adjectives, or trademarks.

Cross-entries direct the reader from one point in the index to another related point where more information is to be found:

Diskettes. <u>See also</u> Floppy disks.
　in word processing systems, 42–81.

In the example, "<u>See also</u> Floppy disks" is a cross-entry. When the reader turns to the main entry *Floppy disks,* more information is at hand:

Floppy disks (diskettes), 22–32
　microdiskette, 25–32
　minidiskette, 23–24
　standard, 22

Cross-entries are introduced by the underscored and initially capitalized words "<u>See also</u>" followed by the main entry to which the reader is referred in initial capital letters (i.e., Floppy disks), followed by a period.

Two commonly used index formats are the indented and the run-in. The writer should indicate which of the two indexing formats is to be used. The indented format (used in our earlier examples) is preferable, for it provides quicker information retrieval. Note that each entry is typed on a separate line:

Disk storage media, 85–95
    operating systems on, 96
    software on, 94
    in word processing systems, 42, 82–90

The run-in format occupies less page space but is more difficult for the reader to use since all subentries are run in together:

Disk storage media: 85–95,
    operating systems on, 96;
    software on, 94; in word
    processing systems, 42,
    82–90

An index features minimal punctuation. Follow these guidelines for punctuating index entries:

1. Use a comma between an entry and any term(s) modifying it and between an entry and the page number relating to it:

Disk storage media, 85–95
    in word processing systems, 42, 82–90
Disks, standard, 22–24

2. Use a semicolon to separate entries only in the run-in index:

Disk storage media: 85–95;
    operating systems on, 96;
    ....

3. Use a colon after a main entry just before its pagination only in the run-in index:

Disk storage media: 85–95;
    ....

4. Terminate a cross-entry with a period; do not use periods elsewhere:

<u>See also</u> CRT.

Tables, graphics, and other visual aids. All visual aids should be titled either in capital letters or in capital and lowercase letters, and sequentially numbered: FIGURE 1, FIGURE 2; TABLE 1, TABLE 2, and so on. Titles may be centered or positioned flush left. Select one style and stick to it for the sake of consistency.

Word processors with graphics capabilities have alleviated most of the drudgery in preparing tabular and graphic exhibits. However, you must have a feel for the length of the table as it will appear in typewritten form and the approximate number of character spaces to be allowed between columns so that you can instruct the machine properly. In general, six character spaces are allowed between columns, especially in tables that are to be typed horizontally. Tables involving more than four columns are generally set up horizontally — that is, the standard page is flipped on its side. The title of the table should appear at the top (i.e., along what used to be the left margin of the vertical sheet) and the end of the table should appear at the bottom (i.e., along what used to be the right margin of the vertical sheet). In this way, the tabular data will face outside and not toward the gutter of the bound report.

Tabular entries and subentries can be capitalized in their entirety, capitalized and lowercased by key word, initially capitalized, or lowercased in their entirety. Main headings are usually capitalized in their entirety as shown in the next example. Once you have selected a style, stick to it throughout all of the tables for the sake of consistency:

TOTAL NET SALES
MANUFACTURING COSTS
ROYALTY EXPENSES
TOTAL COST OF SALES
   % of net
EXPENSES
   Editorial
   Plate
   Sales
   Advertising
   Fulfillment
   Administration

In the previous example, the capitalized items are considered main entries and the indented, capitalized, and lowercased entries are considered secondary to the main entries. Secondary entries can be indented as shown here or set flush with the left margin. Choose one style and adhere to it.

Numerical data in tables must be aligned to the right, as:

UNIT SALES TO DATE
12,700
34,000
 6,000
  765

Tabular entries consisting of numerals and symbols such as plus and minus signs, percentage signs, or dollar signs must be aligned vertically. Decimal points also must be so aligned:

$800,000.00	−14 points	45.9%
4,000.98	−12 points	6.4%
55,896.00	−33 points	28.0%
564.34	+12 points	60.2%

Avoid the use of vertical and horizontal rules in tables constructed on conventional machines: while the horizontal rules can be done easily on the machine, the vertical ones will have to be drawn in by hand, and hand-drawn rules often look messy.

If the table exceeds one page in length, type a continued heading in capital and lowercase letters, as: "Table 3, continued" and center it on the page. Continue typing the tabular data, using the same tabbing and margins as those on the first sheet. Maintain consistent entry and subentry style.

Displayed lists are useful especially in executive summaries and in sections detailing conclusions and/or recommendations, for the displayed matter is clearly visible to the busy reader. Use of the lowercase *o* followed by one space and the text is a neat way of presenting important data (a spaced period also can be used in this manner to highlight significant data):

• Generating business information
• Analyzing business information
• Transmitting/distributing business information

Sometimes the writer will include pie charts and graphs to illustrate points made in the body of the report. These should be roughed out by the writer and then submitted to the company's special media department for professional production. In a company lacking such a support department you may be called on to assist the writer in preparing these visual aids. If so, you'll need the following materials: press-on or contact tone sheets, rules, and letters (available in a graphic arts supply store); T-square, ruler, and compass; nonrepo blue pencil or pen; designer's fine-line black pen; rubber cement or a glue stick; art gum; scissors; artist's knife (sharp, triangular blade); graph paper; and hard-finish drawing paper. Graphs are usually laid out as rectangles on an average scale of 4:3 or 7:4. The title may appear at the top or bottom entirely in capitals or in capital and lowercase letters. Choose one style and stick to it. Position the labels and key lines horizontally on the page for easy reading. You can typewrite the title, labels, and key lines or you can use the press-on letters available in art supply houses. If you use the press-on letters (or numbers) be sure to choose a size compatible with the overall size of the graph. Letters that are too large detract from the visual impact of the illustration. With line graphs you can ink in the lines by hand or you can use the press-on rules available in art stores. The press-on rules come on rolls. Using the nonrepro blue pencil or pen and a ruler, draw in the lines of the graph. Using the artist's knife, cut the press-on rules to fit the outline of the graphed matter. Pull off the backing and affix the rules where appropriate. With bar graphs, you will need press-on tone sheets showing, for instance, dark areas, striped areas, or dotted areas. Many different styles and designs are available. Using the nonrepro pencil or pen and a ruler, measure and construct the various bars called for. Using the artist's knife and the ruler, cut the tone sheets to fit the various bars, peel off the backing, and affix the tones to the graph. You also can shade the bars by hand, but hand shading does not look as professional as the tone-sheet shading. Ensure that there is a color/tone separation of at least 30% between different shadings and tints in the graph; otherwise the shadings and tints will all look alike when reproduced in black-and-white. The press-on sheets usually contain color separation percentages.

The pie (or circle) chart is a useful way of depicting percentages, say, of corporate growth or market shares. Use a compass fitted with a nonrepro blue pencil to construct the circle. Then use the compass to mark off sectors in degrees corresponding to the desired percentages. Typically used percentage values of a circle are these:

360°	=	100%
180°	=	50%
90°	=	25%
36°	=	10%
18°	=	5%
3.6°	=	1%

Cut the press-on tone sheets to fit the marked-off sectors of the circle and then affix them to the chart. Use press-on letters and numbers to label the sectors. If the color/tone contrast between the parts of the circle and the labels is adequate you can insert the labels within the circle itself. But if the contrast is inadequate or if space is tight, you should put the labels outside the circle and use press-on key lines or arrows to connect the labels with the applicable sectors of the circle.

How to make an overhead. Before attempting to make an overhead audiovisual, also called a *transparency*, make sure that the brand you plan to use is appropriate for the copying machine you have at hand. The packaging for the transparencies will list the machines and model numbers in which that brand of transparency can be used. For example, some copiers require transparencies to bear a white sensing strip. Additionally, you must determine which way the white strip should face when you load the tray; loading the transparencies the wrong way may result in the machine becoming jammed.

Once you have read the instructions for the brand of transparency you are using, you are ready to begin. Follow these procedures:

1. Load the transparencies properly on top of a moderate base of paper in the paper tray.
2. Secure the paper tray.
3. Set the machine for one copy.
4. Place the document that is to be made into a transparency on the glass in the correct image area for $8\frac{1}{2}''$ × 11″ paper.
5. Close the cover.
6. Activate the machine.
7. Always allow for one transparency to be processed through the copier and dropped into the output tray before activating the machine again.
8. Delete imaged areas with perchloroethylene (tetrachloroethylene) or the suggested solution for the particular brand if corrections must be made. New data may be added with a grease pencil or solvent marker.

Transparencies are made of plastic film, and therefore will not perform with the same high reliability as plain paper. The toner image cannot penetrate into the transparent film, so be careful not to scratch the finished transparency. If the copier jams more than twice during a single job, the problem is probably with the machine. In these cases, a repairperson should be called. Should the copier become jammed, find the defective transparency (look carefully on the drum if it is nowhere else to be found) and remove it. If you cannot find the transparency, *do not operate the copier* until a repairperson has serviced the machine.

You may notice a thin oily coating on the transparency. This is normal and will eventually wear off. You can remove it by gently wiping both sides of the transparency with a dry tissue or by moistening the tissue with rubbing alcohol. You should note that this oily coating contains silicone which can cause irritation to your eyes if contact is made. Should this happen, flush your eyes thoroughly with clean water.

One other point: before attempting to make the transparency you should ensure that the chart, table, or other information to be displayed has been typed or drawn in such a way as to fit the screen size of the audiovisual machine (overhead projector) to be used. Cardboard mats similar to the ones used in picture frames are available in various sizes keyed to the projectors; a common size is $7\frac{1}{2}''$ × 10″. Using a nonrepro blue pencil, you can draw this measure around the material to be reproduced, thus ensuring inclusion of all data.

AGENDA

An agenda is a list of all issues to be discussed at a meeting. The agenda for an informal meeting lists only the items to be discussed during the meeting. The agenda for a more formal meeting could list times, events,

Agenda for an Informal Meeting

AGENDA

Editorial Meeting

April 16, 19--

1. Call to order

2. Roll call

3. Minutes of previous meeting (corrections, omissions)

4. Publisher's report

5. Production Manager's report

6. Unfinished business

    a. works in progress

    b. staff

7. New business

    a. budget

    b. new proposals

8. Announcements (including date of next meeting)

9. Adjournment

---

speakers, rooms, and activities (an illustration is provided in Chapter 11). Always type the agenda with at least three line spaces between each item.

ITINERARY

An itinerary is a chronological outline of travel plans. It includes:

- Dates and times of departures and arrivals. Include the day as well as the date, and note all time zones.
- Destination city, including name of airport. Use the local time and indicate the number of hours of flying time and layover time, if applicable.
- Airline, flight numbers, meals provided, and seat assignments.
- Car rental agency. Include telephone number, confirmation number, type of charge, and credit card used.
- Airport transportation. Include telephone numbers of shuttle and limousine service.
- Lodging accommodations. Include confirmation numbers, telephone and fax numbers, and credit card used.
- Appointments for each day. Include dates, times, locations, and addresses. Also include names of attendees and reason for meeting.

MINUTES OF A MEETING

Arrive at the meeting before everyone else does to ensure that everything is ready. To take the minutes, you should have plenty of materials — whatever the medium — to get you through a lengthy dictation session. Make sure you have a copy of the agenda for yourself. Even if it is not followed in exact order, you will need it to key your notes, a process addressed later in this section.

The most difficult part of taking minutes is deciding what information has to be written down verbatim, what can be paraphrased, and what is unessential for the official record. Minutes are meant to be concise, factual, and objective recordings of what has happened during the course of a meeting. You cannot inject personal preferences into your notes. You cannot give more weight to what certain people say and not record the pertinent remarks of others. You must be able to interpret statements for what is truly being said, not what you hear by way of the deliverer's voice inflections, intonations, or mannerisms. It can be very difficult to discriminate from among all the opinions and facts just what should be recorded in the minutes. For example, if the implementation of a new procedure is being discussed and it appears that the motion for its institution will be passed, it is equally important to write down why the Publisher feels the procedure will not work, as it is to record why the editors feel that it will.

Itinerary

Itinerary - Stephen Kaye
December 6-7

Thursday, December 6

1:36 p.m.	Leave San Francisco Airport American Airlines Flight 650 Nonstop; lunch
7:05 p.m.	Arrive Dallas/Fort Worth Hotel Transportation Available Hotel: Sheraton Central Park Phone: (214) 633-3700 Dates: December 6 Confirmation No. 582137C Guaranteed Arrival

Friday, December 7

8 a.m.	Breakfast with Elisabeth Callahan and Robert Jordan, Sheraton's Cafe
10:30 a.m.	Meeting with Michael Diehl of Union Carbide 3750 Merrit Way, North Dallas
12:00 p.m.	Luncheon - on your own
2:00 p.m.	Presentation for AMA Sheraton Park Central Topic: Win-Win Communication
6:07	Leave Dallas/Fort Worth American Flight 405 Nonstop; dinner
5:36	Arrive San Francisco Airport

You must listen carefully *and* take down information even when more than one person is talking at the same time. You will have to do some quick sorting in your mind in order to record facts accurately without distortion, while at the same time making sure you attribute all statements to their correct sources. In corporate or organizational meetings, it is necessary to record motions and resolutions verbatim as well as the names of those who made them.

Knowing what you are to be aware of during the progress of the meeting, you are ready to record. Here's how you should do it:

1. Write down the date, location, and time the meeting begins.
2. Record the names of those present and absent (if the number is less than twenty). A quorum check is necessary for larger meetings.
3. Label the meeting (regular, weekly, annual, special, or executive).
4. Name the presiding officer.
5. Record the action. When the meeting begins, key your notes to match the activity. That is, if the discussion is "works in progress" and this subject is item "a" under "7. Unfinished Business," then key your notes "7a" and record the discussion. This relieves you of writing "7. Unfinished Business: a, works in progress." When you type your notes, you simply refer to your agenda to transcribe the key "7a."
6. Record the time of adjournment.

See the section on shorthand for suggestions on coding your stenographic notebook for changes, deletions, and additions while taking minutes.

Drafts

Drafts are like dress rehearsals. Everything is in place, except the audience. If you make a mistake, you can correct it before the audience sees it — and they will never be the wiser. When you sit down to begin formatting, you should have the following materials accessible:

1. the agenda
2. your notes (do not rely on memory)
3. *Robert's Rules of Order* or similar reference books on parliamentary procedure
4. any reports or other documents distributed at the meeting
5. verbatim copies of motions and resolutions
6. the constitution or bylaws of the group (if applicable)

Prepare the draft in the following manner:

1. The draft should be double-spaced so that handwritten corrections may be easily and clearly inserted.

Minutes

Editorial Scheduling Meeting

October 16, 19--

The weekly editorial scheduling meeting of Friday, October 16, convened at 10 a.m. in the conference room. The presiding officer was Amanda Billings. Members of the staff present included Robert Desmond, Carl Edwards, Denise Jameson, Martha Nichols, and Philip Thompson. Roger Lochman was unable to attend.

The minutes of the previous meeting, held on Friday, October 9, were read and accepted. There were no corrections or omissions.

Mrs. Billings reported that the Corporation is looking to the office products line to balance the shortfall in sales expected in the Secondary Education Division. She asked that everyone keep this goal in mind when ambitious schedules are established for new projects.

Robert Desmond informed the staff that he is preparing an analysis of the titles in progress in relation to their marketability, production costs, production schedules, and longevity. He requested that each editor submit a summary of costs to date for freelance services.

Amanda Billings reminded everyone that they must submit their appropriate sections of the formal publishing plans for the office products line to her by October 23.

Denise Jameson raised the question again as to when a new editor will be hired to replace Tom Westman. Because of the ambitious schedules and short-handed staff, this situation should be addressed as soon as possible.

Mrs. Billings requested that Mr. Desmond and Mr. Edwards submit a preliminary budget for 1992 to her by December 1.

Mr. Desmond gave Amanda Billings a new manuscript he received this week from a retired linguistics professor. His preliminary reaction to the proposal is that it would be better suited to the College Division. The manuscript will be routed in the normal fashion, and a decision will be made at the December 2 meeting.

The next meeting of the editorial staff will be held on Friday, October 23.

The meeting was adjourned at 11:30 a.m.

2. Pages should be numbered consecutively.
3. A heading or subheading should not be separated from the first two lines of the summary that follows it when falling at the bottom of a page.
4. Include all materials that will be attached when final, formal minutes are distributed.

It is good practice (and usually required) to present the presiding officer with a typewritten draft of the minutes. If this is not feasible, then you should present the draft to your supervisor before typing the final copy. Either person will be able to weed out any misinterpretations or extremely sensitive material that should not be published.

Final copy

The final copy may be single- or double-spaced. Check copies of previous minutes for your organization's preferred style. The paper used also depends on precedent. Some groups have specially printed stationery for official minutes, while others use white bond paper of second-sheet quality. When designing your minutes, refrain from using distracting symbols or excessive, heavy lines to mark different topics of discussion or to separate portions of the meeting. Make sure that significant points are easily identifiable in the typewritten minutes, but do not overdo it. Simple, straightforward documents will be much more attractive than pages marred with repetitive asterisks, ellipses, and underscores. Most minutes today are written in a narrative style, compared with the perfunctory outline style once used. Because of this significant change, it is especially important that your summaries of the discussions succinctly express the scope of the conversations. If you have not conveyed what went on during the meeting, your efforts have been for naught. See the illustration on page 132 for an example of acceptable official minutes.

6

Records Management

RECORDS MANAGEMENT is that field of information management which is concerned with the systematic analysis and control of the operating records created or maintained by business, government agencies, nonprofit institutions, and other organizations. As used in this context, the term *records* denotes a wide variety of information carriers. Since its inception, records management has emphasized the analysis and control of paper documents ranging from 3" × 5" index cards to engineering drawings and charts measuring 3' × 4' or larger. The vast majority of office documents are letter-size ($8\frac{1}{2}''$ × 11"), legal-size ($8\frac{1}{2}''$ × 14") or, increasingly, computer printout size (11" × 14"). These records can be a valuable resource and a source of problems at the same time. They contain information essential to decision-making and daily work routines. Records in any form are vulnerable to loss resulting from disaster, inadvertent destruction, theft, misfiling, or mishandling. The records management methodologies discussed in this chapter are designed to address these problems.

While paper documents remain its primary focus, records management is increasingly concerned with problems of information storage and handling posed by nonpaper records. Such nonpaper records include photographic negatives and prints, microforms, and videotapes. Similarly, the diskettes, tape cassettes, and other machine-readable magnetic media created by word processors, microcomputers, and other automated office systems constitute an increasingly important records category. Large quantities of machine-readable records are likewise maintained by centralized computing facilities. Such records account for a rapidly growing percentage of most organizations' information resources. Like their paper counterparts, photographic and machine-readable records require appropriate storage facilities, must be carefully organized for effective retrieval, and must be protected from inadvertent damage or destruction.

The Secretary's Role

Interest in records management as a formal discipline has steadily intensified as expanded business and government activities — combined with the widespread use of technology — have increased the volume of record production and the complexity of record-keeping activities. Today, records management is a multifaceted discipline. It draws on methodologies and technologies developed in a variety of related fields, including data processing, information science, industrial engineering, library science, and business administration. Consequently, a records management program can include many elements. It is often difficult to separate clearly records management from other information processing activities.

The structure of records management programs is also varied. Some mid- to large-sized corporations, government agencies, or other organizations have formal centralized records management programs staffed by one or more full-time professionals. In such organizations, departmental secretaries typically serve as liaison persons who provide the records management staff with essential information about departmental files and record-keeping requirements. In most departments, the secretary is the person most familiar with record-keeping practices, and the liaison role is critical to the success of a records management program. In many smaller organizations — and some larger ones — there is no formal records management program. Consequently, the individual secretaries must assume full responsibility for records management activities in their departments. While some aspects of records management require specialized technical expertise, many records management concepts are based on common sense and an orderly approach to problem solving. The following sections explain the major facets of a records management program and provide guidelines for their implementation by secretaries working in a broad range of office environments.

MANAGING RECORDS

Most records management programs include a combination of elements designed to address the problems of both active and inactive records. Activity and inactivity are determined by the frequency with which given groups of records are referenced. While some documents may be referenced on a daily basis, most records are actively referenced only for a brief initial period of time. As an example, correspondence, memorandums, and other routine office documents are usually referenced once or twice shortly after creation but may never be consulted again. Similarly, legal case records, insurance claim files, medical history files, technical project files, and other such documents may remain unused for months or years after the termination of a given transaction or activity. Later, however, they may be referenced frequently if and when the matters to which they pertain require further action.

But while they are not needed to support daily operations, many inactive records must be retained for some period of time to meet legal requirements, in anticipation of possible future reference, or — in some cases — because of their historical or research significance.

The Records Inventory

The secretary should maintain a records inventory and update it frequently. This inventory is a listing of all types of records a company has, how long these items are kept, and their location. Even though inactive records are not frequently referenced, they may contain important information that must be retained and protected. To reduce existing floor space requirements and provide space for future file growth, useless inactive records must be identified and discarded. Inactive records of continuing value can be microfilmed or transferred to economical off-site storage for appropriate periods of time.

Records Scheduling

As indicated above, the records inventory provides information used in the formulation of record retention and disposal schedules. A retention and disposal schedule is a listing that specifies the periods of time for which given record types are to be retained and, if appropriate, the storage location and format. For records to be discarded, it further specifies the date, and, where special security precautions are required, the mode of destruction.

A retention and disposal schedule is a procedural document recognizing that the records created and maintained by an organization are its property and are not to be discarded without proper authorization. Retention and disposal schedules are an essential element in any space conservation program and can yield significant reductions in future filing cabinet purchases.

Organizations with formal centralized records management programs sometimes utilize "document-oriented" or general retention and disposal schedules that list documents by name or type without regard to the specific departments or offices in which they are maintained. As a supplement or alternative, "activity-oriented" retention and disposal schedules are specifically designed for individual departments or offices and list the records maintained by only that department or office. Such activity-oriented schedules are necessarily more time-consuming to prepare than document-oriented schedules, but they usually result in more comprehensive and effective retention guidelines.

RETENTION PERIODS

Whether general or activity-oriented schedules are employed, each record or document type falls into one of three groups:

Short-term retention. Many records are needed for a brief period but have little continuing utility and will be discarded a short time — perhaps several months to two years — after their creation or receipt. Such records are typically retained in office locations until discarded.

Medium-term retention. Other records must be retained for a specified period of time — perhaps for one to ten years — but eventually will be discarded. Such records are often retained in office locations during a relatively brief initial period of active reference and, when reference activity subsides, are transferred to lower-cost, off-site storage facilities from which they are eventually discarded.

Long-term retention. A final, often large, group of records must be retained indefinitely. In many cases, such records are microfilmed to save space and the original paper documents discarded. The microfilm versions may be stored in office locations or off-site, depending on anticipated reference activity.

Groups of Criteria

Three broad groups of criteria — legal/fiscal, administrative, and research — are utilized to assign specific record series to one of the retention groups.

Legal/fiscal criteria. While legal/fiscal criteria receive much publicity, only a small percentage of federal, state, and local laws and regulations specify retention periods for particular types of records, and relevant record retention laws are often difficult to identify and interpret. Legally mandated retention periods are most commonly encountered in industries such as banking or pharmaceuticals, and in activities such as waste disposal or pension fund management, all of which are subject to government regulation. In the absence of specific legal mandates, most record retention decisions are based on anticipated administrative reference requirements to support both daily operations and long-term goals.

Administrative criteria. Even where laws or regulations mandating retention exist, administrative requirements may prove more stringent and warrant longer retention for specific record series. The most effective administrative retention decisions are based on previous reference experience with particular record types. In some cases, the continuing administrative utility of specific records can be established with confidence. Too often, however, records are retained by default. In the absence of reliable information about previous reference activity, their anticipated reference value cannot be assessed, and the organization is reluctant to discard them. Since record destruction is irreversible, many records managers prefer such a conservative approach.

Research criteria. In some organizations, a small percentage of records are retained for their historical or other research significance. Such records typically document important programs or events, the activities of important persons, or the formulation of significant public or business policies.

Where a formal records management program exists, individual departmental secretaries can provide valuable information about reference activity and anticipated administrative value to assist the records management staff in the formulation of appropriate retention periods for various record series. In some organizations, secretaries are asked to draft preliminary retention and disposal schedules for discussion, modification, and eventual approval by the records management unit, department heads, and other appropriate persons. In the absence of a formal records management program, the secretaries must prepare retention schedules for their own departments. Records management textbooks available at bookstores and libraries often include retention recommendations for commonly encountered records and summarize federal and state regulations pertaining to record retention. Publications dealing with record retention and related records management concerns are likewise available from the Association of Records Managers and Administrators (ARMA), the Association for Information and Image Management (AIIM), and other professional groups.

Once formulated, retention and disposal schedules must be revised periodically. The annual review of retention schedules is strongly recommended. The actual implementation of retention schedules is typically the secretary's responsibility. Some secretaries prefer to allot a specific period of time during a slack period for this purpose. In some organizations, the records management unit performs compliance audits to determine that retention schedules are being appropriately implemented.

Record Centers

A record center is a warehouse-type facility designed specifically for the economical storage of inactive, medium-term records pending their eventual destruction. Records are transferred to the center as indicated in retention and disposal schedules. In most cases, the center will not accept records lacking a specific destruction date. Although some record centers do provide vaults or other special facilities for the long-term storage of microfilm or machine-readable records, the vast majority of records transferred to a record center will be destroyed after a specified period of time, thereby making room for the receipt of additional items.

If the record center is operated by a formal records management department, it will supply standardized containers to departments preparing inactive records for transfer, along with instructions for packing, labeling, and inventorying. The records inventory, often prepared on a special form, lists the contents of each container in a given shipment and is essential for later retrieval of the records. Depth of inventorying varies. Some record centers request only a general description of the contents of each container, while others require a detailed listing of individual folder titles.

In the absence of a formal records management program, a record center may be shared by several departments, each of which services its own records. Where a formal records management program exists, the record center is usually operated by a small staff. In such organizations, the record center functions as a custodial agency rather than a generally accessible reference library. Reference requests generally require departmental approval. Prior to contacting the record center, the department will consult its copies of the records inventory sheets to determine the shipment number and container location of the desired records. The record center typically responds to reference requests by returning the requested containers or file folders to the transmitting office. If only a few items are involved, some record centers will provide photocopies.

MICROGRAPHICS

Micrographics and microimaging are two terms for reproduced information in reduced form on film, either microfilm or microfiche. It is estimated that about 4 percent of business information is stored in this form. Document miniaturization through micrographics is the preferred alternative for records designated for long-term retention. Storing information on microfilm or microfiche has saved companies money, space, and retrieval time. Records are photographed onto film so that numerous small images will appear on a reel of 16-millimeter or 35-millimeter film. These images are viewed in enlarged form on a microfilm reader. Microfilm may be stored in cartons and cabinets or in jackets that contain short lengths of film. Similar to microfilm is microfiche, a method of storing microimages on sheets or cards. These sheets or cards can be enlarged through a viewer. A hardcopy version can also be printed. Microfiche can be filed in alphabetical file folders for easy access.

Introduced in the 1920s, the earliest business applications of micrographics technology emphasized the long-term storage of inactive records. In such applications, microfilming can yield very dramatic space savings.

Many organizations now use micrographics to facilitate the management of active records as well. By miniaturizing records, micrographics can make them more accessible and easier to handle.

Microforms are an excellent method for storing both active and inactive files. Since they take up only one third of the space needed for paper documents, they save space and money. Microforms are also more durable than paper and can be easily duplicated and economically mailed. It is important to note that microforms also have several disadvantages. Readers are necessary, and the initial cost of such equipment is high. The equipment is large and takes up desk space. Also, different readers are required for microfilm and microfiche.

COMPUTER SOFTWARE

Records management software, also called document management software, stores, retrieves, and indexes information. This software has many advantages.

- Reports show who has taken a file and when it is due.
- Files not in the filing cabinet can be tracked.
- Possibility of lost or misplaced files is reduced.
- Files that should be removed can be determined.

Records management software can be developed in-house. This software can be highly specialized to fit your company's applications. Its development costs, however, are usually high and considerable time is invested. Database software is available at a reasonable cost. It can also be tailored to meet your company's needs. Also available is document management software. It can be implemented quickly and easily and is relatively inexpensive.

Besides the records management software and networking capabilities, there are several components required:

- Computer
- Screen that displays the stored document
- Laser printer
- Method to enter documents into the system
- High-capacity storage system

To effectively and efficiently manage electronic files, use consistent procedures for naming documents, clean up files periodically, and back up important documents.

FILING SYSTEMS FOR ACTIVE RECORDS

The Official File

The organization of files for later retrieval is the primary concern of active records management. Conservation of space and filing equipment, while important considerations, are of secondary significance. Many records managers believe that a comprehensive file management program must begin with the establishment of an official file as the sole, complete, and authoritative repository for records created or maintained by a given activity. Official files are common in insurance claims processing, accounts receivable, purchasing, and other transaction-oriented activities where work is performed in readily identifiable stages by office employees, each of whom contributes information to the file. Official files are less frequently encountered in scientific research, engineering, architecture, and similar project-oriented activities where the work is performed in a discretionary manner by professional employees.

In such work settings, individual employees often maintain so-called "personal" files. These files, storable in individual offices or in adjacent secretarial work areas, offer the convenience associated with close proximity, but they can vary greatly in scope and content. Too often, personal files are incomplete. They may be arranged in a manner that only their creator can comprehend, and are consequently inaccessible to other workers who may need to retrieve information when the creator of the filing system is out of the office. If the creator of a personal file leaves the organization prior to completion of a project or other activity, the record of work accomplished can be very difficult to reconstruct.

These problems can be addressed successfully through the implementation of a procedure stating that participants in project-related activities must route all documents to an official file. This file then serves as a complete and authoritative point of reference for questions that can be answered from project-related documents. The existence of an official file will eliminate time-consuming searches in multiple personal files, and the completeness of the file will increase the likelihood of retrieving the accurate information required for effective decision-making. Workers will remain free to make copies of documents needed in their own offices.

In terms of physical location, an official file may be centralized or decentralized. Centralization typically occurs at the department or division level, with a common pattern being the establishment of a centralized repository for the official files of all projects undertaken by a given department. Complete centralization of all files at the organizational level is rare. But regardless of the level, centralization can facilitate the development of filing systems and the standardization of filing practices. Staff training is simplified and work performance is enhanced, largely because personnel can give their full attention to filing work rather than dividing their time among a variety of clerical tasks. When compared to an equivalent quantity of scattered files, centralization usually requires fewer file maintenance people. In addition, file control and security are usually improved. As potential disadvantages, the distance between workers and the central file area often necessitates some delay in retrieval, and document routing procedures must be strictly enforced if the central file is to have the completeness essential to user confidence.

Basic Filing Systems

An efficient filing system is one that separates information into categories and assures its rapid and accurate retrieval. The basic filing systems are alphabetical, numeric, alphanumeric, chronological, and geographic.

Alphabetical filing. Almost 90 percent of all filing is alphabetically organized. Alphabetical arrangements are widely used for file folders, index cards, and many other types of records in which the filing unit consists of a name, subject heading, or similar character string. While basic alphabetical concepts are familiar to all literate people, special rules must be implemented for certain situations:

1. Personal names are inverted for filing in surname, forename, and middle initial sequence.

Name	*Indexing Order*
Stephen Kaye	Kaye Stephen
John R. Michaels	Michaels John R.
T. M. Carlson	Carlson T. M.

2. A single letter is indexed as a single word.

Name	*Indexing Order*
MRE Publishers	M R E Publishers

3. The article *the* and words such as *and, for, on, in, by,* and *of* are disregarded in indexing.

Name	*Indexing Order*
Sam the Plumber	Sam (the) Plumber
The Chicago Times	*Chicago Times (The)*
Joyce and Sam Clothing	Joyce (and) Sam Clothing

4. Abbreviations such as *St.* and *Mr.* are indexed as though they are spelled in full.

Name	*Indexing Order*
St. Patrick's Cathedral	Saint Patrick's Cathedral
Mr. Ed's Auto Repair	Mister Ed's Auto Repair

5. Prefixes such as *D', De, Del, Di, Mac, Mc, O'* and others are indexed as written and treated as one word.

Name	*Indexing Order*
Robert De Luca	De Luca Robert
Patrick MacDonald	MacDonald Patrick
Ruth E. O'Brien	O'Brien Ruth E.

6. A personal or professional title is not indexed.

Name	*Indexing Order*
Richard Cline, Ph.D.	Cline Richard (Ph.D.)
Dr. Elizabeth Parsons	Parsons Elizabeth (Dr.)
James E. Johns, M.D.	John James E. (M.D.)

7. Hyphenated firm names are indexed as separate names.

Name	*Indexing Order*
Johnson-Cook Lumber	Johnson Cook Lumber
Williams-Michaels Company	Williams Michaels Company

8. Hyphenated individual names are indexed as one unit.

Name	*Indexing Order*
Louella Miles-Sinclair	Miles-Sinclair Louella
Jennifer Rhodes-Hale	Rhodes-Hale Jennifer

9. A number is indexed as if it were spelled in full.

Name	*Indexing Order*
The 21 Club	Twenty-One Club (The)

10. The ampersand symbol (&) is disregarded.

Name	*Indexing Order*
Johnson & Johnson	Johnson (&) Johnson

Numeric filing. Numeric arrangements are widely used for case files, transaction files, financial records, and similar applications in which documents are numbered and requested by an identifying number. In most instances, a name-to-file index must be maintained as a record of what words the numbers stand for.

Sequential numeric filing is the simplest and most widely encountered type of numeric arrangement. It features the consecutive arrangement of numbered folders, with the highest numbers being added to the end of the file. Preprinted or customized guides can be used to subdivide the file into readily identifiable segments, and color-coded ones are available to simplify misfile detection. Sequential numeric filing systems are easily learned and implemented. Numeric filing has several advantages:

• It permits unlimited expansion.
• It enables quick and accurate refiling.
• Data processing systems work more efficiently with numbers.

Several disadvantages, however, limit the utility of numeric filing. For one thing, in transaction processing and similar applications in which numbers are sequentially assigned to newly created folders, the most active records will be clustered at the end of the file. In large centralized filing situations, requests for those portions of the file may be numerous. A related limitation is the inequitable distribution of reference and other file maintenance activity. A further limitation is that sequential numeric systems typically require the time-consuming movement or "backshifting" of folders to make room at the end of the file for newly created records as older records are purged. Finally, it is time-consuming to maintain the auxiliary card index and to have to make two searches — one of the index and one of the files — every time papers are withdrawn or filed.

Terminal digit filing techniques address these limitations. They are especially useful in accounts payable, accounts receivable, insurance claims adjustment, and similar transaction-processing applications. They are also widely used in medical records management.

The terminal digit approach requires a folder or other record identifier of six digits or longer. When shorter record numbers are involved, the number sequences can be padded with zeros to attain the required length. For filing purposes, the folder number is rewritten as three pairs of two digits each, with the resulting pairs being separated by hyphens. Thus, the number "365461" would be subdivided as "36-54-61," where "61" is described as the primary pair of digits, "54" as the secondary pair, and "36" as the tertiary pair. The digit pairs are rearranged accordingly, and the resulting number is filed as if it were "615436." It will be physically adjacent to folders numbered "355461" and "375461." Folder number "365462," which would normally follow "365461" in a conventional sequential numeric system, will be filed as "625436" and will be located in a different part of the file between folders numbered "355462" and "375462." The resultant scattering of sequentially numbered folders allows a more equitable distribution of filing, reference, purging, and other file maintenance activity. Furthermore, the backshifting of folders following purging is eliminated.

Generally, the original transaction number, case number, or other identifier is not changed on the folder itself. The required transpositions are made by clerical workers at the time the folders are to be filed or retrieved. Initial clerical orientation may be slightly longer than with sequential numeric systems, but terminal digit techniques are soon learned. As with sequential numeric arrangements, terminal digit systems commonly employ preprinted or customized numeric guides to divide the file into easily recognizable segments. Color-coded folders also can be used.

Variations of numeric filing. Two additional variations of numeric filing are widely encountered. *Chronological filing* arranges records by date. It is commonly used for correspondence and transaction files. *Alphanumeric* systems, in which the folder identifier contains a mixture of alphabetical characters and numeric digits, combine alphabetical and sequential numeric filing techniques. Depending on the procedure used, numerals may be sorted before or after alphabetical characters.

Geographic Filing

Geographic arrangement — a variant form of alphabetical filing — is widely used in sales offices, distribution outlets, and similar organizations. The purpose of geographic files is to cluster together the records pertaining to particular sales or distribution territories. The typical geographic file is initially subdivided by state or other territorial grouping, and is arranged alphabetically. Each state then may be subdivided into cities or regions, again arranged alphabetically. Within each of these subdivisions, folders for correspondents or customers are arranged alphabetically. In addition, this type of file requires a separate cross-reference index listing the customer name in alphabetical order.

The rule to follow when indexing geographic names is to consider each word as a unit.

Name	*Indexing Order*
New Jersey	New Jersey
North Dakota	North Dakota
New Bedford	New Bedford

When a geographic name is not of English origin, it is treated as a single indexing unit, even if the non-English name is made up of more than one word.

Name	*Indexing Order*
San Francisco	SanFrancisco
Des Moines	DesMoines
Bank of Santa Fe	Bank SantaFe (of)

Filing Equipment

Because of the increasing amount of paper generated today in offices, storage of files is a major concern. Filing equipment is available in a wide range of designs and sizes to help solve this problem. *Desk-size filing units and two-*

Lateral Files

Courtesy of TAB Products Co.

or three-drawer file cabinets are used for files that are accessed daily. *Four- or five-drawer vertical file cabinets* are used for active files. *Lateral-file cabinets* are available with two to six shelves or drawers. When open, all files are visible. *Open shelf file units* have open shelves like a bookcase. Therefore, all records are visible, and filing and retrieval are carried out quickly and easily. *Rotary files* bring records to the user with little effort. Records are filed flat or vertically and only one request can be processed at a time.

7

Telecommunications

A N ENORMOUS PROPORTION of any modern organization's business is conducted over the telephone. Effective use of the telephone depends on an understanding of the functioning and capabilities of the hardware and an awareness of proper telephone techniques.

OFFICE TELEPHONE SYSTEMS

Office telephone systems can be generally divided into key systems and PBXs. Continuing technical advances have, however, blurred the distinction between the two types. With computerization, functions once performed by add-on devices can now be built into the system.

Key Systems

In telephone jargon, a *key* is a pushbutton. A key system is a group of pushbutton desk telephones interconnected so that they all can be used to share a group of outside lines and make intercom calls to each other. The basic unit is the key telephone. The most common size has six buttons, one of which is the hold button. The switching gear for the system is contained in a cabinet called the *key service unit*. Large systems also have panels of connectors called *terminal blocks*.

Intercom calls. On small systems such as one linking a secretary and an executive, a button is pushed to alert the person being called, who then pushes the intercom button, lifts the handset, and speaks. The buzzer buttons are usually in a separate box attached to the telephone. With a dial-selective intercom, you push the intercom button and then dial one, two, or three digits to reach another person.

Hold. Any key system worthy of the name will allow you to put a call on hold. Options include a periodic tone (so that the caller will not think the line has gone dead) or music or a taped message. *Exclusive hold* means that only the person who put the call on hold can take it off hold. *Recall from hold* means that after a set period on hold the telephone will start buzzing.

Call transferring. This feature allows you to transfer a call to another telephone number either by dialing a special code or by momentarily depressing the switch-hook and then dialing the new number.

Automatic dialing. Also called *speed dialing, memory dialing,* or *abbreviated dialing,* this feature allows you to program a list of telephone numbers (intercom or outside) into your desk telephone. Depending on the system, a programmed number can be reached, either by pushing a button or by dialing code numbers.

Last number redial. Last number redial is like automatic dialing, except that the number in the memory unit is the last number you dialed, which in most systems can be redialed by pressing the # button. This feature is useful when making attempts to get through to a busy number.

Remote station answering. With remote station answering, you can answer someone else's telephone from your own telephone by dialing a special code or pushing a specific button. A similar feature is night answering, which allows all calls to be routed to a single telephone.

Message waiting. With message waiting, a special light or tone on your telephone is activated to show that the receptionist has a message for you. Some companies have message centers to which all calls are routed if not answered after three rings. Most modern systems can be programmed to route an unanswered call back to the receptionist.

Privacy. This feature prevents other people from accessing a line already in use. It is also possible to get an override feature so that an executive can still break into a conversation, but in most cases only after a warning tone has announced the override.

Do not disturb. Using the do not disturb feature prevents calls from arriving on your line. Depending on the system, the caller may get a busy signal, or the call may be routed to another number. This feature is particularly useful in the office of a very busy executive, especially when both executive and secretary are unable to answer the telephone.

Conferencing. With call conferencing you can be connected to several outside lines at once. All the parties can talk and hear each other. While conferencing is often limited to three lines, it can be expanded further to as many as six or perhaps more.

Camp on. If your line is busy, the attendant can use camp on to attach a call to your line, and the call will go through as soon as you have hung up.

Dial restrictions. A dial restrictions device prevents unauthorized people from dialing restricted outside numbers, exchanges, Area Codes, any long-distance numbers, or any outside numbers at all. Such systems are usually not as sophisticated as PBX long-distance control systems.

PBX Systems

PBX stands for Private Branch Exchange. You also may see the initials PABX (Private Automatic Branch Exchange) or CBX (Computerized Branch Exchange) or other variants. But PBX is the generic name for the office switchboard and its descendants — a system allowing inside telephones to call each other and share a limited number of outside lines. Key systems often exist within PBX networks. The principal difference between a PBX and a key system is that all of a PBX's switching takes place within a central mechanism, triggered by dialing code numbers instead of pushing buttons. For instance, instead of pushing a line button to make an outgoing call, you usually dial "9." Incoming calls go through an attendant unless a Direct Inward Dial system is in use. A PBX can support far more telephones than a key system can, while providing similar features. Features that you may encounter on a PBX or on peripheral equipment attached to one in addition to those found on a key system are explained in the next few paragraphs.

Least cost routing. When you make a long-distance call, the system tries to find the cheapest way of placing your call. This usually means waiting a pre-set period for a WATS line or other discount transmission facility to become available. If none becomes available, your call is placed via direct-distance dialing (DDD). How long you have to wait usually depends on the priority assigned to your telephone — executives might get through immediately, for example.

Long-distance control system. Often offered with least cost routing, a long-distance control system (LDCS) requires that you dial in special access codes before you are allowed to make a long-distance call. For instance, you may be required to dial "88" to reach the controller, followed by your personal code number and the number you wish to reach; then you wait for the least cost router to find an unused WATS line. Depending on the limitations put on your code number, you may be prohibited from making international calls, calls to certain areas, or any outside calls at all.

Station message detail recorder. The obvious enhancement of an LDCS, a station message detail recorder (SMDR) keeps track of all the calls you make, what numbers they went to, how long they lasted, how much they cost, and so on. Most SMDRs can produce management reports breaking the call traffic down into categories such as department, caller, or time of day.

Call detail recorder. A call detail recorder is basically a simplified SMDR. It logs outgoing calls, their length, destination, and cost, but it has no way of identifying who made the calls.

WATS extender. A WATS extender attached to a PBX allows you to call the PBX from another telephone and use the system's WATS line.

Digital transmission. Some modern PBX systems use not only computerized switching mechanisms but also computerized telephone instruments. The telephone encodes your voice as a high-speed digital bit stream. Since computers also use digital transmission techniques, it may be possible to connect computer equipment directly to the office telephone network and transmit at speeds as high as 56,000 baud. This advantage does not extend to outside (nondigital) lines. Fancier digital telephones often include a one-line alphanumeric readout that can give the number of the calling party (for intercom calls only), show the cost of your call while still in progress, or display other information while at the same time doubling as a digital clock.

Direct Inward Dial Systems

Direct Inward Dial (DID) systems allow telephone numbers within a company to be reached by dialing them directly from the outside without going through an attendant. However, outgoing calls are subject to the office's PBX or key system. Calls between numbers within the DID system can be placed as conference calls by dialing the last four digits. The DID system may be installed in addition to the PBX, it may be a feature of the PBX, or it may be embodied in special wiring at the telephone company's facilities. This last variant is often called a *Centrex system.*

Other Equipment

Automatic call distributors. Organizations such as airline reservation offices experiencing a lot of incoming calls will usually set up a department of call takers served by an automatic call distributor (ACD). The ACD distributes incoming calls to the call takers and calls that cannot be answered are put on hold with music and a reassuring message. Sophisticated ACDs can gather statistics on how many calls were abandoned or how many busied out, can break down the traffic by time of day, and can monitor the productivity of the individual call takers such as airline ticket agents.

Speakerphones. These devices allow you to speak on the telephone without lifting the receiver. Because of small echoes in the room, the person at the other end may think he or she is listening to you through a rain pipe. This problem can be alleviated to some extent by experimenting with the placement of the microphone or by installing sound-absorbing curtains or carpet. Speaker telephones that suppress or avoid the echoes are also available.

Answering machines. These devices answer the telephone with a recording and then record whatever message the caller cares to leave. Advanced features include a remote key allowing you to call in from another telephone and listen to whatever messages have been left. Units with a speaker can be used for call screening: you leave the machine on, and if you hear someone whom you want to talk to leaving a message, you can then break in and speak to that caller.

Pocket beepers. A beeper is a pocket-sized paging device that alerts the bearer that a telephone message has been received. Beepers are worn by people such as physicians or news photographers who must always remain accessible to their offices. To alert a beeper user, you call the telephone number associated with that person's beeper and leave a message. The pager company then sends out a radio signal triggering the beeper's alarm mechanism. Some systems also will broadcast your recorded message, and some other beepers with digital readouts will display the telephone number the user is supposed to call.

Security. Scrambler telephones, such as those used by the military, are available on the civilian market. They range from inexpensive devices whose encoded output may still be understood by the practiced ear to sophisticated devices intended to thwart professional cryptanalysts. But an unused telephone also can be a security threat. A device called an *infinity transmitter* can be installed in your telephone allowing someone to call it, keep it from ringing, and then listen to everything being said in your office. Therefore, if you're in a sensitive business, you should always greet unexpected "telephone repair people" with skepticism.

TRANSMISSION FACILITIES

The ten-digit telephone number (such as 311–555–6611) is standard in the United States and Canada. The first three digits (311 in this example) designate your Area Code, or *numbering plan area* in telephone jargon. The next three digits (555) designate the central office or exchange to which your line is attached. The last four digits (6611) designate your line. In many areas, long-distance numbers must be preceded by the digit "1." If you are in the same Area Code as the party you are trying to reach, you do not need to dial the Area Code. In some rural areas you do not have to dial the exchange number if you and the person you are calling are both in the same exchange.

All telephones are connected to a central office where the switching takes place. Calls between numbers of the same prefix are handled within the central office. Calls to numbers with a different prefix must be routed over interoffice trunk lines. In large cities with many central offices, interoffice calls are routed through tandem offices. Calls to another Area Code are routed through your central office's associated toll center. The call may be routed through various other switching centers, depending on destination and line traffic, until the connection has been completed. Even if you call the same long-distance number many times, the routing could be different each time. Many long-distance calls are routed through microwave relay links, using a signal subdivided into smaller bandwidths, with one conversation on each band. If you should hear crosstalk, that means your band has overlapped with another.

Each telephone line requires at least two wires and is referred to as the *customer loop*. In a single-line telephone cable the green and red wires (also called *tip and ring*) are the ones needed to operate your telephone. There may be others (such as the black and yellow ones) but they either are spares or are used for a specialized purpose. Multiline cables use a more complicated color scheme.

TELEPHONE COMPANY SERVICES

Message Telecommunications Service

Message Telecommunications Service is also called POTS (Plain Old Telephone Service) and is exemplified by the service used by most residences. In most places, your base monthly bill allows you to make unlimited free local calls. In some areas you are charged for local calls. Local charges may be based on a flat charge per call or on a complex scheme taking into account the length of the call, the distance, and the time of day.

Direct-distance Dialing

Direct-distance dialing (DDD) involves ordinary long-distance calls that you dial yourself. You can dial directly to any number in the United States, Canada, Northwest Mexico, and Mexico City.

Wherever you are, there are two different rate structures — interstate and intrastate. Calls are billed by the minute, figured to the next highest minute, so that 61 seconds is billed as 2 minutes. The first minute is billed at a higher rate than the subsequent minutes. Calls that cover more distance cost more, but not in a proportional way — a 2,000-mile call may cost only twice as much as a 20-mile call. Interstate calls made in the evening (5 P.M. to 11 P.M.) are 40 percent cheaper, while night calls (11 P.M. to 8 A.M.) are 60 percent cheaper. (Intrastate discounts may differ.) While you once could call someone at 7:59 A.M. and talk all day at the night rate, this is no longer the case. Every minute after 8 A.M. will be charged at the day rate, at least for interstate calls.

International Calls

Numbers in Canada and parts of Mexico can be dialed directly using the ten-digit system previously described. Numbers in many other nations can be reached via direct dialing using international access codes. There are four steps involved in international dialing:

1. Dial the international access code — 011.
2. Dial the country code (two or three digits).
3. Dial the city code (one to four digits — none in small countries).
4. Dial the local telephone number.

After dialing all the numbers you should then push the # button if you have a pushbutton telephone. This is supposed to speed up the processing of the call, which can take 45 seconds. To make an operator-assisted international call (such as a collect, credit card, or person-to-person call) use "01" as the international access code. Country codes and some city codes for places that can be reached by direct dialing should be listed in your telephone directory. You will have to call the operator to place calls to other countries not listed there. For questions about international dialing, you can call 1–800–874–4000.

Marine Radiotelephone

Ships in port or near a coastal city can be reached through the marine operator in that city, obtainable through your local operator. Your call is patched through a shortwave radio link to the ship's radio room. You cannot reach ships at sea this way. Properly equipped ships at sea can be reached through the maritime satellite network (INMARSAT) with the same procedure used for international calls. You just have to know what ocean the ship is in and the ship's telephone number. You dial the international access code (011), the ocean code, the ship's seven-digit number, and the # button if you have a pushbutton telephone. Ocean codes are 871 for the Atlantic, 872 for the Pacific, and 873 for the Indian. INMARSAT calls are billed per minute, and if it is long-distance to the satellite uplink facility, you are billed for that, too.

WATS

Wide Area Telephone Service (WATS) is a special telephone line installed at your office that allows outgoing long-distance calls under a billing arrangement that *may* result in lower telephone costs. (WATS lines cannot be used for incoming calls.) There is a widespread myth that WATS calls are free — a myth that can prove costly to those who believe it. The cost of an interstate WATS line is based on usage, just like the cost of using a regular telephone line. The advantage of WATS is that the rates are lower than those for regular telephone calls, and the calls are timed by the second rather than to the next full minute. If you make no calls, all you pay is a basic service fee.

Inward WATS

Inward WATS lines use the 800 Area Code and are toll-free to the caller. The calls are automatically paid for by the receiver. Printing 800 numbers in advertisements is said to raise the response rate by 20 percent or more, an important factor to consider in marketing. At one time you had to get separate 800 numbers for intrastate and out-of-state callers, but now this procedure is unnecessary. Other recent enhancements include customized call routing so that calls from different areas of the country will be routed to different offices, and variable call routing so that after-hours calls will be routed to a separate office. The Information operator for toll-free numbers can be reached at 1–800–555–1212.

Operator-assisted Calls

Operator-assisted calls can be made by dialing "0" and then the number you are trying to reach. The operator will come on before the call goes through. Operator-assisted calls cost more than regular calls except when they are used to overcome a line problem. The surcharge varies. It is usually considered onerous on short calls but less significant on long calls.

Collect calls. When the operator comes on, you give your name and explain that you are making a collect call. When the call is answered the operator asks if the call recipient will accept the charges. If you ask to speak to a specific person, the call becomes a person-to-person collect call, whether you realize it or not, and the cost is increased.

Third-party calls. You can call from one number to another number and charge it to a third number, presumably your home or office telephone. The operator may call that number and see if you are authorized to charge calls to it. In some places you might not be allowed to make third-party calls at all from a pay telephone.

Credit card calls. You give the operator your telephone company credit card number, assuming you have been issued one. In some cases you will be turned over to a recording that will ask you to dial in your credit card number.

Time and charges. You tell the operator you want time and charges, and then you stay on the line after the call is completed. The operator or a recording will come on and tell you the length of the call and its cost. If you forget and hang up at the end of the call, the operator should call you back immediately and give you the time and charges.

Person-to-person. You tell the operator the name of the party you are trying to reach, the operator stays on the line until you speak to that person, and charging begins only at that moment. While this may take the risk out of making a long-distance call to someone who might not be in, the surcharge is as much as you might pay for a half dozen short calls. Also, if your party is not there and the operator asks if you want to talk to someone else and you agree, you'll have made an ordinary call for the price of a person-to-person call.

Conference calls. You should call the operator direct and announce your plans, giving the names and numbers of the people you want to talk to. You should schedule the call with the conferees well in advance.

Foreign Exchanges and Tie Lines

If your office makes a lot of calls to a specific city, you can get a foreign exchange (FX) to that city. An FX is essentially a direct line. When you lift the handset of an FX telephone, you are getting a dial tone from the city it is connected to. There is no usage fee — only the monthly lease for the line. A tie line is a similar leased line between two PBXs in distant cities.

Custom Calling

For an extra fee your local telephone company may be able to provide ordinary telephones with features similar to some of those built into office telephone systems. These features include speed dialing, automated answering services, and three-way calling.

ADVANCED BUSINESS TELECOMMUNICATIONS

Videoconferencing

While some organizations may have Picturephones linking various offices or individuals, the use of televised communication has come to mean video teleconferencing between groups of people in specially equipped rooms. Several hotel chains offer such facilities. A firm can build its own videoconferencing system using transmission facilities provided by any of several

Videoconferencing

One-way videoconferencing system. Courtesy of PictureTel.

companies. Videoconferencing can involve one-way or two-way television transmission. One-way transmissions are essentially private TV transmissions to a select audience and are used for activities such as announcing new policies to a company's national sales force. (See the illustration above.) The salespeople meet in a videoconferencing room in their city and watch corporate management's televised presentation. Questions can be fielded through a telephone hookup. The advantages to videoconferencing are that everyone gets the message at the same time, and executives are not tied up for weeks putting on traveling road shows to educate a widely scattered sales force.

Two-way videoconferencing involves smaller more elaborate facilities. The standard configuration is a soundproofed room with a conference table and one or more wide-screen TV monitors on a wall at one end of the table. Two cameras are often used, either to provide coverage from different angles or to project charts or other written material on the screen. Fax machines also may be included. The cost of two-way videoconferencing can be several thousand dollars per session, but its advantage is its cost-effectiveness over executive travel time to an off-site location.

Cellular Telephones

Cellular telephones are modernized versions of the old mobile car radio-telephones. Cities with cellular telephone systems are divided into circular cells. As you drive from one cell to the next you are handed off to the transmitter in the next cell without your being aware of it. Using a cellular telephone is much like using an ordinary pushbutton telephone. You make calls from it by dialing the telephone number and people reach you by dialing your car's telephone number. A red indicator light shows that your telephone is tuned to a cellular transmitter.

Voice Mail

With a voice mail system, messages are sent, retrieved, and saved on a computer. Voice mail has the following features:

- Incoming calls are answered and routed at once.
- Direct dialing from different locations is used to retrieve messages.
- Calls to other locations can be forwarded.
- The length of the communication is reduced because it is one-way.
- People in different time zones can stay in touch 24 hours a day.
- The same message can be sent to many people at preprogrammed phone numbers.

AUDIX® Voice Messaging

ACTIVITY MENU

Record Messages 1	Get Messages ABC 2	Administer Greetings DEF 3
Review Messages GHI 4	Password/Lists JKL 5	MNO 6
Scan Messages PRS 7	TUV 8	WXY 9
*	0	#

**R Re-log in
Q=7 Z=9

AUDIX® Voice Messaging system redrawn by Tech-Graphics with permission of AT&T.

It is important to remember that rotary phones cannot access this information. Also, some people prefer to talk with people instead of machines. Voice mail should give the person the option to access the operator. This avoids getting callers caught in an endless loop of pressing buttons and not getting results.

TELEPHONE COST CONTROL

In firms where no effort is made to control telephone costs, as much as a third of the telephone bill may result from call abuse — i.e., employees using the office telephones to make personal long-distance calls. If you have been given the job of dealing with call abuse, your best tool may be to remind everyone that long-distance calls are not a salary perk and telephone abusers can expect to be caught. Pressure also can be brought to bear on them by circulating a copy of the telephone bill and requiring each person to read and sign it, or by simply posting the bill on the bulletin board. You may see the telephone bill drop even if you take no further action. A station message detail recorder also could help identify the call abusers, but nothing will be of much help unless management demonstrates its continuing resolve to take action against phone abusers.

Proper training is important in cost control, especially when you realize that one way of making a phone call can be ten times more expensive than another. Employees should be warned against making person-to-person calls and repeatedly reminded that WATS calls are not free. You also may wish to check inventory and ensure that all the lines and equipment you are being billed for have in fact been installed. In large organizations undergoing constant change there is a good chance that an expensive mistake has been made. Telephone system management is a broad subject requiring specialized knowledge. Any information supplied by an account representative or equipment salesperson should be taken with the realization that he or she has a financial interest in your decisions.

TELEPHONE TECHNIQUES

Telephone Courtesy

Telephone courtesy is important to create a positive company image. Below are listed several suggestions:

* Speak directly into the phone. Do not eat, chew gum, drink, or smoke cigarettes while speaking on the telephone.
* Use a calm, professional tone of voice.
* Vary your pitch. Do not speak in a monotone.
* Speak loud enough to be heard, and enunciate clearly.
* Avoid slang.

- Be confident, reliable, cheerful, and positive.
- Keep background sounds low and to a minimum.
- Avoid talking on the phone and to a coworker at the same time.
- Address people by their names and titles.
- Use courteous phrases such as "thank you" and "please."

All of us have encountered rude or nasty people on the telephone. If, for instance, you have a billing problem with a department store and the person in the credit department is rude and not particularly helpful, you might hang up the phone in frustration and declare that you will never shop in that store again. That's not saying much for that particular company's corporate image in your eyes. Occasionally, a call might come in from someone who has a question or is seeking information about your company and has been transferred from office to office to office, hearing only "You're on the wrong line" or "I can't help you." By the time the caller gets to your office, he or she is angry and frustrated. When answering calls like that, try to avoid having to transfer a caller once again unless you can be sure the person he or she is being switched to can definitely provide the correct information. Rather than passing the buck, it's sometimes necessary to find out exactly what it is the caller wants, take down his or her name and number and, when you have ascertained the information, get back to him or her as soon as possible, or have someone in the appropriate division or department return the call.

Incoming Calls

Answer the phone according to company policy and in such a way that a caller knows it is the right number. Below are some ways to answer the phone:

To answer your own phone:
"Marketing, George Carr speaking."

To answer another person's phone:
"Ms. Comstock's office, Janet speaking."

To answer for a department:
"Marketing, Pam Monroe speaking."

To answer for the company:
"Good afternoon, Wilson, Inc."

or

"Wilson, Inc., Jack speaking."

The following suggestions will help create a positive company image:

- Answer immediately, on the first ring if possible.
- Have a pen or pencil, a message pad, a watch for noting the time, the

executive's appointment calendar, extension numbers, and telephone books available.

- Determine who is calling if it is not stated at the onset.
- Repeat the caller's name to verify the pronunciation.
- Avoid disclosing personal information such as "Ms. Ross is at the dentist until noon."
- Dispose of calls appropriately. Determine which calls are urgent and decide on the appropriate person.

A ringing phone should never go unanswered. Whether you are assigned to answer someone else's phone, or you just happen to walk by another office where the phone is ringing, you should be as helpful as possible. It might be necessary to explain to the caller that it's not your office, and rather than saying, "I don't know" or "I can't help you," there's nothing wrong with saying, "I'm afraid there's no one in the office right now. May I have Mr. London or his secretary get back to you?"

If you ask a coworker to answer your phone, it is your responsibility to explain how the phone should be answered, what calls might be expected by the executive, where the executive can be reached if necessary, and any other pertinent information. Be sure to alert your coworker if the executive is expecting a particular call or, as sometimes happens, if the executive does not want to accept certain calls. Explain how the executive prefers to have the phone answered. You might call the executive by a nickname, but it doesn't necessarily mean that he or she wants the phone answered that way. *Charles* London might be preferable to *Chuck* London.

Correct hold procedures. No one likes to be put on hold, but of course it's inevitable in a business office. The following guidelines help promote goodwill:

- Ask permission to put the caller on hold and wait for a response.
- Check back every 30–40 seconds. Ask if he or she wishes to continue to hold or prefers to have the call returned.
- If it may be a long period of time, let the caller know.

Transferring calls. If it's necessary to transfer a call — whether because it came in on the wrong line or because the executive wants to take the call in another office — explain to the caller what you're doing. Don't just say "Hold on." If the call does come in on the wrong line, handle it this way: "I'm sorry, Ms. Slocum is not on this extension. If you'll hold a moment, I'll transfer you to the correct line." It's a good idea to give the correct extension to the caller in case he or she gets cut off or wants to call back later. If the executive wants to take the call on another extension, you can say, "Mr. London is in another office right now but would like to speak with you. Please hold on and I'll transfer you." Stay on the line, and when someone answers the second extension, explain that you're transferring a call and who it's for.

Screening calls. Screening calls involves determining whether to transfer a call or take a message. Avoid giving the impression that the calls are being screened. For example, do not ask the caller's name and then say the executive is not available. At the outset state that the executive is unavailable and ask if the call can be returned. If it turns out to be someone the executive wants to speak with, you can transfer the call, or you can say, "May I put you on hold to determine if I can interrupt?" Transfer a call if it is an emergency.

Rude or persistent callers can try anyone's patience, and there may not necessarily be a general rule of thumb for dealing with them. In some instances, the nicer you are to someone who is barking at you, the more flustered the other person becomes, and little by little that person's rudeness evaporates to stunned politeness. But for some people, dealing with rude callers is in fact annoying, and all the sweetness in the world won't work. In that case patience should prevail, as difficult as it may be.

Message-taking procedures. For every message taken, general information is to be recorded: the time of the call, the name of the caller, his or her title and company, the phone number — including Area Code and extension — and the reason for the call. It's a good idea to repeat the number to the caller in order to verify it. It can be rather embarrassing to return a call for the executive — or for the executive to return the call — and have the wrong number.

In many cases, callers will be known to the secretary but if not, it's a good idea to ask what the call is about. If the executive is unavailable, there's always a chance that someone else can help the caller or that the caller is talking with the wrong office anyway.

Occasionally, you will end up playing "telephone tag" with callers — i.e., someone calls the executive in your office, who isn't in, and when you return the call, the caller isn't in. It gets rather silly after a while.

Diplomatic termination of calls. Some callers tend to ramble on as though you have nothing better to do than spend time on the phone with them. These calls can be time-consuming and difficult to terminate. It takes skill to end a call with the tact to make the caller feel good about the conversation. When terminating a call, give a short explanation such as "I'm sorry, but I have an appointment waiting." You can also make plans to get back to the caller, if the situation warrants.

Domestic Time Zone Map

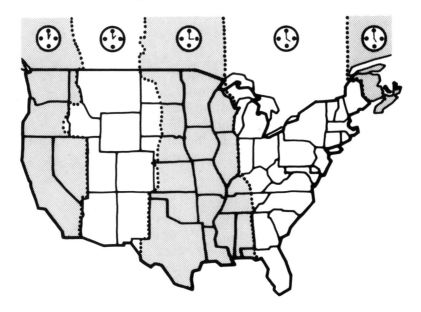

Subtract two hours from Pacific Time to obtain Alaska-Hawaii Time.

Outgoing Calls

The proper handling of outgoing calls is just as important as the proper handling of incoming calls. Before placing an outgoing call, know the reason for calling and the end result desired. This means gathering information and planning before placing the call. Below are some suggestions that may prove helpful:

- Know the name of the person you are calling and how to pronounce it. If you are unsure, check with a colleague or, if possible, call the operator of the company.
- Make an outline or write a brief script to follow.
- Avoid calling between the hours of noon and 2 P.M.
- Take different time zones into consideration.
- Identify yourself immediately.
- Ask if it is convenient to talk. If it is not, determine a time that would be convenient to call back.

8
Incoming and Outgoing Mail

L IKE THE TELEPHONE and computer terminal, conventional mail is a communication lifeline in business and industry today. Although many messages are sent by telex and facsimile or through electronic mail and voice mail, most offices still send and receive a heavy volume of mail conventionally. Written correspondence, unlike sophisticated electronic devices, is relatively inexpensive and technologically uncomplicated. In addition, conventional mail is the most private medium and the one least likely to be monitored or tampered with, without your knowledge. In today's very competitive domestic and multinational workplace, security of communications is a factor to be reckoned with as we have seen from the highly publicized activities of computer hackers and telephone eavesdroppers.

The procedures discussed in the following section will help keep the tasks of sorting, opening, reading, evaluating, logging, and routing the incoming mail from becoming overwhelming. Similar procedures are given for treatment of outgoing mail, always with a view to fast delivery in a cost-effective manner. The procedures established for your office should be arrived at only after consultation with your employer.

HANDLING INCOMING MAIL

Some office functions still cannot be relegated completely to automation. Sorting and slicing open the mail are prime examples, not to mention reading, annotating, and evaluating the contents.

Categories for Sorting

After the mail is delivered, arrange it according to importance. Sort the mail in a clear area to avoid mixing with other material. Check the address

163

to make sure it has been delivered to the correct address. The following are suggested mail categories:

Priority A   E-mail messages, such as faxes, telegrams, and telexes; express mail; certified, insured, registered, and special delivery.

Priority B   Personal or confidential mail. This mail should not be opened unless you have permission to do so. If you have permission, attach a note to indicate that the envelope was marked as such.

Priority C   First-class mail, interoffice mail, priority mail, and airmail.

Priority D   Packages.

Priority E   Second-class mail; newspapers and magazines.

Priority F   Third-class mail; catalogs, pamphlets, booklets, and advertising material.

Opening the Mail

The following procedures are recommended for opening the mail:

- Open all envelopes first and then remove and unfold the contents. Make sure you remove all contents and clip them together.
- Once the contents have been removed, date and stamp each document.
- Check for PERSONAL or CONFIDENTIAL notations and be sure a return address is given. If no return address is given in the letter, attach the envelope to the letter even if no return address is on the envelope.
- If an envelope was opened by accident, write "opened by mistake" and initial it.
- Verify receipt of all enclosures and affix them to the letter. If something is missing, circle the enclosure line and indicate that the item is missing. Record the missing item and contact the sender as soon as possible.

Distribution

Once the mail is sorted by importance, read it and divide it into categories:

- Requires immediate action
- Reply — routine mail
- No reply needed — information only
- Magazines, newspapers
- For reading — reports, advertisements.

Place incoming mail in the same place on the manager's desk. Route materials to other departments or employees by routing slips. If there are a number of people who must see the document, photocopying may be more appropriate, depending on the size of the document.

Daily Mail Record

Some offices require maintenance of a record in which the receipt of important pieces of mail is recorded. A mail record allows you to refer again to basic data about a letter without pulling it from the file. A typical log records the date and time of receipt, the date of the letter itself, the name and affiliation of the correspondent, the nature of the letter, the name of the addressee, and the nature and date of the final disposition. It should also include a column to indicate the type of mail — E-mail, fax, telex, and so on. If filing space is limited, use of a mail log precludes the need to save originals. Such records can be stored in your computer system. It also may be advisable to keep a log as a record of outgoing mail, too.

Submitting the Mail

The final step in the processing of incoming mail is submission of the sorted stack of files to your employer. Arrange the mail in the order of importance, with the most important letters on top. You could also check with your employer to determine if color-coded folders would be helpful. If several people should see the correspondence, use a routing slip. The standard routing slips have places to check the action you wish to have taken.

- For your information
- For your approval
- For your comments
- Please forward
- Please file

Check the section, staple the form to the correspondence, and forward to the individuals to whose attention it is directed.

OUTGOING MAIL

Proofreading

The typewriting and formatting of business letters are discussed in Chapter Four. However, the final proofreading before signature and mailing is important enough to be discussed again here. The truly professional secretary scrutinizes all outgoing correspondence for correct spelling, proper syllable divisions, and good syntax as well as for the presence of excessive strikeovers and corrections. Your goal is to compose or transcribe a letter calling attention to itself because of its correct format, substantive content, and original ideas. Remember that all outgoing letters represent your employer and the corporation to others. The better you make them look, the better you will look, too.

Signature

Letters, contracts, checks, or forms in need of signing may be submitted to the executive in several ways. Place all such paperwork in a file folder labeled "To Be Signed," indicate on each piece where the signature and date are to appear (use a self-sticking note), and submit the folder for signing at the executive's convenience. It is preferable to submit a stack of documents all at one time rather than seeking signatures several times throughout the day. However, a letter, contract, or form sometimes must get out posthaste, and you will not be able to wait until you've amassed numerous documents. That's when a clipboard comes in handy. A clipboard allows your employer to sign a letter in the absence of desk space, e.g., while sitting at a word processing terminal or in a reading chair. Another advantage of using a clipboard is that your employer need not be concerned with smudging the document, a primary consideration for one who handles newsprint all day. This technique works especially well for one-page letters.

Enclosures

If enclosures are to be included in an outgoing letter, type the standard notation *Enc.*, or one of the other conventional forms of it, flush left below the signature line. When sending two or more items, indicate the number and type it next to the enclosure notation. (See Chapter 4 for specific stylings of enclosure notations.) It is also useful to itemize the enclosures and include a brief description of each one as a way of avoiding omissions. Overlooking enclosures is, at the least, annoying to the addressee and an embarrassment to you. When proofreading a letter, you might want to attach a self-sticking note to the edge of the letter and jot down a list of the required enclosures if you haven't already itemized them in the enclosure notation itself.

Copy Notation

The abbreviation notation *cc* covers carbons, photocopies, and pressure-sensitive copies. The copy notation belongs below the enclosure notation (if any), flush left, and a few lines below the signature. (See Chapter 4 for specific guidelines regarding the styling of copy notations, illustrated by typewritten facsimiles.) When sending copies to more than one recipient, put a check mark next to the name of each person to whom you are mailing the material.

With blind copies, the notation *bcc* appears only on the copy and not on the original. Placement of this abbreviation can vary. The typed *bcc* notation is traditionally positioned flush left with the upper or lower margin of the page.

File Copies

Don't forget to retain copies for your files. Depending on the set-up of your filing system and the space available, put a copy of the letter in the appropriate file or files. (See Chapter 6 for information on various filing systems.)

Outgoing Mail Record

If your filing system is solid, sensible, and spacious, then a mail record may not be necessary. However, if you do keep one of them, you may want to keep the other to make your records more meaningful and complete. Data to be included in an outgoing mail record are the date of issue, the name and address of the recipient, a description of the material sent, the method of dispatch (class of mail service, telegram, courier, fax, E-mail, etc.), and the description and date of any subsequent follow-up activity.

Envelope Selection and Folding

Standard letterhead. Letters should be folded and inserted according to the kind of envelope selected. Standard letterhead and half-size, memo-style stationery are folded into traditional thirds. If you're mailing multiple sheets of the same size, attach everything together and insert them into the proper envelopes so that when the letter is open and unfolded, the text will be right side up. If you're sending several different-sized sheets, fasten everything together so that when the letter is removed from the envelope the pages, clippings, or other enclosures will not scatter. (See Chapter 4 for detailed information on envelope sizes and applications.)

Envelopes and mailers made of glossy paper have been known to shed their stamps before reaching the intended recipients — a situation having several undesirable effects: the letters may be returned to you for postage, thus delaying delivery or they may be delivered to the addressee with postage due. If you have a large mailing and a problem such as this develops, notify your post office. Mail handlers will look for the problematic pieces and will help you to rectify the difficulty.

Oversized mailers. When including a letter with a larger item, you have several options. You can fold and insert the letter into its matching envelope and pack it with the enclosure in a larger mailer. Or you can put both letter and enclosure into a single large envelope. If you choose not to fold them, use a piece of corrugated cardboard to prevent damage in transit. Use padded mailers for books, small manuscripts, press kits, files, or similar materials. The mailers cushioned with plastic bubbles or Styrofoam are preferable to those lined with lint because they are neater and lighter. However, the bubble-lined bags are more costly than the ones filled with lint. It is more

Folding and Inserting Stationery into Envelopes

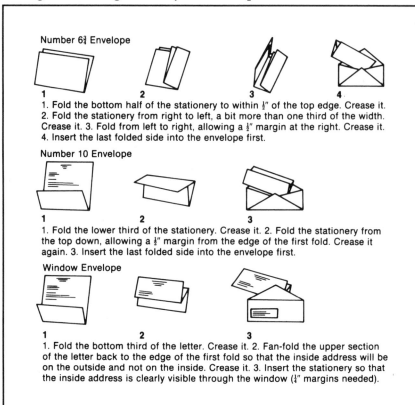

Number 6¾ Envelope

1 **2** **3** **4**

1. Fold the bottom half of the stationery to within ½″ of the top edge. Crease it.
2. Fold the stationery from right to left, a bit more than one third of the width. Crease it. 3. Fold from left to right, allowing a ½″ margin at the right. Crease it.
4. Insert the last folded side into the envelope first.

Number 10 Envelope

1 **2** **3**

1. Fold the lower third of the stationery. Crease it. 2. Fold the stationery from the top down, allowing a ½″ margin from the edge of the first fold. Crease it again. 3. Insert the last folded side into the envelope first.

Window Envelope

1 **2** **3**

1. Fold the bottom third of the letter. Crease it. 2. Fan-fold the upper section of the letter back to the edge of the first fold so that the inside address will be on the outside and not on the inside. Crease it. 3. Insert the stationery so that the inside address is clearly visible through the window (¼″ margins needed).

NOTE: Some printed letterhead intended exclusively for window applications is marked to indicate placement of the inside address. Printed fold lines are often included.

economical to maintain an ongoing supply of the bubble-lined bags in several sizes for use only with particularly important mailings. The cheaper shipping bags or large manila envelopes can be used for less important oversized pieces.

Specialized envelopes. Offices issuing a lot of international mail may wish to use the commercially available overseas airmail envelopes that are lighter than standard office envelopes. A rubber stamp can be used to customize them. Window envelopes, often used in mass mailings, require careful insertion of letters. If the recipient's name and address do not appear through the window, then the time you have saved by not addressing the envelope separately will have been wasted. Some letterhead stationery has a line indicating where to fold the page so that the recipient's name and address will show through the window. Generally, though, the procedure is to fan-fold the sheet in thirds with the inside address outside on the top, as opposed to folding it so that the top third folds over the bottom third with the address block on the inside. (See the section on envelopes in Chapter 4.)

Addressing

The United States Postal Service has modernized its operations with automated scanning and sorting devices that improve dissemination of the mail. To get the most from these mail processing advancements, consider the post office's needs when addressing envelopes:

1. Use envelopes no smaller than $3\frac{1}{2}''\times 5''$ and not exceeding $6\frac{1}{8}''\times 11\frac{1}{2}''$.
2. Center the address and single-space each line flush with the left edge of the line above it. This is called *blocking*. Do not indent the lines of the address.
3. Avoid the slanted address styling. Typewrite the lines parallel to the top and bottom edges of the envelope.
4. Include all information within this block as described in Chapter Four.

Note that attention references, suite numbers, and other nonaddress information should appear within the address block, not set apart from it. The ZIP code should appear on the same line as the city and state.

Special-handling, eyes-only, and other such notations are typed in uppercase letters below the postage line and above the top address line, one third of the way in from the right edge of the envelope. The name of a foreign country should appear in capitals as the last line of the address block. (Follow these fundamental guidelines also when addressing mailing labels for larger containers. Since the label can loosen from the mailer, you ought to secure it with a label cover or tape.) The return address should appear in the upper left corner or on the obverse of the envelope. Be neat and precise. Include the name of the person posting the item, his or her suite or mail stop number, department, and any other information that will ensure the parcel's safe return to sender in the event it is refused or returned by the addressee.

Make certain that the degree of color contrast between the envelope or mailing label and the typed address is sharp enough to be detected by optical character scanners. Contrast is not a problem with standard-colored stationery (white, ecru, or manila). However, if the mailer is of a color that reduces contrast or if the type is not dark, you may inadvertently obstruct the mail's distribution.

Sealing

There are a half dozen ways to seal a mailing container. A sponge or transparent tape may be used if the quantity of the letters is excessive or if the glue is especially evil-tasting. Large numbers of outgoing envelopes can be moistened all at once by stacking them with their flaps open, glue side facing you, one behind the other, with the glue strips touching but not overlapping. Pass a wet sponge over the glue strips all at one time. Then, working from the top envelope, fold the flaps down one by one (see the figure below). For mailing bags, staples work well, as does strapping tape, especially the kind reinforced with strands of fiber. Boxes should be sealed with strapping tape and tied with string. Make sure that you have not left loose edges on the parcel that will jam up the post office's equipment.

Sponge-sealing of Many Envelopes

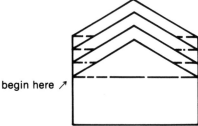

begin here ↗

POSTING THE MAIL

Presorting

From deposit to delivery, a letter passes through many steps at the post office. By sharing the sorting workload yourself, you may obtain reduced postal rates and faster delivery. If you generate a consistently high volume of first-class letters (or a minimum of 500 pieces per mailing), presorting them yourself can save you a substantial amount of money on postage.

The mail is initially sorted by ZIP code from low-numbered zones to high and each piece of mail must bear this code. When a ZIP code has been omitted or when an incorrect ZIP code appears on a parcel, mail room or postal employees must look it up or correct the error. And that's not their job; it's yours. A ZIP code directory should be part of a professional secretary's desk library. It contains the codes of course, as well as other pertinent mailing information such as the standard two-letter state abbreviations. ZIP code directories can be purchased from the post office. With the advent of the expanded nine-digit ZIP code called *ZIP + 4*, directories of all the codes have become real necessities. The additional digits in ZIP + 4 allow the Postal Service to process much more mail with greater speed and efficiency. The program is intended to eliminate all manual mail sorting. (See Chapter 4 for more information regarding ZIP + 4 and its use on envelopes.) Letters going to the same post office (i.e., letters bearing the same five digits in the ZIP code) should be bundled together. Mail destined for one major city (i.e., mail whose ZIP codes share the same first three digits) also ought to be bound together.

Postage for presorted mail must be paid by postage meter, permit imprint, or precanceled stamps. For mailings exceeding fifty pieces, a postage meter and/or envelopes preprinted with your permit number are preferable. If you use precanceled stamps, affix them with a roller or a wet sponge. If presorted letters have not been stamped with precanceled stamps having the printed notation "presorted first-class mail," the letters must be annotated by hand. If your office does not meet the minimum mail volume to qualify for the presort postage rate, you can still hasten the mail's delivery by separating it into broad categories (i.e., local, intrastate, interstate, and international) and by arranging the pieces from low to high ZIP codes. Separating the mail by other classes (second, third, and fourth) and by ZIP code within those classes also will speed delivery.

Stamping

You have several options for stamping outgoing mail. These include postage meters, imprints, and manual methods — all to be discussed. But regardless of the method chosen, you should have at hand an accurate postage scale and lists of the current postage rates applicable to the classes of mail service that your office uses if it lacks a mail room.

Postage meters. Postage meters apply postage in any amount (you set the denominations) directly onto an envelope fed into the machine or onto a label then affixed to the parcel. Each time the meter is used the descending register, which keeps a current tab on the balance of postage remaining in the meter, is reduced by the denomination of postage affixed to the piece of mail. The ascending register then increases by that amount, thus reflecting the amount of postage used. If an incorrect unit of postage has been printed on the envelope or on a label or if the envelope or label has been in some way defaced after having had postage applied, a partial refund (and in some cases, a full one) can be obtained from the post office. However, you must bring the unusable pieces of mail to the post office and complete some forms within one year of the date appearing on the metered postage in order to obtain the refund.

One major benefit of a meter is that the postmarked dated item requires no further cancellation at the post office, thus bypassing another processing activity and thereby expediting delivery. Remember, though, that five or more pieces of metered mail must be bundled together; otherwise they will be processed and canceled in the usual fashion. Postage meters also allow for customized postmarks. And, of course, meters are faster than manual affixation of stamps.

Permit imprints. Permit imprints allow an organization to print postage directly onto envelopes or post cards. Generally, the organization's return address is also printed at the same time in the upper left corner on the face of the envelope, on the obverse, or in the address block on a self-addressed stamped return envelope. Permit inprints are popular with mass mailing programs and are used in all classes of service (first through fourth). Regardless of class, permit-imprinted mail must be sorted by the sender, an extra activity that can neutralize the benefits and conveniences afforded by preprinted permit postage.

Other stamping methods. Another stamping method includes the use of commercial postage stamp dispensers that require neither lease nor license. One such hand-held gadget called a Postafix holds a roll of stamps. A press of the hand dispenses the postage, one stamp at a time. If you have a uniform stack of envelopes or cards, you can speed matters by fanning the upper right edge with one hand and stamping them with the other. Stamps in roll form or in sheets also can be applied rapidly without a special device. Tear off a manageable number of stamps, moisten the first one while it is still attached to the rest of the section, apply it to the letter, and then tear it at the perforation.

MAIL CLASSIFICATIONS

The U.S. Postal Service offers a variety of domestic and international mail delivery service. Domestic mail consists of all classes of mail in the United States. International mail consists of mail received from or mailed to foreign countries. It is important to be familiar with the various classifications of mail: first, second, third, fourth, priority, and express. To improve your service, clearly label your mail according to its appropriate classification.

First-Class Mail

First-class mail includes letters and materials sealed against postal inspection, including:

• Handwritten and typed correspondence
• Postcards and postal cards
• Bills, statements, and invoices

First-class mail can be sent special delivery, certified, COD, and registered. To qualify as first-class, items must weigh 11 ounces or less and be at least 0.0077 inch thick.

Priority Mail

Priority mail is first-class mail weighing from 12 ounces to 70 pounds. Priority is a class of mail, not a special-handling service. It receives the same treatment as first-class parcels weighing under 12 ounces.

Second-Class Mail

Second-class mail is the least expensive to send and is used for unsealed periodicals such as newspapers and journals in bulk. To be eligible, certain requirements must be met to receive a permit:

- Items must be published at least four times a year.
- Publications should be informational and not strictly promotional material.
- A list of recipients must be available for examination by the post office personnel.
- Enclosures are limited to subscription orders and receipts.

Third-Class Mail

Third-class mail includes such items as circulars, catalogs, booklets, printed matter, photographs, keys, and general merchandise. It must weigh less than 16 ounces. If it is heavier, fourth-class or priority mail must be used.

Also available are third-class bulk rates, which apply to material with the same message sent to different addresses. To qualify, you must mail 20 pieces or the weight must be 50 pounds.

Third-class bulk must be labeled, sorted, and bundled, and put in bags. There are six sorting options:

- basic
- basic ZIP + 4
- presort 3 or 5 digits
- 5 digit ZIP + 4
- ZIP + 4 bar-coded
- carrier route

Check with the post office for bulk mail options and procedures.

Fourth-Class Mail

Fourth-class mail consists of pieces weighing one pound (16 ounces) or more that are not required to be sent first class and are not classifiable as second. Packages must weigh 70 pounds or less and cannot measure more than 108 inches in combined length and girth.

Written materials such as instructions, a packing slip, or an invoice may be included in the package at no extra charge. When a letter is sent, attach it to the outside of the parcel and pay for the letter at the first-class rate and for the parcel at fourth-class. Another option is to place the letter inside and mark the package "letter enclosed." There are several categories of fourth-class mail:

- *Parcel Post.* To qualify, 300 pieces or 2,000 pounds must be mailed. The items must be identical in weight but not necessarily in size or content. Rates for parcel post depend on weight, distance mailed, and whether the package is mailed and delivered within a certain service center.
- *Library Rate.* Included in this service are books, theses, printed music, recordings, periodicals, manuscripts, and museum materials.
- *Bound Printed Material.* This category includes educational, promotional, and advertising materials. The materials must be permanently bound with binding, stitching, or staples. At least 90 percent of the sheets must be imprinted with letters, figures, or characters. The material must weigh between 1–10 pounds. To qualify for bulk rate, 300 or more pieces must be mailed.

Express Mail

Express mail is the fastest service that the U.S. Postal Service provides. It is reliable for mailing documents, letters, or packages up to 70 pounds. Advantages of using Express Mail include insurance against loss or damage at no additional cost and the convenience of using a postage meter or stamps. Express Mail is more than just next-day delivery, although that feature is by far the best known. Express Mail service includes:

- *Same-day airport service.* The parcel is posted from an airport mail facility and must be claimed by the addressee at the destination airport mail facility.
- *Airport to addressee.* The parcel is shipped from an airport mail facility but is delivered directly to the addressee by the post office.
- *Office to airport.* Your parcel is picked up at your office by the post office, but the recipient must claim it at the destination airport mail facility.
- *Pick-up and delivery.* The post office picks up and delivers the parcel, door-to-door.
- *Next-day service.* A more accurate appellation would be "next business-day delivery." Post — or have your letter picked up — prior to 5 P.M. (the earlier the better), and it will arrive no later than 3 P.M. the following business day.
- *International Express Mail.* An overseas mailing will arrive at its destination in three days. Many major cities now offer this service.

Extra charges are added for collections from your office, and pick-up arrangements generally require a service contract between your organization and the United States Postal Service. Express mail may be sent COD. If you pay an extra fee, you may also request a return receipt. Check with your post office to determine which services are offered there and which options would be best for your needs.

SPECIAL SERVICES

Registered Mail

Registered Mail is used to protect highly important, often irreplaceable domestic first-class mail. A receipt is issued by the accepting post office, a card is returned to you when delivery has been made, a record of delivery is maintained at the originating and destination post offices, and the mail is monitored through all the steps in between. If the item is lost or spoiled, the post office will award restitution to the sender. Special attention is needed to prepare registered mail. Full names and addresses of the sender and receiver are necessary. The receipt issued for the cost of registered service shows the name of the recipient and the date of delivery. You may specify "restricted delivery": the piece will be delivered only to the person you've designated. Registered mail will be forwarded if the addressee has submitted a change of address notice to the post office. The post office will report the new address to you, should you request that information.

Certified Mail

Certified mail is used when the sender of an article with no intrinsic value wishes to have proof of mailing and delivery. The destination post office keeps a record of delivery for two years. No receipt is issued unless you request one, so you need not bring outgoing certified mail to the post office in person; it can be dispatched with ordinary items in a collection box. For an additional fee, restricted delivery and return receipts are available for certified mailings. The major differences between certified mail and registered mail are cost and speed. Because of the manpower spent monitoring registered mail, the cost is greater and the delivery process is slower than for certified mail. Essentially, registered mail should be used for protection of extremely valuable materials.

Special Delivery Mail

Although special delivery mail will receive special handling at the destination post office, it will probably be shipped from the originating post office with the regular post. This service is available only on classes first, third, and fourth. Special delivery mail is supposed to be delivered to the addressee the day it arrives at the destination post office, even on Sundays and holidays. However, to ensure immediate — and overnight — delivery, consider the United States Postal Service's Express Mail or the services of one of its private-sector competitors.

COD

With COD (collect on delivery) mail, the cost of purchased goods and the cost of mailing the goods are absorbed by the addressee. The maximum collectible COD payment is $300.00. The COD charges also include insurance against nonpayment, damage, or loss. For an additional fee you can be notified of nondelivery before the package is returned to you. First-, third-, and fourth-class mail can be sent by COD. Some private-sector carriers also deliver COD packages.

DOMESTIC TELEGRAPH SERVICE

You can send a telegram through your telex network, by computer, by fax, or you can telephone Western Union and send a traditional telegram.

Fast telegram. The fast telegram is the fastest class of service. It is hand-delivered two to five hours after being received. The charge is based on a minimum of 15 words, with an additional charge for each word over 15. The address and signatures are not counted as words.

Mailgram. The Mailgram provides another form of next-business-day delivery. If the Mailgram is received by 7 P.M., it will be delivered with the next-day regular delivery. The cost depends on the number of words, and there is no charge for address and signature.

Night letter. A night letter is less expensive than the fast telegram, with delivery on the morning of the next day. It may be filed at any time up to 2 A.M. The charge is based on a minimum of 100 words, with an additional charge for each group of 5 words above 100. The address and signature do not count as words.

Remember to have a confirmation copy sent to you. There is an additional fee for such a copy, but you will want a file copy and an opportunity to check the message for any errors in transcription or transmission. If an error occurs, Western Union will send, at no additional cost to you, a revised mailgram, telegram, or night letter.

PRIVATE-SECTOR CARRIERS

Private shipping, delivery, and courier companies offer services that rival those of the United States Postal Service and challenge its former monopoly on mail delivery. In some instances, these operations feature services that the post office does not provide. Most private carriers will establish an account providing for regular billing and will supply you with preprinted mailing forms. The urgency of your mailings and your own budgetary concerns will affect your choice of mailing methods.

Local messengers. Local messenger services offer same-day service within your city. They will collect a parcel from your office and deliver it across town, often within the same hour. Of course, the cost can be high compared with the cost of posting the same parcel through the United States mail. However, the impact of a hand-delivered letter often offsets the expense. Many lobbyists and politicians distribute their "media advisories" (as press releases are now known) via messenger because hand-delivered items are usually treated with higher priority in the recipients' offices. Check the messenger's references carefully.

Couriers. Courier services also provide rapid surface deliveries to nearby metropolitan locations. Check your local Yellow Pages for specific information.

Bus parcel. Bus parcel service is more economical than air package delivery. Services and companies offering these services vary throughout the continental United States. Common options include door-to-door pick-up and delivery, and terminal-to-terminal pick-up and delivery wherein the parcel is taken to the bus depot by the sender and claimed at the destination bus terminal by the addressee. This second option may be combined with the services of a local messenger, who can claim delivery at the destination depot and deliver it to the appropriate office. Before sending parcels, packages, and pouches in this fashion, it is wise to check on the security measures taken at each bus terminal.

United Parcel Service. United Parcel Service (UPS), serving intrastate and interstate destinations, is one of the Postal Service's prime competitors. The advantages of using UPS are fast service, low rates, and the fact that packages shipped with them suffer virtually no damage or loss. A package can be taken to a UPS office or picked up at your office by a UPS driver. If you choose to have it collected from your place of business, you can call UPS to arrange for pick-up the next day. No matter how many package collections a UPS driver makes from your office each week, a one-time weekly pick-up surcharge is added to the shipping fee. If you use UPS often, it is a good idea to arrange for a driver to come by your office the same time each day, thus precluding a telephone call and a day's wait for parcel pick-up.

Air couriers. Air courier services function as air freight forwarders. Parcels are taken to local offices or collected from yours and are shipped by regularly scheduled commercial carriers or by the courier's own fleet of planes.

SPECIAL MAILING PROBLEMS

Military Mailings

Letters, packages, and other parcels destined for Army, Air Force, or Fleet Post Offices overseas are sent to the nearest domestic gateway city where they are pouched and airmailed to their destinations. Overseas government mail is treated in a similar manner. Parcel Airlift (PAL) mail is flown from the city of origin to the point of embarkation. Space Available Mail (SAM) is transported via regular parcel post (i.e., via surface mail) to the gateway city. Both PAL and SAM mail are assessed postage for service from the point of origin to the point of overseas embarkation (the United States gateway city). PAL costs more than SAM because you pay a fee for air service plus the regular parcel post rate. (See Chapter 6 for specific instructions regarding the methods of addressing military mail.)

Overseas Customs Data

Incoming mail. Incoming international mail is first shipped to United States Customs for inspection. Pieces not requiring duty payments are turned over to the Postal Service and are then delivered to the addressee. Parcels requiring payment of import tariffs are issued mail-entry forms stating the duty due. They are returned to the post office, which then delivers them and collects the fees. You may challenge the duty assessed on any international parcel if you believe the customs fee to be incorrect. This is done in one of two ways. Pay the duty and lodge your protest by sending a copy of the mail-entry form affixed to the package along with a covering letter to the customs office listed on the form. The import duty originally charged will be reviewed and a refund issued, if deemed proper. Or you may refuse the parcel and submit a letter to the holding post office objecting to the import duty levied. The original assessment will be reexamined by customs.

Freight. International freight shipments either clear customs at the initial port of entry or travel to another customs port for clearance. You are responsible for arranging clearance of international freight coming to your office. There are at least two ways to do so. For example, a freight forwarder will, for a fee, arrange clearance and forward your parcel to you. Or you may name an unpaid agent to act on your behalf. The agent must have in hand a letter addressed to the attention of the officer in charge of customs stating that the bearer of the letter is acting for you.

Express. Express shipments arriving from foreign nations are generally cleared at customs by the express carrier and then are delivered to you.

Forwarding

The best way to redirect mail is to place over the old address a label bearing the forwarding address and conforming to standard scannable format. That's how the post office does it when they've been informed of a change in address. For misdirected letters, you may cross out the incorrect address and write the correct one directly on the envelope. However, forwarding a piece of mail in this way reduces the likelihood of its being electronically scanned, thus delaying its delivery. It would be ideal both for you and for the post office if no mail had to be forwarded in this fashion. There are several ways to inform correspondents of address changes:

1. The post office provides free change-of-address kits. They're fine if you've only a handful of people to alert.
2. You can have announcements of your imminent move printed. In addition to the new address, include the effective moving date and new telephone numbers, if they also will change.
3. Preprinted Rolodex cards are a special courtesy; you may want to send them to clients and customers in addition to change-of-address notification cards.
4. And don't forget to notify your old post office and the new one, too.

TROUBLESHOOTING AND REVIEW

Incoming Mail

1. Unless you are told otherwise, do not open items marked PERSONAL or CONFIDENTIAL.
2. Suspicious-looking parcels and letters should be brought to your employer's attention and to the attention of your company's security officer. If need be, contact the police or the Postal Inspection Service. This kind of mail includes suspected letter or package bombs and written threats.

3. If a letter or its envelope bear no return address, clip both items together before submitting them to your employer.

4. Maintain accurate correspondence files or mail logs. Few things are
   less professional than having to request from the sender a copy of a
   letter to your employer because it has been misfiled, discarded, or
   otherwise lost.

Outgoing Mail

1. Inspect all outgoing letters. Are words broken into their proper syl-
   lables at the ends of lines? Do verbs agree with their subjects? Are
   margins neat? Take the time to retype any correspondence in which
   the answer to any of the above questions is "no."

2. Be sure that all required signatures are in place; that enclosures, attachments, and other referenced items have been included; that
   courtesy copies have been duly noted and posted; that file copies
   have been made; and that the mail logs are updated. Ensure that
   letters are inserted into their proper envelopes.

3. Business correspondence prepared by an executive is always typed,
   and the envelope or address label should also be typed. Remember
   to style all address information in block format.

4. Sharp contrast between the mailer and the address information is a
   requirement for faster mail processing.

5. There is not much hope for a parcel whose mailing label has fallen
   off unless the return address appears directly on the mailer, in which
   case the parcel will be returned to you. Tape labels to containers or
   use mailing label holders for added security.

6. Envelopes with weak glue should be sealed with tape.

7. Clearly note the desired class of service on all outgoing mail. With
   distinctive air mail or green-edge first-class envelopes, further designation of class is unnecessary.

8. Use a postal scale and current rate charts to determine proper postage. When in doubt of the proper rate, call your post office or private carrier. Answers to usual and unusual questions can be obtained
   over the telephone, in person, or from brochures.

9. Whether you use the United States Postal Service or a private carrier,
   consider time, expense, and indemnity. Why send a parcel by overnight air when bus parcel achieves the same result and is less costly?

10. Investigate the reliability of the company to which you plan to en-
    trust your mail. What recourse will you have in the event of delay,
    spoilage, or loss?

11. Mail early in the day to reduce delivery time by almost one full day.

ELECTRONIC COMMUNICATIONS

Fax Machines

Facsimile transmission is perhaps the oldest form of electronic communication. A *fax* is a popular method for sending information in the form of a precise duplicate of the original being sent. Facsimile transmission is uncomplicated, versatile in what can be transmitted, and relatively inexpensive.

A fax machine can send photographs, diagrams, statistics, graphs, charts, drawings, and handwritten and typed copy to another fax machine at any location served by a telephone line. Information can be sent between locations in the same building, within the same city, or across continents.

To send a message, you place the document in the tray of the fax machine, dial the telephone number at the receiving terminal, and push the transmit button. The material is scanned, and the light and dark areas are converted into signals that can travel across the telephone lines. You cannot add any information at the machine. Facsimile machines can only transmit what is already prepared.

If your company does not have a facsimile machine, there are many businesses that offer fax services, as well as pickup and delivery services.

Electronic Mail

An electronic mail or E-mail system allows employees to send messages to other employees in the same building or to branch offices. Employees in one firm can send messages to other firms in the same city or across the country.

E-mail delivery systems have several advantages:

- Speed.
- They do not require paper.
- "Telephone tag" is avoided.
- Systems are operable 24 hours a day.
- Messages can be sent to several destinations at one time.
- Messages may be sent when rates are lower.
- Sender and recipient do not have to be available to conduct business.

The following guidelines will help you use E-mail properly.

- Keep the messages short. People dislike paging through several screens to find the important information.
- Although in-house messages are usually less formal, be careful in choice of words, spelling, grammar, and so forth.

Electronic Mail Systems

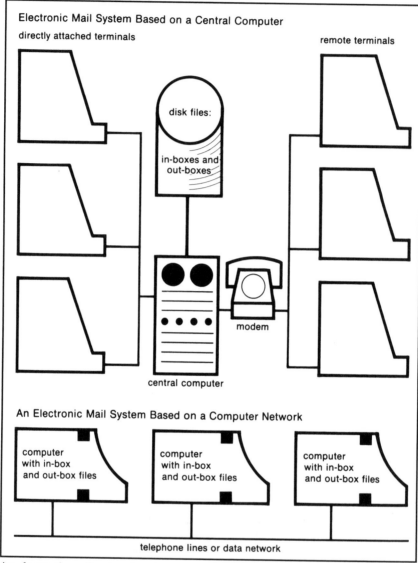

An electronic mail system based on a central computer (top) can be compared with a bulletin board. The computer's files store messages, and users can get to them through terminals attached to the system or by calling in from remote terminals. An electronic mail system based on a computer network (bottom) can be compared with a private Telex network. The computers transmit messages to each other over telephone lines or data network. The two methods overlap, since central computer systems also may exchange mail with computers in other offices.

- Since security can be a problem, do not send confidential information.
- Do not use E-mail to avoid encounters or conflict. Using E-mail to handle problems often creates a negative reaction.
- Routine memos and reports usually do not require electronic transmittal. Determine the urgency of what you are sending and use the appropriate method.

9
Business Style Guide

THE KEY TO EXCELLENCE in business writing is impeccable use of the language. The importance of proper capitalization, punctuation, spelling, and numeral use cannot be overemphasized. These are the fasteners holding together business communications. Improper use of them can result in sentence construction that detracts from the content of the letter, memo, report, speech, or press release.

BASIC RULES OF CAPITALIZATION

First Words

Capitalize the first word of:

* Every sentence.

    The dinner was postponed until Tuesday.
    Personal income rose 0.9 percent in December from November.

* A direct quotation.

    "We shook hands with the minister," he said.

* Every line in a poem.

    For thy sweet love remembered such wealth brings
    That then I scorn to change my state with kings.

* Each item displayed in a list or outline.

    Four things to remember:
    1. Speak clearly.
    2. Speak confidently.

3. Be articulate.
4. Know your audience.

• The salutation and complimentary close of a letter.

Dear Mr. Adams   Very truly yours

Proper Nouns

Capitalize:

• Names of people, corporations, organizations, councils, congresses, and historical periods and events.

Hillary Rodham Clinton
Environmental Protection Agency
the Civil War
Roman Catholic Church
a Republican
the Democratic party
American Airlines

• Names of places and geographic divisions, districts, regions, and locales.

Wall Street   North Pole
New York   the South
Pennsylvania   China
Brooklyn Bridge   New England

• Names of rivers, lakes, mountains, seas, and oceans

Atlantic Ocean   Mississippi River
Blue Ridge Mountains   Lake Erie

• Names of nationalities, peoples and tribes, and languages.

Americans   Sioux
Bantu   French
Gaelic   Old Church Slavonic

• Words that are derived from proper nouns when used in their primary senses.

European cities   British royalty

Do not capitalize words indicating compass points unless a specific region is referred to.

Turn north onto Interstate 84.
Do not head west on Route 30.

Titles of People

Capitalize:

• Words indicating kinship relationships when preceding a person's name and constituting a title.

    Aunt Barbara   Uncle Ed

• Civil, corporate, military, royal, religious, and honorary titles when preceding a name.

Chief Justice William Rehnquist	General George S. Patton
Mayor Jordan	Pope John Paul II
Queen Elizabeth	Governor Cuomo

Titles of Publications and Artistic Works

Capitalize:

• All key words in titles of literary, dramatic, artistic, and musical works.

the book *A Place Called School*
the short story "The Plague"
the poem "The Highwayman"
the play *Cats*
the movie *Gone With the Wind*

• The word *the* in the title of a newspaper if considered an integral part of the publication's entire title.

The Wall Street Journal
the *Washington Post*

Days, Months, and Holidays

Capitalize the days of the week, months of the year, holidays, and holy days.

Monday	Passover
March	Christmas
Memorial Day	Ramadan

Courts

Capitalize the names of specific judicial courts.

The Supreme Court of the United States
The United States Court of Appeals for the Seventh Circuit

Abbreviations and Acronyms
Capitalize many abbreviations and acronyms derived from proper nouns.

Dec.	Wed.
Dr. Jones	Lt. Gov. Sinclair
IBM	OPEC

Treaties and Laws
Capitalize the names of treaties, pacts, accords, acts, laws, and specific amendments.

Fifth Amendment	Civil Rights Act
Warsaw Pact	Equal Rights Amendment

Names for the Deity and Sacred Works
Capitalize names for a Supreme Being, other deities, and sacred books.

the Almighty	the Savior
the Holy Spirit	Jehovah
Allah	the Messiah
the Bible	the Koran

Trademarks and Service Marks
Capitalize trademarks and service marks as the owner styles it.

Xerox	Kleenex
Band-Aid	Ping-Pong
Teletype	Plexiglas
Post-it	TelePrompTer

Scientific Names
Capitalize scientific terms such as:

- Names of geologic eras, periods, epochs, and strata and the names of prehistoric divisions:

Paleozoic Era	Age of Reptiles
Pleistocene	Bronze Age

- Names of constellations, planets, stars, and other celestial bodies.

the Milky Way	Neptune
Earth	the Big Dipper

- Genus—but not species—names in binomial nomenclature (these should be in italic as well).

    Chrysanthemum leucanthemum
    Macaca mulatta
    Rana pipiens

- Latin names of classes, families, and all groups higher than genera in botanical and zoological nomenclature.

    Gastropoda   Nematoda

BASIC RULES OF PUNCTUATION

Comma

The comma functions primarily to set off nonessential expressions that interrupt the flow of thought and to separate elements within a sentence to clarify their relationship to one another. Use a comma or commas to set off:

- Words, phrases, and clauses that break the flow of a sentence.

    Janet Sims, rather than Steve Marks, has been named president.

- Words, phrases, or clauses loosely added on to the end of a sentence.

    Let me know the results, please.
    I am happy about the results, really!

- Nonessential expressions that are not necessary for the meaning or completeness of the sentence.

    Jane would prefer, however, to schedule the appointment later.
    There is, no doubt, an explanation for the change in plans.

- A nonrestrictive clause or phrase—one that if eliminated would not affect the meaning of the sentence.

    There is a fine line between editing and formatting, which is covered in the following sections.

The comma should not be used when the clause is restrictive—one that is essential to the meaning of the sentence.

    The manager that was on the committee has years of experience.

- Words or phrases in apposition to a noun or noun phrase.

    Dennis Jennings, our newly appointed manager, held an exciting meeting.

- Words used to introduce a sentence.

  Clearly, we did not make a mistake.
  Indeed, Florida does have humid summers.

- Transitional words and short expressions that require a pause in reading or speaking.

  The computer age, at least for a while, could create economic problems.

- City and state in addresses and names of geographic places.

  Denver, Colorado
  Miami, Florida, at 10 a.m.

- Year from the month and day in full dates. Note that a comma also follows the year.

  The meeting was held on February 6, 1991, in Chicago.

- Words used in direct address.

  Mr. Stone, please be ready to submit your report.

- Some titles, degrees, and honorifics from surnames and from the rest of a sentence.

  Sandra O'Connell, Esq., stated
  John P. Jamison, Jr., wrote
  Susan H. Greenfield, Ph.D., presented

- The clauses of a compound sentence connected by a coordinating conjunction, such as *and, but, for, or, nor.*

  A lot of people did not attend the meeting, but they want to attend the dinner.

  The comma may be omitted in short compound sentences.

  We have prepared the case and we are ready to present it.

- An introductory participial phrase.

  Waiting for an appropriate opening, James presented his view.

- An introductory infinitive phrase unless the phrase is the subject of the sentence.

  To make sure the conference was a success, Susan worked day and night.

- Three or more items in a series, unless all the items are joined by *and* or *or*.

  The conference will take time, effort, and planning.

  The conference will take time and effort and planning.

- Two or more adjectives modifying the same noun if *and* could be used between them. (Read the sentence with *and* between *interesting* and *well-written*. If it sounds correct, a comma is needed.)

  The interesting, well-written book is on the desk.

- A tag question from the rest of the sentence.

  It didn't take long to get the election results, did it?

- Series of four or more figures into thousands, millions, and so on.

5,000	$15,000
145,000	5,000,000

Semicolon

Use a semicolon:

- To separate the clauses of a compound sentence having no coordinating conjunction, such as *and, but, for,* or *nor.*

  Some firms went bankrupt; others have survived.

- When one or both clauses have internal commas.

  The issues that top security analysts favor include Bristol Myers, NYSE, $42, among drug companies; McDonald's, NYSE, $72, in restaurants; and Lockheed, NYSE, $115, in aerospace.

- To separate clauses of a compound sentence joined by a transitional expression such as *nonetheless, however,* or *for example.*

  We will produce the product; however, it will cost $15.

Colon

Use a colon:

- To introduce words, phrases, or clauses that explain, amplify, or summarize what has preceded.

  There are several courses you can take: anthropology, psychology, or sociology.

  The verdict is in: We need to accept the proposal now.

Notice that in the second example *we* is capitalized because it begins another complete sentence.

* To introduce a list.

  In the session we will also discuss:
  1. Current consumption data
  2. Sales projections

* To separate hour and minute in time.

  3:45 p.m.   7:30 a.m.

* Following a salutation in a business letter.

  Ladies and Gentlemen:
  Dear Mr. Kane:

Apostrophe

Use an apostrophe to indicate:

* The possessive case of singular and plural nouns.

  Sam's final report
  the man's red tie
  my friends' parties

* The plurals of figures, letters, or words. Note that it is possible to omit such apostrophes.

  the 1900's *or* the 1900s

* An omission of letters in contractions.

  isn't   it's   can't

* An omission of figures in dates.

  the class of '84

Exclamation Point

Use an exclamation point to terminate an emphatic or exclamatory sentence or emphatic interjection.

  I need to know now!
  No! I won't go.
  Encore!

Hyphen

Use a hyphen:

* To join the elements of some compounds.

  cost-effectiveness
  self-employed

- To join the elements of some compound modifiers preceding nouns.

  cost-of-living index
  heavy-duty press

- To indicate that two or more compounds share a single base.

  three- and four-ton stamping machines
  eight- and ten-year old foundries

- To substitute for the word *to* between figures or words.

  1–2 years

- To indicate that part of a word or more than one syllable has been carried over from one line to the next.

  Other litigants are expected to make a separate legal effort.

Parentheses

Use parentheses to enclose:

- Material that is not an essential part of the sentence and that if not included would not alter the meaning.

  The Pittsburgh television (KDKA) anchor Bill Doe is highly respected throughout the industry.

- Figures following and confirming written-out numbers, especially in legal and business documents.

  We placed twelve (12) telephone calls to Europe.

- Abbreviations of written-out words when the abbreviations are used for the first time in a text and may be unfamiliar to the reader.

  The national meeting of the American Medical Association (AMA) will be held in San Francisco.

Period

Use a period:

- To complete a declarative sentence.

  He completed the work on time.

- For abbreviations.

  Inc.   etc.   Ltd.

Question Mark

Use a question mark to terminate a direct question.

When is the meeting?

Ampersand

The ampersand (&) is a symbol meaning "and." It should not be used in formal writing except when it is part of the official name of a company.

Johnson & Johnson

Dash

Use a dash:

* To indicate a sudden break or change in continuity.

    Last year Graceland attracted over 500,000 people—more than Jefferson's Monticello.

* To set apart a defining or emphatic phrase.

    It is important—very important—to read the book.

* To set off a summarizing phrase or clause.

    Now GM, Ford, Chrysler, American Motors—it's up to you.

* To set apart parenthetical material:

    The income from retail ads was almost three times as much as from national ads—$22 billion v. $8 billion.

Italics

Use italics:

* For the titles of books, plays, and long poems.

    the book *In Cold Blood*
    the play *A Man for All Seasons*

* For the titles of magazines and newspapers.

    the *Saturday Review*
    The New York Times
    The Atlantic

* For the titles of motion pictures and radio and television series.

    When Harry Met Sally   *L.A. Law*

- For the names of paintings and sculptures.

  Mona Lisa
  Pietà

- When referring to words, letters, or numbers.

  I think *don't* would be more forceful.
  The *60* in an earlier memo should be *600*.

- For foreign words and phrases not yet assimilated into English.

  garçon   *pâtissiers*   *c'est la vie*

- For the titles of long musical compositions.

  Messiah   *Götterdämmerung*

Quotation Marks

Use quotation marks:

- To enclose direct quotations.

  "We discovered that we couldn't complete the work."
  "There is always room at the top."

- To enclose words or phrases to clarify their meaning or to indicate they are being used in a special way.

  The theme, "It's not too late," was chosen.

- To set off the titles of articles, chapters, essays, short stories, short poems, individual television and radio programs, and songs and short musical pieces.

  Read Chapter 2, "The Structure of Language," in *Linguistics: An Introduction.*
  Pushkin's short story "The Queen of Spades"

Ellipses

Use three spaced points to indicate omission of words or sentences within quoted matter.

  "I would like to convince him of their . . . aggressive intentions."

Use four spaced points to indicate omission of words at the end of a sentence.

  "I would like to convince them. . . . I do not expect difficulties."

RULES OF SPELLING

Plurals

The plural of nouns is formed by adding *s*.

books   groups   meetings

With words ending in *s, x, ch, sh,* and *z*, the plural is formed by adding *es*.

bosses   churches   quizzes
boxes   sashes

Some words are spelled differently in the plural form.

man   men
woman   women
child   children

Words ending in *o* preceded by a vowel form the plural by adding *s*. Words ending in *o* preceded by a consonant form the plural by adding *es*, and a few by adding *s*.

studios   radios
potatoes   heroes
memos   solos

Words ending in *y* preceded by a vowel form the plural by adding *s*. Words ending in *y* preceded by a consonant change the *y* to *i* and add *es*.

attorneys   days
lady   ladies
county   counties

The plural of proper names is always formed by adding *s*.

The Kennedys   The Mimos   The Cabrinis

The plural of an abbreviation is usually formed by adding *s*.

months   mos.
numbers   nos.

Generally, the plural of a compound term is formed by making the most important word plural.

ambassadors at large   attorneys general
bills of lading   brothers-in-law

Words Ending in Silent *e*

Usually drop the *e* before a suffix or verb ending that starts with a vowel.

owe	owing
use	using/usable
judge	judging
argue	arguable

Exception: dye/dyeing

Retain the *e* before suffixes beginning with a consonant unless another vowel precedes the final *e*.

hate	hateful
excite	excitement
argue	argument

Exceptions: acknowledgment, judgment, abridgment

FORMING POSSESSIVES

To form a possessive of a singular noun add an 's to the noun. Singular nouns that end in an *s* sound also form the possessive by adding 's.

June's advice
judge's verdict
California's beauty
Arkansas's economy
boss's request
witness's answer
Ms. Diaz's office

For a plural noun that ends in *s*, add only an apostrophe to form the plural possessive.

witnesses' testimony   attorneys' advice

For an irregular plural noun (one that does not end in *s*), add an 's to form the plural possessive.

men's golf clubs

To form the singular possessive of a compound noun, add an 's to the last word of the compound.

my daughter-in-law's visit
notary public's office hours

To form the plural possessive of a compound noun, first form the plural. If the plural form ends in *s*, add only an apostrophe.

businesspersons   businesspersons'
vice presidents   vice presidents'

If the plural form does not end in an *s*, add an *'s*.

mothers-in-law   mothers-in-law's

To form the singular possessive of an abbreviation, add an *'s* to the singular form.

J.B.'s opinion   CPA's bill

To form the plural possessive, add an *s'* to the singular form.

CPAs' meeting   the M.D.s' conference

To form the possessive of a personal or organizational name, add an *'s* at the end of the complete name.

Rawlins Co.'s location
Bank of America's new office
Houghton Mifflin's plan
James Franklin, Jr.'s, announcement

The possessive form has come to be accepted in many common expressions that refer to time and measurement in phrases implying personification.

one day's notice   an hour's time
two years' work   this morning's meeting

Possessives in holidays are usually singular.

Father's Day   Valentine's Day
Washington's Birthday   New Year's Eve

NUMERAL USE

Numbers

Spell out numbers from zero to ten and use figures for numbers 11 and above.

seven applicants
13 candidates
371 tons of iron ore

When a sentence begins with a number, spell it out.

Fifteen thousand feet of wire was lost.
But: We lost 15,000 feet of wire.

Calendar years, however, are the exception.

1993 promises to be a profitable year.
We expect double earnings in 1993.

When two or more numbers appear in one sentence, spell them out if both are below ten, use figures if they are both above 10, and use figures if one is below 10 and the other above 10.

We have five new publications and three revisions.
Order 15 reams of paper and 20 boxes of envelopes.
About 15 orders were delivered on 2 trucks.

When two numbers come together in a sentence and both are in figures or both are in words, separate them with a comma.

On page 162, 15 new rules are presented.
On June 15, 13 new staff members were hired.

When two numbers come together and one is part of a compound modifier, express one of the numbers in figures and the other in words. Spell out the first number unless the second number would make a shorter word.

500 four-page newsletter   three 5-room houses

Always use figures with abbreviations and symbols. Note that there is no space between number and symbol.

$88   52%   80°

If a number forms part of a corporate name or a set phrase, use the exact style on the letterhead or check with the telephone directory or *Thomas Register.*

Ten Speed Press
Twentieth Century-Fox Film Corp.
Saks Fifth Avenue
Fortune 500

Always write decimals in figures.

100.23 mm.

Use figures to express scores and voting results.

a score of 90 on the test
a vote of 10 to 6

Always use figures to express numbers referred to as numbers.

The number *13* is considered unlucky.

My lucky number is *3*.

Money

Use figures to express exact or approximate amounts of money.

$12

$18.50

about $1,500

nearly $25,000

Do not add a decimal point or zeros to a whole dollar amount when it occurs in a sentence.

Enclosed is my check for $32.

This brand is $12.50; your brand is $12.

Money in even amounts of a million or more may be expressed partially in words.

$15 million $8.5 billion

Spell out indefinite amounts of money.

a few million dollars

several thousands of dollars

For amounts under a dollar, ordinarily use figures and the word *cent*.

This item has been reduced 50 cents.

Dates

When the day precedes the month or stands alone, express it in ordinal numbers that are spelled out or abbreviated.

the fifth of March

the 1st of June

When the day follows the month, express it in cardinal numbers (1, 2, 3).

June 5   November 23

Percentages

Express percentages in figures and spell out the word *percent* (notice *percent* is one word).

The interest is 5 percent a year.

The items will be discounted 20 percent.

The percent sign (%) may be used in tables, business forms, and in statistical matter.

Clock Time

Always use figures with *a.m.* or *p.m.* Note that *a.m.* and *p.m.* are expressed in small letters without spaces.

> The bus leaves at 7:15 a.m.
>
> The meeting will start precisely at 2 p.m.

For time "on the hour," zeros are not needed to denote minutes.

> 9 a.m.   5 p.m.

Do not use *a.m.* or *p.m.* with the word "o'clock." Note that the expression *o'clock* is more formal than *a.m.* or *p.m.*

> 4 o'clock *or* 4 p.m.

Use a colon (without space before or after) to separate hours from minutes.

> 3:50 p.m.   12:20 a.m.

Measurements

Measurements are expressed in figures.

> A higher rate is charged on packages over 3.5 kilograms.

Expressing Numbers in Roman Numerals

Roman numerals are used mainly for proper names, important divisions of literary and legislative material, for main topics in outlines, and in dates on public buildings.

King Edward VII	Part VI
Chapter X	Volume IV
World War I	MCMLXXXV (1985)

To form Roman numerals, consult the following table:

1	I	15	XV	100	C
2	II	16	XVI	200	CC
3	III	17	XVII	300	CCC
4	IV	18	XVIII	400	CD
5	V	19	XIX	500	D
6	VI	20	XX	600	DC
7	VII	21	XXI	700	DCC
8	VIII	30	XXX	800	DCCC
9	IX	40	XL	900	CM
10	X	50	L	1000	M
11	XI	60	LX	1500	MD
12	XII	70	LXX	1900	MCM
13	XIII	80	LXXX	1945	MCMXLV
14	XIV	90	XC	2000	MM

10
Business English

THE ABILITY TO WRITE accurately and concisely is essential in business communication. The first step in developing effective communication skills is knowing and understanding the basics of good grammar and usage. The following guide will help you ensure that the message you are trying to convey is the same message that gets heard.

PARTS OF SPEECH

Nouns

A noun is a word that names a person, place, thing, quality, or action. Nouns can be classified as common, referring to one of a kind or class such as *dog* or *paper*, or proper, referring to a specific person, place, or thing such as *Macbeth* or *Boston*. Nouns can also be classified as abstract or concrete. An abstract noun is the name of an idea, quality, action, or state such as *capitalism* or *beauty*. A concrete noun refers to a person or a thing such as *farmer* or *flower*. Nouns can show possession and number (singular or plural). Following are some examples of how nouns can function in sentences:

as a subject of a sentence:

The *housing industry* is in trouble.

as the direct object of a verb:

Spiraling interest rates and inflation have softened the *housing industry*.

as the object of a preposition:

This is one of the hottest issues in the *housing industry*.

or as the indirect object of a verb:

Give the *housing industry* a chance and it may recover.

Collective nouns. A collective noun denotes a group of persons or things regarded as a unit. It takes a singular verb when it refers to the group as a whole and a plural verb when it refers to the members of the group as separate persons or things:

The *committee was* in executive session.
The *committee have* all left for the day.

A collective noun should not be treated as both singular and plural in the same construction:

The *company is* determined to press *its* (not *their*) claim.

Among the most common collective nouns are *committee, company, clergy, enemy, group, family, people,* and *team.*

Nouns as modifiers. Nouns often occur as modifiers of other nouns. In the following examples, the italicized words function as modifiers.

office systems management   *product* quality
cost analysis   *work distribution* chart

Pronouns

A pronoun is a word that takes the place of a noun and refers to a person or thing that has already been named or is understood in a particular context. It performs all the functions of a noun but is not as specific. Pronouns refer to people or objects and must agree with their antecedents — the nouns or other pronouns they refer to — in person, number, and gender:

Has the supervisor finished dictating *his* memo?
The management and union negotiators refused to budge from *their* positions.
The Publishing Committee has given us *its* unanimous approval.
The CEO has not given us *her* comments yet.

Personal pronouns. Personal pronouns designate the person speaking, the person spoken to, or the person or thing spoken of. Personal pronouns have grammatical case (nominative, objective, or possessive), number (singular or plural), person (first, second, or third), and gender (masculine, feminine, or neuter).

Personal Pronouns

Person	Case	Singular	Plural
1st person	nominative	I	we
	objective	me	us
	possessive	my, mine	our, ours
2d person	nominative	you	you
	objective	you	you
	possessive	your, yours	your, yours
3d person	nominative	he, she, it	they
	objective	him, her, it	them
	possessive	his, her, hers	their, theirs
		its	

Demonstrative pronouns. Demonstrative pronouns point out or identify specific objects.

> *This* is my workstation. *That* is yours.
>
> *These* are my diskettes. *Those* are yours.

Reflexive pronouns. Reflexive pronouns direct or reflect the action back to the subject. In form they represent a compound of one of the personal pronouns and *-self* or *-selves*.

> He did *himself* a great disservice by being uncooperative.

Indefinite pronouns. Indefinite pronouns do not have clear or explicit antecedents. Examples of those most frequently used are listed below:

all	everybody	none
another	everyone	no one
any	everything	one
anybody	few	other
anything	many	several
both	much	some
each	neither	somebody
either	nobody	someone

Reciprocal pronouns. Reciprocal pronouns, such as one another, or each other, denote interaction between two or more members of a group:

> They helped *one another* with the mailing lists.
>
> The two secretaries answer *each other's* phones.

Interrogative pronouns. Interrogative pronouns include *who, whom, whose, which,* and *what* and are used in direct questions.

> *Who* is calling?
>
> *Which* is your typewriter?
>
> *What* are your feelings about the situation?
>
> *Whom* did you travel with to Chicago?

Verbs

A verb is a word that expresses action or a state of being:

> She *performs* well under pressure. (action)
>
> He *is* the chief operating officer. (state of being)

A verb can indicate tense (present, past, or future), person (first, second, or third), number (singular or plural), voice (active or passive), and mood (indicative, subjunctive, or imperative). A regular verb forms the past tense and past participle by adding *-d* or *-ed: play, played, played.* An irregular verb undergoes a vowel change when it forms the past tense and the past participle. The past participle also or instead may end in *-n* or *-en: take, took, taken; write, wrote, written.*

Subject/Verb Agreement

The verb must agree with its subject in number and person:

> The *company officers were* unavailable for comment. (plural subject and verb)
>
> The *company president was* unavailable for comment. (singular subject and singular verb)

Certain words and expressions, however, sometimes pose problems in connection with subject/verb agreement.

Collective nouns. Collective nouns such as *committee, jury,* and *group* usually take singular verbs but can take plural verbs if the constituents of the collective unit are being considered individually:

> The *Publishing Committee has* unanimously vetoed the project.
>
> The *Publishing Committee were* divided about the viability of the project.

Extraneous expressions. Don't be misled by the presence of plural nouns in phrases that intervene between the subject and its verb:

> The *executive,* together with two secretaries, a chauffeur, and four bodyguards, *has* arrived. (*executive* is the subject)
>
> *She,* and not any of her associates, *is* responsible. (*she* is the subject)

Singular subject + *to be* + plural complements. The number of the verb *to be* must agree with the subject, not with the complement. A complement is a predicate noun or adjective coming after the verb:

> The *topic* of my memorandum *is* fiscal irresponsibility and managerial incompetence.

The singular subject is *topic,* with which the singular verb *is* agrees. The compound phrase *fiscal irresponsibility and managerial incompetence* is the complement.

Singular subjects preceded by *each, every, many a, such as,* or *no.* These words take a singular verb even when several such subjects are linked by *and:*

> *Each* manager and *each* division chief *has* urged the employees to invest in the thrift plan.
>
> *No* department head and *no* divisional manager *has* ever commented.

Unitary compounds and singular verbs. When referring to a unit, such as an organization or corporate entity, a singular verb is correct:

> *Hutchins/Young & Rubicam has* prepared an elaborate presentation.

Either/or and neither/nor. If the subjects in these constructions are both singular, use a singular verb, and if both are plural, use a plural verb:

> Either the *general management* or the *publisher decides* that.
>
> Neither the *managers* nor their *secretaries have* responded.

If one subject is singular and the other plural, the number of the verb is usually governed by the number of the subject closest to it:

> Neither the supervisor nor the *union members are* willing to negotiate.
>
> Neither the union members nor the *supervisor is* willing to negotiate.

There. The word *there* frequently precedes a linking verb such as *be, seem,* or *appear* at the beginning of a sentence or clause. The number of the verb is governed by the subject, which in such construction, follows the verb:

> There *has been a great deal* of uncertainty as to the exact meaning of the law.
>
> There *seem* to be *many options.*

But a singular verb is also possible before a compound subject whose parts are joined by a conjunction or conjunctions, especially when the parts are singular:

> There *is* much *work* and *planning* involved.

Adjective

An adjective is a word that modifies a noun or pronoun. In modifying another word, an adjective serves to describe it, qualify it, limit it, or make it distinct and separate from something else.

a tall building   a reasonable offer
a two-story building   a red fox

Adjectives have positive, comparative, and superlative forms. The comparative form is used to compare two persons or things, or to compare a person or a thing with a class. The comparative is usually formed by the addition of -er to the base form of the adjective:

This report is *longer* than the one I received last week.

When the comparative is used to compare a person or a thing with a class of which it is a part, the word *other* or *else* must be used:

Mr. Jordan is always *busier* than the *other* managers.
That desk is *bigger* than anything *else* in the room.

The superlative is used to compare more than two persons or things. It is usually formed by the addition of -est to the base form of the adjective:

Ms. Davis receives the *highest* salary in the company.

Adjectives can also be compared by using the words *more, most, less,* or *least* before the base form:

This project is *more* important than that one.
Chris Jacobs was the *most* impressive of all the candidates.

Some adjectives can be compared in two ways:

clear   clearer   clearest
clear   more clear   most clear

A small group of adjectives have irregular comparative and superlative forms:

good   better   best
bad   worse   worst

Adverb

An adverb is a word that modifies a verb, an adjective, or another adverb. Adverbs characteristically end in -ly, although not always, as in the case of *there, now, so.*

spoke *thoughtfully* (*thoughtfully* modifies verb)
exactly right (*exactly* modifies adjective)
very badly (*very* modifies adverb)

Adverbs also have positive, comparative, and superlative forms. Some adverbs add *-er* (comparative) or *-est* (superlative). They may also be preceded by *more, most, less,* or *least:*

| early | earlier | earliest |
| soundly | more soundly | most soundly |

Some adverbs can be compared in two ways:

| loud | more loud | most loud |
| loud | louder | loudest |

Preposition

A preposition is a word that connects a noun or pronoun with another word or words and shows the relationship between the two. Some examples of prepositions include: *to, of, for, in, on, with, between, among, about,* and *since.*

We will leave *for* Chicago *on* Monday.

The results came *from* the doctor.

Joe attended the meeting *with* several colleagues.

We drove *to* the city.

Conjunction

A conjunction is a word that connects other words, phrases, clauses, or sentences. The coordinating conjunctions such as *and, but,* and *or* link words, phrases, or clauses of equal rank.

The staff includes a secretary, an assistant, *and* a receptionist.

The life is busy *but* lonely.

You can go *or* you can stay.

Mr. Sinclair *and* Ms. Jones will conduct the meeting.

Appositive

An appositive is a word or phrase that explains or identifies another word or phrase.

Kent Adams, *an account manager,* is known for his speaking ability.

Ms. Smith's assistant *Peter* has worked here for two years.

Article

The adjectives *a* and *an* are known as indefinite articles, and *the* is known as a definite article.

A computer has arrived.

An entertainment unit was ordered.

The shipment has been delayed.

WORDS THAT SOUND ALIKE

The list below contains two types of words: words that are pronounced exactly alike, though spelled differently; and words that look and sound somewhat alike.

accede	to comply with; to give consent
exceed	to surpass
accent	stress in speech or writing
ascent	act of rising
assent	consent
accept	to take; to receive
except	to exclude (*v.*); excluding (*prep.*)
access	admittance
excess	surplus
ad	shortened version of advertisement
add	to join
adapt	to adjust
adept	proficient
adopt	to choose
addition	something added
edition	one version of a publication
adverse	hostile; unfavorable
averse	disinclined
advice	information; recommendation (*n.*)
advise	to recommend; to give counsel (*v.*)
affect	to influence; to change; to assume
effect	result; impression (*n.*); to bring about (*v.*)
allusion	an indirect reference
illusion	an unreal vision
delusion	a false belief
already	previously
all ready	all prepared
alternate	substitute (*n.*); to take turns (*v.*)
alternative	one of several choices (*n.*)
altogether	entirely
all together	everyone in a group
always	at all times
all ways	all means or methods

anyone	anybody
any one	any one person in a group
anyway	in any case
any way	any method
appraise	to set a value on
apprise	to inform
are	a form of to be
our	belonging to us (*pron.*)
hour	sixty minutes
assistance	help
assistants	those who help
awhile	for a short time
a while	a short period of time
biannual	occurring twice a year
biennial	occurring once in two years
billed	charged
build	to construct
born	brought into life
borne	carried; endured
breath	respiration
breathe	to inhale and exhale
breadth	width
calendar	a record of time
calender	a machine used in finishing paper and cloth
capital	city serving as the seat of government; a principal sum of money; a large-sized letter (*n.*); chief; foremost; punishable by death (*adj.*)
capitol	the building in which a state legislative body meets
census	statistics of population
senses	mental faculties
choose	to select
chose	did choose (past tense of *choose*)
cite	to quote; to summon (*v.*)
sight	a view; vision
site	a place
coarse	rough; common
course	direction; action; a way; part of a meal

complement	something that completes
compliment	a flattering speech or comment (*n.*); to praise (*v.*)
conscience	the sense of right and wrong (*n.*)
conscious	cognizant; sensible; aware (*adj.*)
correspondence	letters
correspondents	those who write letters; journalists
corespondents	parties in divorce suits
council	an assembly
counsel	an attorney; advice (*n.*); to give advice (*v.*)
consul	a foreign representative
cue	a hint
queue	a line of people
decent	proper; right
descent	going down
dissent	disagreement
deference	respect, regard for another's wishes
difference	dissimilarity; controversy
deposition	a formal written statement
disposition	temper; disposal
device	a contrivance
devise	to plan
disinterested	unbiased; impartial
uninterested	bored; unconcerned
dual	double
duel	a combat
elicit	to draw forth
illicit	unlawful
eligible	fitted; qualified
illegible	unreadable
emerge	to rise out of
immerge	to plunge into
emigrate	to go away from a country
immigrate	to come into a country
eminent	well-known; prominent
imminent	threatening; impending
ensure	to make certain
insure	to protect against loss
assure	to give confidence to someone

everyday	daily
every day	each day
everyone	each one
every one	each one in a group
expand	to increase in size
expend	to spend
explicit	easily understood
implicit	unquestioning
farther	at a greater distance
further	to a greater extent or degree
formally	in a formal manner
formerly	before
forth	away; forward
fourth	after third
hear	to perceive by ear
here	in this place
interstate	between states
intrastate	within one state
its	possessive form of *it*
it's	contraction for *it is*
knew	understood
new	fresh, novel
know	to understand
no	not any
later	more recent; after a time
latter	second in a series of two
lay	to place
lie	falsehood (*n.*); to recline; to tell an untruth (*v.*)
leased	rented
least	smallest
lessen	to make smaller
lesson	exercise for study
loose	not bound (*adj.*); to release (*v.*);
lose	to suffer the loss of
loss	something lost
nobody	no one
no body	no group

overdo	to do too much
overdue	past due
past	time gone by (*n.*); gone by (*adj., adv.,* or *prep.*)
passed	moved along; transferred
patience	composure; endurance
patients	sick people
peace	calmness
piece	a portion
persecute	to oppress
prosecute	to sue
personal	private
personnel	the staff
peruse	to read
pursue	to chase
precede	to go before
proceed	to advance
principal	chief; leading (*adj.*); a capital sum of money that draws interest; chief official of a school (*n.*)
principle	a general truth; a rule
propose	to suggest
purpose	intention
quiet	calm; not noisy
quite	entirely; wholly
quit	to stop
right	correct (*adj.*); privilege (*n.*)
rite	a ceremony
write	to inscribe
scent	odor
sent	did send
cent	penny
sense	meaning
stationary	fixed
stationery	writing materials
their	belonging to them
there	in that place
they're	contraction of *they are*

to	toward (*prep.*)
too	more than enough; also
two	one plus one
weather	state of the atmosphere (*n.*); to come through safely (*v.*)
whether	if

A CONCISE GUIDE TO USAGE

The following notes are intended to help you with usage problems commonly encountered in writing. They are entered in alphabetical order according to key words.

about

The construction *not about to* is often used to express determination: *We are not about to negotiate with strikebreakers.* Many consider this usage acceptable in speech but not in formal writing.

above

The use of *above* as an adjective or noun in referring to a preceding text is most common in business and legal writing. In general writing its use as an adjective (*the above figures*) is acceptable, but its use as a noun (*read the above*) is often objected to.

acquiesce

When *acquiesce* takes a preposition, it is usually used with *in* (*acquiesced in the ruling*) but sometimes with *to* (*acquiesced to management's wishes*).

admission

Admission has a more general meaning than *admittance,* which is used only to denote the obtaining of physical access to a place. To *gain admittance to the board* is to enter its chambers; to *gain admission to the board* is to become a member. One pays *admission* to a theater (to become a member of the audience) in order to be allowed *admittance* (physical entry to the theater itself).

advance

Advance, as a noun, is used for forward movement (*the advance of our sales-people into the new market*) or for progress or improvement in a figurative sense (*a sales advance of 35 percent this year*). *Advancement* is used mainly in the figurative sense (*career advancement*). In the figurative sense, moreover, there is a distinction between the two terms deriving from the transitive and intransitive forms of the verb *advance.* The noun *advancement* (unlike *advance*) often implies the existence of an agent or outside force. Thus, *the advance of research and development* means simply the progress of the company's R & D efforts, whereas *the advancement of research and development* implies progress resulting from the action of an agent or force: *The addition of $1.5 million to last year's budget has resulted in the advancement of our research efforts.*

affinity
Affinity may be followed by *of, between,* or *with* — thus, *affinity of persons, between two persons,* or *with another person.* In technical writing, *affinity* (meaning "a chemical or physical attraction") is followed by *for* (*a dye with an affinity for synthetic fabrics*). In general usage *affinity* should not be used as a simple synonym for *liking.*

affirmative
The expressions *in the affirmative* and *in the negative,* as in *The client answered in the affirmative,* are generally regarded as pompous. *The client answered yes* would be more acceptable even at the most formal levels of style.

agenda
Agenda, meaning "list" or "program," is well established as a collective noun taking a singular verb.

ago
Ago may be followed by *that* or *when: it was a week ago that* (or *when*) *I saw the invoice.* It may not be followed by *since: It was a week ago since the order arrived. Since* is properly used without *ago,* as in *It has been a week since the order arrived.*

alibi
Alibi (noun) in its nonlegal sense of "an excuse" is acceptable in written usage.

alleged
An *alleged burglar* is someone who is said to be a burglar but against whom no charges have yet been proved. An *alleged incident* is an event that is said to have taken place but which has not yet been verified. A man arrested for murder may be only an *alleged murderer,* for example, but he is a real, not an *alleged, suspect* in that his status as a suspect is not in doubt.

all right
It is still not acceptable to write *all right* as a single word.

allude
Allude and *allusion* are often used where the more general terms *refer* and *reference* would be preferable. *Allude* and *allusion* apply to indirect reference that does not identify specifically. *Refer* and *reference,* unless qualified, usually imply direct, specific mention.

alumni
Alumni is generally used to refer to both the *alumni* (masculine plural) and *alumnae* (feminine plural) of a coeducational institution. Some may prefer *alumni and alumnae* or *alumnae/i.*

a.m./p.m.

In general, *12 a.m.* denotes midnight and *12 p.m.* denotes noon, but there is sufficient confusion over them to make it advisable to use *12 noon* and *12 midnight* where absolute clarity is required.

and

Although frowned upon by some, the use of *and* to begin a sentence has a long and respectable history: "And it came to pass in those days . . . " (Luke 2:1).

and/or

And/or is widely used in legal and business writing. Its use in general writing to mean "one or the other or both" is also acceptable but can appear stilted.

apparent

Used before a noun, *apparent* means "seeming": *For all its apparent wealth, the company was leveraged to the hilt.* Used after a form of the verb *to be,* however, *apparent* can mean either "seeming" (as in *the virtues of the deal were only apparent*) or "obvious" (as in *the effects of the drought are apparent to anyone seeing the parched fields*).

as well as

As well as in the sense of "in addition to" does not have the conjunctive force of *and.* Consequently, in the following examples the singular subjects remain singular and govern singular verbs: *The parent company, as well as its affiliate, was named in the indictment. Harris, as well as Lewis, has bought a personal computer.* *As well as* is held to be redundant in combination with *both.* Therefore, the following example should be avoided: *Both in theory as well as in practice, the idea is unsound.* Acceptable alternatives are *both in theory and in practice; in theory, as well as in practice.*

back

the expression *back of* is an informal variant of *in back of* and should be avoided in writing: *There was a small loading dock in back of* (not simply *back of*) *the factory.*

backward/backwards

The adverb may be spelled *backward* or *backwards,* and the forms are interchangeable; *stepped backward; a mirror facing backwards.* Only *backward* is an adjective: *a backward view.*

bad/badly

The adverb *badly* is often used idiomatically as an adjective in sentences like *I felt badly about the ruined press run,* where grammar would seem to require *bad.* This usage is parallel to the use of the adverb *well* in sentences like *you're looking well* and is acceptable, though *bad* is less likely to cause objections. The use of *bad* and *good* as adverbs, while common in informal speech, should be avoided in writing. Formal usage requires: *My tooth hurts badly* (not *bad*). *He drives well* (not *good*).

bait/bate
The word *bait* is sometimes used improperly for *bate* in the phrase *bated breath.*

baleful/baneful
Baleful and *baneful* overlap in meaning, but *baleful* usually applies to that which menaces or foreshadows evil (*a baleful look*). *Baneful* is used most often of that which is actually harmful or destructive (*the baneful effects of government regulations*).

because
Because is the most direct of the conjunctions used to express cause or reason. It is used to state an immediate and explicit cause: *The company went bankrupt because the management was incompetent.* The expression *the reason is because* is redundant and so should be avoided at all levels. When *because* follows a negative verb or verb phrase, it should be preceded by a comma when the *because* clause gives the subject's reason for not doing something: *I didn't leave, because I was busy* means roughly "I stayed because I had a lot of work to do." When no comma is used, the *because* clause is understood as part of what is being negated. *I didn't leave because I was busy* means "My reason for staying was not because of work, but because of something else."

behalf
In behalf of and *on behalf of* have distinct senses and should not be used interchangeably. *In behalf of* means "in the interest of" or "for the benefit of": *We raised money in behalf of the United Way.* *On behalf of* means "as the agent of" or "on the part of": *The lawyer signed the papers on behalf of the client.*

besides
In modern usage the senses "in addition to" and "except for" are conveyed more often by *besides* than *beside.* Thus: *We had few options besides the course we ultimately took.*

better/best
Better is normally used in a comparison of two: *Which accounting firm does the better job?* However, *best* is used idiomatically with reference to two in certain expressions: *Put your best foot forward. May the best man or woman win!*

bias
Bias has generally been defined as "uninformed or unintentional inclination"; as such, it may operate either for or against someone or something. Recently *bias* has been used in the sense of "adverse action or discrimination": *Congress included a provision in the Civil Rights Act of 1964 banning racial bias in employment.*

bimonthly/biweekly
Bimonthly and *biweekly* mean "once every two months" and "once every two weeks." For "twice a month" and "twice a week," the words *semimonthly* and *semiweekly* should be used. But there is a great deal of confusion over the distinction, and a writer is well advised to substitute expressions like "every two months" or "twice a month" whenever possible.

black
When referring to a person, the noun and the adjective *black* are usually but not invariably uppercased.

blatant/flagrant
Blatant and *flagrant* are often confused. In the sense that causes the confusion, *blatant* has the meaning of "outrageous" or "egregious." *Flagrant* emphasizes wrong or evil that is glaring or notorious. Therefore, one who blunders may be guilty of a *blatant* (but not a *flagrant*) error; one who intentionally and ostentatiously violates a pledge commits a *flagrant act*.

both
Both is used to underscore that the activity or state denoted by a verb applies equally to two entities, where it might have been expected that it would apply only to one. *Both the employees have exasperated me*, for example, emphasizes that neither employee escapes my impatience. As such, *both* is improperly used with a verb that can apply only to two or more entities. The expression *the both*, as in *the office manager gave it to the both of them*, should be avoided in formal writing and speech. In possessive constructions, *of both* is usually preferred: *the shareholders of both companies* (rather than *both their shareholders*); *the fault of both* (rather than *both their fault* or *both's fault*).

bring
Bring is used to denote movement toward the place of speaking or the point from which the action is regarded: *Bring the letter to me now. The Wall Street Journal brought good news about the economy. Take* denotes movement away from such a place. Thus, one normally *takes* checks to the bank and *brings* home cash, though from the banker's point of view, one has *brought* him checks in order to *take* away cash.

but
But is used to mean "except" in sentences like *No one but a company officer can read it*. This use of *but* is perhaps better thought of as a preposition, since the verb always agrees with the subject preceding *but*. Accordingly, this use of *but* should properly be accompanied by pronouns in the objective case, like *me* and *him: Everyone but me has received an answer. But* is often used in informal speech together with a negative in sentences like *It won't take but an hour*. The construction should be avoided in formal style; write *It won't take an hour. But what* is informal in sentences like *I don't know but what we'll get there before the boys do*. In writing, substitute *whether* or *that* for *but. But* is

also informal when used in place of *than* in sentences like *It no sooner started but it stopped* (in writing use *than*). *But* may be used to begin a sentence, even in formal style. *But* is usually not followed by a comma.

callous

The noun is spelled *callus* (*a callus on my foot*), but the verb and adjective are spelled *callous* (*calloused skin; a callous disregard for human rights*).

can

Generations of grammarians have insisted that *can* should be used only to express the capacity to do something, while *may* must be used to indicate permission. Technically, correct usage therefore requires: *The supervisor said that anyone who wants an extra day off may* (not *can*) *have one. May* (not *can*) *I have that pencil?* In speech, however, *can* is used by most speakers to express permission, and the "permission" use of *can* is even more frequent in British English. The negative contraction *can't* is frequently used in coaxing and wheedling questions like *Can't I have the car tonight?*

cannot

In the phrase *cannot but,* which is sometimes criticized as a double negative, *but* is used in the sense of "except": *One cannot but admire the takeover strategy* (that is, "one cannot do otherwise than admire the strategy"). Thus, the expression is not to be classed with the double negative that occurs when *but* in the sense of "only" is coupled with a negative. Alternative phrasings are *can but admire, can only admire, cannot help admiring.*

center

Center as an intransitive verb may be used with *on, upon, in,* or *at.* Logically, it should not be used with *around,* since the word *center* refers to a point of focus. Thus: *The discussion centered on* (not *around*) *the meaning of the law* (with a possible alternative being *revolved around*).

certain

Although *certain* appears to be an absolute term, it is frequently qualified by adverbs, as in *fairly certain.*

close proximity

Strictly speaking, the expression *close proximity* says nothing that is not said by *proximity* itself.

compare

Compare usually takes *to* when it denotes the act of stating or representing that two things are similar: *They compared the odor from the smokestack to the smell of rotten eggs.* It usually takes *with* when it denotes the act of examining the ways in which two things are similar. *The painter compared the new batch of red paint with the old one. The investigators compared the forged will with the original.* When *compared* means "worthy of comparison," *with* is used: *The plastic imitation can't be compared with the natural wood cabinet.*

complete

Complete is sometimes held to be an absolute term like *perfect* or *chief,* which is not subject to comparison. It can be qualified by *more* or *less,* however, when its sense is "comprehensive, thorough," as in *A more complete failure I could not imagine.* Also acceptable: *That book is the most complete treatment of the subject available today.*

comprise / compose

The traditional rule states that the whole *comprises* the parts; the parts *compose* the whole. In strict usage: *The Union comprises fifty states. Fifty states compose* (or *constitute* or *make up*) *the Union.*

continuance / continuation / continuity

Continuance, except in its legal sense, is sometimes interchangeable with *continuation. Continuance,* however, is used to refer to the duration of a state or condition, as in *the president's continuance in office. Continuation* applies especially to prolongation or resumption of action (*a continuation of the board meeting*) or to physical extension (*the continuation of the railroad spur beyond our plant*). *Continuity* is used to refer to consistency over time; one speaks of *the continuity of foreign policy. The continuity of a story* is its internal coherence from one episode to the next; *the continuation of a story* is that part of the story that takes up after a break in its recitation.

convince

According to a traditional rule, one *persuades* someone to act but *convinces* someone of the truth of a statement or proposition: By *convincing* me that no good could come of continuing the project, the director *persuaded* me to shelve it altogether. If the distinction is accepted, then *convince* should not be used with an infinitive: *They persuaded* (not *convinced*) *me to go.*

criteria

Criteria is a plural form only, and should not be substituted for the singular *criterion.*

critique

Although *critique* is widely used as a verb (*critiqued the survey*), it is regarded by many as pretentious jargon. Substitute, *go over, review,* or *analyze.*

data

Data is the plural of the Latin word *datum* (something given) and traditionally takes a plural verb: *These data are nonconclusive.* The singular construction is widely used and is also acceptable.

depend

Depend, indicating condition or contingency, is always followed by *on* or *upon,* as in *It depends on* (or *upon*) *who is in charge.* Omission of the preposition is typical of casual speech.

deprecate
The first and fully accepted meaning of *deprecate* is "to express disapproval of." But the word has steadily encroached upon the meaning of *depreciate*. It is now used, almost to the exclusion of *depreciate*, in the sense "to belittle or mildly disparage": *The cynical employee deprecated all of the good things the company had to offer.* This newer sense is acceptable.

dilemma
Dilemma applies to the choice between evenly balanced alternatives, most often unattractive ones. It is not properly used as a synonym for *problem* or *predicament*. A sentence such as the following, therefore, is unacceptable: *Highjacking has become a big dilemma for our trucking subsidiary.*

disinterested
According to the traditional rule, a *disinterested* party is one who has no stake in a dispute and is therefore presumed to be impartial. By contrast, one is *uninterested* in something when one is indifferent to it. These two terms should not be used interchangeably despite an increasing tendency among some writers to do it.

distinct
A thing is *distinct* if it is sharply distinguished from other things (*a distinct honor*); a property or attribute is *distinctive* if it enables us to distinguish one thing from another. *This carpeting has a distinctive feel to it* means that the feel of the carpet enables us to distinguish it from other carpets. *Thick-pile carpeting is a distinct type of floor covering* means that the thick-pile carpeting falls into a clearly defined category of floor coverings.

done
Done, in the sense of "completely accomplished" or "finished," is found most often, but not exclusively, in informal usage. It is acceptable in writing in the following example: *The entire project will not be done until next year.* In some contexts this use of *done* can be unclear, as in *The work will be done next week.* Alternatives, dependent on the meaning, would be: *The work will get done next week. The work will be done by next week.*

doubt
Doubt and *doubtful* are often followed by clauses introduced by *that, whether,* or *if.* A choice among the three is guided by the intended meaning of the sentence, but considerable leeway exists. Generally, *that* is used when the intention is to express more or less complete rejection of a statement: *I doubt that they will even try* (meaning "I don't think they will even try"); or, in the negative, to express more or less complete acceptance: *I don't doubt that you are right.* On the other hand, when the intention is to express real uncertainty, the choice is usually *whether: We doubt whether they can succeed. It*

is doubtful whether our opponents will appear at the hearing. In fact, *whether* is generally the only acceptable choice in such examples, though some experts would accept *if* (which is more informal in tone) or *that. Doubt* is frequently used in informal speech, both as verb and as noun, together with *but: I don't doubt but* (or *but what*) *they will come. There is no doubt but it will be difficult.* These usages should be avoided in writing; substitute *that* or *whether* as the case requires.

due

The phrase *due to* is always acceptable when *due* functions as a predicate adjective following a linking verb: *Our hesitancy was due to fear.* But objection is often made when *due to* is used as a prepositional phrase: *We hesitated due to fear.* Such a construction is unacceptable in writing, though it is widely used. Generally accepted alternatives are *because of* or *on account of.*

each

When the subject of a sentence begins with *each,* it is traditionally held to be grammatically singular, and the verb and following pronouns must be singular as well: *Each of the designers has* (not *have*) *his or her* (not *their*) *distinctive style.* When *each* follows a plural subject, however, the verb and following pronouns generally remain in the plural: *The secretaries each have their jobs to do.* The expression *each and every* is likewise followed by a singular verb and singular pronouns in formal style: *Each and every packer knows what his or her job is supposed to be.*

each other

According to some traditional grammarians, *each other* is used of two, *one another* of more than two. This distinction has been ignored by many of the best writers, however. When speaking of an ordered series of events or stages, only *one another* can be used: *The Caesars exceeded one another* (not *each other*) *in cruelty* means that each Caesar was crueler than the last. *Each other* cannot be used as the subject of a clause in formal writing. Instead of *we know what each other are thinking,* one should write *each of us knows what the other is thinking.* The possessive forms of *each other* and *one another* are written *each other's* and *one another's: The machinists wore each other's* (not *each others'*) *hard hats. The district managers had forgotten one another's* (not *one anothers'*) names.

either

Either is normally used to mean "one of two," although it is sometimes used of three or more: *either corner of the triangle.* When referring to more than two, *any* or *any one* is preferred. *Either* takes a singular verb: *Either plant grows in the shade.* Sometimes it is used informally with a plural verb, especially when followed by *of* and a plural: *I doubt whether either of them are available.* But such use is unacceptable to many in formal writing.

elder

Elder and *eldest* apply only to persons, unlike *older* and *oldest,* which also apply to things. *Elder* and *eldest* are used principally with reference to seniority: *elder statesman; Pat the Elder.* Unlike *older, elder* is also a noun (*the town elders; ought to listen to your elders*).

else

Else is often used redundantly in combination with prepositions such as *but, except,* and *besides: No one* (not *no one else*) *but that witness saw the accident.* When a pronoun is followed by *else,* the possessive form is generally written thus: *someone else's* (not *someone's else*). Both *who else's* and *whose else* are in use, but not "*whose else's*": *Who else's appointment book could it have been? Whose else could it have been?*

everywhere

The only acceptable word is *everywhere* (not *everywheres*). The use of *that* with *everywhere* (*everywhere that I go*) is superfluous.

except

Except in the sense of "with the exclusion of" or "other than" is generally construed as a preposition, not a conjunction. A personal pronoun that follows *except* is therefore in the objective case: *No one except them knew it. Every member of the committee was called except me.*

excuse

The expression *excuse away* has no meaning beyond that of *excuse* (unlike *explain away,* which has a different meaning from *explain*). *Excuse away* is unacceptable: *The general manager's behavior cannot be excused* (not *excused away*).

explicit / express

Explicit and *express* both apply to something that is clearly stated rather than implied. *Explicit* applies more particularly to that which is carefully spelled out (*the explicit terms of ownership contained in the licensing agreement*). *Express* applies particularly to a clear expression of intention or will: *The corporation made an express prohibition against dealers' selling cars below list prices.*

fatal / fateful

Although the senses of *fatal* and *fateful* have tended to merge in recent times, each has a different core of meaning. The contrast between *fatal,* in the sense of "leading to death or destruction," and *fateful,* in the sense of "affecting one's destiny or future," is illustrated by the following sentence: *The fateful decision to relax safety standards led directly to the fatal car crash.*

fault

Fault as a transitive verb meaning "to criticize or find fault with" is attested as far back as the 16th century but has recently come into much wider use.

This usage is acceptable: *One cannot fault management's performance. To fault them is grossly unfair.*

few/fewer
Few and *fewer* are correctly used in writing only before a plural noun (*few cars; few of the books, fewer reasons, fewer gains on the stock market*). *Less* is used before a mass noun (*less music; less sugar; less material gain*). *Less than* is also used before a plural noun that denotes a measure of time, amount, or distance (*less than three weeks; less than sixty years old; less than $400*).

finalize
Finalize is frequently associated with the language of bureaucracy and so is objected to by many writers. The sentence *we will finalize plans to remodel twelve stores this year* is considered unacceptable. While *finalize* has no single exact synonym, a substitute can always be found among *complete, conclude, make final,* and *put in final form.*

firstly
Firstly may be used in a sequence: *firstly, secondly, thirdly,* and so on. Another alternative, since all these ordinal numbers can be used adverbially, is the somewhat more forceful *first, second,* or *third.*

flammable/inflammable
Flammable and *inflammable* are identical in meaning. *Flammable* has been adopted by safety authorities for the labeling of combustible materials because the *in-* of *inflammable* was understood by some people to mean "not."

flaunt/flout
Flaunt and *flout* are often confused. *Flaunt* as a transitive verb means "to exhibit ostentatiously": *The manager flaunted a corporate credit card and expense account.* To *flout* is "to defy openly": *They flouted all social proprieties.*

follow
As follows (not *as follow*) is the established form of the phrase, no matter whether the noun that precedes it is singular or plural: *The new operating procedures are as follows* (or *procedure is as follows*).

forbid
Forbid may be used with an infinitive: *I forbid you to smoke in the elevators;* or a gerund: *I forbid your smoking;* but not with *from: I forbid you from smoking.*

forceful/forcible/forced
Forceful, forcible, and *forced* have distinct, if related, meanings. *Forceful* is used to describe something that suggests strength or force (*a forceful marketing campaign*). *Forceful* measures may or may not involve the use of actual physical force. *Forcible,* by contrast, is most often used of actions accomplished by the application of physical force: *There had clearly been a forcible entry into the storeroom. The suspect had to be forcibly restrained. Forced* is used to describe a

condition brought about by control or by an outside influence (*forced labor; a forced landing; a forced smile*).

former
The former is used when referring to the first of two persons or things mentioned. It is not used when referring to the first of three or more. For that purpose one may use *the first* or *the first-named* or repeat the name itself.

fortuitous
Fortuitous is often confused with *fortunate. Fortuitous* means "happening by chance." A *fortuitous* meeting may have either fortunate or unfortunate consequences. In common usage, some of the meaning of *fortunate* has rubbed off on *fortuitous* so that even when it is properly used, *fortuitous* often carries an implication of lucky chance rather than unlucky chance. But the word is not synonymous with *fortunate* and should not be used unless it refers to something that came about by chance or accident. The following example is unacceptable: *The meeting proved fortuitous; I came away with a much better idea of my responsibilities.*

forward/forwards
Forwards may be used in place of *forward* only in the adverbial sense of "toward the front" (*move forward* or *move forwards*). In specific phrases the choice of one or the other is often idiomatic (*look forward; from that day forward; backwards and forwards*).

fulsome
Fulsome is often misused, especially in the phrase *fulsome praise,* by those who think that the term is equivalent merely to *full* and *abundant.* In modern usage *full* and *abundant* are obsolete as senses of *fulsome.* The modern sense of *fulsome* is "offensively flattering or insincere"; hence, *fulsome praise* really means insincere, unctuous compliments.

get
Get has a great number of uses, some of which are acceptable at all levels and others of which are generally felt to be informal (though never incorrect). Some uses to be avoided in writing are (1) the use of *get* in place of *be* or *become* in sentences such as *The executive got promoted;* (2) the use of *get* or *get to* in place of *start* or *begin,* as in *Let's get* (or *get to*) *working now;* and (3) the use of *have got to* in place of *must* in sentences like *I have got to go now.*

gift
Gift (verb) has a long history of use in the sense "to present as a gift; to endow": *We gifted the charity with a $1,000 donation.* In current general use, however, *gift* in this sense is sometimes regarded as affected and should be avoided.

good
Good is properly used as an adjective with linking verbs such as *be, seem,* or *appear: The future looks good. The soup tastes good.* It should not be used as an

adverb with other verbs: *The plant runs well* (not *good*). Thus: *The designer's new suits fit well and look good.*

government
In American usage *government* always takes a singular verb.

group
Group as a collective noun can be followed by a singular or plural verb. It takes a singular verb when the persons or things that make up the group are considered collectively: *The planning group is ready to present its report.* *Group* takes a plural verb when the persons or things that make it up are considered individually: *The group were divided in their sympathies.*

half
The phrases *a half, half of,* and *half a* are all correct, though they may differ slightly in meaning. For example, *a half day* is used when *day* has the special sense "a working day," and the phrase then means "four hours." *Half of a day* and *half a day* are not restricted in this way and can mean either four or twelve hours. When the accompanying word is a pronoun, however, the phrase with *of* must be used: *half of them.* The phrase *a half a*, though frequently heard, is held by some to be unacceptable.

hanged
Hanged, as the past tense and past participle of *hang,* is used in the sense of "put to death by hanging." In the following example *hung* would be unacceptable: *Frontier courts hanged many a prisoner after a summary trial.* In all other senses of the word, *hung* is the preferred form as past tense and past participle.

hardly
Hardly has the force of a negative; therefore, it is not used with another negative: *I could hardly see* (not *couldn't hardly see*). *They listened to the presentation with hardly a smile* (not *without hardly a smile*). A clause following *hardly* is introduced by *when* or, less often, by *before: We had hardly merged with one restaurant chain when* (or *before*) *a second chain made us an attractive offer.* Such a clause is not introduced by *than* in formal style: *Hardly had I walked inside when* (not *than*) *the downpour started.*

harebrained
The first part of the compound *harebrained* is often misspelled "hair" in the belief that the meaning of the word is "with a hair-sized brain" rather than "with no more sense than a hare."

headquarter
The verb *headquarter* is used informally in both transitive and intransitive senses: *Our European sales team will headquarter in Paris. The management con-*

sulting firm has headquartered its people in the New York Hyatt. Both of these examples are unacceptable in formal writing.

headquarters

The noun *headquarters* is used with either a singular or a plural verb. The plural is more common: *Corporate headquarters are in Boston.* But the singular is sometimes preferred when reference is to authority rather than to physical location: *Headquarters has approved the purchase of desktop computers for our engineers.*

here

In formal usage *here* is not properly placed before a noun in a phrase such as *this here house.* In constructions introduced by *here is* and *here are* the number of the verb is governed by the subject, which appears after the verb: *Here is the annual report. Here are the quarterly reports.*

historic / historical

Historic and *historical* are differentiated in usage, although their senses overlap. *Historic* refers to what is important in history (*the historic first voyage to outer space*). It is also used of what is famous or interesting because of its association with persons or events in history (*Edison's historic lab*). *Historical* refers to whatever existed in the past, whether regarded as important or not: *a historical character.* Events are *historical* if they happened, *historic* only if they are regarded as important. *Historical* refers also to anything concerned with history or the study of the past (*a historical society; a historical novel*). The differentiation between the words is not complete, though: they are often used interchangeably, as in *historic times* or *historical times.*

hopefully

The use of *hopefully* to mean "it is to be hoped," as in *hopefully we'll exceed last year's sales volume,* is grammatically justified by analogy to the similar uses of *happily* and *mercifully.* However, this use of *hopefully* is still not accepted by some critics.

how

How is often used in informal speech where strict grammar would require *that,* as in *The president told us how he was penniless when he started in this business.* The use of *as how* for *that* in sentences like *they said as how they would go* is informal and should be avoided in writing. Similarly, one should avoid in writing the expressions *seeing as how* and *being as how.*

however

However is redundant in combination with *but.* One or the other but not both should be used in the following examples: *We had an invitation but didn't go. We had an invitation; however, we didn't go.* The use of *however* as the

first word of a sentence is now generally considered to be acceptable but is
still avoided by some.

identical
Some authorities on usage specify *with* as the preferred preposition after
identical. But either *with* or *to* is now acceptable: *a model identical with* (or *to*)
last year's.

idle
Idle is now accepted in the transitive sense of "to make idle." The following
example is accepted on all levels of speech and writing: *The dock strike had
idled many crews and their ships.*

if/whether
Either *if* or *whether* may be used to introduce a clause indicating uncertainty
after a verb such as *ask, doubt, know, learn,* or *see: We shall soon learn whether*
(or *if*) *it is true. If* should be avoided when it may be ambiguous, as in the
following: *Let me know if the vice-chairman is invited.* Depending on the meaning, that could be better phrased: *Let me know whether the vice-chairman is
invited. Let me know in the event that the vice-chairman is invited.* Often the
phrase *if not* is also ambiguous: *The discovery offered persuasive, if not conclusive,
evidence.* This could mean "persuasive and perhaps conclusive" or "persuasive but not conclusive." A clause introduced by *if* may contain either a past
subjunctive verb (*if I were going*) or an indicative verb (*if I was going*) depending on the meaning intended. Traditionally, the subjunctive is used to
describe a situation that is known to be contrary to fact, as in *if America were
still a British colony* or *if Napoleon had been an Englishman.* The main clause of
such a sentence must then contain the modal verb *would* or (less frequently) *should: If American were still a British colony, we would drink more tea
than we do. If I were the President, I should* (or *would*) *make June 1 a national
holiday.* When the situation described by the *if* clause is not known to be
false, however, that clause must contain an indicative verb, and the choice
of verb in the main clause will depend upon the intended meaning: *If Ham-
let was really written by Marlowe, as many have claimed, then we have underesti-
mated Marlowe's genius. If the main switchboard was out all day, as you say, then I
understand why we didn't get any responses to our advertisement.* The indicative is
also required when the situation described by the *if* clause is assumed to be
true: *If I was short with you a moment ago, it is only because I wasn't paying attention. If Rome is the loveliest city in Italy, Milan is the most elegant.* When an *if*
clause is preceded by *ask* or *wonder,* only the indicative should be used: *He
asked if Napoleon was* (not *were*) *a great general. I wonder if the tax attorney was*
(not *were*) *serious.* There is a growing tendency to use *would have* in place of
the subjunctive in contrary-to-fact *if* clauses, but this usage is still considered
incorrect. Instead of *if I would have been promoted two years earlier,* write *if I had
been promoted;* instead of *if I would have been president,* write *if I were.*

impact

Impact (verb) has been used principally in the sense of "to pack together": *Traffic impacts the area during rush hour.* Recently it has come into more general use in the sense of "to have an impact on." Sometimes it is used transitively: *These taxes impact small businesses.* At other times it is used intransitively (with *on*): *Social pathologies, common to the inner city, impact most heavily on a plant operating in such a location.* The preceding example is unacceptable to many.

important

The following sentence may be written with the adjective *important: The shareholders' opinion is evident; more important, it is likely to prevail.* It also may be written with an adverb: *The shareholders' opinion is evident; more importantly, it is likely to prevail.* Most grammarians prescribe the adjectival form, in which *important* stands for "what is important." But the adverbial form is also acceptable.

impracticable / impractical

Impracticable applies to that which is not capable of being carried out or put into practice: *Building a highway to the moon is impracticable. Impractical* refers to that which is not sensible or prudent: *Your suggestion that we use balloons to convey messages across town is impractical.* A plan may be impractical if it involves undue cost or effort and still not be impracticable. The distinction between these words is subtle, and *impractical* is often used where *impracticable* would be more precise.

infer

Infer is sometimes confused with *imply,* but the distinction is a useful one. To *imply* is "to state indirectly." To *infer* is "to draw a conclusion." The use of these two terms interchangeably is entirely unacceptable. One should write: *The quarterly report implies* (not *infers*) *that sales are down because of the recession. Because of that implication, investors have inferred* (not *implied*) *that we have something to hide, and our stock has fallen three points.*

input

Input has gained currency in senses not related to physics or computer technology. Example: *The report questioned whether, in such a closed administration, a president thus shielded had access to a sufficiently varied input to have a realistic picture of the nation* (*input* here meaning "a flow of information"). Example: *The nominee declared that he had no input, so far as he knew, in the adoption of the plank on abortion* (*input* here meaning "an active role, a voice in policy making"). These newer uses are unacceptable to some critics.

inside / inside of

Inside and *inside of* have the same meaning. *Inside* is generally preferred, especially in writing, when the reference is to position or location (*inside the warehouse*). *Inside of* is used more acceptably when the reference is to time: *The 300-page report was photocopied inside of* (not *inside*) *ten minutes.*

intend

Intend may be followed by an infinitive (*intended to go*) or a gerund (*intended going*), by a *that* clause with a subjunctive verb (*intended that he be present*), or by a noun and an infinitive (*intended him to receive the prize*).

intrigue

Intrigue is fully established as a noun and as a verb in all meanings except that of "to arouse the interest or curiosity of." In that sense it has been resisted by writers on usage, who regard it as an unneeded French substitute for available English words such as *interest, fascinate, pique,* or *puzzle.* Nevertheless, it has gained increasing acceptance because no single English word has precisely the same meaning. The following example is therefore acceptable: *The announcement of a special press conference intrigued the financial writers in the manner of a good suspense novel.*

its/it's

Its, the possessive form of the pronoun *it,* is never written with an apostrophe. The contraction *it's* (for *it is* or *it has*) is always written with an apostrophe.

kind

When *kind of* is used to mean "more or less," it is properly preceded by the indefinite article *a* in formal writing: *a kind of genius* (not *kind of a genius*). The use of *kind of* to mean "somewhat," as in *we were kind of sleepy,* is generally regarded as informal.

kudos

Kudos is one of those words, like *congeries,* that look like plurals but are historically singular, and so it is correctly used with a singular verb: *Kudos is due the committee for organizing a successful company picnic.*

lack

Lack can be used in the present participle with *in: You will not be lacking in support from the finance committee.* It is also used by itself or with *for: You will not lack* (or *lack for*) *support from the finance committee.* In that example, *lack* is preferred over *lack for.* In some cases, however, the two phrasings can convey different meanings: *The millionaire lacks nothing* (the millionaire has everything). *The millionaire lacks for nothing* (the millionaire has everything he needs).

latter

Latter, as used in contrast to *former,* refers to the second of two: *Jones and Smith have been mentioned for transfer to our London office, but the latter may decline the post. Latter* is not appropriate when more than two are named: *Jones,*

Smith, and Kowalski have been nominated. Kowalski should then be referred to as *the last, the last of these, the last named,* or simply *Kowalski.*

lay/lie

Lay ("to put, place, or prepare") and *lie* ("to recline or be situated") are frequently confused. *Lay* is a transitive verb and takes an object. *Lay* and its principal parts (*laid, laying*) are correctly used in the following examples: *The messenger laid* (not *lay*) *the computer printouts on the desk. The executive dining room table was laid for four. Lie* is an intransitive verb and does not take an object. *Lie* and its principal parts (*lay, lain, lying*) are correctly used in the following examples: *The founder of the company often lies* (not *lays*) *down after lunch. When I lay* (not *laid*) *down, I fell asleep. The rubbish had lain* (not *laid*) *in the dumpster for a week. I was lying* (not *laying*) *in bed when I received the call. The valley lies to the east.* There are a few exceptions to these rules. The idioms *lay low, lay for,* and the nautical sense of *lay,* as in *lay at anchor,* though intransitive, are well established.

learn

Learn in modern usage is nonstandard in the sense of "to teach": *The instructor taught* (not *learned*) *them cardiopulmonary resuscitation.*

leave/let

Leave alone is acceptable as a substitute for *let alone* in the sense of "to refrain from disturbing or interfering." The following examples are acceptable: *Leave them alone and they will work well. Left alone, they were quite productive.* Those who do not accept these examples generally feel that *leave alone* should be restricted to the sense of "to depart and leave one in solitude": *They were left alone in the wilderness.* In formal writing *leave* is not an acceptable substitute for *let* in the sense "to allow or permit." Only *let* is acceptable in these examples: *Let me be. Let us not quarrel. Let matters stand.*

lighted

Lighted and *lit* are equally acceptable as past tense and past participle of *light.* Both forms are well established as adjectives also: *a lighted* (or *lit*) *cigarette.*

like/as/as if

Like has been used by the best writers as a conjunction since Shakespeare's time. But the usage has been so vehemently attacked by critics in recent times that the sensible writer will avoid it lest the the readers pay more attention to the words than to the content. Prudence requires *The machine responds as* (not *like*) *it should.* Constructions like *looks like, sounds like,* and *tastes like* are less likely to offend, but *as if* is better used in formal style: *It looks as if* (not *like*) *there will be no action on the bill before Congress recesses.* There can be no objection to the use of *like* as a conjunction when the following verb is not expressed: *The new senator took to politics like a duck to water.*

likewise

Likewise, not being a conjunction, cannot take the place of a connective such as *and* or *together with,* as in *The mayor risked his credibility, likewise his honor.* Properly, *The mayor risked his credibility and* (or *and likewise*) his honor.

literally

Literally means "in a manner that accords precisely with the words." It is often used to mean "without exaggeration." Users should be certain that in such use unintentionally comic images are not created, as in *the boss was literally breathing fire.*

loan/lend

Loan has long been established as a verb, especially in business usage, though some hold that *lend* is the preferred form, in general as well as formal writing. Many phrases and figurative uses require *lend* (*lend an ear; distance lends enchantment*).

lost

The phrase *lost to* can sometimes be ambiguous, as in *As a result of poor preparation, the court battle was lost to the defense attorney* (lost by the defense attorney or lost by the plaintiff's attorney to the defense attorney?). Unless the context makes the meaning clear, the sentence should be reworded.

majority

When *majority* refers to a particular number of votes, it takes a singular verb: *Her majority was five votes.* When it refers to a group of persons or things that are in the majority, it may take either a plural or singular verb, depending on whether the group is considered as a whole or as a set of people considered individually. So we say *the majority elects* (not *elect*) *the candidate it wants* (not *they want*), since the election is accomplished by the group as a whole; but *the majority of our employees live* (not *lives*) *within five miles of the office,* since living within five miles of the office is something that each employee does individually. *Majority* is often preceded by *great* (but not by *greater*) in expressing, emphatically, the sense of "most of": *The great majority has decided not to throw good money after bad.* The phrase *greater majority* is appropriate only when considering two majorities: *A greater majority of the workers has accepted this year's contract than accepted last year's.*

man

The use of *man* to mean "a human being, regardless of sex" has a long history, but is now much less generally accepted. For many people, its use in the primary sense of "adult male human being" has made it no longer broad enough to serve as the superordinate term: *The men who settled America's frontier were a sturdy race. Twentieth-century man has made great strides in improving health care. The man of the future will eat his meals in tablet form.* Many people feel that in such cases the sense of "male" is predominant over that of "person." Other means of expressing the idea while avoiding this possible confusion are: *men and women, humans,* and *human beings. Man* in the sense of "mankind" is also sometimes felt to be too exclusive. Its use in phrases such as *the evolution of man* can be avoided with similar substitutions: *the evolution of humans.* Many occupational titles in which *man* occurs as an element are being replaced, sometimes officially, by terms considered neutral. For example, *firefighter* is used instead of *fireman,* or *Members of Congress* instead of *Congressmen.* Caution is, however, advisable in recasting such terms with the use of *person.* For example, *policeperson* as an alternative for *policeman* might sound awkward or strained to some people; use *police officer* instead.

masterful

Masterful has the undisputed meaning of "strong-willed, imperious, domineering." It is widely used also as a substitute for *masterly* in the sense of "having the skill of a master." Some feel that the distinction between the two words should be respected, as in *a masterly* (not *masterful*) *sales presentation.*

means

In the sense of "financial resources," *means* takes a plural verb: *Our means are quite adequate for this acquisition.* In the sense of "a way to an end," it may take a singular or plural verb; the choice of a modifier such as *any* or *all* generally determines the number of the verb: *Every means was tried. There are several means at our disposal.*

meantime / meanwhile

Meantime serves principally as a noun: *In the meantime we made plans for an unfavorable Federal Communications Commission ruling.* In expressing the same sense as a single adverb, *meanwhile* is more common than *meantime: Meanwhile, we made plans for an unfavorable ruling.*

migrate / emigrate / immigrate

Migrate is used with reference to both the place of departure and the destination and can be followed by *from* or *to.* It is said of persons, animals, and birds and sometimes implies a lack of permanent settlement, especially as a result of seasonal or periodic movement. *Emigrate* pertains to a single move by a person, and implies permanence. It refers specifically to the place of departure and emphasizes movement from that place. If the place is mentioned, the preposition is *from: Since many people have emigrated from the Soviet Union, we see a new demand for Russian-language books. Immigrate* also pertains to a single move by persons and likewise implies permanence. But it refers to destination, emphasizes movement there, and is followed by *to: Many illegal aliens have immigrated to the United States in recent months.*

minimize
According to traditional grammar, *minimize* can mean only "to make as small as possible" and is therefore an absolute term, which cannot be modified by *greatly* or *somewhat*.

most
The adverb *most* is sometimes used in the sense of "almost": *Most all the clients accepted the provisions in the contract.* However, this usage is generally considered unacceptable in formal writing. In the sense of "very," as an intensive where no explicit comparison is involved, *most* is acceptable both in writing and in speech: *a most ingenious solution.*

mostly
Mostly is used at all levels of style to refer to the largest number of a group: *The trees are mostly evergreens. The police arrested mostly juveniles.* In speech and informal writing, it is also used to mean "in the greatest degree" or "for the most part," but this usage is to be avoided in formal writing: *Those most* (not *mostly*) *affected are the lathe operators in Building C. For the most part* (not *Mostly*), *Northern Telecom is the supplier of our communications equipment.*

movable
Something is *movable* if it can be moved at all (*movable office furniture; a movable partition*): it is *mobile* if it is designed for easy transportation (*a mobile electric generating unit*) or if it moves frequently (*a mobile drilling rig*).

myself
In informal speech, reflexive pronouns like *myself* and *yourself* are often used for emphasis in compound subjects and objects: *The utility's board of directors and myself are undecided about the cost benefits of building a nuclear reactor. I would assign the new project to either Pat or yourself.* Both constructions are to be avoided in writing.

nauseous
Traditionally, *nauseous* means "causing nausea"; *nauseated* means "suffering from nausea." The use of *nauseous* in the sense of *nauseated* is unacceptable to many and should be avoided in writing.

neither
According to the traditional rule, *neither* should be construed as singular when it occurs as the subject of a sentence: *Neither of the reports is* (not *are*) *finished.* Accordingly, a pronoun with *neither* as an antecedent also must be singular: *Neither of the doctors in the lawsuit is likely to reveal his or her* (not *their*) *identity.*

no
When *no* introduces a compound phrase, its elements should be connected with *or* rather than with *nor.* Thus we write: *The candidate has no experience or interest in product development* (not *nor interest*). *No modification or change in operating procedures will be acceptable to them* (not *nor change*).

nominal

Nominal in one of its senses means "in name only." Hence a *nominal payment* is a token payment, bearing no relation to the real value of what is being paid for. The word is often extended in use, especially by sellers, to describe a low or bargain price: *We acquired 600,000 barrels of new oil reserves at a nominal extra cost.*

not

Care should be taken with the placement of *not* and other negatives in a sentence in order to avoid ambiguity. *All issues are not speculative* could be taken to mean either "all of the issues are not speculative" of "not all of the issues are speculative." Similarly, the sentence *We didn't sleep until noon* could mean either "We went to sleep at noon" or "We got up before noon."

nothing

Nothing takes a singular verb, even when it is followed by a phrase containing a plural noun or pronoun: *Nothing except your fears stands* (not *stand*) *in your path.*

number

As a collective noun, *number* may take either a singular or a plural verb. It takes a singular verb when it is preceded by the definite article *the: The number of skilled workers is small.* It takes a plural verb when preceded by the indefinite article *a: A number of the workers are unskilled.*

numerous

Numerous is not used as a pronoun in standard English. In writing, expressions like *numerous of the firefighters* should be avoided.

odd

Odd, when used to indicate a few more than a given number, should be preceded by a hyphen in order to avoid ambiguity: *thirty-odd salespeople in the showroom. Odd* in that sense is used only with round numbers.

off

Particularly in written usage, *off* should not be followed by *of* or *from: The speaker stepped off* (not *off of* or *off from*) *the platform.* Nor should *off* be used for *from* to indicate a source in a sentence such as: *I got a loan from* (not *off*) *the credit union.*

on/onto/upon

To indicate motion toward a position, both *on* and *onto* can be used: *The guard dog jumped on the counter. The dog jumped onto the desk. Onto* is more specific, however, in indicating that the motion was initiated from an outside point. *The child wandered onto the field* means that the child began wandering at some point off the field. *The child wandered on the field* may mean that the wandering began somewhere on the field. In constructions where *on* is an adverb attached to a verb, it should not be joined with *to* to form a single word *onto: The meeting moved on to* (not *onto*) *the next subject; hold on to* (not *onto*) *the railing as you climb the stairs.* In their uses to indicate spatial relations, *on* and *upon* are often interchangeable: *The container was resting on* (or *upon*) *the flatcar. The welder took it on* (or *upon*) *himself to finish the job before nightfall. We saw a robin light on* (or *upon*) *the lawn.* To indicate a relation between two things, however, instead of between an action and an end point, *upon* cannot always be used: *Hand me the book on* (not *upon*) *the file cabinet.* Similarly, *upon* cannot always be used in place of *on* when the relation is not spatial: *We will be in Des Moines on* (not *upon*) *Tuesday. A good book on* (not *upon*) *word processing has just come out.*

onetime / one-time
Onetime (single word) means "former." *One-time* (hyphenated) means "only once." Thus *a onetime employee* is a former employee; *a one-time mayor* was mayor only once.

only
When used as an adverb, *only* should be placed with care to avoid ambiguity. Generally this means having *only* adjoin the word or words that it limits. Variation in the placement of *only* can change the meaning of the sentence, as the following examples show: *Dictators respect only force; they are not moved by words. Dictators only respect force; they do not worship it. She picked up the receiver only when he entered, not before. She only picked up the receiver when he entered; she didn't dial the number.* Though strict grammarians insist that the rule for placement of *only* should always be followed, there are occasions when placement of *only* earlier in the sentence seems much more natural. In the following example, *only* is placed according to the rule: *The committee can make its decision by Friday of next week only if it receives a copy of the latest report.* Placement of *only* earlier in the sentence, immediately after *can*, would serve the rhetorical function of warning the reader that a condition on the statement follows. *Only* is often used as a conjunction equivalent to *but* in the sense of "were it not that": *They would have come, only they were snowed in.* Many experts consider this example unacceptable in writing.

ought to
Ought to is sometimes used without a following verb if the meaning is clear: *Should we begin soon? Yes, we ought to.* The omission of *to*, however (as in *no, we ought not*) is not standard. Usages like *one hadn't ought to come* and *one shouldn't ought to say that* are common in many varieties of American English. They should be avoided in written English, however, in favor of the more standard variant *ought not to.*

pair
Pair as a noun can be followed by a singular or plural verb. The singular is always used when *pair* denotes the set taken as a single entity: *This pair of shoes is a year old.* A plural verb is used when the members are considered as

individuals: *The pair are working more harmoniously now.* After a numeral other than *one, pair* itself can be either singular or plural, but the plural is now more common: *Six pairs* (or *pair*) *of stockings are defective.*

partly / partially
Partly and *partially* are not always interchangeable. *Partly* is the better choice when reference is made to a part as opposed to the whole, especially when speaking of physical objects: *The letterhead is partly red and partly green. Partially* is used to mean "to a degree" when referring to conditions or states: *Our marketing efforts have only partially penetrated into New England.*

party
A person may be called a *party* in the sense of "participant" (*a party to the industrial espionage ring*) or in a humorous sense (*a wise old party*). But except in legal usage, *party* should not be used as a general synonym for *person*, as in this example: *The party who stole $12,000 worth of inventory was taken into custody.*

peer
Peer is sometimes misused in the sense of "a superior": *That manager is the equal, if not the peer, of any executive on the committee. Peer* refers to an equal, not a superior. *Peer* is properly used in the expressions *peer group* and *a jury of one's peers.*

people / persons
People and *persons* are distinguished in usage. *People* is the proper term when referring to a large group of individuals, collectively and indefinitely: *People use a wide variety of our products at work and at home. Persons* is applicable to a specific and relatively small number: *Ten persons were fired.* In modern usage, however, *people* is also acceptable with any plural number: *I counted twenty people.* The possessive form is *people's* (*the people's rights*) except when *people* is used in the plural to refer to two or more groups considered to be political or cultural entities: *the Slavic peoples' history.*

per
Per is used with reference to statistics and units of measurement (*per mile; per day; per person*). Its more general use (as in *per the terms of the contract*) is acceptable in business writing.

percent
Percent is generally used with a specific figure. The number of a noun that follows it or is understood to follow it governs the number of the verb: *Twenty percent of the stock is owned by a conglomerate. Forty-seven percent of our sales come from consumer appliances.*

percentage
Percentage, when preceded by *the,* takes a singular verb: *The percentage of un-skilled workers is small.* When preceded by *a,* it takes either a singular or plu-

ral verb, depending on the number of the noun in the prepositional phrase that follows: *A small percentage of the workers are unskilled. A large percentage of the defective press run was never shipped.*

perfect
Perfect has traditionally been considered an absolute term, like *chief* and *prime,* and not subject to comparison with *more, less, almost,* and other modifiers of degree. The comparative form nonetheless has the sanction of the United States Constitution, in the phrase *a more perfect union,* and must be regarded as entirely correct, especially when *perfect* is used to mean "ideal for the purposes," as in *A more perfect spot for our broadcasting station could not be found.*

perfectly
In writing, *perfectly* is sometimes objected to when it is used as a mere intensive denoting "quite," "altogether," or "just," as in *perfectly good* and *perfectly dreadful.* But it is widely used by educated speakers in this sense.

permit
Permit of is sometimes used for the transitive verb *permit* (to allow, to admit) as in *permits of two interpretations.*

person
Person is increasingly used to create compounds that may refer to either a man or a woman: *chairperson; spokesperson; anchorperson; salesperson.* These forms can be used when reference is to the position itself, regardless of who might hold it: *The committee should elect a new chairperson at its meeting.* They are also appropriate when speaking of the specific individual holding the position: *She was the best anchorperson the local station had ever had. The group asked him to act as its spokesperson.* In such cases, the alternatives *anchorwoman* and *spokesman* also would be appropriate, and sometimes are preferred by the holder of the position. See also the note at **man** on pages 232–233.

personality
Personality, meaning "celebrity" or "notable," is widely used in speech and journalism. In more formal writing, however, it is considered unacceptable by critics.

personnel
Personnel is a collective noun and never refers to an individual; therefore, it is unacceptable when used with a numeral. It is acceptable, however, to use another qualifying word: *A number of armed forces personnel* (not *six armed forces personnel*) *testified.*

plead
In strict legal usage, one is said to *plead guilty* or *plead not guilty,* but not to *plead innocent.* In nonlegal contexts, however, *plead innocent* is well established.

plus
Traditionally, *plus* as a preposition does not have the conjunctive force of *and*. Therefore, when *plus* is used after a singular subject, the verb remains singular: *Two* (the numeral considered as a single noun) *plus two equals four. Our production efficiency plus their excellent distribution system results in a new industry leader. Plus* is sometimes used loosely as a conjunction to connect two independent clauses: *We had terrible weather this year, plus the recession affected us adversely.* Such use in writing is considered unacceptable by many, and should be avoided.

poor
Poor is an adjective, not an adverb. In formal usage it should not be used to qualify a verb, as in *did poor* or *never worked poorer. Poorly* and *more poorly* are required in such examples.

practicable / practical
Practicable describes that which can be put into effect. *Practical* describes that which is also sensible and worthwhile. It might be *practicable* to build a bullet train between New York and Omaha, but it would not be *practical.*

practically
Practically is used unexceptionally in its primary sense of "in a way that is practical." In other senses it has become almost interchangeable with *virtually.* Such use is acceptable when the meaning is "for all practical purposes." Thus, a man whose liabilities exceed his assets may be said to be *practically bankrupt,* even though he has not been legally declared insolvent. By a slight extension of this meaning, however, *practically* is often used to mean "nearly" or "all but": *They had practically closed the deal by the time I arrived.* Such use, sometimes considered informal, is widely encountered in reputable writing.

première
Première as a verb is unacceptable to a great number of people, despite its wide usage in the world of entertainment.

presently
Presently is now used primarily in the sense of "soon." Confusingly, it is also used in the sense of "at the present time." Writers who use the word should take care that the meaning is clear from the context.

protagonist
Protagonist denotes the leading figure in a theatrical drama or, by extension, in any work or undertaking. Sometimes in modern usage the sense of singularity is lost: *There are three protagonists in the takeover fight.* This watered-down meaning, though well established, is unacceptable to a great many people. *Protagonist* is informally used to indicate a champion or advocate.

prove

The forms *proved* and *proven* can both be used in: *You have proved* (or *proven*) *your point*. *Proven* is commonly used as an adjective directly before a noun (*a proven talent; a proven point*).

quick / quickly

Both *quick* and *quickly* can be used as adverbs. *Quick* is more frequent in speech: *Come quick!* In writing, the slightly more formal *quickly* is preferred: *When the signal was relayed to our parts center, we responded quickly*. In the latter example, *quick* would be unacceptable to many experts.

quote

Quote (transitive verb) is appropriate when words are being given exactly as they were originally written or spoken. When the reference is less exact, *cite* is preferable. *Quote* (noun) as a substitute for *quotation* is considered unacceptable by many traditionalists.

raise

Raise is properly used as a transitive verb: *Raise the loading bay doors*. For intransitive uses, *rise* is standard: *The platform rises*. However, *raise* is sometimes used as an intransitive verb: *The window raises easily*. *Raise* (noun), rather than *rise*, is now standard in the United States for an increase in salary, though one still speaks of a *rise in prices*.

rare / scarce

Rare and *scarce* are sometimes interchangeable, but *scarce* carries an additional implication that the quantities involved are insufficient or inadequate. Thus we speak of *rare books* or of *the rare qualities* of someone we admire, but of *increasingly scarce oil reserves*.

rarely

The use of *ever* after *rarely* or *seldom* is considered redundant. Thus, the example *he rarely* (or *seldom*) *ever makes a mistake* is unacceptable in speech and writing to a majority of experts. The following constructions, using either *rarely* or *seldom*, are standard, however: *rarely if ever; rarely or never* (but not *rarely or ever*).

rather

Rather is usually preceded by *should* or *would* in expressing preference: *They would rather not diversify the company*. But *had* is equally acceptable: *I had rather be dead than be unemployed*. In a contraction such as *he'd*, either *would* or *had* can be understood.

regard

Regard is traditionally used as a singular in the phrase *in* (or *with*) *regard to* (not *in regards to*). *Regarding* and *as regards* are used in the same sense of "with reference to." In the same sense *with respect to* is acceptable, but *respecting* is not. *Respects* is sometimes preferable to *regards* in the sense of "particulars": *In some respects* (not *regards*) *we are similar to our competition*.

relatively

Relatively is appropriate when a comparison is stated or implied: *The first question was relatively easy* (that is, in comparison to the others). In formal style *relatively* should not be used to mean simply "fairly," as *I am relatively sure of it.*

repel / repulse

The verbs *repel* and *repulse* both have the physical sense of driving back or off. *Repulse* also may apply to rebuffing or rejecting discourteously, but only *repel* should be used in the sense of causing distaste or aversion: *Your arrogance repelled us. He repulsed with rudeness all of our attempts to help him.*

replete

Replete means "abundantly supplied": *a takeover battle replete with scandal, mudslinging, and threats.* It should not be used to mean simply "complete" or "equipped": *a club replete with pool, tennis courts, and golf courses.*

responsible

Some usage experts say that *responsible* should be used only with reference to persons, not things, since only persons can be held accountable. The word is commonly used, however, with reference to things: *Defective welds were responsible for the buckled axle.*

restive / restless

Restive and *restless* are now commonly used as equivalent terms. *Restive,* however, implies more than simply "nervous" or "fidgety": it implies resistance to some sort of restraint. Thus, a patient who is sleeping poorly may be *restless;* but the same patient is *restive* only if kept in bed against his or her will.

sacrilegious

Sacrilegious, the adjective of *sacrilege,* is often misspelled through confusion with *religious.*

said

The adjective *said* is seldom appropriate to any but legal writing, where it is equivalent to *aforesaid: the said tenant* (named in a lease); *said property.* In similar contexts in general usage, *said* is usually unnecessary and *the tenant* or *the property* will suffice.

same

Only in legal writing is *the same* or just *same* used as a substitute for *it* or *them.* In general writing, one should avoid sentences like *The charge is $5; please remit same.*

scarcely

Scarcely has the force of a negative; therefore, it is not properly used with another negative: *I could scarcely believe it* (not *I couldn't scarcely believe it*). A clause following *scarcely* may be introduced by *when* or, less often, by *before* but not by *than: The meeting had scarcely begun when* (or *before* but not *than*) *it was interrupted.*

seasonal / seasonable

Seasonal and *seasonable,* though closely related, are differentiated in usage. *Seasonal* applies to what depends on or is controlled by the season of the year: *a seasonal rise in unemployment. Seasonable* applies to what is appropriate to the season (*seasonable clothing*) or timely (*a seasonable intervention in the dispute*). Rains are *seasonal* if they occur at a certain time of the year. They are *seasonable* at any time if they save the crops.

see

The phrase *see where* sometimes occurs in speech as an informal equivalent of *see that,* as in this sentence: *I see that everything is running smoothly at the grain elevator.* The same applies to *read where.* These informal usages, permissible in speech, should be avoided in formal writing.

slow

Slow sometimes may be used as a variant form of the adverb *slowly,* when it comes after the verb: *We drove the car slow.* In formal writing *slowly* is generally preferred. *Slow* is often used in speech and informal writing, especially when brevity and forcefulness are sought: *Drive slow! Slow* is also the established idiomatic form with certain senses of common verbs: *The watch runs slow. Take it slow.*

so

In formal writing the conjunction *so* is preferably followed by *that* when it introduces a clause stating the purpose of or reason for an action: *The supervisor stayed late so that he could catch up on his paperwork. So* generally stands alone, however, when it is used to introduce a clause that states the result or consequence of something: *The canning process kills much of the flavor of the food, so salt is added.*

sometime

Sometime as an adjective is properly employed to mean "former."

sooner

No sooner, as a comparative adverb, should be followed by *than,* not *when,* as in these typical examples: *No sooner had I arrived than I had to leave for an emergency meeting. I had no sooner made an offer than they said the property had been sold to another person.*

stratum

The standard singular form is *stratum:* the standard plural is *strata* (or sometimes *stratums*) but not *stratas.*

than as

In comparisons, a pronoun following *than* or *as* may be taken as either the subject or the object of a "missing" verb whose sense is understood. Thus, in a sentence such as *John is older than I,* the nominative *I* is traditionally required on the grounds that the sentence is equivalent to *John is older than I am.* In *It does not surprise me as much as him,* the use of the objective *him* is justified by analogy to the sentence *It does not surprise me as much as it surprises him.*

there

There (adverb) meaning "in that place" comes after the noun in constructions introduced by the demonstrative *that: That truck there should be moved away from the front gate.* Use of *there* before the noun, as in *that there truck,* is inappropriate in formal English.

this/that

This and *that* are both used as demonstrative pronouns to refer to a thought expressed earlier: *The door was unopened; that* (or *this*) *in itself casts doubt on the guard's theory. That* is sometimes prescribed as the better choice in referring to what has gone before (as in the preceding example). When the referent is yet to be mentioned, only *this* is used: *This* (not *that*) *is what bothers me. We have no time to consider late applications. This* is often used in speech as an emphatic variant of the indefinite article *a: This friend of mine inquired about working here. I have this terrible headache.* This usage should be avoided in writing.

tight

Tight as an adjective appears after the verb when it is used to qualify the process denoted by the verb (*hold on tight; close it tight*). In a few cases *tight* is the only form that may be used (*sit tight; sleep tight*). In most cases the adverb *tightly* also may be used in this position (*close it tightly*). Before a verb only the adverb is used: *The money supply will be tightly* (not *tight*) *controlled.*

together

Together with, like *in addition to,* is often employed following the subject of a sentence or clause to introduce an addition. The addition, however, does not alter the number of the verb, which is governed by the subject: *The chairman* (singular), *together with two aides, is expected in an hour.* The same is true of *along with, as well as, besides, in addition to,* and *like: Common sense as well as training is a requisite for a good job.*

too

Too preceded by *not* or another form of negative is frequently employed as a form of understatement to convey humor or sarcasm: *The workers were not too pleased with the amount of their raises. This applicant is not too bright.* When used for effect, it is employed on all levels. *Too* can often be eliminated from such sentences without loss, but if deletion gives undue stress to the negative sense, the writer may find *not very* or *none too* preferable choices.

torn

Torn, never *tore,* is the standard past participle of the verb *tear. I have torn the book* (not *tore*).

transpire

Transpire has long been used in the sense of "to become known": *It soon transpired that they intended to gain a controlling interest in the corporation.* The meaning "to happen" or "to take place" has come into use more recently: *The board wondered what would transpire next.* This use is still considered pretentious or pompous by some.

try

Try and is common in speech for *try to,* especially in established combinations such as *try and stop me* and *try and get some rest.* In most contexts, however, it is not interchangeable with *try to* unless the level is clearly informal. For instance in formal writing, the following would be unacceptable to many critics: *It is a mistake to try and force compliance with a regulation that is so unpopular* (preferably *try to force*).

type

Type is most appropriate when reference is being made to a well-defined or sharply distinct category, as in *that type of chassis, this type of aspirin.* When the categorization is vaguer or less well accepted, *kind* or *sort* is preferable: *That is not the sort of analysis one can trust. This is the kind of annual report that puts you to sleep after the first page.*

unexceptional

Unexceptional is often confused with *unexceptionable.* When the desired meaning is "not open to objection" or "above reproach," the term is *unexceptionable: unexceptionable arguments.*

verbal

In the sense "by word of mouth," *verbal* is synonymous with oral. In other senses *verbal* has to do with words, whether written or spoken: *verbal communication* (as opposed, say, to gestures). *Verbal,* when applied to terms such as *agreement, promise, commitment,* or *understanding,* is well established in the sense of *oral.* But anyone who fears misunderstanding may use *oral* instead.

want

When *want* is followed immediately by an infinitive construction, it does not take *for: I want you to go* (not *want for you*). When *want* and the infinitive are separated in the sentence, however, *for* is used: *What I want is for you to finish that one first. I want very much for you to take the other company's offer.*

–ward

Since the suffix *–ward* indicates direction, there is no need to use *to the* with it: *The containerized cargo ship is sailing westward* (or *to the west* but not *to the westward*).

way

Way, not *ways,* is the generally accepted form in writing when the term refers to distance: *a long way to go.* The phrase *under way* (meaning "in motion" or "in progress") is written thus in all contexts, including the nautical (not as *under weigh*).

what

When *what* is the subject of a clause, it may be construed either as singular or as plural, depending on the sense. It is singular when it is taken as equivalent to *that which* or *the thing which: What seems to be a mechanical problem in the stamping equipment is creating defective panels.* It may be plural when it is equivalent to *those which* or *the things which: What were at first minor incidents have now become major problems in the chemical disposal system.* But when a *what* clause is the subject of a sentence, it will not in general take a plural main verb unless it is the subject of a plural verb in its own clause. Thus we say *what most surprise me are the remarks at the end of the study,* where the main verb *are* is plural because the verb *surprise* is plural in the subordinate clause. But we say *what the person was holding in his lap was* (not *were*) *four letters,* because *what* is not the subject of a plural verb in its own clause.

whatever

Whatever (pronoun) is used in questions and statements: *Whatever made them say that?* When a clause beginning with *whatever* is the subject of its sentence, no comma should be used: *Whatever you do is right.* Otherwise, a comma may be used: *Whatever you do, don't forget to record your expenses.* When the phrase preceding a restrictive clause is introduced by *whichever* or *whatever, that* should not be used in formal writing. It is held to be incorrect to write *whatever book that you want to look at;* one should write instead *whatever book you want to look at will be sent to your office* or *whichever book costs less* (not *that costs less*) *is fine with us.*

when

In informal style *when* is often used to mean "a situation or event in which," as in *A dilemma is when you don't know which way to turn.* This usage should be avoided in formal writing.

where

When *where* refers to "the place from which," it requires the preposition *from: Where did you come from?* When it refers to "the place to which," it requires no preposition: *Where did they go* (better than *where did they go to?*). When *where* refers to "the place at which," it also requires no preposition: *Where are they* (not *where are they at?*).

which

Which sometimes refers to an entire preceding statement rather than to a single word: *The drilling failed to turn up any new reserves, which disturbed the geologist.* When *which* follows a noun, the antecedent may be in doubt and ambiguity may result: *The inspector filed the complaint, which was a surprise.* If *which* is intended to refer to the entire first clause rather than to *complaint,* the desired sense would be expressed more clearly by this construction: *We learned that the inspector had filed the complaint, and that discovery came as a surprise to us.*

whose

Whose, as the possessive form of a relative pronoun, can refer to both persons and things. Thus, it functions as the possessive of both *who* and *which.* The following example, in which *whose* refers to an inanimate object, is acceptable on all levels: *The car, whose design is ultramodern, is typical of the new styles.* The alternative possessive form *of which* is also used in referring to things but is sometimes cumbersome in application.

–wise

The suffix *–wise* has a long history of use in the sense "in the manner or direction of" (*clockwise, likewise, otherwise,* and *slantwise*). In recent times, *–wise* has been in vogue as a suffix meaning "with relation to" and attachable to any noun: *saleswise, inflationwise.* Most new or temporary coinages of this sort are unacceptable in writing and are considered by many to be inappropriate in speech.

with

With does not have the conjunctive force of *and.* Consequently, in the following example the verb is governed by the singular subject and remains singular: *The governor, with her aides, is expected at the trade show on Monday.*

wreak/wreck

Wreak is sometimes confused with *wreck,* perhaps because the wreaking of damage may leave a wreck: *The storm wreaked* (not *wrecked*) *havoc along the coast.* The past tense and past participle of *wreak* is *wreaked,* not *wrought,* which is an alternative past tense and past participle of *work.*

CLICHÉS

The word *cliché* means "a trite or overused expression or idea." The English language is, of course, full of clichés, many of which originated as metaphors, proverbs, or brief quotations. Historical changes in the language through the ages have rendered them virtually meaningless. For example, what does *fell* in *one fell swoop* mean? And *do one's thing* and *keep a low profile* illustrate how such expressions have lost their original force through relentless use. Since most clichés express rather clear meanings, every writer will have to determine whether a cliché doesn't actually offer a shade of meaning that is hard to convey by fresher alternative wording. A cliché, properly used, can sometimes prevent strained, wordy, or ambiguous discourse. Writers of fresh, original prose, though, should avoid most clichés.

a little of that goes a long way	add insult to injury	albatross around one's neck
absence makes the heart grow fonder	age before beauty	all in a day's work
	agonizing reappraisal	all in all
	agree to disagree	

all in the same boat
all over but the
   shouting
all things being equal
all things considered
all things to all men (*or*
   people)
all work and no play
apple of one's eye
apple-pie order
armed to the teeth
arms of Morpheus
as luck would have it
as the crow flies
at a loss for words (*or*
   never at a loss . . .)
at first blush
at one fell swoop
(an) axe to grind
babe in the woods
backhanded
   compliment
bag and baggage
bark up the wrong tree
bated breath
bathed in tears
battle of the giants
battle royal
beard the lion in his
   den
beat a dead horse
beat a hasty retreat
beat around the bush
before hell freezes over
beg to disagree
beggar description
bend (*or* lean) over
   backward
best foot forward
best-laid plans
best of all possible
   worlds
best of both worlds
better late than never
between a rock and a
   hard place
between the devil and
   the deep blue sea

beyond the call of duty
beyond the pale
bigger than all
   outdoors
bigger than both of us
bigger (*or* larger) than
   life
bite off more than one
   can chew
bite the bullet
bite the hand that feeds
   one
bitter pill to swallow
black-and-white issue
bloody but unbowed
bloom is off the rose
bloom of youth
blue-sky thinking (*or*
   idea)
blush of shame
blushing bride
boggle the mind
bolt from the blue
bone of contention
boom to bust
born with a silver spoon
   in one's mouth
bosom of the family
brave the elements
breathe a sign of relief
bright and early
bright as a button
bright-eyed and bushy-
   tailed
bright future
bring home the bacon
brown as a berry
budding genius
bull in a china shop
burn the midnight oil
busy as a bee
butter wouldn't melt in
   one's mouth
by leaps and bounds
by the same token
calm before the storm
can't see the forest for
   the trees

carry (*or* have) a chip
   on one's shoulder
carry its share of the
   burden
(a) case in point
cash cow
caught on the horns of
   a dilemma
caught red-handed
chip off the old block
clear as a bell
clear as mud
coals to Newcastle
coin a phrase
cold as ice
(a) cold day in July (*or*
   Hell)
come (with) hat in
   hand
compare apples to
   oranges
conspicuous by one's
   absence
cool as a cucumber
cross the Rubicon
crying need
crying shame
cut a long story short
cut off one's nose to
   spite one's face
cynosure of all eyes
daily repast
David and Goliath
dead as a doornail
dead giveaway
dead in the water
deaf as a post
death warmed over
defend to the death
   one's right to . . .
depths of despair
diamond in the rough
die in harness
die is cast
distaff side
do it up brown
do one's thing
dog in the manger

dog of a company
dollars to doughnuts
doom is sealed
doomed to
    disappointment
down in the dumps
down in the mouth
down one's alley
down-side risk
draw the line
drown one's sorrows
drunk as a lord (*or*
    skunk)
dull thud
dyed in the wool
ear to the ground
early bird gets the
    worm
early to bed, early to
    rise . . .
easier said than done
eat one's hat (*or* words)
epoch-making
eternal reward
eyes of the world
face the music
fair sex
fall between the cracks
fall on deaf ears
far be it from me
(a) far cry
fast and loose
fate worse than death
fat's in the fire
feather in one's cap
feather one's nest
feel one's oats
festive board
few and far between
few well-chosen words
fiddle while Rome
    burns
fight like a tiger
fill the bill
filthy lucre
fine and dandy
first and foremost
fit as a fiddle

flash in the pan
flat as a flounder (*or*
    pancake)
flesh and blood
fly off the handle
fond farewell
food for thought
fool's gold
fool's paradise
fools rush in
foot in one's mouth
foot in the door
foot the bill
foregone conclusion
forewarned is
    forearmed
frame of reference
free as a bird (*or* the
    air)
fresh as a daisy
generous to a fault
gentle as a lamb
get the jump on the
    competition
get down to brass tacks
get one's back (*or* dan-
    der) up
get one's ducks in a row
get one's feet wet
gift of gab
gild the lily
go belly up
(a) good time was had
    by all
goose that laid the
    golden egg
grain of salt
grand and glorious
graphic account
green-eyed monster
grin like a Cheshire cat
grind to a halt
hail fellow well met
hale and hearty
hand that rocks the
    cradle
handsome is as hand-
    some does

handwriting on the wall
hapless victim
happy as a lark
happy pair
hard row to hoe
haughty stare
haul (*or* rake) over the
    coals
have a foot in the door
have a leg up
head over heels
heart of gold
heave a sigh of relief
heir apparent
hew to the line
high and dry
high as a kite
high on the hog
hit the nail on the head
hit the spot
hitch one's star to
hook, line, and sinker
hook or crook
horse and pony show
hot as a firecracker (*or*
    pistol *or* six-shooter)
hue and cry
hungry as a bear (*or*
    lion)
if (the) truth be told
in full swing
in no uncertain terms
in on the ground floor
in seventh heaven
inspiring sight
in the final (*or* last)
    analysis
in the limelight
in the long run
in the nick of time
in this day and age
iron out a difficulty
irons in the fire
irony of fate
irreparable damage (*or*
    loss)
it goes without saying
it is interesting to note

it never rains but it
  pours
it's a small world
it's an ill wind
it's six of one and a half
  a dozen of the other
it stands to reason
it takes all kinds to
  make a world
it takes two to tango
(the) jig is up
just deserts
keep a low profile
keep a stiff upper lip
keep one's chin up
keep (or lose) one's
  cool
keep one's ear to the
  ground
knock into a cocked hat
knock on wood
labor of love
land of milk and honey
land of opportunity
land office business
land war in Asia
last but not least
last straw
law unto one's self
lead to the altar
lean and hungry look
lean over backward
leave holding the bag
leave in the lurch
leave no stone
  unturned
left-handed
  compliment
leg up on the
  competition
lend a helping hand
lest we forget
let one's hair down
let the cat out of the
  bag
let well enough alone
lick into shape
lick one's wounds

lid of secrecy
light at the end of the
  tunnel
like a house afire (or on
  fire)
like a newborn babe
limp as a dish rag
lock, stock, and barrel
long arm of the law
look a gift horse in the
  mouth
look for a needle in a
  haystack
(as) luck would have it
mad as a hatter (or
  March hare)
mad as a hornet (or wet
  hen)
mad dash
make a clean breast of
make a long story short
make a virtue of
  necessity
make bricks without
  straw
make ends meet
make hay while the sun
  shines
make no bones about
mantle of snow
matter of life and
  death
meaningful dialogue
meek as Moses
meet one's Waterloo
method in one's
  madness
milk of human
  kindness
mince words
mind one's p's and q's
miss the boat
moment of truth
monarch of all one
  surveys
month of Sundays
moot question (or
  point)

more easily said than
  done
more sinned against
  than sinning
more than meets the
  eye
(the) more the merrier
motley crew
naked truth
name is legion
necessary evil
needs no introduction
neither fish nor fowl
neither here nor there
neither hide nor hair
never a dull moment
never say die
nip in the bud
none the worse for wear
no holds barred
no sooner said than
  done
not to be sneezed at
not wisely but too well
not worth its salt
not worth the paper it's
  printed on
nothing new under the
  sun
of a high order
old before one's time
on cloud nine
on one's uppers
on the ball (or stick)
on the best (or unim-
  peachable) authority
on the bum (or the fritz)
on the lam
on the other hand
on the QT
on the wagon
once in a blue moon
one man's meat is
  another man's poison
one's own worst enemy
open and shut case
open secret
opportunity knocks

other side of the coin
other things being
    equal
out of the frying pan
    and into the fire
over a barrel
overcome with emotion
paint the town red
pandemonium reigned
part and parcel
pay the piper
paying its own freight
penny for one's
    thoughts
pennywise, pound
    foolish
perfect gentleman
pet peeve
pillar of society
pillar to post
pinch pennies
plain and simple
plain as day
plain as the nose on
    one's face
play fast and loose
play hardball
play it by ear
play second fiddle
play the devil's advocate
(a) plum of a job (or
    position)
plumb the depths
(at this) point in time
point with pride
poor but honest
(the) powers that be
pretty as a picture
pretty kettle of fish
pretty penny
psychological moment
pull no punches
pull the wool over one's
    eyes
pure as the driven snow
put on the dog
put on the Ritz
quick and dirty

quick as lightening (or a
    flash)
quiet as a mouse
rack one's brains
rain cats and dogs
raise Cain
raise the roof
read the riot act
(the) real McCoy
red as a beet
red-letter day
reign supreme
render a decision
rest assured
ring true
ripe old age
rising star
roll up one's sleeves
rollercoaster earnings
rub one the wrong way
run it up the flagpole
    and see if anyone
    salutes it
sadder but wiser
sad to relate
save for a rainy day
seal one's fate (or
    doom)
second to none
seething mass
sell like hot cakes
separate the men from
    the boys
separate the sheep
    from the goats
shoot from the hip
short end of the stick
(a) shot in the arm
shout from the roof-
    tops
show one's hand
show one's true colors
show the white feather
sick and tired
sight to behold
silver lining
sing like a bird
skeleton in one's closet

small world
smell a rat
sow one's wild oats
spinning (or turning
    over) in one's grave
spinning straw into gold
stagger the imagination
stair-step earnings
start the ball rolling
steal one's thunder
stem to stern
stick in one's craw
stick out like a sore
    thumb
stick to one's guns
stick to one's knitting
stir up a hornet's nest
straight and narrow
straight from the
    shoulder
straw in the wind
straw that broke the
    camel's back
strictly speaking
strong as an ox
stubborn as a mule
sweat of one's brow
sweet sixteen
sweet smell of success
sweeten the pot (or
    kitty)
take a dim view of
take a raincheck
take it easy
take off one's hat to
take the bull by the
    horns
take up the cudgels
talk through one's hat
tell someone who cares
that is to say
that's for sure
throw caution to the
    wind
throw in the towel (or
    sponge)
throw one's hat in the
    ring

throw the book at
time hangs heavy
time immemorial
time of one's life
tip the scales
tit for tat
to tell the truth
to the manner born
too funny for words
too little, too late
tried and true
trip the light fantastic
true blue
turn over a new leaf
ugly duckling
uncharted seas
up and comer
up the creek without a
  paddle

up to one's ears
up-side potential
usually reliable
  source(s)
vale of tears
viable option
view with alarm
walk on eggshells
wash one's hands of
wax poetic (*or*
  eloquent)
wear two hats
wee (small) hours
well worth one's while
  (*or* trouble)
wet behind the ears
wet to the skin
what makes the world
  go 'round

when all is said and
  done
when you come right
  down to it
whistle Dixie
whistle in the dark
wide-open spaces
wise as an owl
without a doubt
without further ado
wolf in sheep's clothing
work one's fingers to
  the bone
worst-case scenario
you can bank on that
you can bet your
  bottom dollar
you can take that to the
  bank

REDUNDANT EXPRESSIONS

Redundancy — needless repetition of ideas — is one of the principal obstacles to writing clear precise prose. The list below gives some common redundant expressions. The elements repeated in the phrases and in the brief definitions are italicized. To eliminate redundancy, delete the italic elements in the phrases.

anthracite *coal*
(a hard *coal* having a high carbon content)

old **antique**
(an object having special value because of its *age,* especially a work of art or handicraft more than 100 years *old)*

ascend *upward*
(to go or move *upward)*

assemble *together*
(to bring or gather *together)*

pointed **barb**
(a sharp *point* projecting in reverse direction to the main point of a weapon or tool)

first **beginning**
(the *first* part)

big *in size*
(of considerable *size)*

bisect *in two*
(to cut *into two* equal parts)

blend *together*
(to mix or go well *together)*

capitol *building*
(a *building* in which a legislative body meets)

coalesce *together*
(to grow or come *together* so as to form a whole)

collaborate *together* or *jointly*
(to work *together* in a *joint* effort)

fellow **colleague**
(a *fellow* member of a profession, staff, or academic faculty)

congregate *together*
(to bring or come *together* in a crowd)

connect *together*
(to join or fasten *together*)

consensus *of opinion*
(collective *opinion*)

courthouse *building*
(a *building* in which judicial courts or county government offices are housed)

habitual **custom**
(a *habitual* practice)

descend *downward*
(to move, slope, extend, or incline *downward*)

doctorate *degree*
(the *degree* or status of a doctor)

endorse a check *on the back*
(to write one's signature *on the back of,* e.g., a check)

erupt *violently*
(to emerge *violently* or to become *violently* active)

explode *violently*
(to burst *violently* from internal pressure)

real **fact**
(something with *real,* demonstrable existence)

passing **fad**
(a *transitory* fashion)

few *in number*
(amounting to or made up of a *small number*)

founder *and sink*
(to *sink* beneath the water)

basic **fundamental**
(a *basic* or essential part)

fuse *together*
(to mix *together* by or as if by melting)

opening **gambit**
(a remark that is intended to *open* a conversation)

gather *together*
(to come *together* or cause to come *together*)

free **gift**
(something bestowed voluntarily and *without compensation*)

past **history**
(a narrative of *past* events; something that took place *in the past*)

hoist *up*
(to raise or haul *up* with or as if with a mechanical device)

current or *present* **incumbent**
(one *currently* holding an office)

new **innovation**
(something *new* or unusual)

join *together*
(to bring or put *together* so as to make continuous or form a unit)

knots *per hour*
(a unit of speed, one nautical mile, or 1.15 statute miles, *per hour*)

large *in size*
(greater than average *in size*)

merge *together*
(to blend or cause to blend *together* gradually)

necessary **need**
(something *necessary* or wanted)

universal **panacea**
(a remedy for *all* diseases, evils, or difficulties)

continue to **persist**
(to *continue* in existence)

individual **person**
(an *individual* human being)

advance **planning**
(detailed methodology, programs, or schemes worked out *beforehand* for the accomplishment of an objective)

chief or *leading* or *main* **protagonist**
(the *leading* character in a Greek drama or other literary form; a *leading* or *principal* figure)

original **prototype**
(an *original* type, form, or instance that is a model on which later stages are based or judged)

protrude *out*
(to push or thrust *outward*)

recall *back*
(to summon *back* to awareness; to bring back)

recoil *back*
(to kick or spring *back;* to shrink *back* in fear or loathing; to fall *back*)

new **recruit**
(a *new* member of a body or organization, especially of a military force)

recur *again* or *repeatedly*
(to occur *again* or *repeatedly*)

temporary **reprieve**
(a *temporary* relief, as from danger or pain)

revert *back*
(to *return* to a *former* state)

short *in length* or *height*
(having very little *length* or *height*)

shuttle *back and forth*
(to move, go, or travel *back and forth*)

skirt *around*
(to move or pass *around* rather than across or through)

small *in size*
(characterized by relatively little *size* or slight dimensions)

tall *in height*
(having greater than average *height*)

two **twins**
(one of *two* offspring born at the same birth; one of *two* identical persons, animals, or things)

completely **unanimous**
(being in *complete* harmony, accord, or agreement)

visible *to the eye*
(perceptible *to the eye*)

from **whence**
(*from* where; *from* what place; *from* what origin or source)

11

A Style Guide for Technical
and Scientific Material

T HE ROLE OF THE PROFESSIONAL secretary in preparing technical
and scientific material is not well established and may vary over
a broad range of responsibilities, depending on the employer's needs and
the nature of the organization. In this respect the secretary's role is more
fluid than it is in traditional business settings. Because such a role presents
both challenges and opportunities, it is important that the secretary try to
establish the employer's expectations as early as possible.

Many institutions that deal routinely with technical and scientific material, such as government or private organizations and large aerospace companies, employ a staff of technical writers or editors who are responsible for
turning draft manuscripts into finished products. Such organizations often
have, in addition, a technical word processing center especially trained to
deal with technical and scientific material. In such cases, the secretary's role
may be limited to typing from handwritten material rough-draft manuscripts that are then sent to the editorial staff for further processing. In
other institutional settings, such as colleges or universities, the secretary's
role may be significantly expanded, with the employer relying more heavily
on the secretary to produce a final manuscript.

Whatever the institutional setting, however, the secretary who is expected
to deal with technical and scientific material in any capacity faces special
challenges. These challenges can be frustrating or surprisingly rewarding,
depending on how you approach them. First, it is misleading to think of
"science" as a single cohesive body of knowledge. There are many sciences,
each with its own subject matter, tradition, specialized vocabulary, guiding
principles, and techniques. Being exposed to a science for the first time is
a little like being confronted with a new language and the underlying ideas
it expresses. The sooner you learn the language of whatever field you are
working in, the more interesting your job will become and the more

254

effectively you will carry out your assignments. A number of books have been written for the scientific layperson in almost every field. Don't hesitate to ask the scientists you work with to recommend one that deals with their subject. In addition, several good general periodicals are devoted to explaining advances in the sciences. *Scientific American,* available on most newsstands, is one of the oldest and most comprehensive of these.

Most sciences have two aspects, basic science and applied science. Basic science attempts to understand how the things in the natural world come to be as they are and why things happen as they do: the origin of mountain chains, the causes of the weather, the shape of a galaxy, the pattern of a snowflake, the source of the sun's light, the reasons that objects have different colors, the origin of the universe, and countless other problems. Applied science uses this understanding to devise new or improved ways of doing things. Many of our modern technologies — computers, stereo systems, space flight, lasers, new fabrics and materials, new energy sources, to mention only a few — were made possible by new insights into why things happen.

Another challenge to the secretary employed in a technical setting arises from the fact that many of the sciences rely heavily on the language of mathematics. It is possible to understand much of this notation without formal training in mathematics and without a detailed understanding of the more complex mathematical procedures that scientists use. This chapter describes procedures for preparing various kinds of scientific and technical material, explains the role of some of the notation used in the sciences, and provides some rules of style. It is by no means comprehensive, and you will find that, as in any field, much of what you will need to know will be acquired on the job by asking questions in the same spirit of adventure that scientists bring to their work.

PARTS OF A SCIENTIFIC MANUSCRIPT

Like any other narrative account, a scientific or technical report must have a beginning, a middle, and an end. This seems elementary, but it is surprising how many professional scientists ignore this precept in practice. Although you cannot be expected to rewrite a paper (that is the author's or the editor's job), you can be alert to obvious omissions, especially when preparing material for a professional journal. There are, of course, many different forms of scientific and technical writing, from an article written for a general audience to a journal paper, a meeting paper, an internal document, a published report, or a grant application. Each has its own special format and requirements. Here, we focus on the parts of a typical scientific report.

A report can serve a variety of purposes: it can present the results of experiment, it can be a purely theoretical study, it can compare the results of experiment with theory, or it can survey and review the current status of a particular topic. In addition to its substantive portions — the beginning, middle, and end — a report contains certain parts that may be regarded as "housekeeping"; that is, it contains parts that provide the standard information normally included in scholarly writing. These usually brief parts may be some or all of the following:

1. *Title*   Titles may be subject to restrictions (especially by journals). For example, some journals limit the number of words in a title or specify that a title cannot be a question.

2. *By-line and supplementary information*   This includes such information as the name of the author or authors and address or institutional affiliation.

3. *Abstract*   An abstract summarizes in a few sentences the research problem addressed and the author's principal conclusions. Printed with the paper, they provide a brief overview of its content. Abstracts are also printed in journals dedicated solely to abstracts of work in a particular field.

4. *Acknowledgments*   In the acknowledgments, an author may give credit to others who contributed significantly to the work reported; these may be individuals, institutions, or funding agencies.

5. *References*   Many authors are careless about the accuracy, completeness, and style of their references. The secretary may be asked to verify references or to complete fragmentary references by consulting the source. (Nearly all journals specify a style for references; your institution may have a preferred style for its reports.) Make sure that every reference cited appears in the list of references and that every reference listed is cited.

6. *Index codes or key words*   These list the principal topics addressed in a report in a form appropriate for computerized search. In most sciences there is a standard index from which index codes or key words may be drawn.

PREPARING MATERIALS FOR SCIENTIFIC JOURNALS

The number of specialized scientific and technical journals and their publication costs have grown enormously over the past few decades. As a result, the editorial resources of many journals have been stretched so thin that most submitted manuscripts cannot be edited, and careless preparation may be cause for rejection. Although authors are aware of their responsibility for a paper's content and technical accuracy, many are careless about details of style. The secretary is often the one person who must ensure proper formatting and perform routine copy-editing — tasks that require thorough familiarity with the style requirements of specific journals.

All journals provide, in some form, specifications that detail format and style requirements. These usually include instructions governing such matters as length, title, abstract, types of headings used, numbering of sections, abbreviations, mathematical conventions, use of metric units, and preparation of artwork and photographs. Such a guide may appear in each issue of a journal or at intervals throughout the publication cycle. Some journals (or institutions publishing several journals) provide a more comprehensive style guide which may be ordered, and still others refer their authors to a general style guide such as the University of Chicago's *Manual of Style.*

The secretary preparing a manuscript for a journal should obtain a copy of its current style specifications. These should be followed as closely as possible. No journal, however, is likely to provide complete guidance on every aspect of style. Accordingly, it is important for you to obtain copies of one or more recent issues of the journal and to follow these when in doubt. If the articles vary in details of style that are not covered in the journal's style guide, choose any standard guide and follow it consistently.

What the Secretary Can Contribute to a Journal Article

The most important contributions that you can make to a manuscript being prepared for journal submission are adherence to style specifications, notational consistency, neatness, and legibility. Keep in mind that you are not designing an article for the compositor: the journal editor will mark up the manuscript for typesetting and in doing so will indicate size and styles of type for text, subheads, figure captions, and so forth. Your job is to ensure that the manuscript is as complete and as accurate as possible. Signs and symbols should be typed whenever feasible. When they are not available they may be entered neatly and legibly in the text with a black pen. The first time a sign or symbol (other than an English letter) is used, its name enclosed in a circle should be noted opposite it in the margin. This enables the compositor, who will be typesetting the manuscript, to interpret the symbols in the text. Some signs and symbols, especially if they are hand-lettered, are easily confused. Table 1 shows some of these symbols. If you are uncertain what the author intends, ask. Remember that the compositor will typeset what he or she thinks is there, not what you (or the author) know is there. In addition to annotating a symbol in the margin, you may be asked to prepare a list of all symbols used in the manuscript, together with their names. (Most journals require such a list.) Provision of a list of symbols affords additional insurance that they will be typeset correctly. Underscoring of Roman letters used in a mathematical context may be required if they are to be italicized in print. Follow the specifications of the individual journal, for house styles vary.

Neatness, legibility, and correctness are especially important when the paper being submitted is camera-ready copy (that is, it will be photographically copied for publication rather than typeset). This method is often used with symposium proceedings, for example. In other words, what you see is

Table 1.   **Some Easily Confused Symbols**

Symbol	Identification	As typeset	Symbol	Identification	As typeset
a	cap aye	A	ψ	lc psi	ψ
a	lc aye	a	Ψ	cap psi	Ψ
α	lc alpha	α	φ	lc phi	ϕ
∝	proportional to	$\propto$	Φ	cap phi	Φ
∞	infinity	∞	Σ	cap sigma	Σ
c	lc cee	c	Σ	summation	Σ
C	cap cee	C	s	lc ess	s
|	vertical bar	|	S	cap ess	S
/	solidus	/	V	cap vee	V
'	prime	$'$	v	lc vee	v
I	one	1	ν	lc nu	ν
l	lc ell	l	γ	lc gamma	γ
e	lc ee	e	υ	lc upsilon	υ
∈	an element of	$\in$	u	lc you	u
ε	lc epsilon	ϵ	μ	lc mu	μ
ε	eh	ε	W	cap double-you	W
K	cap kay	K	w	lc double-you	w
k	lc kay	k	ω	lc omega	ω
κ	lc kappa	κ	x	lc ex	x
n	lc en	n	X	cap ex	X
η	lc eta	η	×	multiplication sign	$\times$
°	degrees	°	χ	lc chi	χ
o	lc oh	o	z	lc zee	z
O	cap oh	O	Z	cap zee	Z
0	zero	0	2	two	2
ρ	lc rho	ρ	⟨⟩	angle brackets	$\langle \, \rangle$
p	lc pee	p	<,>	less than	$<$
P	cap pee	P		greater than	$>$
π	lc pi	π	†	dagger	†
Π	cap pi	Π	+	plus	$+$
Π	product symbol	Π			

*Adapted with permission from the American Institute of Physics *Style Manual* (3rd ed.).
†The second column gives acceptable ways of spelling out a symbol in the margin when marking copy for typesetting.

what you get. In such a case, marginal annotation and symbol lists are dispensed with, but it is wise to use rub-on symbols in the interest of appearance when symbols are unavailable on a typing element. It is also important in such a case to follow specifications for manuscripts *exactly*.

Illustrations

All journals provide specifications for illustrations submitted with manuscripts. These can include charts and graphs, line drawings, and photographs. Normally, graphs and other drawn illustrations will be produced by a professional technical illustrator prior to manuscript submission. You should provide a copy of a journal's specifications along with the hand-drawn illustrations when submitting them to an illustrator. Most journals will reject a paper if the illustrations have not been drawn to their specifications. For example, many journals must photographically reduce artwork to fit space limitations and format requirements. If the correct typesize has not been used on labels and callouts, these will appear either too small or too large when reduced and therefore will be unacceptable. It is the technical illustrator's job to ensure that such requirements are met. Photographs, if used, also should satisfy the journal's specifications regarding such matters as size, and callouts. Since very few professional journals print color photographs, it is best to submit black-and-white glossy prints to ensure that the salient features will be visible in black-and-white reproduction. Previously screened photographs (i.e., images that have been treated to produce a dot pattern) are usually unacceptable. Placement of figures in a manuscript is indicated by simply making a note in the margin, such as "Fig. 2," or "Fig. 3 should appear about here," at an appropriate point (normally the first time a figure is mentioned). Circle these notations.

Submitting a Manuscript

After a final check of the manuscript against the journal's specifications, the original and any extra copies requested by the journal can be packaged for submission. *Always* keep at least one file copy of the manuscript; in case the original is lost or damaged. A manuscript is usually accompanied by a covering letter.

Proofs

Before a journal prints a paper, it will send typeset galley or page proofs to the author. (Galley proofs are uncut text; page proofs are fully laid-out pages.) This is the author's last chance to correct any errors; therefore, the proofs must be read with great care, especially if the paper contains mathematical material. Compositors and editors can make errors or misinterpret instructions. After reading the proofs, the author may ask you to proofread the typeset copy as a double check. Any errors that you find should be called to the author's attention and corrected neatly and legibly in the margin,

260   Technical and Scientific Material

Table 2.   Examples of Selected Proofreaders' Marks

Mark	Instruction
Copper is highly toxic ^to^ many aquatic organisms.	Insert indicated letter, word, phrase, or sentence.
Copper is highly toxic #to many aquatic organisms.	Insert space.
Copper is highly toxic to many aquatic organisms ⊙	Insert period.
Copper is highly toxic to many aquatic organisms and . . .	Insert punctuation (or subscript).
We have measured the mussels sensitivity to copper.	Insert apostrophe (or superscript).
Copper is highly toxic to many aquatic organisms.5	Raise to superscript.
Copper (29Cu) is highly toxic to many aquatic organisms.	Lower to subscript.
Copper is highly toxic to to many aquatic organisms.	Delete.
Copper is highly toxic to ^many^ all aquatic organisms.	Delete and insert.
Copper is highly toxic to many aqua tic organisms.	Close space.
Copper is highly toxic to many aquatic organisms.	Delete and close.
Copper is highly toxic to many aquatic organisms.	Let it stand.
copper is highly toxic to many aquatic organisms.	Capitalize letter.
Copper is highly toxic to many aquatic Organisms.	Lowercase letter.
Copper is highly toxic to many AQUATIC organisms.	Lowercase word.
Copper is highly toxic to many aquatic organisms.	Transpose letters.
Copper is highly to toxic many aquatic organisms.	Transpose words.
¶ Copper is highly toxic to many aquatic organisms.	Begin new paragraph.
No ¶ Copper is highly toxic to many aquatic organisms.	No new paragraph.

Table 2. (*continued*)

Mark	Instruction
Copper is highly toxic to many aquatic ⌐ organisms.	Move left as indicated.
Copper is highly toxic to many aquatic organisms. ⌐	Move right as indicated.
⌐Copper is highly toxic to many aquatic organisms.	Raise as indicated.
Copper is highly toxic to many aquatic ⌊ organisms.	Lower as indicated.
⌐ APPENDIX A ⌐	Center.
Copper is highly toxic to ⌐ many aquatic organisms.	Run in.
APPENDIX A	Italics or underscore.
APPENDIX A	Boldface.

using standard proofreaders' marks. Since resets are costly, the author (or institution) may be billed for any such changes or additions. Nearly all journals today levy page charges for papers accepted. Page charges are normally billed to the institution rather than to the author, but a bill may be included along with the page proofs. You should find out how your organization handles these charges. At the time the corrected proofs are returned to the journal, the author may request reprints of the paper for distribution to colleagues. The publisher ordinarily includes with the proofs a form for ordering reprints.

FORMATTING MATHEMATICAL MATERIAL

This section introduces you to some of the basic ideas and notations used in mathematics and to some of the rules of style for formatting mathematical material. You will find it very helpful if you learn to recognize some of the different kinds of mathematical expressions and understand the roles played by the various signs and symbols they contain. Although it is not feasible in a brief survey to discuss all of the special symbols and notations you are likely to encounter, this section is designed to convey some of the flavor of what mathematics is about. The ability to see the *form* of a mathematical expression will help you to type it more accurately.

Some Basic Mathematical Ideas

The commonest form of mathematical "statement" in the sciences is the equation. An equation may be thought of as a kind of symbol machine that transforms one number (or set of numbers) into another. We can write an algebraic equation in the general form

$y = f(x)$,

Where $f(x)$ means "a function of x." When used to designate a function, it does *not* mean "x multiplied by f" (and thus should not be broken at the end of a line). A function of x stands for any mathematical expression in which x is the only variable. (A *variable* is a letter that takes on the value of any number we substitute for it.) Because the numerical value of x can be any number, it is known as the *independent* variable. The letter y is called the *dependent* variable because its numerical value is equivalent to, and depends on, the value of $f(x)$. As we have not yet specified the particular mathematical expression that $f(x)$ stands for, our imaginary function machine for $f(x)$ looks like this:

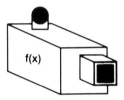

If we now replace $f(x)$ with a specific function of x, say $2x$ (x multiplied by 2), the function machine looks like this:

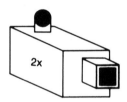

Substituting a numerical value for x is like dropping it into our imaginary function machine. Suppose this number is 4. If we drop 4 into the hopper of the machine and turn the crank, the machine grinds away and multiplies 2 and 4 to produce the resulting value of y:

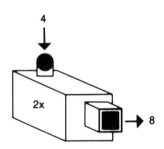

and the result is different for each number that we drop into the hopper. We can make the function $f(x)$ as complicated as we please; we can even add terms containing other variables w and z so that our original equation becomes

$$y = f(x, w, z)$$

The principle is the same: every time we drop a number or set of numbers into a particular function machine and turn the crank, we get another value of y.

The use of equations in the sciences depends on this number-generating property of functions. For example, when a scientist studying a physical system (such as an atom) can write down an equation describing the time behavior of the system in the form of a specific mathematical function, he or she can predict how the system will change over time by substituting numbers for the independent variables. Because the quantities they contain can be precisely manipulated, equations also enable us to find the values of quantities that we cannot directly measure by using the values of quantities that we can directly measure.

How to Read a Mathematical Expression

Although a mathematical expression may appear complicated, with a little practice it can be mentally broken down into smaller units. This way of looking at an equation enables us to see its general *form* and can be very helpful when an equation is being typed. Mathematics, like music, uses a special notation to convey information. The mathematical expressions used in the sciences are made up of several kinds of signs and symbols: English (or Roman) and Greek letters, signs of operation, fences, and special symbols.

Letter symbols. The letters in a mathematical expression may stand for variables (whose values range over a set of numbers), constants (whose numerical values are fixed and must be specified in a particular context), abbreviations of English words such as *sin* or *exp,* or other kinds of symbols such as index numbers. The meaning of each letter, abbreviation, or symbol should be clearly defined the first time it is used, with an indication of whether it is a variable, a constant, or another kind of symbol.

In addition to Roman letters, letters of the Greek alphabet are often used in mathematical expressions. (Greek letters are used for certain kinds of quantities for historical reasons.) Table 3 lists the letters of the Greek alphabet, their names and pronunciations, and their English equivalents. Because they are used extensively, you should learn to recognize them. Even the Roman and Greek alphabets together, however, may not contain enough letters for an author's needs. Further, an author may wish to use similar symbols for closely related but different quantities. The solution to both of

Table 3.   **Greek Alphabet**

Uppercase	Lowercase	Name	Pronunciation *
A	α	alpha	(ăl′fə)
B	β	beta	(bā′tə)
Γ	γ	gamma	(găm′ə)
Δ	δ	delta	(dĕl′tə)
E	ε	epsilon	(ĕp′sə-lŏn′)
Z	ζ	zeta	(zā′tə)
H	η	eta	(ā′tə, ē′tə)
Θ	θ	theta	(thā′tə, thē′tə)
I	ι	iota	(ī-ō′tə)
K	κ	kappa	(kăp′ə)
Λ	λ	lambda	(lăm′də)
M	μ	mu	(myoo͞, moo͞)
N	ν	nu	(noo͞, nyoo͞)
Ξ	ξ	xi	(zī, sī, ksē)
O	o	omicron	(ŏm′ĭ-krŏn′)
Π	π	pi	(pī)
P	ρ	rho	(rō)
Σ	σ, ς	sigma	(sĭg′mə)
T	τ	tau	(tou, tô)
Υ	υ	upsilon	(ŭp′sə-lŏn′, yoo͞p′sə-lŏn′)
Φ	φ	phi	(fī)
X	χ	chi	(kī)
Ψ	ψ	psi	(sī, psī)
Ω	ω	omega	(ō-mĕg′ə, ō-mē′gə, ō-mā′gə)

*The pronunciations shown here are taken from *The American Heritage Dictionary of the English Language, Third Edition.*

these problems is the use of superscripts, subscripts, or primes. Thus, an author may mean completely different things by a and a_o or p_{ij} and p_{ik} or f' and f''. This means that the secretary must be *very* careful to type every character as the author wants it. Typographical errors in mathematics are much more serious than in ordinary text. An error like "typwriter" is easy to spot in a draft, and the meaning is still clear; but dropping an *e* from a mathematical quantity may go unnoticed and can make an equation wrong.

It is also important to note that letter symbols maintain their identities throughout a discussion. In algebra, we are taught that the unknown is always x (or some other letter), no matter what the variable stands for. This does not mean that a symbol can stand for anything at different places. Most characters used in a paper or article mean the same thing, whatever it is, throughout. For example, if the author writes "the Boltzmann constant, k," at one point in a paper, you can be reasonably sure that when k appears again it still stands for the Boltzmann constant. (This does not necessarily apply to superscripts and subscripts used as indexes, such as i, j, or k, which may stand for different numbers in different places.)

In handwritten equations, authors often do not distinguish between the letter "oh" (uppercase or lowercase) and the numeral zero. Ordinarily, the secretary can guess the meaning from the context. When "oh" or zero is used in a superscript or subscript, however, the context may not help. If you cannot decide, ask. Thereafter, you can assume that the character is the same in identical contexts.

A word about the displayed expressions in this chapter. Displayed mathematical expressions, that is, expressions set on a separate line, when typeset, conventionally appear with the symbols representing entities such as variables styled in *italics*. But in this book we have purposely set the symbols in our *displayed* expressions in roman, for that is the way you may encounter them in handwritten or typewritten draft formats. When you keyboard a document for typesetting, use an italic font for the symbols or underscore them. (Mathematical expressions that have been run into the text itself have been italicized in order to set them off from the rest of the text.)

Signs of operation. Signs of operation (sometimes called *operators* or *operational signs*) indicate specific mathematical operations, such as addition $(+)$, substraction $(-)$, multiplication $(\times)$, or division $(\div)$, that are to be carried out on the letter symbols. In multiplication and division, the signs $\times$ and $\div$ are usually implicit rather than written out. For example, instead of writing $a \times b \times c$, we write abc, where the multiplication signs between the letters are understood. Another way of indicating multiplication is used when a symbol is multiplied by itself; rather than writing aaa, we write a^3 ("a cubed" or "a to the third power"). Similarly, in division, instead of writing $x \div y$ we use the fractional form x/y (read as "x divided by y" or "x over y").

Expressions that appear complicated often consist of the familiar operations of arithmetic carried out on various letter symbols. For example,

$$ax + by + 4x^2 - 2y + y/x$$

means "ax (or a times x) plus by (or b times y) plus $4x^2$ (4 times x squared) minus $2y$ (2 times y) plus the quantity y divided by x (or y over x)." The constants a, b, 4, and 2 are known as the *coefficients* of the variables they multiply.

Operations are also indicated by the superscript (exponent) of a quantity. For example, a^n ("a raised to the nth power" or "a to the nth") means n of the quantities a multiplied together. The symbol for the root of a quantity $(\sqrt{})$ is called the *radical* symbol, as in $\sqrt{x}$, read as "the square root of x." The same quantity also can be written as $x^{1/2}$, read as "x raised to the one-half power." Similarly, $^4\sqrt{x}$ ("the fourth root of x") can be written as $x^{1/4}$ ("x raised to the one-fourth power"). Using this same notation, we can write the expression $^3\sqrt{x^2}$ ("the third root of the quantity x squared") as $x^{2/3}$, or "x to the two-thirds power."

Mathematical expressions also can have more complicated exponents; for example, x^{2n+1}, read as "x raised to the power $2n$ plus 1" or "x to the quantity $2n$ plus 1." One special function often used in mathematics is called the exponential function, e^x, where e is a fixed quantity called the base of natural logarithms and the exponent x can be any expression. If the exponent of e is a complicated expression that includes a fraction, as in

$$e^{t^2/4k^2},$$

writing it in this form can be awkward, especially if the expression occurs in text. Scientists therefore sometimes use *exponential* notation, in which "exp" replaces e and the exponent is written on the same line. In this notation, the expression above is written $\exp(t^2/4k^2)$.

Other signs of operation stand for more complicated mathematical processes such as *differentiation* and *integration*. These are operations that change the *form* of a function. They may be thought of as changing the machinery in the function machine. Roughly speaking, differentiation is a procedure that enables us to study the rate at which the value of a function changes with respect to a change in its independent variable. If our equation, in functional form, is

$$y = f(x),$$

differentiation is often indicated by the symbols

$$\frac{dy}{dx} = f'(x)$$

(read as "the derivative of y with respect to x equals f prime of x" or "dy over dx equals . . ."), where $f'(x)$ is the new function arrived at by differentiation. If y represents distance traveled as a function of time t, for example, differentiating $f(t)$ will tell us how distance changes with time, or in other words, the *velocity* of whatever it is that we are describing.

Similarly, if we differentiate the function in our example a second time, indicated by

$$\frac{d^2y}{dx^2} = f''(x),$$

we obtain the rate at which the velocity *changes,* or the *acceleration.*

Differentiation can also be symbolized by what is called the "dot" notation. For example,

$$\dot{y} = f'(x)$$

means the same as

$$\frac{dy}{dx} = f'(x)$$

and

$$\ddot{y} = f''(x)$$

means the same as

$$\frac{d^2y}{dx^2} = f''(x).$$

Finally, functions with more than one independent variable can be differentiated by a process called *partial differentiation,* in which one variable at a time is differentiated while the others are held constant. Partial differentiation of a function $y = f(x, z)$ is indicated by the symbolism

$$\frac{\partial y}{\partial x} = f_x(x, z)$$

$$\frac{\partial y}{\partial z} = f_y(x, z),$$

where the symbol $\partial y/\partial x$ is read as "the partial derivative of y with respect to x" or "partial y over partial x."

Because the operation of *integration* is the reverse of differentiation, it is sometimes known as *antidifferentiation.* Integration may be thought of as a procedure that sums up an infinite number of elements whose size becomes gradually smaller; it is indicated by the symbol $\int$. For example, in the function

$$y = \int x^2 \, dx$$

(read as "integral of x squared dx"), the function to be integrated (called the *integrand*) is x^2. (The dx specifies the variable x on which the operation is to be performed; it does *not* mean "d multiplied by x").

The expression just given is called an *indefinite integral* because it does not specify the range of values of x over which integration is carried out. When such a range of values is specified, the resulting expression is called a *definite integral.* An example is the function

$$y = \int_0^\infty 2x^3 \, dx.$$

The symbols of zero and infinity (∞) at the bottom and top of the integral sign are said to indicate the *limits* of the integration (that is, the two ends of the range). Each integral may have its own limits. You also may see an

Table 4.   **Common Mathematical Operators**

+	plus
−	minus
±	plus or minus
∓	minus or plus
×	multiplication sign
Σ	summation
Π	product symbol
∂	backcurling delta (partial derivative sign)
∇	del (vector operator)
∇	bold del
∀	inverted sans serif aye (for all)
∃	inverted sans serif ee (there exists)
∧	wedge, roof (outer product sign; conjunction sign)
∨	inverted wedge or roof (disjunction sign)
∩	intersection sign
∪	union sign
√	radical
∫	integral
∮	contour integral

Adapted with permission from the American Institute of Physics *Style Manual* (3rd ed.).

integral sign with a circle at its center: $\oint$. This is known as a *contour integral* and represents integration over a closed path. As in differentiation, we can also integrate a function of more than one variable; for example,

$$y = \iint (x^2 + 2y) \; dxdy$$

or

$$y = \iiint (x^2 + 2y - z) \; dxdydz$$

Other signs of operation are the product sign Π (capital Greek *pi*) and the summation symbol Σ (capital Greek *sigma*). These are used when a series of mathematical terms is multiplied or added, respectively. For example,

$$\prod_{i=1}^{n} x_i,$$

read as "the product from i equals 1 to n of x sub i," means that we start with x_1 and multiply each term by the next (x_2, x_3, etc.) and end with x_n, whatever number n may be: $x_1 \times x_2 \times x_3 \times x_4 \times \ldots \times x_n$. The expression operated on by the product sign is called the *multiplicand*. In summation, we simply add the terms

$$\sum_{i=1}^{n} x_i$$

(read as "summation from *i* equals 1 to *n* of *x* sub *i*") instead of multiplying them. The expression operated on by the summation sign is called the *summand*.

The summation and product signs are *large* Greek capital letters, larger than those you may have on a typing element. You should therefore hand-letter these symbols or use rub-ons. Since the integral sign is unique, you can use the sign on a scientific typing element, especially for in-text expressions. Any of these signs must always be as high as the expressions they apply to.

Trigonometric functions also specify operations that are performed on letter symbols that represent angles. Some of the simpler trigonometric functions are $x = \sin \theta$, $y = \cos \theta$, and $z = \tan \theta$, where "sin" is the abbreviation for "sine," "cos" for cosine," "tan" for "tangent," and θ is an angle (other characters may be used for the angle). In the right-angle triangle, the lengths of the three sides are *a*, *b*, and *c*. The sine of the angle θ is defined as b/c, the cosine of θ is defined as a/c, and the tangent of θ is defined as b/a.

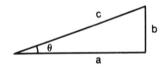

Another sign of operation you may often encounter (especially in the mathematics of probability) is the *factorial* symbol !, as in *n*! (read as "*n* factorial"). In mathematical notation, ! is not an exclamation point but indicates the product of all the integers (whole numbers) from *n* to 1. For example, if $n = 6$, $n! = 6 \times 5 \times 4 \times 3 \times 2 \times 1 = 720$. We have described in this section only a few of the most common mathematical operations; there are many others. Table 2 includes some additional operators and their meanings.

Signs of relation. In contrast to signs of operation, signs of relation indicate the relationships among the various terms in a mathematical expression. We have already seen how one common sign of relation, the equality sign, is used. Other often used signs of relation play similar roles. For example, < and > mean "less than" and "greater than," respectively; the expression $a < b$ is read as "*a* is less than *b*," and $a > b$ is read as "*a* is greater than *b*." Table 4 includes some additional signs of relation.

Table 5. Common Mathematical Signs of Relation

$=$	equals; double bond
$\neq$	not equal to
$\triangleq$	corresponds to
$\equiv$	identically equal to; equivalent to; triple bond
$\not\equiv$	not identically equal to; not equivalent to; not always equal to
$\sim$	asymptotically equal to; of the order of magnitude of
$\approx$	approximately equal to
$\simeq$	approximately equal to
$\cong$	congruent to; approximately equal to
$\propto$	proportional to
$<$	less than
$>$	greater than
$\not<$	not less than
$\not>$	not greater than
$\ll$	much less than
$\gg$	much greater than
$\leq$	less than or equal to
$\geq$	greater than or equal to
$\lessapprox$	less than or approximately equal to
$\gtrapprox$	greater than or approximately equal to
$\subset$	included in, a subset of
$\supset$	contains as a subset
$\not\subset$	not included in, not a subset of
$\subseteq$	contained within
$\supseteq$	contains
$\in$	an element of
$\ni$	contains as an element
$\notin$	not an element of
$\rightarrow$	approaches, tends to; yields; is replaced by
$\leftrightarrow$	mutually implies
$\perp$	perpendicular (to)
$\parallel$	parallel (to)

Adapted with permission from the American Institute of Physics *Style Manual* (3rd ed.).

Fences. Fences, sometimes called *symbols of inclusion,* are the punctuation marks of mathematics. Their role is to prevent ambiguity by setting off from one another the different terms in a mathematical expression. Fences include left and right parentheses ( ), brackets [ ], braces { }, and other specialized symbols. The accepted convention for the order in which fences are used is { [( )] }. If more fences are needed, this order may be repeated with larger fences. An example illustrates the way fences are used. In the expression

$$n + 2n + 1^2 - 2n + a - 1^3u - n$$

it is not clear, in the absence of fences, on which terms the operations are to be performed. Proper use of fences makes the meaning clear:

$$\{[(n + 2)(n + 1)^2 - 2n + (a - 1)^3]u\} - n^2.$$

There is one important rule about fences: except in very special cases, every left fence of a given kind must have a corresponding right fence. In complicated expressions, we can be sure that every kind of fence has a mate by counting the fences. If we find that an expression has, say, five parentheses, we can be reasonably sure that somewhere a parenthesis has been omitted. The same rule applies to special symbols that define what they enclose, such as the symbol for absolute value $|a|$ (read as "the absolute value of a"), where the vertical bars mean that the quantity a is to be used without regard for its sign (positive or negative). Another set of such symbols is the angle brackets $\langle a \rangle$ (not to be confused with the "less than" or "greater than" symbols), which indicate that the quantity they enclose is an average. Another notation for showing an average is the overbar $\bar{a}$. The overbar should extend over the entire expression to which it applies. Fences should be as high as the expressions they enclose. Rub-on or hand-drawn fences should be used if an expression such as a_i^2 is taller than a single letter symbol.

Rules of Style for Mathematical Material

In typing mathematical material, you not only will be dealing with signs and symbols that may be unfamiliar, but you also may be working with handwritten drafts that are barely legible. Perhaps the most effective way of coping with this situation, and the one you may find the most rewarding, is to familiarize yourself with the subject matter you will be dealing with.

If you simply cannot make out a symbol in a handwritten draft, you can guess, leave a space with a question mark, or ask the author. In the last case it is preferable, if there are several questionable symbols, to mark them for clarification in a single conference with the author.

In typing mathematical material, decisions about the use of typed, handlettered, or rub-on symbols will depend on the variety of symbols available, the kind of manuscript you are preparing (rough draft, camera-ready copy, journal article, or conference paper, for example), and the stage of a particular draft (preliminary, intermediate, or final). In some cases you may find it more convenient, unless otherwise instructed, to hand-letter all symbols in each successive draft except for the final, where you may need to use rub-on symbols or carefully annotated hand-lettered symbols.

When hand-lettering the symbols or using rub-ons, you will find that it is distressingly easy to drop some of them inadvertently in successive drafts, especially if you are working with a computer-linked printer not equipped with a special symbol element. One way to avoid this problem is to write or draw in the symbols neatly in each draft with a highly visible ink (such as red).

Although mathematics has been called the universal language of the sciences, it is fair to say that there is no generally observed standard for formatting mathematical expressions. Stylistic conventions may differ from one science to another and even from journal to journal within a particular science. Whatever set of rules is used, however, the result must be clear, consistent, and unambiguous. Many technical journals provide a style sheet for authors. If you know you will be preparing materials mostly for a particular journal or set of journals, you should obtain such a guide, either from your employer or from the journal (see the section on preparing journal articles). The American Institute of Physics, for example, publishes a useful *Style Manual.* Companies that produce their own technical reports often provide a style guide for authors, editors, and secretaries. You should ask whether such a guide is available. The rules of style given here thus should be regarded as default rules; they can be used if no other formal guidance is available.

Spacing of symbols.   Proper spacing of mathematical symbols is important both to avoid ambiguity and to give a clean, uniform appearance to a manuscript. Although the rules given here may seem tedious at first, with a little practice you should be able to apply them almost automatically in most cases. There is one important caveat in deciding how to space symbols: unless you know that an author is meticulous about writing mathematics (and, surprisingly, most are not), *you cannot rely on what you see,* either in a handwritten draft or in one that has been typed by the author. This is one of those cases in which you probably will be more familiar with the rules than the author is and thus can provide a valuable service.

1. Do not space:
    - between quantities multiplied together when no multiplication sign is used, as in xy, $2ab$, or $2x_r e^x$.
    - between a symbol and its subscript and superscript, as in x^n, x^{2y+c}, or Q_{max}.

- before and after fences, as in $(2x + b)(6y + c)$ or $[(x_i^2 - 2y^2)(x + 2)]u_i$.
- in names of functions or between names of multiplied functions, as in $f(x)$ or $f(x)f(y)$.
- between a sign and its quantity in signed quantities ± 6, -7, $+10$.
- when a sign of relation is used with a single quantity: "a value >6," "a length of ~ 3 meters."

2. Use one space:
   - before and after a binary sign of operation (an operation involving two quantities), as in $a + b$ or $a - b$ (note that this is different from a signed quantity). An exception is when a binary operator or sign of addition appears in a superscript, subscript, or limit, in which case no spaces are used:

     $$u^{n-1} \qquad \sum_{i=1}^{\infty}.$$

   - before and after a sign of relation: $a = 2b$, $x < y$, $g \subset r$.
   - before and after abbreviations that are set in roman type: $2 \sin \theta$, $\log b$, $2x \exp 4y$. An exception to this is when the abbreviation is preceded or followed by an expression in fences or a superscript or subscript. In such cases, use no space:

     $$(6n - m)\log a, \exp[(2x - y)/4], \sin^2\theta.$$

   - before and after a unary sign of operation (an operation on one expression), as in

     $$\omega \int_0^{\infty} (6x^2 - 4y)\ dx,\ iq\ \frac{\partial\psi}{\partial t},\ \sum_{n=1}^{\infty} x_n,\ \text{or}\ \frac{dy}{dx}\ f(x).$$

     Note: if an expression includes limits, count one space before and after the beginning and end of the limit, as in

     $$\lim_{y\to\infty}\ f(y).$$

     If limits are written as superscripts or subscripts, count one space after the last character to the right, as in

     $$g(t)\ =\ \frac{1}{2\pi i} \int_{a-i\infty}^{a+i\infty} e^{xt}f(x)\ dx.$$

   - after commas in sets of symbols, as in $(r,\ \theta,\ \phi)$ and $f(x,\ y)$.

3. Use three spaces:
   - between two or more equations that are in sequence on the line: $z = a^2 + b^2 + c^2$, $x = 2a + 3b + c$.

- between an equation and a condition on that equation:
  $d = u_a k \quad (a = 1, 2, 3, \ldots, n)$.
- between an equation and any parenthetical unit of measure:
  $a = v/t \quad (\text{m} \cdot \text{s}^{-2})$.
- between an equation and a following phrase in a displayed expression: $f(x) \to 0 \quad \text{as } x \to \infty$.

In-text and displayed equations. To avoid awkwardness or to conserve space, equations or expressions set in text are often formatted differently from equations set on a separate line (displayed). For example, in

$$\frac{h^2}{4\pi^2 k e^2 m} = \frac{a_0}{Z}$$

the fractions are "built up." In text, such an equation should be typed with the solidus (slash) instead of the fraction bar: $h^2/4\pi^2 ke^2 m = a_0/Z$. When reformatting, however, it is sometimes necessary to add fences to avoid ambiguity. For example,

$$z = \frac{a + y}{b}$$

does not mean the same as $z = a + y/b$. It is necessary to place the numerator in parentheses to preserve the meaning: $z = (a + y)/b$. Similarly, the expression

$$e^{2\pi i/\sqrt{(x^2+y^2)}}$$

can be typed in text as $\exp[2\pi i/\sqrt{(x^2 + y^2)}]$, but the brackets are necessary. If an in-text expression is sufficiently complex, however, it is preferable to display it. You should seek the author's advice when reformatting an equation. Even in displayed equations, it is best to avoid expressions that are doubly built up. For example,

$$y = \frac{x}{b} + \frac{x^2}{4/a}$$

is preferable to

$$y = \frac{x}{b} + \frac{x^2}{\frac{4}{a}}.$$

Displayed equations are often numbered. The rule of thumb is that if a displayed equation is subsequently cited, it should be numbered. All numbered equations should be displayed, but not all displayed equations need be numbered.

The rules for indenting displayed equations vary from style to style;

equations are sometimes centered, sometimes indented slightly to the right, and sometimes typed flush left. In the absence of specific guidance, you will probably find it convenient to indent them or type them flush left, a practice that avoids counting the spaces to the center and tabbing. Whatever spacing you use, be consistent. In numbered equations, the equation number is enclosed in parentheses and set flush with the right margin:

$$f' = \sum_{n=0}^{\infty} na_n u^{n-1} . \tag{1}$$

Punctuation after in-text mathematical expressions is the same as in ordinary English. In a displayed equation, however, leave one space between the last character and any following punctuation (period, comma, or semicolon).

Breaking an equation. If they will not fit on a single line, lengthy displayed equations may be broken (carried over to the next line). An equation should be broken, if at all possible, only preceding a sign of relation (equal, less than, etc.) or preceding a sign of operation (plus, minus, integral symbol, etc.):

$$u'(t) = b^0 a_0^{-1} \sum_{r=1}^{\infty} \exp(srt) p_r t \quad (\textit{line break can come here})$$

$$- b_1 a_0^{-1} \sum_{r=1}^{\infty} \exp[s_r(t - \omega)] p_r \, (t - \omega) . \tag{2}$$

The second line may be typed as a standard indentation from the left margin (to allow space for an equation number) or, as in Eq. (2), aligned one space to the right of a sign of relation. Whatever style you use, however, consistency is the watch-word.

If a displayed equation is broken between multiplied numbers, the multiplication sign (which is usually implicit) should be inserted at the beginning of the new line. Thus,

$$\Delta m = m_2 - 2m_1 = 2m_1 \left[\left(1 - \frac{u^2}{c^2} \right)^{-1/2} - 1 \right]$$

becomes

$$\Delta m = m_2 - 2m_1 = 2m_1$$

$$\times \left[\left(1 - \frac{u^2}{c^2} \right)^{-1/2} - 1 \right] .$$

Fractions, expressions within fences, and expressions within a radical sign ($\sqrt{\ }$) should not be broken unless absolutely necessary. Do not break an expression containing an integral sign until d(variable) occurs, as in

$$\overline{K}(s, t) = - K(s, t) + \int_a^b K(s, r)K(r, t) \, dr$$

$$- \int_a^b \int_a^b K(s, r)K(r, w)K(w, t) \, dr \, dw.$$

"Where" lists. Displayed equations are often followed by lists that define the symbols they contain, called "where" lists since they are preceded by the word *where*. If a where list contains few or only simple definitions, it may be run into the text, as in

$$\text{"L} = n \frac{h}{2\pi} = n\hbar,$$

where $\hbar$ is Planck's constant and n is an integer."

When a list is lengthy (say, four or more lines) or itself contains built-up expressions, it should be displayed separately and the definitions aligned with the "equals" sign. For example, an author might say:

"We may write

$$F^{3/4} = \left(\frac{bW_v - c}{2yL} \right)^m,$$

where b = proportionality constant,
       W_v = vapor mass rate,
       c = intercept as $W_v = 0$,
       $2yL$ = cross-sectional area normal to flow,
       L = tube length per crosspass,
       m = positive exponent."

The symbol definitions are listed in the same order in which they appear in the equation. Note that each line is punctuated by a comma except for the last, which ends with a period because it is the end of the sentence.

Some miscellaneous rules:

• Fraction bars should extend over or under the longest expression in a fraction, with the shorter expression centered on the bar. For example, in

$$\frac{2E_0(P_1 - P_2)}{2}$$

the bar extends under the entire numerator, and the denominator is centered.

• In a signed fractional expression, the sign should be aligned on the fraction bar, as in

$$X = - \frac{mA}{R}$$

- Complicated expressions involving a radical sign, as in

$$\sqrt{[3J/(J + 1)]T_Nm^2},$$

are more conveniently typed as

$$\sqrt{\{[3J/(J + 1)]T_Nm^2\}}.$$

Note the added braces, which are essential to indicate the extent of the radical. Alternatively, an expression such as

$$\sqrt{\frac{[3J/(J + 1)]T_Nm^2}{E_n - B_n^2b^2T_N}}$$

may be written as

$$\left\{\frac{[3J/(J + 1)]T_Nm^2}{E_n - B_n^2b^2T_N}\right\}^{1/2}$$

If the radical sign is used, it must extend over the entire expression it applies to.

- To avoid awkward spacing, limits for in-text signs of operation (integration, summation, etc.) may be written as superscripts or subscripts rather than above or below the operator without causing confusion. For example,

$$\prod_{n=0}^{\infty} a_n$$

can be typed as $\prod_{n=0}^{\infty} a_n$. This is *always* done with the limits of an integral sign.

- In a symbol having both a superscript and a subscript, they should be aligned as in x_n^2 (not $x^2{}_n$), unless the author specifies otherwise.

FORMATTING CHEMICAL MATERIAL

Basic Chemical Terminology

The basic unit of matter is the *atom.* There are many different kinds of atoms. Each kind of atom is called an *element.* The chemical properties of an element are governed by its atomic structure. Every atom has a central part, the *nucleus,* in which most of its mass (or weight) is concentrated. The nucleus consists of two kinds of particles: the *proton,* which has one positive unit of electrical charge, and the *neutron,* which is electrically neutral. The number of protons in the nucleus is called its *atomic number.* The total number of neutrons and protons in a nucleus is called its *atomic mass number.* The nucleus is surrounded by a swarm of much lighter, fast-moving particles called *electrons,* each of which carries one negative unit of electrical charge.

The electrons are bound to the nucleus by the attractive force between their negative charges and the positive charge on the nucleus.

An electron is not free to move anywhere in the space around the nucleus. Each electron is constrained by a set of rules to move only in a certain volume of space around the nucleus called a *shell.* The rules partition the space around the nucleus so that only a certain number of electrons can occupy a particular shell. Some shells are relatively close to the nucleus and some are farther away. After the innermost shell (which has no more than two electrons), each shell can accommodate various numbers of electrons (with the number varying from shell to shell). The outermost shell is known as the *valence shell,* and its electrons are called the *valence electrons.* The electrons in the outermost shell are those that give an atom its chemical properties.

When the number of protons (positively charged) in the nucleus equals the number of electrons (negatively charged) around the nucleus, the charges cancel one another and the atom is electrically neutral. In general an atom is more stable if its valence shell contains eight electrons. Hence, an atom of chlorine, which has seven electrons in its valence shell, is more stable if it accepts an electron from another atom (filling its valence shell for a total of eight electrons). Because the resulting chloride atom has one more electron than proton, it carries one unit of negative charge. Similarly, an atom of sodium, which has one electron in its valence shell, is more stable if it gives up an electron (so that the next shell in contains eight electrons). The resulting sodium atom carries one unit of positive charge.

An atom that has one or more units of charge, positive or negative, is called an *ion.* The transfer of an electron from one atom to another forms an *ionic bond.* Ordinary table salt (sodium chloride) consists of sodium and chlorine atoms bonded to one another. Other atoms *share* their valence electrons to fill up their valence shell, forming *covalent bonds.* A nitrogen atom, for example, has five valence electrons. If two nitrogen atoms share three electrons apiece, they form three covalent bonds and effectively fill their valence shells. The process by which atoms form chemical bonds is called a *chemical reaction.* Atoms can undergo a chemical reaction with other atoms, or groups of atoms, combining to form a *molecule.* Likewise, molecules can combine chemically with other molecules or atoms.

The chemical properties of the various elements depend, as we have noted, on the number of electrons in their valence shells and also the readiness with which their atoms accept, give up, or share electrons. As we increase the number of protons and electrons in an atom, the number of electrons in the valence shell repeats in a regular pattern. Atoms having the same number of valence electrons tend to have similar chemical properties. This periodic pattern enables us to group elements with similar chemical properties; the result is known as the *periodic table of the elements,* shown on pages 280–281.

The table also lists the names of the elements, their chemical symbols, their atomic numbers, and their atomic mass numbers. Since a chemical symbol is *not* an abbreviation, it is *not* followed by a period. The atomic mass number is not always a whole number because the nuclei of atoms of the same element can contain different numbers of neutrons, such atoms are called *isotopes*. The atomic mass numbers in the table thus represent an *average* for a particular element as it is found in nature.

Chemical Notation

Chemists generally divide all chemical compounds into two major kinds, *inorganic* compounds and *organic* compounds. Inorganic compounds are those that are composed of elements other than the element carbon (atomic number 12). Organic compounds are those that contain carbon atoms. The reason for this division is twofold. Historically, the first carbon compounds studied were products of the human body; hence, they were called organic compounds. Secondly, because of its chemical properties, the element carbon forms a countless variety of different compounds, and the molecules of carbon compounds can be very large. Such compounds have given rise to a separate field of study. In observing this division, we first discuss the notation for inorganic compounds and then the notation for organic compounds, although the notation overlaps in many respects.

Inorganic chemistry. The *name* of a chemical element appearing in text should be spelled out the first time it is used. The name of an element is not capitalized (unless, of course, it is the first word in a sentence):

Oxygen and hydrogen react to form water.

The first letter of each chemical *symbol* is always capitalized; the second letter, if there is one, is never capitalized:

The material was found to consist of C, H, Cl, and Br.

There is a conventional notation for indicating the atomic number, atomic mass number, ionic charge, and number of atoms of an element in a compound. This is done by the use of appropriate index numbers (superscripts and subscripts) attached to the chemical symbol. There is no space between a chemical symbol and its index number.

1. The atomic number is indicated by the lower-left index number: $_1H$, $_8O$, $_{12}Mg$, $_{50}Sn$. (The atomic number is usually omitted in a chemical formula, as it is unique to an element.)
2. The atomic mass number is indicated by an upper-left index number: ^1H, ^{16}O, ^{24}Mg, ^{118}Sn. Another way of indicating the atomic mass

Table 6. Periodic Table of the Elements

The periodic table arranges the chemical elements in two ways. The first is by **atomic number,** starting with hydrogen (atomic number = 1) in the upper left-hand corner and continuing in ascending order from left to right. The second is by the number of electrons in the outermost **shell.** Elements having the same number of electrons in the outermost shell are placed in the same column. Since the number of electrons in the outermost shell in large part determines the chemical nature of an element, elements in the same column have similar chemical properties.

This arrangement of the elements was devised by **Dmitri Mendeleev** in 1869, before all the elements were yet known. To maintain the

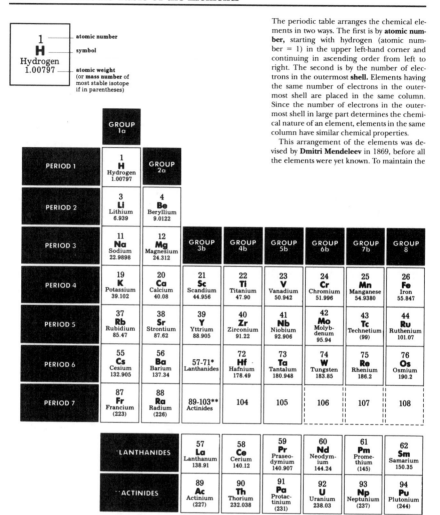

Table 7. The Chemical Elements

ELEMENT	SYMBOL	ATOMIC NUMBER	ELEMENT	SYMBOL	ATOMIC NUMBER	ELEMENT	SYMBOL	ATOMIC NUMBER	ELEMENT	SYMBOL	ATOMIC NUMBER
Actinium	Ac	89	Cadmium	Cd	48	Element 104	–	104	Holmium	Ho	67
Aluminum	Al	13	Calcium	Ca	20	Element 105	–	105	Hydrogen	H	1
Americium	Am	95	Californium	Cf	98	Erbium	Er	68	Indium	In	49
Antimony	Sb	51	Carbon	C	6	Europium	Eu	63	Iodine	I	53
Argon	Ar	18	Cerium	Ce	58	Fermium	Fm	100	Iridium	Ir	77
Arsenic	As	33	Cesium	Cs	55	Fluorine	F	9	Iron	Fe	26
Astatine	At	85	Chlorine	Cl	17	Francium	Fr	87	Krypton	Kr	36
Barium	Ba	56	Chromium	Cr	24	Gadolinium	Gd	64	Lanthanum	La	57
Berkelium	Bk	97	Cobalt	Co	27	Gallium	Ga	31	Lawrencium	Lr	103
Beryllium	Be	4	Copper	Cu	29	Germanium	Ge	32	Lead	Pb	82
Bismuth	Bi	83	Curium	Cm	96	Gold	Au	79	Lithium	Li	3
Boron	B	5	Dysprosium	Dy	66	Hafnium	Hf	72	Lutetium	Lu	71
Bromine	Br	35	Einsteinium	Es	99	Helium	He	2	Magnesium	Mg	12

overall logic of the table, Mendeleev allowed space for undiscovered elements whose existence he predicted.

The table has since been filled in, most recently by the addition of Element 104 and Element 105. The solid lines around these elements indicate that they have been isolated experimentally although not officially named. Broken lines around elements 106–109 indicate that these elements, though not yet isolated, are known to exist.

The **lanthanide** series (elements 57–71) and the **actinide** series (elements 89–103) do not conform to the **periodic law** and are therefore placed below the main body of the table.

GROUP 0
2 **He** Helium 4.0026

GROUP 3a	GROUP 4a	GROUP 5a	GROUP 6a	GROUP 7a
5 **B** Boron 10.811	6 **C** Carbon 12.01115	7 **N** Nitrogen 14.0067	8 **O** Oxygen 15.9994	9 **F** Fluorine 18.9984	10 **Ne** Neon 20.183
13 **Al** Aluminum 26.9815	14 **Si** Silicon 28.086	15 **P** Phosphorus 30.9738	16 **S** Sulfur 32.064	17 **Cl** Chlorine 35.453	18 **Ar** Argon 39.948

GROUP 8	GROUP 8	GROUP 1b	GROUP 2b						
27 **Co** Cobalt 58.9332	28 **Ni** Nickel 58.71	29 **Cu** Copper 63.546	30 **Zn** Zinc 65.37	31 **Ga** Gallium 69.72	32 **Ge** Germanium 72.59	33 **As** Arsenic 74.9216	34 **Se** Selenium 78.96	35 **Br** Bromine 79.904	36 **Kr** Krypton 83.80
45 **Rh** Rhodium 102.905	46 **Pd** Palladium 106.4	47 **Ag** Silver 107.868	48 **Cd** Cadmium 112.40	49 **In** Indium 114.82	50 **Sn** Tin 118.69	51 **Sb** Antimony 121.75	52 **Te** Tellurium 127.60	53 **I** Iodine 126.9044	54 **Xe** Xenon 131.30
77 **Ir** Iridium 192.2	78 **Pt** Platinum 195.09	79 **Au** Gold 196.967	80 **Hg** Mercury 200.59	81 **Tl** Thallium 204.37	82 **Pb** Lead 207.19	83 **Bi** Bismuth 208.980	84 **Po** Polonium (210)	85 **At** Astatine (210)	86 **Rn** Radon (222)

109

63 **Eu** Europium 151.96	64 **Gd** Gadolinium 157.25	65 **Tb** Terbium 158.924	66 **Dy** Dysprosium 162.50	67 **Ho** Holmium 164.930	68 **Er** Erbium 167.26	69 **Tm** Thulium 168.934	70 **Yb** Ytterbium 173.04	71 **Lu** Lutetium 174.97
95 **Am** Americium (243)	96 **Cm** Curium (247)	97 **Bk** Berkelium (247)	98 **Cf** Californium (251)	99 **Es** Einsteinium (254)	100 **Fm** Fermium (257)	101 **Md** Mendelevium (256)	102 **No** Nobelium (255)	103 **Lr** Lawrencium (257)

ELEMENT	SYMBOL	ATOMIC NUMBER	ELEMENT	SYMBOL	ATOMIC NUMBER	ELEMENT	SYMBOL	ATOMIC NUMBER	ELEMENT	SYMBOL	ATOMIC NUMBER
Manganese	Mn	25	Palladium	Pd	46	Rubidium	Rb	37	Terbium	Tb	65
Mendelevium	Md	101	Phosphorus	P	15	Ruthenium	Ru	44	Thallium	Tl	81
Mercury	Hg	80	Platinum	Pt	78	Samarium	Sm	62	Thorium	Th	90
Molybdenum	Mo	42	Plutonium	Pu	94	Scandium	Sc	21	Thulium	Tm	69
Neodymium	Nd	60	Polonium	Po	84	Selenium	Se	34	Tin	Sn	50
Neon	Ne	10	Potassium	K	19	Silicon	Si	14	Titanium	Ti	22
Neptunium	Np	93	Praseodymium	Pr	59	Silver	Ag	47	Tungsten	W	74
Nickel	Ni	28	Promethium	Pm	61	Sodium	Na	11	Uranium	U	92
Niobium	Nb	41	Protactinium	Pa	91	Strontium	Sr	38	Vanadium	V	23
Nitrogen	N	7	Radium	Ra	88	Sulfur	S	16	Xenon	Xe	54
Nobelium	No	102	Radon	Rn	86	Tantalum	Ta	73	Ytterbium	Yb	70
Osmium	Os	76	Rhenium	Re	75	Technetium	Tc	43	Yttrium	Y	39
Oxygen	O	8	Rhodium	Rh	45	Tellurium	Te	52	Zinc	Zn	30
									Zirconium	Zr	40

number of an element, usually when it stands alone or is mentioned in text, is to place it after the hyphenated name or chemical symbol of the element: uranium-238, curium-247, carbon-14. Note that we may infer the number of neutrons in a nucleus by subtracting the atomic number from the atomic mass number. Hence, the isotope ^{235}U has 143 neutrons (235 minus 92) and ^{238}U has 146 neutrons (238 minus 92).

3. Ionic charge is indicated by an upper-right index number: H^+, F^-, O^{2-}, Fe^{3+}, Co^{3+}, U^{5+}, Mn^{4+}. If an ion has only one plus or minus charge, the numeral 1 is omitted. When an atom gives up valence electrons, it is said to be *oxidized* or in an *oxidation state*. Some atoms can give up different numbers of valence electrons. The *oxidation number*, which specifies how many electrons have been given up, is indicated by a Roman numeral in parentheses following the chemical symbol: Fe(II), Fe(III), Co(III), U(V), Mn(IV). There is no space between the chemical symbol and the parenthetical numeral.

4. The number of atoms of an element in a molecule is indicated by a lower-right index number: H_2, O_2, $C_{16}H_{34}$, K_2CO_3.

The same notation, with some additional features, is used for chemical compounds or molecules. Such an expression is known as a *chemical formula*. For example, the formula for the water molecule, which consists of two atoms of hydrogen and one atom of oxygen, is expressed in chemical notation by H_2O. (Note that we use only the index numbers that are relevant in a particular context. Atomic number and atomic mass number are usually included in a formula only when we deal with reactions of the nucleus. To write the formula for the carbon dioxide molecule when we wish to draw attention to the atomic mass number of the carbon atom because it is radioactive, we would write $^{14}CO_2$.)

Some molecules are also ions; that is, they have a net electrical charge, indicated by using fences (parentheses and brackets) in much the same way as they are used in mathematical notation. For example, the expression $Fe[(CN)_6]^{4-}$ indicates an ion composed of one iron atom (Fe^{2+}) and six cyano groups (CN^-), and the ion has a net charge of -4. The unshared electron of a free radical is indicated by a raised period to the right of the chemical symbol: $H_3C\cdot$, $C_6H_5\cdot$, $HO\cdot$. The same notation is used to indicate water of hydration: $Na_2SO_4\cdot H_2O$).

The physical state — solid (s or c), liquid (ℓ or l), or gas (g) — of an element or compound is specified by including the abbreviation in parentheses after the chemical symbol: $H_2(g)$, $Br_2(l)$, $S(s)$. Note that there is no space between the abbreviation and the chemical symbol. A chemical reaction (that is, the chemical combination of atoms or molecules) is indicated by linking the reacting species with a "plus" symbol, followed by an arrow indicating the direction of the reaction, and finally by the formula(s) of the reaction product(s). The number of each species participating in the reaction is given by a coefficient preceding the chemical symbol:

$$Ca_3(PO_4)_4 + 3H_2SO_4 \rightarrow 2H_3PO_4 + 3CaSO_4$$

$$2AgCl + 2Hg \rightarrow Hg_2Cl_2 + 2Ag.$$

The first of these expressions tells us that one molecule of $Ca_3(PO_4)_4$ combines with three molecules of H_2SO_4 (sulfuric acid) to form two molecules of H_3PO_4 and three molecules of $CaSO_4$. The second expression tells us that two molecules of AgCl combine with two atoms of Hg (mercury) to form one molecule of Hg_2Cl_2 and two atoms of Ag (silver). As in mathematical notation, we leave one space on both sides of the "plus" symbol and on both sides of the arrow (chemical sign of relation). If a reaction proceeds in both directions, two single-headed arrows are used to indicate a balance in which the forward and reverse reactions are proceeding at equal rates:

$$Zr + H_2 \rightleftharpoons ZrH_2.$$

An expression for a chemical reaction may also contain additional information describing the conditions of the reaction, the physical state of the reactants, or other reaction products:

$$WF_6(g) + 3H_2(g) \xrightarrow[\text{Excess } H_2]{\text{Heat}} W(s) + 6HF(g).$$

Organic chemistry. As mentioned previously, organic chemistry is the study of the compounds of the element carbon. Because a carbon atom can form covalent bonds with as many as four other atoms, it is known as a *tetravalent* element. The spatial orientation of other atoms when they bond to carbon, and the number of bonds they form with carbon, strongly affect the properties of the resulting molecule. For example, two molecules containing carbon may have the same chemical formula (with regard to the total number of atoms in the molecule) but may have quite different physical or chemical properties because of the way the other atoms are attached to the carbon atoms. For this reason, formulas describing carbon compounds are often given in *structural* form. A *structural formula* displays the spatial relationships among the atoms in a unique and unambiguous way. A structural formula thus contains more *information* about a compound than does its chemical formula. This becomes especially important when we deal with the very large molecules that carbon is capable of forming. (The long and complex molecules that comprise the genetic material in a biological cell, for example, can contain many thousands of carbon atoms.) In general, a carbon atom can bond to its neighbors in four different ways; each kind of bond is represented by a special notation:

1. a single bond, in which two electrons are shared, is represented by a single line drawn from the carbon atom to another atom, as in

$$
\begin{array}{c}
\text{H} \\
| \\
\text{H}-\text{C}-\text{H} \\
| \\
\text{H}
\end{array}
$$

2. a double bond, in which four electrons are shared, as in

$$
\begin{array}{cc}
\text{H} & \text{H} \\
\diagdown & \diagup \\
& \text{C}=\text{C} \\
\diagup & \diagdown \\
\text{H} & \text{H}
\end{array}
$$

3. a triple bond, in which six electrons are shared, as in

$$\text{H}-\text{C}\equiv\text{C}-\text{H}$$

4. a hydrogen bond, represented by a dotted line, in which a hydrogen atom bonded to atom *A* in one molecule makes an additional bond to atom *B* in either the same or another molecule, as in

$$
\begin{array}{c}
\text{O} \\
\diagup \quad \diagdown \\
\text{H} \qquad \text{H} \\
\vdots \\
\text{O} \\
\diagup \quad \diagdown \\
\text{H} \qquad \text{H}
\end{array}
$$

Hydrogen bonds are generally not shown unless they are specifically discussed.

Especially in biological molecules, carbon tends to bond with oxygen, nitrogen, and hydrogen. As we have already seen, a hydrogen atom has one electron to share, and thus forms a single bond with carbon. Oxygen shares one or two electrons and can form a single or double bond with carbon:

$$
\begin{array}{ccc}
\diagdown & \quad | & \quad | \quad\quad | \\
\text{C}=\text{O} & -\text{C}-\text{OH} & -\text{C}-\text{O}-\text{C}- \\
\diagup & \quad | & \quad | \quad\quad |
\end{array}
$$

Nitrogen can share one, two, or three electrons to form a single, double, or triple bond:

$$-\overset{|}{\underset{|}{C}}-NH_2 \qquad \overset{\diagdown}{\underset{\diagup}{C}}=NH \qquad H-C\equiv N$$

We are now able to see the importance of structural formulas, for the same formula, for example, C_3H_6O, can represent more than one geometrical structure, as in

$$H-\overset{H}{\underset{H}{\overset{|}{C}}}-\overset{H}{\underset{H}{\overset{|}{C}}}-\overset{O}{\underset{H}{\overset{\diagup\!\!\!\diagup}{C}}} \qquad or \qquad H-\overset{H}{\underset{H}{\overset{|}{C}}}-\overset{}{\underset{O}{\overset{|}{C}}}-\overset{H}{\underset{H}{\overset{|}{C}}}-H$$

Some of the bonds in a structural formula can be omitted if it can be done without ambiguity. The resulting formula is a hybrid between a chemical formula and a structural formula. For example, $CH_3(CH_2)_6CH_3$ is a shortened form of

$$CH_3-CH_2-CH_2-CH_2-CH_2-CH_2-CH_2-CH_3.$$

When bonds are shown explicitly, they are always drawn *between* atoms and not to the center of a *group* of atoms:

$$H-\overset{COOH}{\underset{OH}{\overset{|}{C}}}-H \qquad or \qquad H-\overset{\overset{O\diagdown\!\diagdown\,C\,\diagup OH}{}}{\underset{OH}{\overset{|}{C}}}-H$$

$$not \qquad H-\overset{COOH}{\underset{OH}{\overset{|}{C}}}-H$$

We know that the second formula cannot be correct because it shows an oxygen atom, which has two bonding electrons, sharing electrons with three other atoms (top) and hydrogen, which has one bonding electron, sharing electrons with two other atoms (bottom).

This simplification can be carried even further when no ambiguity results. For example, besides the straight-chain carbon molecules we have so far discussed, carbon can form other kinds of chemical structures. A *ring structure* is one common form, as in the benzene ring, which can be drawn as

Note that the alternating double bonds that link the carbon atoms appear in a different position in each molecule, although the structures are chemically equivalent. This representation can be further simplified to

without loss of information. Finally, the same structure can be shown as

We have so far discussed organic compounds as if they all lay in the plane of the page. Actually, carbon's four bonds are arranged in a three-dimensional tetrahedral structure, and to distinguish among different possible configurations in space, we sometimes wish to show this structure. In one widely accepted convention, three different kinds of lines are used: solid lines for atoms (or groups) in the plane of the page, dashed lines for atoms behind the plane of the page, and wedge-shaped lines for atoms that lie above the plane of the page. For example,

Ring structures may also be represented in three dimensions with the same conventions:

$$HOCH_2$$
$$HOCH \quad O \quad H$$
$$HO \quad H$$
$$H \quad OCH_3$$
$$H \quad OH$$

SCIENTIFIC NOTATION

Because scientists often deal with very large or very small numbers, they have developed a special *scientific notation* that enables them to name such numbers without using an excessive number of zeros. This notation is based on powers of $10(10^n$, where the exponent n is any number). For example, the number 1000 (one followed by three zeros) is written more compactly as 10^3 ("ten to the third power") because $10 \times 10 \times 10 = 1000$. We can see the usefulness of this notation when we consider a larger number such as one billion (1 000 000 000 or one followed by nine zeros). In scientific notation, this is written as 10^9. Using this notation, we can quickly write numbers as large as we please without bothering to count zeros, even numbers that are so large they have no name, such as 10^{28} ("ten to the 28th power"), or one followed by 28 zeros. We can use this notation to write numbers less than one. The general form for numbers less than 1 is 10^{-n} (read as "ten to the minus n"), where the minus sign means 1 divided by 10^n, or $1/10^n$. For example, one billionth is written 10^{-9} $(1/10^9)$. We also can combine this notation with decimal numbers to express numbers that lie between powers of ten. This is done by multiplying the base number by another number, or in general, $m \times 10^n$. For example, 240 000 may be written 240×10^3. Using this notation, we can easily rewrite numbers in whatever form is most convenient by moving the decimal point in m any number of spaces to the left or right and increasing or decreasing the exponent by the same number. For example, 240×10^3 can be rewritten as 24×10^4 (moving the imaginary decimal point after 24 one place to the left and increasing the exponent by 1). Similarly, 3.5×10^8 can be written as 35×10^7 (moving the decimal point one space to the right and reducing the exponent by 1). The same rules hold for negative exponents.

Scientific notation also makes it easy to multiply or divide large or small numbers quickly. The general form for multiplication is

$$10^a \times 10^b = 10^{a+b},$$

where a and b are added algebraically. For example, $10^{16} \times 10^4 = 10^{(16+4)}$ or 10^{20}. Similarly, $10^{-16} \times 10^8 = 10^{-16+(8)}$ or 10^{-8}. (Remember that we add *algebraically*.) For division, the general form is $10^a/10^b = 10^{a-b}$, where again the subtraction is algebraic. For example, $10^{16}/10^{-4} = 10^{16-(-4)}$ or 10^{20}.

Here we have subtracted -4 algebraically, changing its sign and adding. With a little practice, numbers written in scientific notation can be easily manipulated. As we shall see, this system of notation is very useful when we use the metric system of measurement, which is based on units of ten.

THE METRIC SYSTEM

The metric system, also called the International System of Units (or SI for short), is a standardized system of expressing units of measurement. SI units have been officially adopted in nearly every country in the world because of their simplicity and ease of manipulation. Although the use of metric weights and measures was legalized in the United States as long ago as 1866, Americans have in general preferred the traditional English system of measurement (such as *foot, pound,* and *degree Fahrenheit*), and conversion to SI has gone more slowly here than elsewhere. (Even English measures, however, are now officially defined in SI units.) In 1975, the United States Congress passed legislation to coordinate a voluntary policy of increasing the use of SI in this country as well. This means that eventually all measurements in the United States are to be expressed in SI units. Liquid and weight measures are now often listed on labels in both English and SI units.

Base Units

Table 8 gives the SI base and supplemental units and their abbreviations. You may find that the SI units for mass (the kilogram), length (the meter), and time (the second) are the most familiar of these. The other base units (and their derived units) are also used extensively in the scientific

Table 8. **SI Base and Supplemental Units**

Quantity	Unit	Symbol
length	meter*	m
mass	kilogram	kg
time	second	s
electric current	ampere	A
temperature	kelvin	K
amount of matter	mole	mol
luminous intensity	candela	cd
plane angle	radian	rad
solid angle	steradian	sr

*The approved SI style of spelling is *metre, centimetre, litre,* and so on.

literature. Each SI base unit has been defined with great precision in terms of measurable physical quantities. For example, the metre has been defined as the distance light travels in $1/299{,}792{,}458$ of a second. To deal with very large and very small measurements, SI provides prefixes for the base units. Table 9 gives the SI prefixes, their equivalents in scientific notation, and their official symbols.

Derived Units and Conversion

The derived units of SI are obtained by combining the base and supplementary units. Table 10 gives the approved derived units that have special names. For those accustomed to the traditional English units, it may help to understand SI units by comparing them to their equivalents in the English system. Table 11, called a *conversion table,* lists some common SI units and their English equivalents. To convert from English to SI, we multiply the number of English units by their equivalent in SI units. For example, to convert 6 miles to kilometers, we multiply 6 by 1852 to obtain 11,112 meters, or 11.112 kilometers.

Some conversion tables give the conversion factor as a decimal number followed by the letter E plus or minus a two-digit number: $4.184 \text{ E} + 03$.

Table 9.   **SI Prefixes**

Symbol	Prefix	Multiplication Factor
E	exa	10^{18}
P	peta	10^{15}
T	tera	10^{12}
G	giga	10^{9}
M	mega	10^{6}
k	kilo	10^{3}
h	hecto	10^{2}
da	deca	10^{1}
d	deci	10^{-1}
c	centi	10^{-2}
m	milli	10^{-3}
μ	micro	10^{-6}
n	nano	10^{-9}
p	pico	10^{-12}
f	femto	10^{-15}
a	atto	10^{-18}

This notation means that the conversion factor 4.184 is multiplied by 10^3. As a rough rule of thumb, we suggest the following reminders:

A liter is a quart and a little more.

A kilogram is two pounds and a little more.

A kilometer is 1/2 mile and a little more.

SI Style

Because a small change in the way SI units are written or typed can change their meaning completely, it is important to type them correctly. Adherence to a few simple rules can avoid confusion.

1. The full names of SI units are always written in lowercase letters unless one is the first word in a sentence. Some SI units (newton, kelvin, watt, pascal) are named after famous scientists; if so, the *symbol* begins with an uppercase letter (N, K, W, Pa). An exception is the (non-SI but commonly used) unit for temperature, the degree Celsius, which is always capitalized.
2. SI units are not italicized because they are not mathematical symbols.
3. Do not put a period after SI symbols, except at the end of a sentence; they are *not* abbreviations.
4. Do not mix unit names and their symbols. For example, do not write km/second. Write either km/s or kilometer/second.
5. Do not pluralize symbols. For example, write 800 km, not 800 kms. Full unit names are pluralized normally, by adding an *s* (meters, kilograms).
6. Always space between a symbol and its numerical value; 500 s, not 500s (which appears to be the plural of 500). The exception is the degree Celsius (°C), where the degree and Celsius symbols are written flush with the numerical value (40°C).
7. When a prefix symbol (M, G, etc.) is combined with a unit symbol, do not leave a space between them: GHz, not G Hz.
8. Derived units involving multiplication, such as Newton metre, should be separated from one another with a raised dot (N·M) or, if your typing element lacks this symbol, with a period (N.M).
9. Derived units involving division can be written using either the solidus (/) or the negative exponent combined with the dot multiplier. For example, kilograms per cubic meter may be written kg/m^3 or $kg·m^{-3}$. When preparing a manuscript for a journal, you should consult its style specifications on this point. Whatever style is used, it is best to be consistent.
10. When numerical values are written in SI, use a space rather than a comma to separate groups of three digits to the left and to the right

Table 10.   **Some Common SI-derived Units**

Derived Units

Most of the units in the International System are derived units, that is units defined in terms of base units and supplementary units. Derived units can be divided into two groups—those that have a special name and symbol, and those that do not.

Without Names and Symbols

Measure of	Derivation
acceleration	m/s^2
angular acceleration	rad/s^2
angular velocity	rad/s
density	kg/m^3
electric field strength	V/m
luminance	cd/m^2
magnetic field strength	A/m
velocity	m/s

With Names and Symbols

Unit	Measure of	Symbol	Derivation
coulomb	electric charge	C	$A \cdot s$
farad	electric capacitance	F	$A \cdot s/V$
henry	inductance	H	$V \cdot s/A$
hertz	frequency	Hz	$cycles/s$
joule	quantity of energy	J	$N \cdot m$
lumen	flux of light	lm	$cd \cdot sr$
lux	illumination	lx	lm/m^2
newton	force	N	$kg \cdot m/s^2$
ohm	electric resistance	Ω	V/A
pascal	pressure	Pa	N/m^2
tesla	magnetic flux density	T	Wb/m^2
volt	voltage	V	W/A
watt	power	W	J/s
weber	magnetic flux	Wb	$V \cdot s$

of the decimal point, as in the standard American style. Thus, ten thousand is typed 10 000 rather than 10,000 and one millionth as 0.000 000 1 rather than 0.000,000,1. This convention was adopted because Europeans traditionally use a comma where we use a decimal point and periods to space groups of three numbers. However, numbers with only four digits to the right or left of the decimal point are written without either a space or a comma (9856 and 0.0011). In decimal numbers less than one, the decimal point is *always* preceded by a zero: 0.068, not .068.

Table 11. **Measurement**

Length		
U.S. Customary Unit	**U.S. Equivalents**	**Metric Equivalents**
inch	0.083 foot	2.540 centimeters
foot	$\frac{1}{3}$ yard, 12 inches	0.305 meter
yard	3 feet, 36 inches	0.914 meter
rod	$5\frac{1}{2}$ yards, $16\frac{1}{2}$ feet	5.029 meters
mile (statute, land)	1,760 yards, 5,280 feet	1.609 kilometers
mile (nautical, international)	1.151 statute miles	1.852 kilometers

Area		
U.S. Customary Unit	**U.S. Equivalents**	**Metric Equivalents**
square inch	0.007 square foot	6.452 square centimeters
square foot	144 square inches	929.030 square centimeters
square yard	1,296 square inches, 9 square feet	0.836 square meters
acre	43,560 square feet, 4,840 square yards	4,047 square meters
square mile	640 acres	2,590 square kilometers

Weight		
U.S. Customary Unit (Avoirdupois)	**U.S. Equivalents**	**Metric Equivalents**
grain	0.036 dram, 0.002285 ounce	64.798 milligrams
dram	27.344 grains, 0.0625 ounce	1.772 grams

Table 11.   (*continued*)

Weight		
U.S. Customary Unit (Avoirdupois)	**U.S. Equivalents**	**Metric Equivalents**
ounce	16 drams, 437.5 grains	28.350 grams
pound	16 ounces, 7,000 grains	453.592 grams
ton (short)	2,000 pounds	0.907 metric ton (1,000 kilograms)
ton (long)	1.12 short tons, 2,240 pounds	1.016 metric tons
Apothecary Weight Unit	**U.S. Equivalents**	**Metric Equivalents**
scruple	20 grains	1.296 grams
dram	60 grains	3.888 grams
ounce	480 grains, 1.097 avoirdupois ounces	31.103 grams
pound	5,760 grains, 0.823 avoirdupois pound	373.242 grams

Volume or Capacity		
U.S. Customary Unit	**U.S. Equivalents**	**Metric Equivalents**
cubic inch	0.00058 cubic foot	16.387 cubic centimeters
cubic foot	1,728 cubic inches	0.028 cubic meter
cubic yard	27 cubic feet	0.765 cubic meter
U.S. Customary Liquid Measure	**U.S. Equivalents**	**Metric Equivalents**
fluid ounce	8 fluid drams, 1.804 cubic inches	29.573 milliliters
pint	16 fluid ounces, 28.875 cubic inches	0.473 liter
quart	2 pints, 57.75 cubic inches	0.946 liter
gallon	4 quarts, 231 cubic inches	3.785 liters
barrel	varies from 31 to 42 gallons, established by law or usage	

Table 11. (*continued*)

U.S. Customary Dry Measure	U.S. Equivalents	Metric Equivalents
pint	½ quart, 33.6 cubic inches	0.551 liter
quart	2 pints, 67.2 cubic inches	1.101 liters
peck	8 quarts, 537.605 cubic inches	8.810 liters
bushel	4 pecks, 2,150.420 cubic inches	35.239 liters

British Imperial Liquid and Dry Measure	U.S. Customary Equivalents	Metric Equivalents
fluid ounce	0.961 U.S. fluid ounce, 1.734 cubic inches	28.413 milliliters
pint	1.032 U.S. dry pints, 1.201 U.S. liquid pints, 34.678 cubic inches	568.245 milliliters
quart	1.032 U.S. dry quarts, 1.201 U.S. liquid quarts, 69.354 cubic inches	1.136 liters
gallon	1.201 U.S. gallons, 277.420 cubic inches	4.546 liters
peck	554.84 cubic inches	0.009 cubic meter
bushel	1.032 U.S. bushels, 2,219.36 cubic inches	0.036 cubic meter

The Metric System
Length

Unit	Meters	U.S. Equivalent	Unit	Meters	U.S. Equivalent
myriameter	10,000	6.214 miles	meter	1	39.370 inches
kilometer	1,000	0.621 mile	decimeter	0.1	3.937 inches
hectometer	100	109.361 yards	centimeter	0.01	0.394 inch
decameter	10	32.808 feet	millimeter	0.001	0.039 inch

Table 11. (*continued*)

Area

Unit	Square Meters	U.S. Equivalent
square kilometer	1,000,000	0.386 square mile
hectare	10,000	2.477 acres
are	100	119.599 square yards
deciare	10	11.960 square yards
centare	1	10.764 square feet
square centimeter	0.0001	0.115 square inch

Volume

Unit	Cubic Meters	U.S. Equivalent	Unit	Cubic Meters	U.S. Equivalent
decastere	10	13.079 cubic yards	decistere	0.10	3.532 cubic feet
stere	1	1.308 cubic yards	cubic centimeter	0.000001	0.061 cubic inch

Capacity

			U.S. Equivalents	
Unit	Liters	Cubic	Dry	Liquid
kiloliter	1,000	1.308 cubic yards		
hectoliter	100	3.532 cubic feet	2.838 bushels	
decaliter	10	0.353 cubic foot	1.135 pecks	2.642 gallons
liter	1	61.024 cubic inches	0.908 quart	1.057 quarts
deciliter	0.10	6.102 cubic inches	0.182 pint	0.211 pint
centiliter	0.01	0.610 cubic inch		0.338 fluid ounce
milliliter	0.001	0.061 cubic inch		0.271 fluid dram

Mass and Weight

Unit	Grams	U.S. Equivalent	Unit	Grams	U.S. Equivalent
metric ton	1,000,000	1.102 tons	gram	1	0.035 ounce
quintal	100,000	220.462 pounds	decigram	0.10	1.543 grains
kilogram	1,000	2.205 pounds	centigram	0.01	0.154 grain
hectogram	100	3.527 ounces	milligram	0.001	0.015 grain
decagram	10	0.353 ounce			

Table 11.   (*continued*)

Metric Conversion Chart—Approximations

When You Know	Multiply By	To Find	When You Know	Multiply By	To Find
Length			**Mass and Weight**		
centimeters	0.39	inches	grams	0.035	ounce
			kilograms	2.21	pounds
meters	3.28	feet	tons (100kg)	1.10	short tons
meters	1.09	yards			
kilometers	0.62	miles	ounces	28.35	grams
inches	25.40	millimeters	pounds	0.45	kilograms
inches	2.54	centimeters	short tons (2000 lb)	0.91	tons
feet	30.48	centimeters	**Volume**		
yards	0.91	meters	milliliters	0.20	teaspoons
miles	1.61	kilometers	milliliters	0.06	tablespoons
Area			milliliters	0.03	fluid ounces
square centimeters	0.16	square inches	liters	4.23	cups
			liters	2.12	pints
square meters	1.20	square yards	liters	1.06	quarts
			liters	0.26	gallons
square kilometers	0.39	square miles	cubic meters	35.32	cubic feet
hectares (10,000m²)	2.47	acres	cubic meters	1.35	cubic yards
square inches	6.45	square centimeters	teaspoons	4.93	milliliters
square feet	0.09	square meters	tablespoons	14.78	milliliters
square yards	0.84	square meters	fluid ounces	29.57	milliliters
			cups	0.24	liters
square miles	2.60	square kilometers	pints	0.47	liters
			quarts	0.95	liters
acres	0.40	hectares	gallons	3.79	liters

Table 11.   (*continued*)

Metric Conversion Chart—Approximations

When You Know	Multiply By	To Find	When You Know	Multiply By	To Find
Volume			**Speed**		
cubic feet	0.03	cubic meters	miles per hour	1.61	kilometers per hour
cubic yards	0.76	cubic meters	kilometers per hour	0.62	miles per hour

Temperature

$$°C = (°F - 32) ÷ 1.8 \qquad °F = (°C × 1.8) + 32$$

Temperatures in degrees Celsius, as in the familiar Fahrenheit system, can only be learned through experience. The following temperatures are ones that are frequently encountered:

0°C	Freezing point of water (32°F)
10°C	A warm winter day (50°F)
20°C	A mild spring day (68°F)
30°C	A hot summer day (86°F)
37°C	Normal body temperature (98.6°F)
40°C	Heat wave conditions (104°F)
100°C	Boiling point of water (212°F)

12

Time Management: Appointments, Meetings, and Conferences

H ELPING AN EXECUTIVE manage time is an integral part of a secretary's duties. Many of the things that a secretary does for the executive in one way or another lead to enhanced management of time. Effective time management can be achieved through many means, some of which can be very detailed and others very simple, depending on the needs of the individual executive and the practices followed within the company. In an effort to simplify, eliminate as many steps as possible to accomplish a given task. But at the same time, the desired result of the activity must not be changed because of your wish for simplification. Use as many timesaving methods and procedures as possible, within limitations. Undoubtedly, you have realized that some practices and procedures have come to be "set in concrete," thus precluding introduction of more streamlined approaches. Discussed in this chapter are some methods for assisting the executive with appointments, schedules, and meetings.

Calendar Management

Daily, Weekly, and Monthly Scheduling

One of your primary considerations as a time manager should be ensuring that the executive is in the proper location at the proper time, regardless of whether the location is within your own facility or at an outside site. Appropriate scheduling of meetings and appointments and confirmation or cancellation of them is critical in maintaining efficient use of the executive's time. Having a large, monthly desk calendar is a good start. Tentative schedules can be indicated in pencil as far in advance as possible. If a business trip or meeting is scheduled during a particular month, for instance, it can be marked on the calendar along with all available information such as the destination or location, the time, travel arrangements, and so on. As the details are confirmed, appropriate notations can then be added to the calendar. Another method also may be helpful to you in this respect. Keep a monthly calendar book, and have the executive to whom you report keep a duplicate calendar book. Set a time when you can both sit down to go over the calendar, scheduling as far into the future as possible in *both* books. You may have to do it on a daily, weekly, or monthly basis, depending on the nature of the executive's schedule and the practices or needs of your company. Again, as confirmations are received or other details are arranged, note them in the appropriate places in both books. If the executive's schedule often changes erratically and without notice, you should note all activities in the books in pencil to facilitate quick neat changes.

Confirmations and cancellations. A prompt telephone call to confirm or cancel an appointment or meeting should take only a moment or two of your time. This avoids wasting the executive's time later on and precludes any possibility of the executive or a caller appearing at a particular place and time without a confirmed appointment. If a meeting or appointment remains unconfirmed or has been cancelled, that block of time then becomes open for other appointments or other activities.

You may be confronted with a situation in which the executive leaves for a meeting that overruns its allotted time, in which case appointments throughout the rest of the day could become hopelessly backed up. Think ahead: if you know that meetings with certain people tend to run long, call the conference room or office in which the meeting is taking place and confer with the executive. You can then call the scheduled visitors and reschedule their appointments. If you know that some of the visitors have rather flexible schedules, you can call them on your own without conferring with the executive, and say, "Ms. Lee is in a meeting that may last well into the afternoon. I doubt very much that she will be able to see you at one o'clock today, but her schedule tomorrow morning looks very good. Could you come in about 9:30?" If the executive is in a high-level meeting with, say, the chairman or the president, call the secretary to this officer, explain the situation, and ask that a message be conveyed to your executive regarding the upcoming appointments. Your executive can then call you back at a convenient time.

Some executives are very well organized and are always aware of their upcoming activities. They have an excellent sense of time. Managing the time of such a person is relatively easy. Others, however, especially those who are involved in numerous high-priority projects, seem unable to schedule themselves realistically and really entrust their days to their secretaries. If you are in this situation, you'll have to become very familiar with all of the executive's associates and outside visitors so that you can make spot decisions regarding rescheduling and cancellation of appointments. You may be faced with five visitors pacing in the outside office, impatiently waiting for an executive who isn't there. You can put a tracer on the executive by calling all of the offices frequently visited, or you can save yourself a lot of time by suggesting that the executive purchase a beeper. You can beep the executive on or off the company site with reminders that certain activities are scheduled during the rest of the day. You can also use the beeper to alert the executive that visitors are waiting in the office.

Tickler files. Use of a tickler or "suspense" file can be very helpful to you in your daily, weekly, and monthly scheduling. When you know that a particular item (e.g., correspondence, a note, or a reminder) is due on a certain date, put a notation to this effect into a tickler file in your desk and mark your daily calendar "suspense." This notation reminds you that an item in the suspense file will need attention on a certain date. Some of you may wish to use an expansion file tabbed by day, month, or full date, as appropriate. Another extremely useful item is a control sheet that tells you when reports or other materials are to be issued. You can simply use a sheet marked with grid lines. The date is written across the top, either by day or month, and the reports or other projects are listed down the left-hand side. Progress on each can be noted within the grid. The control sheet lets you know at first glance where you stand with upcoming activities from start to finish. It therefore serves as a comprehensive reminder and a progress report.

Many companies have a department which is responsible for the corporate calendar. At the beginning of each year the department may solicit input from various executives and departments as to what activities, such as meeting dates or deadlines for particular documents or reports, should be noted on that calendar. Recurring events and projects with predetermined dates and deadlines, such as shareholders' meetings and the issuance of annual reports, are already indicated on the corporate calendar. This calendar when made final is then issued to all of the executives and secretaries concerned and is followed by updated monthly versions reflecting revisions or other changes as appropriate. In this way high-level corporate communication regarding such activities is ensured. The same system could be used on a smaller scale for the secretary's own needs or as an aid to the executive in outlining daily, weekly, monthly, or annual planning and reporting. Such a calendar would provide a broad outline of the matters to be taken care of by day, week, month, or at any given time during the year. A daily, weekly, or monthly update, as required by the circumstances, will allow progress, changes, or adjustments to be recorded and acted on.

Communication between executive and secretary. Communication between executive and secretary concerning calendar planning and scheduling is necessary to ensure accurate and effective time management. Imagine the embarrassment that could ensue if the executive schedules an appointment with one guest or client, while in the meantime the secretary unwittingly schedules another appointment for the same hour with another guest or a competitive client. One way of avoiding double bookings is to have an understanding with the executive whereby you schedule *tentative* appointments. With this system you notify the visitor that the meeting or appointment is tentative and that confirmation will follow. After having checked with the executive as to the schedule for that date and time, you then can confirm the appointment. The confirmed appointment should be noted in both calendar books. This procedure prevents overbooking of appointments and also keeps you from scheduling unwanted or unscreened appointments. It is far wiser to spend a few minutes on a daily or weekly basis in going over the tentative or confirmed appointment or meeting schedule to avoid situations embarrassing for all concerned. Try to set a specific time for this activity.

"Do not disturb" or quiet time blocks. Every executive should try to set aside quiet or "do not disturb" time periods, either during each day or at some point once or twice each week. If you and the executive are able to set aside such blocks of time, the executive can use it for planning, paperwork, formulating thoughts and ideas, and problem-solving. Staff members should be informed that "Ms. Doe is from now on reserving the time from 9:15 a.m. to 10:15 a.m. for concentrated, undisturbed work and will see no visitors and will take only the most urgent calls during that period." The executive should shut the door; a closed door usually will cause even the more aggressive visitors to pause. You will have to be firm with visitors and callers at first until they realize the executive is truly serious about the need for quiet time.

An ancillary advantage to this arrangement is that it may give you an opportunity to catch up on miscellaneous correspondence, paperwork, filing, and other matters. If you have an assistant, the assistant could answer the telephone for you during this period.

Time Wasters

An enormous amount of time is wasted particularly but not exclusively by the executives themselves. A study of management by Henry Mintzberg of McGill University has shown that executives' biggest time wasters are telephone interruptions, drop-in visitors, ineffective delegation of tasks, and meetings with two or more people in attendance, in that order. You and the executive can work together to make better use of time. For example, you should display initiative in handling as many administrative details as possible and in coordinating effective procedures for an easy flow of paper. Such an arrangement turns on the willingness of the executive to delegate these responsibilities to you and to rely on your good judgment in fulfilling them. As we have learned in Chapter 8, you can and should sort and read incoming mail and other documents. Attaching the appropriate files or back-up information to incoming documents will facilitate later action by the executive. If an incoming letter is a response to a letter from the executive, attach a copy of the executive's original letter to the incoming reply. Include with them any other relevant material, such as a memo. In this way you can save the executive expensive time otherwise wasted while wading through masses of mail, some items of which probably could have been handled by another person or department.

Interruptions. No office is free of interruptions. But the number of interruptions tends to increase as the executive's ongoing responsibilities and projects grow. Your job is to shield the executive from all unnecessary interruptions by screening and redirecting telephone calls as appropriate and by screening visitors. If you are aware of the executive's priority projects and the importance of various callers in relation to the executive's position and projects, you should be able to control the flow of incoming calls and visitors.

Compile a list of frequent callers and the level of priority of their calls. The executive will always talk to certain people whenever they call, but there will be others to whom the executive may not always wish to talk. This list should be kept next to the phone, in full view so that you or anyone else covering for you can see it at a glance. Confer with the executive from time to time to ensure that the list is kept revised and current.

Your office may receive numerous telephone calls that really should be redirected to other departments. Try to assist the caller and whenever possible, forward the call to the proper person or department. If you are not sure of the department, take down the information and tell the caller you will have someone get back in touch and follow through.

A log of incoming telephone calls can be prepared by the secretary. When giving the list to the executive, the secretary can include precise information about the nature of the call together with any relevant attachments and back-up material. Difficult and unfamiliar names should be accompanied by phonetic spellings to aid the executive in pronouncing them correctly — a useful public relations gesture.

A predetermined period during the day can be set aside for making or returning telephone calls. If the executive can block out such a time, either before or after lunch or even late in the day, frequent callers will become accustomed to expecting a return call at a certain time and others can be advised accordingly.

Organizing your own tasks. Set your own task priorities by keeping a list of specific things to be done on a given day and then do them. Divide your tasks into small time blocks and handle each one in order of importance.

Try to schedule short, simple tasks between other activities. Arrange schedules around high-priority projects and do first things first. Extra time always should be allowed for concentration on high-priority matters, and the time of day during which you are at your best should be reserved for such activities. If working on figures, for example, early in the morning might be the best time for you.

If you report to more than one executive, it is wise to do the following:

1. Find out which executive is higher in rank; the work that you do for the higher-ranking executive will take priority. For example, if you work for the chairman and the president, the chairman's assignments should be carried out first. And at the outset, everyone concerned should reach an understanding about priorities-by-rank.
2. If possible, obtain colored in- and out-boxes and assign them to each executive. Label them clearly with the executives' names. Try to get the executives to use these boxes rather than dropping materials onto the middle of your desk.
3. If the executives hand you top-priority tasks all at the same time, ask for the assistance of a temporary worker. You can offload the less complicated tasks onto this person.
4. Set up a back-up system with another secretary who can fill in for you during breaks and on occasions when you are in meetings or are away from the office.
5. Establish set time blocks for performing time-consuming tasks such as mail sorting. Whenever possible, keep up with filing chores on a daily basis so that you are not swamped with unfiled papers at week's end.

Meetings

Although meetings are vital to the conduct of business, many are unnecessary. Some meetings are now being eliminated through the use of telephone conference calls, videoconferencing, and electronic mail. All of these alternatives are in the long run less costly and more efficient than meetings. When a meeting or conference is being discussed, many factors should be considered to determine whether the meeting is truly necessary in the first place. Although the secretary is normally not in a position to make such determinations, his or her input can be of great assistance to the executive. Is there a real objective for the meeting or conference? If the meeting is for gathering or dispersing of information, what will be accomplished as a result? If no concrete actions will be taken, or if the participants will not leave the meeting better informed, why have the meeting in the first place?

If asked, you can encourage your executive to use more time- and cost-efficient methods of discussion and decision-making. These include a quick one-on-one phone call, a conference or videoconferencing call, a short memo, or a scaled-down and tightly controlled meeting devoted only to the pertinent topics. In a scaled-down meeting, the agenda itself can contain specific time limitations for discussion of topics. Example: Marketing Plan — Software (10:30 – 11 a.m.).

Once a meeting has definitely been decided upon, a few simple ploys can be used to make it efficient, controlled, and effective. First of all, the list of those who will attend should include only those who are essential to the objective of the meeting. Ten or twelve people at the most should attend a discussion meeting. If the intent is to give or hear a speech, with or without a question-and-answer period, the number of participants need be restricted only by seating and space availability. After having determined the number of participants, an agenda should be prepared. A preliminary (or "working") agenda can be circulated to the prospective participants. In some cases, the host may wish to solicit input from those participants as to what items might be included or excluded. Upon receiving and reviewing a preliminary agenda, someone may decide to send another representative or not to be represented at the meeting at all. Use of a preliminary agenda enables the host to cut out as much extraneous subject matter as possible. The final agenda is developed from the preliminary model and is distributed to the participants in advance.

ARRANGEMENTS FOR FORMAL MEETINGS AND CONFERENCES

Using the Services of Hotel Meeting Coordinators

Setting up a formal meeting or conference may be simple or complicated, depending on the nature of the event and the kind of advance planning you do. The easiest and most direct way to plan off-site meetings is to get in touch with the hotel or facility where the event will be held. Major domestic and foreign hotels and conference centers usually have individuals or staff responsible for setting up and coordinating meeting arrangements. Why spend time and energy making arrangements that can be handled by others who are trained and paid exclusively to do just that? They may be able to suggest innovative arrangements that you have not even considered. Many hotels do not charge for meeting rooms but may charge for extras, such as audiovisual equipment. After you have outlined the requirements for the meeting, the hotel representative may provide you with printed preregistration cards to send to the participants. They, in turn, make their own reservations directly with the hotel — a process that saves an enormous amount of your time. When the event draws near, check with the hotel to find out who has made reservations and verify their count with your list of respondents. Discrepancies can be straightened out with the participants by telephone. You can have the participants get in touch with you concerning their hotel reservations, and then you can take further steps to coordinate them with the hotel representative.

Other meetings or conferences may require that all arrangements be made in a more personal fashion. Whether you or the hotel or conference site representative does the coordinating, it is extremely important that all possible requirements be known well in advance of the event.

Making Arrangements for Off-site Meetings and Conferences

You can't always rely on the availability of hotel meeting planners at every single meeting site. Furthermore, you need to have planned the activities in advance to a certain degree so that you can tell the hotel representatives the following essential things:

- The date(s) of the meeting.
- The number of participants.
- The size of the conference room(s) and dining room(s) needed and the desired seating plans.
- The number, locations, times, and menus of meals.
- The special equipment required.
- The nonbusiness events planned.

Obviously, you must know well in advance the inclusive dates of the event. The number of participants must be worked out and confirmed well in advance, too, for this figure affects all other planning — the budget for the entire event, the number of hotel reservations required, the selection of conference and dining rooms, the type of seating, the group rates for meals, and so forth. Determine with the hotel the final cutoff date for receipt of acceptances and changes in the list of participants and stick to it. Otherwise, chaos will reign — rooms will not be available, the hotel staff will be upset, and participants arriving without reserved rooms will be annoyed. Take bids from at least three hotels based on the data in the list above. You and the executive can then decide together which hotel is the most competitive. At this point you should give the hotel detailed information on a day-by-day chart showing exactly what is expected of them. Base your chart on the agenda that the executive has written for the meeting. See the illustration on page 306 for a sample of one day's activities.

A detailed conference package ought to be mailed to all participants well in advance. If the conference involves several days of long meetings, type up a separate agenda for each day, allowing ample space between agenda items. Also in the package should be:

- A map indicating the location of the meeting site.
- Ground transportation information.
- Registration materials including name tag.

Meeting Activity Sheet

```
TO:    International Hotel              SUBJECT:  Affiliates' Meeting

FROM:  Janice Sale                     DATES:    May 1, 19-- through
       Executive Assistant to Mart Miller        May 4, 19--
       UBC Network
       45 Green Mountain Tower
       Anywhere, US  98765
       (123) 456-7890

DATE:  February 1, 19--


                    DAY-BY-DAY ACTIVITY GUIDE
```

date	time	room	activity	setup	attendees	equipment
5/4	9:00 a.m. to noon	Colonial	Ratings Review	Panel Plan seats for 200	200	1 dais mike 25 aisle mikes 4 video machines
	10:30 a.m. to 10:45 a.m.	Colonial	Break	4 buffet tables	200	
	1:00 p.m. to 2:00 p.m.	Lee	Luncheon	20 round tables each seating 10 persons	200	
	2:15 p.m. to 5:00 p.m.	Colonial	New Programs	same as 9-12	200	same as 9-12
	3:45 p.m. to 4:00 p.m.	Colonial	Break	same as 10:30-10:45 a.m.	200	
	6:00 p.m. to 7:30 p.m.	Jefferson	Cocktail Party	4 buffet tables 4 open bars	200	

- Information regarding hotel check-in and check-out times, room reservations and payments, meal plans, and payment procedures.
- Description of planned entertainment and a list of available activities and points of interest to be seen during free time.
- Sports facilities description.
- List of doctors in the area.

Seating plans. Various seating plans should be studied with a view toward the nature of the meeting and number of participants. Is it a panel discussion? A formal sales presentation? An informal brainstorming session? A meeting at which a VIP will give a speech? The next illustration shows you some of the more typical seating plans used at meetings.

When developing the seating plans, set up separate smoking and non-smoking areas. One way to indicate them is by affixing the international "smoking permitted" and "smoking forbidden" press-on signs to pieces of folded poster board and placing them on the appropriate tables. Consider round tables for meals — such tables allow for more relaxed conversation. The longer rectangular tables of the T and U formations are more appropriate for formal gatherings, especially those during which video or slide shows are to be presented.

Companies usually plan morning and afternoon breaks during meetings. For the morning break, usually lasting fifteen minutes, you will have to arrange for coffee, tea, juice, and milk as well as snacks.

Ensure that all tables are covered and that they are set with water pitchers, glasses, ashtrays, pens, and writing tablets. If placecards are to be used, check them against your seating charts just before the meeting begins. If you need audiovisual equipment, screens, flipcharts and markers, slide projectors, lecterns, microphones, recorders, or video machines, give the hotel

Seating Plans for Meetings

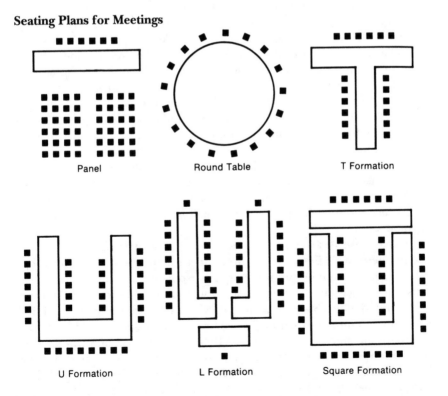

Panel   Round Table   T Formation

U Formation   L Formation   Square Formation

a list of these items and then ensure that they are on hand in the right rooms at the right times. You should find out the dimensions of the screens used with overhead projectors so that the people preparing the transparencies will tailor them to fit the equipment. If the hotel cannot supply all the equipment that you need, check the Yellow Pages for equipment rentals. *Reconfirm* delivery of all rental equipment.

Your role at the meeting. If you are to attend the meeting, you will fulfill many responsibilities which could be grouped under the general heading of *expediter* or *troubleshooter*. You should have several checklists with you on which you have noted the particulars of the meeting plans for each day. Go to the meeting rooms and check the seating, the ventilation, the placecards, the positioning of the equipment, and the arrangements for morning and afternoon break refreshments. Stay in touch with the hotel staff members assigned to your company's event and work closely with them to resolve any last-minute problems. If registration is to take place the night before and early on the first official day of the meeting, be at the registration desk to assist in getting the attendees settled. It is a good idea to hand out a card with your name and room number on it so that anyone who has a problem with a room or a bill can call you for assistance.

You may be asked to assist a speaker with a slide projector, VCR, or an audiovisual projector during a presentation. Take enough time in advance to familiarize yourself with the equipment so that the presentation will run smoothly and professionally. If possible, rehearse the presentation at least once before it is given, especially if you are using a slide projector keyed to a running tape recorder. Be sure that all electrical cords are out of the way; speakers have been known to become entangled in such wiring while walking back and forth during presentations.

If the company has booked a hospitality suite for informal gatherings between events, see to it that the housekeeping staff cleans and airs the room at least once or preferably twice during the day. Stale cigarette smoke and leftover drinks create an unpleasant atmosphere for people who might want to use the suite for phone calls, small informal meetings, or just for relaxation.

You may have to arrange for special secretarial or translation services. Discuss these problems with the hotel; if no help is available, check the Yellow Pages for temporary secretarial persons and for foreign-language translators or schools. Universities are also good sources for translators, as is the United States State Department, which maintains a list of qualified people to accompany foreign visitors on government-sponsored itineraries.

Perhaps the meeting will feature a VIP from the private, political, government, or entertainment sector as a keynote speaker or performer. If this is the case, talk to that person's staff and the hotel staff about any special security arrangements required.

On-site Meetings

On-site meetings can include the following:

1. Sales and other meetings held at corporate headquarters (these involve hotel, restaurant, travel, and entertainment arrangements as indicated in the previous sections).
2. Shareholders' and directors' meetings.
3. Regularly scheduled management and executive committee meetings.
4. Special staff, management, and executive meetings.
5. Employee meetings (such as those called by management to make important announcements).

For regularly scheduled and special meetings you should:

1. Obtain the date, time of day, and location.
2. Reserve an on-site meeting room.
3. Obtain the list of attendees.
4. Prepare and distribute a meeting announcement and an agenda.
5. Alert the attendees and presenters of any special materials that they may have to bring with them.
6. Notify the chair of those who may or will be absent.
7. Just before the meeting is to start (i.e., about thirty minutes ahead of time) check the room for proper ventilation, pens and writing tablets, and the presence of any special equipment that has been requested by the participants).

Sometimes only the members of high-level corporate committees receive copies of the agenda and of the minutes of previous meetings. In such cases, send only a brief memo to the presenters and guests, informing them of the date, time, and location of the meeting and the time at which they are expected to make their presentation(s):

> There will be a meeting of the Publishing Committee at 9 a.m., Tuesday, May 23, 19—, in the Board Room on the 30th floor. Mr. Smith asks that you be prepared to give your presentation from 9:15 a.m. to 9:45 a.m.

Shareholders' meetings. Invitations to shareholders' meetings are very formal and are usually preprinted. They are issued on behalf of the company officers about four weeks prior to the event or at a set time stipulated in the company's by-laws. A proxy form usually accompanies the invitations for use by the shareholders who cannot attend in person. The corporate secretary or general counsel usually handles invitations to these kinds of meetings.

Directors' meetings. If you work in the office of the company chairman or president, you may be called on to issue notices of forthcoming meetings to the board of directors. These gatherings usually occur at a set time during the fiscal year and the procedures in preparation for them are predetermined. Keep a current list of the directors' full names, corporate and home addresses, corporate titles, and telephone numbers. Notify them of the meeting, preferably in writing, at least two or three weeks in advance or in accordance with the provisions of the company's by-laws. Keep a separate list of the directors, in order of seniority on the board, with notations as to the date on which they were notified of the meeting, and a check mark indicating whether or not each person will or will not be able to attend. Total the number of attendees and indicate whether or not a quorum is assured.

You also may have to make arrangements for outside sites for shareholders' meetings. Follow the guidelines given in previous sections of this chapter when doing so. With directors' meetings, you will probably have to make hotel reservations for those living at a distance, and you will be expected to arrange dinners and luncheons for them if your position is in the office of the president or the chairman and chief executive officer.

13

Domestic and International Travel

A GREAT PERCENTAGE of an executive's time may be spent in travel, both domestic and foreign. Of course, the amount of time spent on the road or in the air varies according to the type of business and the responsibilities of the individual manager. These factors, in turn, dictate the amount of pretravel planning time by executive and secretary. Since most trips involve air travel, this chapter will concentrate on that mode of transportation.

TRAVEL ARRANGEMENTS

When an executive tells you that he or she needs to go to a certain destination, some of the questions that must be answered right away are:

1. Where is the destination?
2. How does one get there from here?
3. Where do you look for the necessary travel information or whom do you call?
4. What is the departure date?
5. What is the estimated date of arrival at the destination?
6. What is the date of return?
7. Where is the best place to stay?
8. What travel documents are required (if an international trip)?
9. How much luggage is allowed?
10. What currency is used and what is the basic exchange rate?

In order to locate cities and countries with which you might be initially unfamiliar, we suggest at the outset that you devote one shelf of your bookcase to travel guides, at least two atlases — one international, and the other domestic (i.e., a U.S. road atlas), and current editions of the airline guides discussed later in this section. In many instances you may not have time to go to a library for this sort of information because the executive who travels frequently may have to plan a trip on the spur of the moment.

Obtaining Travel Information

You may get assistance in making travel arrangements from sources such as a travel agency, an in-house travel department, or a company employee designated to handle travel requests. You can also contact airlines, hotels or motels, and car rental agencies directly for up-to-date schedules and rate information. Most airlines, major hotel chains, and car rental agencies have toll-free 800 numbers to call for reservations. If you do not have an 800 phone directory, call 1–800–555–1212 to obtain the 800 number.

Reference publications provide detailed information about transportation and accommodations. Even though travel agencies have this information, you can use these references for preplanning before determining the itinerary and confirming the final reservations.

Official Airline Guide (OAG). This guide contains detailed airline schedules. It comes in two editions — the North American edition, updated twice a month, and the Worldwide edition, updated once a month. Cities are arranged alphabetically and listed by destination. Times are given in local time. Information includes flight numbers, days the flights operate, number and location of stops, type of airplane, food service, baggage allowance, and 800 numbers for airline reservations.

OAG pocket flight guides. These pocket guides are quick references for checking scheduled direct flights. Also included are airline telephone numbers, names of airlines, flight numbers, class of service, type of airplane, and stops en route. The guides, which are updated monthly, are available in four editions: North America, Europe/Middle East/Africa, Pacific/Asia, and Latin America.

OAG Travel Planner Hotel and Motel Redbook. This reference, published four times a year, contains detailed hotel listings, airline and ground transportation information, airport diagrams, country and city maps, and currency conversion rates. A section for each country features a calendar of events, banking and business hours, and travel document requirements. There are two editions — the Pacific/Asia edition and the European edition. A North American edition, *OAG Business Travel Planner,* is also available.

Official Railway Guide. Rail timetables and fares for Amtrak, as well as for trains in Canada and Mexico, are listed in this guide published eight times a year.

Making Reservations

The next thing to do is to determine the degree of flexibility, if any, in the executive's travel plans so that you can obtain the lowest fare. The fare differences applicable to day of week or time of day apply mostly to domestic travel (i.e., travel completely within the United States and some resort destinations, such as those in the Caribbean, Acapulco, or Cancún). Because the executive's time is often limited and is always precious, he or she must often travel during the peak times, but it is certainly worth your while to find out if an off-peak time would still fit the proposed travel schedule.

Since your own time is also valuable, the less spent asking basic questions will allow you more time to attend to other travel details. If you don't have access to the *OAG* or a hotel index, you can still keep your telephone waiting time to a minimum if you know these things in advance: the date of travel, the preferred departure time (such as morning, afternoon, or evening), and the length of stay (approximate, if actual dates are not known; this information may be used to determine fare savings or costs).

When making the actual reservations, you have several options. You can make the reservations directly with the airline, through a travel agency, or through your company's own corporate travel department. In some instances travel agencies have branch offices in large corporations.

If you find that travel is increasing in your company or department, investigate several travel agencies in your area and have one of them set up an account to handle all travel arrangements for you. Most travel agencies will set up such an account for billing purposes, will make all travel and travel-related arrangements for you, will deliver the tickets to your office (and in emergency situations will arrange for airport ticket pickup), and will assist you with international documentation such as visas and tourist cards. They also will provide itinerary sheets with day-by-day reservations and accommodations information. Travel agencies are staffed and equipped to make airline, rail, ship, hotel, rental car, tour, and transfer arrangements.

It should be mentioned here that a travel agency does not charge for the majority of its services because the airlines and hotels pay the agency on a commission basis. The fares charged for an airline ticket purchased from a travel agency will be the same as if the ticket had been purchased directly from the airline. But if the travel agency incurs unusual expenses such as long-distance or international telephone calls for last-minute arrangements or changes, those additional expenses are normally charged back to your company's account.

Of course, you can always make the reservations directly with the airline. In the case of international travel, it is best to get in touch with the airline responsible for the international segment of the itinerary because they have facilities in the destination country through which you can book additional reservations for connecting or continuing travel and hotel accommodations. The airline also can reserve rental cars, request tours, and arrange transfers. As an added convenience, the tickets may be charged to your executive's airline credit card or a major credit card and then mailed to your office or held for pickup at one of the airline's ticket office locations.

Classes of Airline Travel and Types of Flights

Business travelers have three classes of airline services from which to choose: first class, business class, and coach class.

First class is the most pleasant way to travel. The seating configuration is more spacious than that provided for other classes. Some airlines have first-class seating with adjustable foot rests that extend full length to afford a roomy, comfortable seat approximating a bed (in fact, some international airlines do have beds) — a feature greatly appreciated by travelers on long flights, such as transatlantic or transpacific ones. There are many other amenities as well including fine food and complimentary headsets.

Business class is less expensive than first class but slightly more expensive than coach class. However, the difference in price over coach can be well worth the extra dollars because of the desirable accommodations. The roomy seating is usually identical to the first-class seats of those airlines not offering sleeper seats. The service is also more personalized than that of coach. In-flight entertainment headsets are usually complimentary in business class as well. Business class also affords the executive the larger, quieter aircraft cabin for attending to last-minute business details while en route.

Coach class is the least expensive and its seating is less roomy than that found in the business class section. Also, because of the popularity of special fares and tours, the coach-class cabin (or main cabin) is usually more crowded than either first class or business class. First-run movies are shown on virtually all international flights and the headsets for viewing in-flight entertainment must be rented in coach class. Depending on the executive's schedule on the arrival day, coach class can be quite suitable. Of course, some companies restrict the classes of travel to various management levels. You'll have to act within these guidelines if they exist.

Direct flights. If the flight is listed as direct, the plane makes stops in one or more cities, but passengers do not change planes.

Nonstop flights. If the flight is listed as nonstop, the flight has no stops between the departure and the arrival cities.

Connecting flights. A connecting flight stops between departure and destination cities and requires a plane change.

Accommodations

The next travel consideration is the type of hotel accommodations. When traveling internationally, the executive should take into account several hotel rate plans:

1. *Full American Plan*   With this plan, breakfast, lunch, and dinner are included in the price of the room. However, the meals usually must be taken on the hotel property itself and most of the time a particular restaurant within the hotel is stipulated. There may be occasions when several hotels have arranged trades among themselves, offering the traveler diversified meals at different sites. The hotel, of course, can tell you what other hotels, if any, participate in such "trade" plans.

2. *Modified American Plan*   With the Modified American plan, two meals — breakfast and either lunch or dinner — are included in the price of the room. Again, the hotel normally requires that the meals be taken on the hotel property itself, but as with the Full American Plan, reciprocal agreements with other properties in the same city may exist.

3. *Continental Plan*   With this plan, a light breakfast (or continental breakfast) consisting of coffee, juice, and pastries is included in the price of the room.

4. *European Plan*   With the European Plan, no meals are included in the price of the room.

Depending on the individual travel and business schedule, cost savings can be achieved through judicious use of these plans. Adding the cost of the meals to the room rate increases the cost of the room; it could be less expensive in the long run, however, than if the meals were purchased separately. At some locations such as resorts during the peak season, one has no choice of the plans. The various meals are included in the bill whether they are taken or not, and it should be understood that in such a case there is no refund for unused meal plans. This point is particularly important when planning a meeting at a resort during the peak season.

In suggesting hotel accommodations, you will need to keep in mind the nature and scope of the planned activities. Will meetings or appointments be held downtown, or in the "town center," as most European business districts are called? Will the meetings be held at a conference center? Will the scheduled appointments be at several different places throughout a large area? You should have some idea of the type of mobility required before making hotel reservations. If the executive has one appointment and then is scheduled to depart on another flight, suggest accommodations close to the airport or near the train station if the connections out of the city are by rail. If the executive is to be attending a conference, determine the location of the conference hall so that convenient accommodations in the immediate vicinity can be requested. If meetings are to be held in several locations within a large area, suggest accommodations readily accessible to one or more of the meetings places. Good restaurants and shopping areas also ought to be near. Be sure to find out whether or not ground transportation will be required. Most airlines and travel agencies can tell you if taxi service is obtainable. If the executive has several appointments scheduled close together, suggest hiring a private car and driver. The airline or travel agent can arrange that service and provide cost estimates. A private car and driver will be particularly desirable for an executive with a tight schedule.

Hotels normally have noon or early afternoon check-out and check-in times while most flights to and from the United States and European cities depart the United States gateway city in the evening, arriving at their destinations the following morning. During peak travel time or when large conventions are under way, hotels might be booked up and rooms might not be available until some of the guests have checked out. As a result, the executive may have to wait for several hours before the rooms have been cleaned and have been made available for check-in. If an appointment has been scheduled for the same day as the executive's arrival, and if you know that the hotel is heavily booked, reserve a room for the evening *before* the day of the first appointment and ensure that the booking is guaranteed and available for immediate check-in upon the executive's arrival. This procedure will allow the executive time to freshen up, relax, and get settled prior to the first appointment. The extra cost is sometimes half the normal room tariff, but even at the full room rate it is well worth the money. Of course, if the hotel is not filled to capacity, rooms should be readily available for immediate check-in upon arrival. Your job, then, is to find out what the situation is ahead of time.

Car Rental

Car rental agencies use different classifications for their cars, such as deluxe, standard or mid-size, compact, or subcompact. If a car is rented with unlimited mileage, the driver pays a set amount for a designated time period. The payment is not based on the number of miles traveled, as with a limited mileage plan. A liability damage waiver and a collision damage waiver increases the cost of the rental. Most travelers will not need these types of additional coverage if they are covered by their own personal automobile insurance policies.

INTERNATIONAL TRAVEL ARRANGEMENTS

International business travel has increased greatly. Travel agencies provide the best assistance for planning trips to foreign countries. You will need information about travel documents, foreign customs, security, and foreign currency.

Travel Documents

When traveling to a foreign country, a valid United States passport is a must. While some countries require only proof of citizenship, a passport is essential in others, and is, therefore, recommended across the board — especially if several trips are to be made in the course of a few months. The requirements for obtaining a United States Passport follow.

A passport may be obtained by completing the Passport Application form DSP-11, which must be *personally* presented to and executed by a Passport Agent, a clerk of any federal court or state court of record, a judge or clerk of any probate court accepting applications, or a postal employee designated by the postmaster at a post office selected to accept passport applications. If your executive wishes to apply for the passport by mail, the form DSP-82 must be completed. However, the executive must have had another United States passport in his or her name within the past eight years and that passport must be available for submission with the application. Required in court to obtain a passport are proof of citizenship, proof of identity, two photographs, and payment of required fees. When completing the form by mail, send it together with the most recent passport, two photographs, and the fee to one of the Passport Agencies listed in your telephone directory.

Traveler's Advisory: **Travelers should always carry their passports on the person, never packed in their luggage.**

Many countries require a visa or tourist card for entry. The visas are issued by the embassies and consulates of the various countries for a small fee, or in some cases they are free of charge. Be certain to check with the appropriate consulate or embassy or with your airline or travel agent to learn which visas or tourist cards are required for a particular trip; these regulations can change without notice. Since consulates are not located in all United States cities, be sure to allow sufficient time for securing the proper visa application forms, completing them, and applying by mail, especially if several visas are required. It is helpful to maintain a current District of Columbia telephone book if your executive travels abroad a lot; you can find the addresses and telephone numbers of all the embassies in Washington therein.

Under World Health Organization regulations, many countries require that visitors be vaccinated against smallpox, cholera, and yellow fever. While some vaccinations are not required by the World Health Organization, they may be recommended for the traveler's protection. Be sure to consult with your local Public Health Service, your travel agent, or the airline. All vaccinations must be listed on a World Health Organization certificate, obtainable from the Public Health Service in your city. Should the executive be concerned with the possibility of becoming ill during a foreign trip, it is suggested that you contact Intermedic prior to departure from the United States. The organization publishes an international directory of English-speaking physicians. Intermedic's United States headquarters is at 777 Third Avenue, New York, NY 10017; tel: (212) 486–8900. Another suggestion is a membership in the International Association for Medical Assistance to Travelers (IAMAT), a nonprofit, donation-supported foundation located at 736 Center Street, Lewiston, NY 14092; tel: (716) 754–4883. There is no membership fee, although donations are accepted. Upon joining, you are sent a directory of doctors in 450 cities worldwide. All physicians speak English and are available 24 hours a day. A fixed fee is charged for office visits and house or hotel calls. You will also receive world immunization and malaria risk charts.

If the executive is taking special medication, he or she should carry enough of the medication for the duration of the trip, as well as a doctor's certificate verifying the need for the medication. The family physician can provide information relating to prescription refills in case of an emergency. It is a good idea to take along extra medication just in case a business trip lasts longer than expected or in case inclement weather or other untoward circumstances delay the return schedule. As with a passport, the executive should *never* pack medication in luggage that is to be checked in case the luggage does not arrive on the same flight.

Packing and Luggage

Traveling light can add considerably to the comfort and ease of a trip. The travel agent or airline reservations office can assist with updated weather information and can offer suggestions as to the general type and weight of clothing needed. Some countries such as those in the Middle East and parts of Africa have very strict clothing requirements, especially for women, and you should be sure to familiarize the executive with the various social customs and restrictions pertaining to attire. Detailed information can be obtained from the embassies or consulates of these countries.

Choice of luggage is a matter of personal preference, but it is suggested that if possible the luggage be of a size and weight to be carried on board the flight. If the business trip is fairly short, usually all that is needed will be a strong soft garment bag that can be hung in one of the coat closets on board the aircraft or that will fit, folded, into one of the overhead storage bins. A small light bag that will fit beneath the airplane seat can be used for smaller articles. Check with the airline or travel agent for regulations concerning size, weight, or amount of carry-on luggage. If luggage must be checked, be sure that the executive allows sufficient time for airport check-in. The airline or travel agent will provide information concerning minimum check-in times. The airline or travel agent can tell you the maximum weight allowable and pieces that can be checked. This point applies especially to long trips or to trips in which the executive may have to carry special product samples in oversize bags.

Electric current abroad. Throughout Europe, the Mediterranean, and the Far East, the standard electric current is generally 220 volts/50 cycles and the plugs to appliances as well as the electrical outlets differ markedly from ours. If an electric appliance such as a shaver or hair dryer is carried along, the traveler also should take a lightweight, all-purpose transformer and plug adaptor, available at most department or hardware stores.

Currency

Travelers checks are probably the safest and most convenient way to carry money. They can be cashed easily in most cities around the world. And in case of loss or theft, they can be replaced when a report is filed with the bank or agency from which the checks were purchased. And before leaving home, it is always good to have some currency of the host country. Most banks maintain international departments and will exchange dollars for foreign currency. Thus, upon arrival the executive does not have to wait at the airport for a bank to open or queue up to exchange currency. With local currency in hand, one has no delay in getting out of the airport area. Also, one has money for tipping and using pay phones.

The bank when exchanging dollars into foreign currency will usually provide information on the foreign currency purchased, such as denominations and conversion rates. Conversion rates are based on the current buying rate and therefore fluctuate. One day's rate may be slightly more or less on another day. Conversion from dollars to local currency also can be accomplished after arrival at most major cities abroad. Banks and currency exchange booths are located in major airports throughout the world. It should be kept in mind, however, that banking hours vary in different countries. Most hotels abroad can exchange dollars if necessary. However, the conversion rate there may not be as attractive as in the United States since the hotels must pay a percentage to have dollars converted back into the local currency. When you expect to need large amounts of money in a foreign country, it is best to arrange a line of credit with a U.S. bank. Some countries have currency restrictions. Check with the appropriate consulate or embassy for the latest amounts.

Airline Lounges and Clubs

Another item in the list of passenger conveniences is the special private lounge that most airlines maintain at major airports, especially at locations where the airline operates a significantly large number of scheduled flights. The traveler can purchase an annual or lifetime membership. The clubs offer a quiet relaxed setting with easy chairs, sofas, tables, desks, beverage service (in most cases complimentary), and snacks away from the noise and hustle-bustle of the main passenger terminal. After having checked the luggage at the main ticket counter, the traveler can go to the club and check in for the flight. During check-in, the passenger can secure a seat assignment and a boarding pass and then can relax or work while waiting for the flight to be announced. Telephones are readily accessible. Several types of clubs and lounges are available. Some first-class lounges are free of charge for first-class passengers. Most of the clubs, however, charge a membership fee. Membership is valid for the airline's club facilities anywhere in the world that such facilities are maintained.

Language

Most first-time travelers to a foreign country have some concern about language barriers. Every bookstore has foreign-language phrase books for the traveler who is unfamiliar with the language of the country to be visited. It is a courtesy to one's hosts to take a few minutes to learn a few words and phrases in their native language. The executive who has mastered a few common words and phrases not only will please the hosts but also will help get the visit off to a good start. Fluency is not expected; it is the diplomacy and the thought that counts. If necessary professional interpreters can be contracted in advance to translate during meetings and appointments when accuracy is important. The embassy or consulate of the host country can assist in arranging for interpreters' services.

Special Services

If, during a trip, the executive calls you and asks for an important item, there are ways of sending a package abroad quickly and efficiently. Most international airlines have a small package service. A package can be shipped on the next flight for a nominal fee. Special customs clearances are included, but the package should be available for pickup at the destination within a few minutes of its arrival. Check with the airline's small package service for complete details. If you do not find a separate listing in the telephone directory for such a service, the airline reservations office or your travel agent will be able to assist you with the arrangements via telephone. Some of the overnight delivery services such as Federal Express, DHL, and Emery offer similar overseas courier services. Special arrangements can be made through them for electronic transmittal of documents to domestic as well as to international destinations (see the section on electronic mail in Chapter 9).

United States Customs Information

If the executive's permanent residence is in the United States, he or she is allowed an exemption on items for personal use only, providing that he or she has been outside the United States for at least 48 hours and has not claimed an exemption within 30 days. Articles accompanying the traveler in excess of the exemption will be assessed at a flat duty rate. Everything acquired abroad is subject to duty, including items that are used or worn. The goods must accompany the traveler to qualify for exemption. Anything shipped is subject to duty. Included in the exemption are cigars (Cuban cigars may be brought in, provided they were acquired by the traveler in Cuba) and cigarettes. If the traveler is over twenty-one years of age, alcoholic beverages may be included in the exemption. However, some states have restrictions on the number of cigarettes and the amount of liquor that residents may bring back. Families from one household traveling together may pool their exemptions. If the traveler is not a United States resident, an exemption is allowed for gifts accompanying the traveler, providing the stay in the United States is in excess of 72 hours and an exemption has not been claimed within six months.

Antiques and original works of art produced 100 years before the date of entry may be brought into the United States duty free, provided the proper documentation has been obtained to prove authenticity. Galleries and antique dealers where the purchases are made can provide the proper documents with the purchases. Gifts may be sent to the United States free of duty if not more than one parcel per day is addressed to the same person. These gifts (no alcohol, tobacco, or alcoholic perfume, however) need not be declared upon arrival. Fruits, vegetables, plants, seeds, meats, and pets must meet Department of Agriculture or Public Health Service requirements. No one may bring in articles valued over a certain amount or for other than their personal use from Cuba, North Korea, Vietnam, or Cambodia without having a license from the Treasury Department. Wildlife products, such as furs of the cat species and skins of alligators and crocodiles, require special documents to enter the United States. Call the nearest consulate for further details.

There is no limitation in terms of total amount of monetary instruments which may be brought into or taken out of the United States, nor is it illegal to do so. However, if one transports or causes to be transported (including by mail or other means), more than the quota amount in monetary instruments on any occasion into or out of the United States, or if one receives more than that amount, one must file a report (Customs Form 4790) with Customs. Monetary instruments include United States or foreign currency, coin, travelers checks, money orders, and negotiable instruments of investment securities in bearer form. Reporting is required under the Currency and Foreign Transactions Reporting Act of 1970 (Public Law 91–508. 31U.S.C.1101, et seq.). Failure to comply can result in civil and criminal penalties.

Traveler's Advisory: **On trips abroad, be sure to register dutiable items, such as cameras and watches, before departure. This simple step will save you from paying duty on "prior possessions" upon reentry. Registration can be done at the airport or local customs houses in major cities and is valid for life. We suggest keeping all purchases together and having the receipts handy for customs inspection.**

Business Assistance

Throughout the world, the traveler will rarely be too far from communication with an embassy or consulate where expert assistance in arranging local business contacts can be obtained. United States Chamber of Commerce offices that also can be helpful are located in many international cities. Major sources of information in the United States are

World Trade Information Center
Department 1AB
One World Trade Center
New York, NY 10048
(212) 435-4170

Bureau of International Commerce
U.S. Department of Commerce
Washington, DC 20230
(202) 482-2000
(or one of the 43 district offices)

Find/SVP
625 Avenue of the Americas
New York, NY 10011
(212) 645-4500

Information or guidance on business matters also may be obtained from the Economic or Commercial Attaché of any United States embassy or consulate, special overseas trade office, or Chamber of Commerce office abroad.

International Marketing Centers are located in many cities. The marketing centers can provide free information, and, for a nominal fee, office space, a desk, telephone, secretarial services, and an interpreter for a maximum of five days. (The secretarial and interpretative services, however, involve an additional fee.) This service also includes the use of audiovisual equipment and a display rack for samples or brochures. Free local telephone service and access to telecommunications are usually provided too.

A telephone call or visit to the Commerce Department District Office in your state will enable you to make arrangements in advance. A similar service is also available at Export Development Offices, Trade & Commercial Offices, East-West Trade Support Offices, and Chamber of Commerce Offices in many countries. Other useful information can be gained by contacting the commercial officer at the embassy or consulate of the host country.

Itineraries and Appointment Calendars

One of the best aids to the traveling executive is a well-prepared itinerary and schedule of appointments. It is always good to note on the appointment schedule the time differences, if any, so that the executive will know what time it is at home. During a business meeting, if something should arise that warrants a telephone call, the executive can decide when to call the home office. The appointment list also should include the name, address, and telephone number of the limousine service (if any); the name of the driver (if known); the name, address, and telephone number of each hotel; and the name, address, and telephone number of each appointment.

In developing business relationships, it is always advisable to learn in advance as much about the people being visited as possible. Some information can be obtained from the person who has originally set up or suggested the meeting. Another source of information is the international edition of *Who's Who*. If the host is a government official, the local consulate or embassy can usually provide appropriate personal background information. This information should be listed in the order that the appointments are to occur and can be put on small index cards for the executive to review. Having some knowledge of a foreign colleague's interests and family can be of great assistance in getting a meeting off to a pleasant, diplomatic start. For information on preparing an itinerary, refer to Chapter 5.

Transportation Abroad

Public transportation is far more widely used abroad than it is in the United States. Urban and interurban bus travel, especially within Europe, is excellent, and if time permits between appointments, it is an excellent alternate means of travel. Europe and the Far East have some of the most modern, efficient, comfortable, and well-run train networks in the world. Another mode of transportation to consider is a rental car. Reservations for rental cars can be made through your local travel agent, the airline, or the car rental office in your city, for most of the major rental car agencies have offices throughout the world. All countries of Western and Central Europe and the Far East accept a valid driver's license from any state in the United States. An International Driving Permit, required by some countries, can be obtained for a small fee through the American Automobile Association. Driving is not as difficult as might be expected. One drives on the right-hand side of the road in most countries except ones such as the United Kingdom and Ireland. All countries have adopted the International Road Signs.

TRIP FOLLOW-UP

Expense Reports

Sit down with the executive and go over the itinerary sheet as soon as possible after the trip is over. Having kept a copy of the itinerary and having made pertinent notes as the executive has called in during the trip, your own follow-up tasks now should be easier. No doubt the executive will have made notes on the itinerary regarding expenses. If additional currency exchanges have taken place abroad, the rates will usually differ, either from day to day or from city to city. This factor will obviously affect the bottom line of the expense reports. In converting foreign currency to dollars, be sure to use the currency conversion rate that was charged. Remember to take into consideration tips for porters at airports and hotels, and doormen at hotels and clubs. Any cash paid out as tips should be noted. If you remind the executive about the tips, other cash expenses that might not be supported by receipts will come to mind at the same time. If payment for hotels, meals, or limousines was made with a major credit card, it is advisable to complete as much of the expense report as possible and hold it pending receipt of the credit-card charges. (The credit-card accounting office converts the foreign currency to dollars for billing.) If your company prefers that all expenses be submitted immediately upon return, always mention in the Purpose of Trip section of the expense report that a supplemental expense record will follow as soon as all credit-card billings have been received.

Follow-up Correspondence

While going over the itinerary with the executive after the trip, request all business cards that the executive has received during the course of the trip. Put the names, addresses, corporate titles, and phone numbers of the card bearers into the executive's Rolodex. During the review, make a note of any letters of appreciation that should be written. Were any special arrangements made by the host, such as limousine transportation, flowers or fruit baskets in the hotel room, dinners at the host's home or at a club or restaurant, or special tours? Just a short note of thanks will suffice:

Dear Mr. Giraud:

My sincere thanks for the courtesies you extended on my behalf during my recent visit to Paris. The welcome that I received from your fine staff on check-in certainly made me feel right at home. It was especially thoughtful of you to provide the excellent bottle of wine.

The kindness of your personnel was greatly appreciated, and I am looking forward to returning to Paris soon.

Sincerely yours,

Martin I. Benson
President

If the executive has called in during the trip, review any notes made during the course of the conversations. Will some time elapse before plans or agreements made abroad can be put into final form? If so, a note to this effect is called for, reassuring the foreign business colleague that while some work still may be pending, the arrangements discussed are nevertheless proceeding on track:

Dear Mr. Johnson:

Thank you again for the time you afforded me on Thursday, January 19, to discuss our proposal. I have passed the information and changes along to our legal staff for incorporation into the final analysis. As soon as these changes have been approved by the Board, we will be in contact with you.

The many courtesies and kindnesses extended on my behalf during the course of our discussions are greatly appreciated.

Sincerely yours,

Martin I. Benson
President

Written Reports

In reviewing the itinerary, take the opportunity to keyboard all notes or comments made by the executive. Prepare these notes immediately for the executive's review, together with a list of all business cards received. In this way the executive will have raw travel data in a readable, well organized format for reference in writing any post-trip reports. As soon as the executive has given you the full information for the post-trip report, type a draft for editing, additions, and other changes. By following the suggestions outlined, you will be in a position to provide the executive with a problem-free, efficiently scheduled, and productive business trip.

14

Accounting and Data Processing

THE EVOLUTION, over several hundred years, of the practice of accounting as a means of enabling businesses to keep track of past events and provide them with useful information for making future decisions has been important to business expansion in the 1980s. Every business must handle certain financial and tax matters, and subsequently keep records of these transactions as well as report them to various persons and groups outside the organization, including government agencies. A secretary is often required to perform many of the daily functions related to these types of financial transactions. This chapter is intended to help you become familiar with certain accounting principles and definitions, as well as with specific procedures related to recording the transactions in the company's books.

BASIC ACCOUNTING PRINCIPLES

Accounting is called the language of business. The first step in mastering any language is to learn its rules and the meanings of its terms. Present-day accounting practice has produced a number of generally accepted principles which standardize both terminology and methods of recording the activities of the business. This standardization allows a company's accounting reports to be meaningful to managers, bankers, stockholders, creditors, government agencies, and others interested in its financial reports. These generally accepted principles provide the "language of business" that is understood by a diverse group of individuals.

Dual Aspect Concept

If you had to determine the financial status of a business or individual, you might ask, "What does it (or the individual) own of value?" The items of value that a company owns are called *assets*. A company's assets are entered in the records at their original cost to the company, indicating that the value of the assets is equal to their cost. Over time, certain items owned by a company increase or decrease in value. Once an asset is recorded at its original cost, however, it is almost never adjusted to a current market value. Such adjustment could require continual revaluation to reflect the almost daily changes in the real or current market values of a company's numerous assets. Moreover, who could determine the real worth to a company of its desks, carpets, or calculators? This would be a difficult and time-consuming task. Therefore, accounting records are rarely adjusted to reflect the actual or current market value of an asset as opposed to its book (cost) value. Assets owned by a company may include the following:

Cash (in the bank as well as petty cash)

Accounts Receivable

Marketable Securities (stocks, bonds, certificates of deposit)

Prepaid Items (insurance, rent deposits)

Property, Plant, and Equipment (land, buildings, equipment, furniture, fixtures)

Inventory (raw materials, work in process, finished goods)

The money or funds used to acquire assets is provided either by the owners of the company or by creditors of the company. Creditors are individuals or companies that lend money or extend credit to a business for a period of time. When this occurs, they acquire a claim of that amount against the business. Because a business will use its assets to pay off these claims, the claims are *claims against assets*. If a business refuses to pay a claim, the person to whom it is due can sue the business in a court of equity. Thus, *all* claims against assets are called *equities*. A court of equity will usually hold the business liable for the amount of the claim. This helps explain the accounting term for the equity of a creditor, *liability*. Any asset not claimed by a creditor will be claimed by the owners of the business. These claims are called *owners' equity*. The total of all claims cannot exceed what there is to be claimed. This leads to the dual aspect concept: *Assets = Equities* or *Assets = Liabilities + Owners' Equity*, also known as the basic accounting equation:

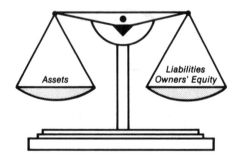

Monetary Concept

An accounting system records only those events that can be expressed in terms of dollars; e.g., the purchase of land or equipment, or the sale of inventory for cash or on account. On the other hand, the morale and health of company personnel cannot be expressed in dollar terms and the accounting system does not consider such factors. Thus, a company's accounting records do not reveal all the facts, or even all the important facts, about a business. The records show only events that have taken place and that can be expressed in monetary terms. The belief that accounting reports tell everything that one needs to know about a business is, therefore, incorrect.

The Business Entity

Accounting records are maintained for the business entity, as opposed to the persons who own, operate, or are otherwise associated with the business. Records reflect only what is happening to the company and not the personal transactions entered into by the people related to the company. For example, if the owner of a business buys a home, this purchase has no bearing on what is happening to the business, since the owner is an entity distinct from the business entity. A business may be operated under any one of several legal forms, such as a corporation, a partnership (two or more owners), or a proprietorship (one owner). Regardless of legal status, the business entity concept applies.

The Accrual Principle

The accrual principle is based on the fact that net income of a business is not related to the flow of cash but rather to changes in the owners' equity resulting from operations of a business. Revenue of a business adds to the owners' equity and expenses decrease the owners' equity. The difference between revenue and expenses is the company's net income. (See later sections of the chapter for additional explanations.)

Other Concepts

Two other generally accepted principles relate to the accrual concept. The first one states that *revenue* is recognized when goods are delivered or when services are performed. This is called the *realization concept.* It does not specifically relate to when cash is received for the sale of goods or services. The second concept, called the *matching concept,* states that *expenses* of a period are costs associated with the revenues or activities of that period. The expenses do not relate to the actual cash disbursements for those expenses.

Most entities account for revenues and expenses as well as cash receipts and cash payments. Many individuals and some small businesses keep track only of cash receipts and cash payments. This type of accounting is called *cash accounting.* If you record your deposits, the checks you write, and your balance in a bank account, you are doing cash accounting. In order to measure the income of a period, we must measure revenues and expenses, and this requires the use of accrual accounting. Accrual accounting is more complex than cash accounting but it is the only one that measures true changes in owners' equity.

ACCOUNTING REPORTS

Accounting information is given to third parties external to the company on three main financial statements. The first, called the balance sheet, shows a company's assets and liabilities and owners' equity at a given point in time. It is like a snapshot, capturing the company's financial position at a specific moment, while recognizing that events may soon occur that will change certain aspects of the items of value that a company owns, as well as claims against those assets by creditors and owners. The presentation shown in the first illustration is fairly typical, although it is also common to find the assets listed on the left-hand side and the liabilities on the right-hand side of a page. In any event, the dual aspect principle is followed, and the total dollar amount of assets will equal the total amount of liabilities and owners' equity. The totals, however, are not indicative of the company's financial condition. It is only after analysis of the various accounts listed on the balance sheet that we can come to any conclusions about the financial health of a company.

The second statement, the income statement, presents the results of a company's operations for a given period of time — a month, three months, or a year. The last day of that period will be the date of the balance sheet information accompanying the income statement. The income statement is also known as the profit and loss report, P & L, or operating statement. In any case, the statement shows sales, the cost of the specific goods or services sold, the other costs associated with selling the goods or services, and the resulting profit or loss (net income, bottom line, or net profit). Thus, this statement shows all sources of revenue generated by the company's operations as well as all related expenses incurred to generate that revenue, following the accrual, matching, and realization concepts. The format and specific revenue and expense classifications will vary but the income statement in the illustration on page 332 is fairly typical.

The third financial statement (see page 333) is the statement of changes in financial position. Although this financial statement is required by certified public accountants, it is not commonly used by persons within a company. The statement presents the results of financing and investing activities of a company for the same period of time covered by the income statement. This information helps inform its readers about events that have occurred within the company but that are not reflected in the other two financial statements (i.e., are not related to the items a company owns at a specific

Andrew Manufacturing Company
Balance Sheet
December 31, 1992

<u>Assets</u>

Current Assets

Cash		$ 10,000
Marketable Securities		13,000
Accounts Receivable, net		72,000
Inventories		101,000
Prepaid Insurance		3,000
Total Current Assets		199,000

Fixed Assets

Land	$120,000	
Buildings	500,000	
Furniture and Fixtures	73,000	
Equipment	104,000	
	797,000	
Less: Accumulated Depreciation	407,000	
Total Fixed Assets		390,000

Other Assets

Long-term Investments	93,000	
Long-term Receivables	10,000	
Goodwill, net	72,000	
Other Assets	17,000	
Total Other Assets		192,000
TOTAL ASSETS		$781,000

<u>Liabilities & Owners' Equity</u>

Current Liabilities

Accounts Payable		$53,000
Bank Loan Payable		100,000
Accrued Wages and Salaries Payable		7,000
Current Portion of Mortgage Payable		5,000
Taxes Payable		10,000
Total Current Liabilities		175,000

Long-term Liabilities

Mortgage Payable	$200,000	
Bonds Payable	150,000	
Total Long-Term Liabilities		350,000
Total Liabilities		525,000

Owners' Equity

Common Stock	100,000	
Retained Earnings	156,000	
Total Owners' Equity		256,000
TOTAL EQUITIES		$781,000

Andrew Manufacturing Company
Income Statement
for the year ended December 31, 1992

Gross Sales		$3,600,000
Less Sales Returns, Allowances, and		250,000
Discounts		
Net Sales		3,350,000
Less Cost of Goods Sold		1,650,000
Gross Profit		1,700,000
Less Operating Expenses		
Selling, General, and Administrative		
Expenses		
Insurance	$12,000	
Office Salaries	311,000	
Selling Expense	175,000	
Heat, Light, and Power	23,000	
Advertising	165,000	
Telephone	57,000	
Office Supplies	17,000	
Automobile Expense	30,000	
Bad Debt Expense	97,500	
Travel Expense	133,000	
Depreciation Expense	20,000	
Miscellaneous Expense	53,500	
Total Selling, General and		1,094,000
Administrative Expenses		
Research and Development Costs		250,000
Other Operating Expenses		16,000
Total Operating Expenses		1,360,000
Operating Profit		340,000
Other Income and Expenses		
Interest Expense	100,000	
Interest Income	(73,000)	
Miscellaneous Income	(10,000)	
Total Other Income and Expenses		17,000
Profit Before Taxes		323,000
Provision for Corporate Income Taxes		147,000
Net Income		$ 176,000

point in time and are not related to the results of operations for a period of time). This financial statement is also known as the source and application of funds statement, or the "where got-where gone" statement. Because it is not commonly used within a business, we will not go into any more detail about its construction or use. Refer to an accounting text for additional information about the statement of changes in financial position.

Before we go into more depth about the types of accounts included in

Andrew Manufacturing Company
Statement of Changes in Financial Position
for the year ended December 31, 1992

Resources Were Provided by:

Operations	$176,000	
Add: Items Not Affecting Working Capital Depreciation	20,000	
Total Resources Provided by Operations		$196,000
Increase in Mortgage Payable		75,000
Sale of Common Stock		50,000
Total Resources Provided		321,000

Resources Were Used To:

Purchase Fixed Assets	153,000	
Acquire Long-term Investments	43,000	
Pay Mortgages Payable	25,000	
Total Resources Used		221,000
Net Change in Working Capital		$100,000

Changes in Working Capital	Increase (Decrease) in Working Capital
Current Assets	
Cash	$ 30,000
Marketable Securities	(10,000)
Accounts Receivable	30,000
Inventories	(19,000)
Prepaid Insurance	3,000
Current Liabilities	
Accounts Payable	(30,000)
Bank Loan Payable	100,000
Accrued Wages and Salaries Payable	(2,000)
Current Portion of Mortgage Payable	—
Taxes Payable	(2,000)
Change in Working Capital	$100,000

the balance sheet and income statement, we should elaborate on the accounting period being covered by the income statement. For most businesses, the official accounting period is one year. Income statements, however, called interim statements, usually are prepared for shorter periods as well. Most companies have income statements prepared on a monthly basis to report the operation of the business during the past month. Thus, the accounting period covered in a monthly income statement is one month. The report is prepared from information accumulated in the accounts of the business. Information often must be reported to various government agencies and banks on a monthly or quarterly basis, so income statements are often generated for these reasons as well.

As we mentioned earlier, the official accounting period is usually one year and for most companies, it is the calendar year; that is, the year which ends on the last day of the calendar, December 31. Some companies, however, end their year at the end of their busy season. This is called a fiscal year end. For example, colleges and universities usually have a June 30 year end. Retailers often end their year at the end of January. Sports-related businesses end their year at the end of the month that their season ends. The accounting period for these businesses is the natural business year, not a calendar year. Of course, companies do not fire their employees and cease operations at the end of an accounting period; they continue from one accounting period to the next. The fact that accounting chops the stream of events into a set period makes the problem of measuring revenue and expenses into that period one of the most difficult problems in accounting, but it does not affect the daily operations of the company. In rare instances, an accounting period may extend beyond one year if the business activities of the company extend beyond twelve months from the time the transaction is initiated until it is completed. This situation occurs in companies dealing with long-term contracts or in those companies whose production processes are lengthy. If your company falls into this category, the accounting period and the income statement covered by it may extend beyond twelve months.

Balance Sheet Accounts

A balance sheet showing a number of items becomes more useful when the items are classified into significant groups of assets and liabilities. It would, of course, be possible to list each individual account receivable, each inventory item owned, each piece of equipment, and each account payable, but this usually provides much more detail than is needed for a balance sheet analysis. For the practical purpose of making the balance sheet more informative, items are grouped into classifications. There is no limit to the number of classifications, but the ones shown in the facsimile are the common ones.

Current assets. The first balance sheet classification is current assets. The current assets classification includes cash and other assets which can reasonably be expected to be realized in cash or sold or consumed during the normal operating period of the business, usually one year. Current assets can be subclassified as indicated in the following list:

1. *Cash* This includes all cash owned by a company, including cash in the bank (in a checking or savings account), petty cash, and so on. The amount of cash a company has will change through the receipt of cash for sales and the payment of bills with cash (or checks). An adequate amount of cash is vital to a company's survival and sufficient

amounts should be available to meet the immediate needs of the company's operations.

2. *Marketable Securities* If a company has more cash on hand than is needed for the immediate future, it may use the excess cash to purchase short-term investments such as certificates of deposit or stock or indebtedness of other companies. The investing company earns short-term returns such as interest or dividends just as an individual's savings account in a bank earns interest. These investments can be readily sold in the marketplace and converted back into cash on very short notice.

3. *Accounts Receivable* This account often comprises a large portion of a company's current assets and represents amounts of money owed to the company by its regular customers. It is collectible within the next twelve months. This account is reported as its net value, which means that the actual value of the receivables has been reduced by an amount equivalent to the company's expectations of receivables that will not be paid. A company maintains detailed records of accounts receivable by customer in a subsidiary accounts receivable ledger. This subsidiary record has a page devoted to each customer and lists all sales "on account" as well as cash collections related to these sales. The total of every page balance in the subsidiary ledger is shown as the amount owed to the company as total accounts receivable.

4. *Inventories* Inventories often represent the largest portion of current assets for a company. For manufacturing firms, inventories include raw materials to be converted into a finished product, work-in-process inventories that include partially completed products, and finished products ready for sale. Inventories generally cannot be converted into cash as quickly as receivables, since it takes time for the goods to be sold (usually resulting in an account receivable) and for the cash to be collected.

5. *Prepaid Items* This represents prepayments for resources such as rent, interest, insurance, deposits, and so on, that will be used up during the next twelve months. Since they have not yet been used up or consumed, they still are assets (items of value) to the company. They are rarely converted into cash (although conversion is possible) and are therefore listed last under current assets.

Fixed assets. The next major asset classification is fixed assets, which may also be called plant assets; property, plant, and equipment; or tangible fixed assets. Fixed assets are relatively long-lived assets that are held for use by the business in the production of goods or sale of goods or services. They are not acquired for resale in the ordinary course of business but must have a useful life of at least one year. The reported value of fixed assets is based on the amount it cost the company to acquire them, called the historical or acquisition cost. Items in this category include:

1. *Land*   (on which the company may have already constructed buildings)
2. *Buildings*   (office or plant locations used in routine business operations)
3. *Equipment*   (office or production machines used by the company)
4. *Furniture and Fixtures*   (desks, chairs, and similar furnishings used by company personnel)

Fixed assets other than land are assumed to have limited lives because time, obsolescence, and normal use eventually reduce their benefit to the business. Those assets are therefore called depreciable assets. The process of allocating the cost of these assets ratably to the accounting periods in which they are consumed and benefit the company is called depreciation. Depreciation expense is taken each accounting period as an expense on the income statement and results from an attempt to systematically allocate the asset's acquisition cost over its anticipated useful life. The depreciation accumulated from all previous periods appears on the balance sheet as a reduction of the related fixed asset account cost. This yields the presumed fixed asset value to the company at the balance sheet date.

The estimated useful life of an asset is an estimate and is subject to many uncontrollable external factors such as obsolescence, technological advancements, and unexpected wear and tear. Therefore, the balance sheet value of fixed assets does not necessarily represent the value a company would receive if the asset were to be sold at the balance sheet date.

The Internal Revenue Service does not use depreciation but has a similar, although not identical, system called the "Accelerated Cost Recovery System," or ACRS. This system allows companies to recover their asset cost by taking deductions on their tax returns at a more rapid pace than allowed for book or internal financial statements.

Other assets. This is the last major asset classification and, if used at all, contains miscellaneous assets difficult to classify as either fixed or current assets. Investments, long-term receivables, and goodwill are examples of assets that the company intends to hold for more than one year. Investments may include securities of other companies that the business has invested in or that the employer owns or controls. Long-term receivables may indicate the sale of expensive items for which payments are spread out over more than one year. Goodwill is associated with the price paid by one company to purchase another; the selling price paid by one company to purchase another company is often higher than the value of the net physical assets acquired. The excess amount paid is called goodwill and reflects the purchaser's belief in the company's potential to earn high profits.

Current liabilities. Recall that liabilities are claims of creditors against the assets of the business. Current debts or obligations that must be paid or otherwise settled within one year or the normal operating cycle of a business are called current liabilities. These are the company's most immediate obligations, and cash or other current assets are necessary to liquidate them. These claims are usually not against a specific asset of the company. Within the classification of current liabilities there are several subclasses:

1. *Accounts Payable* This represents amounts owed to ordinary business creditors for unpaid bills for inventory and supplies. If the claim is evidenced by a note or other written document, it is usually segregated as a note payable.
2. *Bank Loan Payable* This represents money owed by the company to its bank. Because it is shown as a current liability, it implies that it is payable within one year.
3. *Accrued Salaries and Wages Payable* This refers to amounts owed to employees of the business at the time the balance sheet was drawn up. An example of this is when employees are paid on a weekly basis, and the balance sheet has been drawn up at a point during one of the pay periods. As a result, wages and salaries owed to employees but not yet paid to them are recorded as a liability.
4. *Current Portion of the Mortgage Loan Payable* This amount represents the portion of the mortgage principal (not interest) payable within twelve months of the balance sheet date.
5. *Taxes Payable* This amount is owed to the federal, state, or local government for taxes due on income, payroll, inventory, etc., but not yet paid.
6. *Unearned Revenues* These are obligations to provide goods or services to customers who have made advance payments. For example, subscription receipts that have been received by a magazine publisher in advance of sending the magazine issues are unearned revenues. Rent that is received in advance by a landlord is still another example of these types of liabilities.

Long-term liabilities. These claims against assets are due to be paid after the next twelve months. This category includes: property mortgages payable, long-term loans payable, notes payable, and bonds or debentures payable. Unlike accounts payable, these liabilities tend to be evidenced by formal documents indicating a definite obligation to pay at some future time. Often long-term liabilities are a guaranteed claim against some specific assets, known as a *lien*. Any portion of long-term payables becoming due within one year from the balance sheet date should be included in the current liabilities category. Any amount recorded here represents the principal amount due only. These types of obligations usually have an interest payment associated with them; the interest due is not recorded on the balance sheet, however, because interest relates to the use of money or funds over time. Interest is not initially recorded until your company has had the use of someone else's funds for a period of time. Then the expense is recorded in the income statement and the payable recorded separately as a current liability.

Owners' equity. This section of the balance sheet represents claims made against the assets by the owners of the business and is simply the portion of the company not claimed by anyone else. It is also known as book value or net worth. The manner of reporting owners' equity on the balance sheet depends on the type of business for which the balance sheet is prepared. As previously mentioned, a business may be organized as a single proprietorship, a partnership, or a corporation.

The owners' equity section of Andrew Manufacturing Company indicates that it is organized as a corporation. Corporations are created under and regulated by state and federal laws. These laws require that a distinction be made between the amount invested in the corporation by its owners (the original shareholders) and the increase or decrease in owners' equity due to daily operations. The former, called common stock or capital stock, is entered on the balance sheet at its stated value, which might be the price paid for the stock, its par value, or some other figure agreed upon at the time the stock was issued or sold. Subsequently, there is no relationship between the recorded value and the market value of the stock. The latter, called retained earnings, reflects the earnings of the company from daily operations in prior years that have been left in the business and have not been paid out to the owners in the form of dividends. The word *surplus* was used in place of retained earnings in the past but is not in current use today. Retained earnings or accumulated amounts of net income belong to and are a claim of the company's owners and are always shown after common stock in the owners' equity section of the balance sheet.

When a business is owned by one person, it is called a sole or single proprietorship and the single owner's equity may be reported on the balance sheet in either of the following ways:

a. Ryan Andrew, capital $256,000

b. Ryan Andrew, capital, January 1, 1992 $200,000

Net Income for the year ended December 31, 1992	$323,000	
Withdrawals	267,000	
Excess of earnings over withdrawals		56,000
Ryan Andrew, capital, December 31, 1992		$256,000

When two or more persons own a business as partners, changes in their equities resulting from earnings and withdrawals are normally shown in a supplementary financial statement entitled the Statement of Partners' Equity. Only the amount of each partner's equity and the total equities are shown on the balance sheet itself:

Partners' Equity

Ryan Andrew, capital	$128,000
Daniel Andrew, capital	128,000
	$256,000

Thus, in the owners' equity section of the balance sheet, capital (cash or assets) contributed by the owners of the company as well as earnings accumulated since the business began are accumulated as claims against assets.

Income Statement Accounts

Sales. The first entry on the income statement is the sales for the period. It is customary to show gross sales revenue earned by the accrual method and then to deduct any returns, allowances, and discounts given during the period to arrive at net sales. By showing sales returns and allowances separately, attention is called to any unusual amounts (increase) shown in this category.

Sales revenues are inflows of cash and other assets received from others for goods exchanged or services performed. The result is an increase in total assets, a decrease in total liabilities, or a combination thereof. Terms such as *income, revenue, earned,* and *received* preceded by a noun such as *rent, interest,* or *commissions* identify a revenue source. Revenues derived from sales to customers are often described as sales revenue, fees earned, or commissions earned in the income statement. Other revenues unrelated to customer sales include commissions earned, dividends received, interest income, rental revenue, and so forth.

Expenses. In accounting, expenses are considered as the outflow of cash or other resources of the business during a specific period of time. The accrual principle is followed. Expenses relate to the consumption of assets or the incurrence of debt for goods or services consumed by the company in order to produce revenue. The common classifications of expenses are:

1. *Cost of Goods Sold* This represents the cost of goods purchased for resale as well as the cost incurred in manufacturing products for sale to customers. This category should include, to the extent possible, only the costs associated with goods sold during the current accounting period. In a manufacturing company, they include raw materials, direct labor, and manufacturing overhead. Manufacturing overhead

includes all allocated product-related costs other than raw material and direct labor including indirect labor, fringe benefits, supervision costs, plant rent, insurance, freight, light and power, plant depreciation, quality assurance, shipping, and so on. The cost of any goods remaining on hand at the end of the period is shown as inventory in the current assets section of the balance sheet.

2. *Gross Profit*   This represents the amount of sales revenue recognized in excess of the cost of goods sold. This amount must exceed the amount of all remaining expenses of operating the business if the business is to be profitable. Gross profit is also known as gross margin.

3. *Operating Expenses*   Operating expenses are incurred in the normal operations of the business. Operating expenses are not incurred to produce a product; rather, they are considered costs of the period. They are often subclassified by function, such as selling and distribution, research and development, and general and administration expenses. Selling expenses include all expense incurred during the period to perform the sales activities of the firm. Such expenses include salaries paid to sales people, commissions, rental of sales facilities, depreciation on sales equipment, and advertising costs. General and administrative expenses are those incurred during the year in administering overall company activities. They often include office supplies used, officers' salaries, depreciation of the office building and equipment, rental of office space, property taxes, legal fees, accounting fees, office employee salaries, and related fringe benefits. Research and development (R&D) expenses are incurred by the company in pursuit of further improvement of existing products or development of new products. These expenses include salaries of R&D personnel, facilities and equipment expense, and other like expenses incurred for research and development efforts.

4. *Operating Profit*   This represents profit earned from the normal business operations of the firm. It represents sales revenues minus the cost of goods sold and operating expenses. Operating profit also may be called income from operations or net operating revenue.

5. *Other Income and Expense*   These are nonoperating sources of revenues or expenses, not resulting from the daily operations of the business. They include items such as interest income from investments, interest expense on loans or other outstanding debts, profit or loss on the sale of fixed assets, and revenue from nonrelated business operations. They are listed separately to highlight their difference from other revenue and expenses related to the business' primary operations.

6. *Profit Before Taxes*   This is the net difference between all revenues and expenses of the business and also may be called income before taxes.

7. *Provision for Corporate Income Taxes*   Included in this line classification are all federal corporate income taxes. Local and state taxes are sometimes included here as well. If not, they are included with general and administrative expenses. If the company is a sole proprietorship or partnership, the business pays no taxes. Rather, the owners include their pro rata share of the business profit (or loss) on their personal tax returns and pay taxes on this profit individually.

8. *Net Income*   Also known as net profit or "the bottom line," net income represents the amount of profit the company has earned for the period covered by the income statement.

PROCEDURES

Now that you are familiar with accounting as the language of business, you are better able to perform the many duties and functions that you may be called on to do. Included in them are activities related to handling cash such as recording cash receipts and disbursements, controlling petty cash, or performing a bank reconciliation; recording investments in securities; and recording the acquisition of fixed assets. We will go into some depth about performing each function, but first let's explore the various data-gathering accounting information systems.

Accounting Systems

An accounting system consists of all the business papers, records, reports, and procedures used in recording and reporting transactions. Actually an accounting system is a data processing system and it may be manual, mechanical, electronic, or, as is the usual case, a combination of all three. The three approaches may be described briefly as follows.

Manual data processing. With this approach, the accounting work is performed by hand (i.e., manually). This type of system is used extensively in small businesses and for certain parts of the information process in medium- and large-sized businesses. In larger companies, it is useful for discussing and illustrating the application of accounting concepts and principles as well as for explaining the accounting process. The writing-copying-posting procedure when performed manually accomplishes its objectives but is often time-consuming and error-prone. Therefore, procedures that reduce the number of times information is copied and recopied improve the system.

One such system is the one-write, or pegboard, system. It is designed to process all or a large portion of the data of the transaction with one writing. This can be done with payroll, sales, purchases, cash receipts, and cash disbursements. For payroll, the paycheck, employee earnings record, and payroll register are all recorded simultaneously via a system of alignment of documents and carbon copies. Similarly for credit sales, the entry on the customer's month-end statement, the posting to his or her account, and the entry in the sales journal are all made at once.

Mechanical data processing. When repetitive transactions occur in large numbers, mechanical processing of accounting data is often used. Cash registers, adding machines, calculators, and posting machines or punched card equipment are typical of this type of processing. One electric accounting (posting) machine can be used for sales accounting, cash receipts, cash disbursements, accounts payable, payroll, and other accounting applications. When used in sales accounting, for example, the machine will produce the invoice for each charge sale, post to the customer's individual account, update the statement to be sent to the customer at month-end, and enter the sale in the sales journal, all in one operation.

Electronic data processing (EDP). This method uses computers of varying sizes and sophistication (large mainframes to micro- and minicomputers) to process information in a rapid, usually inexpensive fashion. This equipment has a large capacity to store data and the capability to manipulate and recall data with great speed. Electronic data processing involves the use of hardware (the central processing unit and related peripherals) and software (the computer programs that give instructions to the computer as well as other related items for system operations such as training material). The EDP equipment in use today performs many functions that accounting needs, such as arithmetic procedures (add, subtract, multiply, and divide), memory storage (file maintenance), memory recall, comparison of information, repetition of the same set of instructions, and making yes/no decisions.

Computers process data with speed and accuracy. Before a computer can do this, however, a human being must think through the procedures that the computer will use in processing the data, anticipate every processing exception, and then instruct the computer in great detail how to do the job. Although computers are a big help in the processing of accounting information, they are only as good as the people programming them and the correctness of the data being processed. Remember, computers — and those who input data into them — are not infallible.

The Accounting Process

The basic accounting process is the same for all businesses, large and small. The purpose of an information processing system is to facilitate the accu-

The Basic Accounting Record-Keeping System

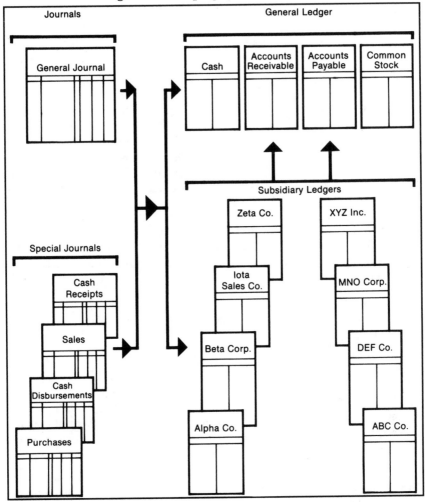

mulation of data needed to make decisions and to prepare financial statements. The basic components of that information processing system, whether manual or electronic, are the same and are shown in the illustration on this page. The components of the system include:

Component	Purpose
General journals and special journals	For formally recording the data obtained from the analysis of individual transactions.

General ledger

For accumulating and summariz-ing the data recorded in the jour-nals in terms of the dual aspect concept for the balance sheet and income statement accounts. There is a separate account page for each general ledger account.

Subsidiary ledgers

To provide a detailed analysis of the balance in a specific general ledger account (accounts receiv-able, notes receivable, marketable securities, inventories, fixed assets, and notes payable).

When a company must record hundreds or thousands of similar transac-tions such as credit sales or purchase of materials, the information process-ing system must handle the transaction as efficiently as possible. This makes the use of special journals which record and summarize like transactions advantageous.

Transaction	Special Journal
Purchase of merchandise or raw materials on credit	Purchases journal
Cash payments	Cash disbursements journal
Credit (and sometimes cash) sales	Sales journal
Cash collections	Cash receipts journal

The formats of special journals vary depending upon the needs of manage-ment. The two special journals we discuss in detail are typical examples but may be modified to meet management's goals for cost and time savings.

The cash receipts journal.   Used to record all cash receipts of the company, this journal is designed to handle not only payments of credit and cash sales but also other revenue sources. The procedures to follow in recording cash receipts are performed daily (see the illustration on pages 346–347):

1. Enter cash received in the cash receipts journal, listing the amount, date, and source (columns 1–3).
2. If the receipt is in payment of a prior credit sale, record the amount in column 5 and record the customer account number from the ac-counts receivable subsidiary ledger in column 4. Someone also should record the receipt on the individual customer's account card in the subsidiary ledger.
3. If the customer in #2 above paid less than the full invoice price be-

cause he or she took an allowable discount for paying within a certain period of time, note the amount of discount taken in column 6.

4. If the receipt is for a cash sale, record the amount in column 7.

5. Each miscellaneous cash receipt is recorded in columns 8–11. Record the general ledger account and account number in columns 8 and 9 (e.g., receipt of proceeds from *bank loan,* sale of old *equipment,* or sale of *marketable securities*). Record the amount in column 10 or 11. (Someone should record the receipt in the specific general ledger account as well.)

6. The columns in the cash receipts journal are totaled on a monthly basis and the totals are recorded in the general ledger accounts. (The total of the miscellaneous account column is not recorded in the general ledger since it represents the sum of amounts already recorded in several different accounts.) Each month, start a new page in the cash receipts journal. Number each page sequentially.

The cash disbursements journal. This journal is used to list all checks written during the period. A sample format is shown in the illustration on pages 348–349. The procedures that should be followed in recording cash disbursements are:

1. Enter each check in the journal in sequential order in columns 1–4.

2. Most checks will normally be issued in payment of a previously recorded account payable. If this is the case, record the amount in column 6 and record the vendor account number from the accounts payable subsidiary ledger in column 5. Someone also should record the payment on the individual vendor account card in the subsidiary ledger.

3. If the payment in #2 above is less than the full invoice price because the company took an allowable discount for paying within a certain period of time, note the amount of the discount taken in column 7.

4. Any other payments should be entered as a miscellaneous payment in columns 8–10. Record the general ledger account and account number in columns 8 and 9 (e.g., payment of *rent, repairs, utilities, notes payable, interest* expense). Record the amount in column 10. (Someone should also record the payment in the specific general ledger account.)

5. The columns in the cash disbursements journal are totaled on a monthly basis and the totals are recorded in the general ledger accounts. (The total of the miscellaneous amount column is not recorded in the general ledger since it represents the sum of amounts already recorded to several different accounts.) Each month, start a new page in the cash disbursements journal. Number each page sequentially.

Andrew Manufacturing Company

Cash Receipts Journal				
			Accounts Receivable (Credit)	
Date	Source/Explanation	Cash Received (Debit)	Subsidiary Ledger Reference No.	Amount
12/4/92	Alpha Co.-Invoice			
	412	723	1011	730
12/7/92	Cash Sale	471		
12/12/92	Sales of Marketable			
	Securities	2000		
12/20/92	Zeton W.-Invoice			
	422	973	9008	1000
12/21/92	Bank Loan	4500		
12/30/92	Delta Co. Invoice			
	425	524	2013	550
		9191		2280
Col. 1	Col. 2	Col. 3	Col. 4	Col. 5

These procedures do not change the basic accounting concepts or process discussed previously. They simply are used to make the recording and summarizing of financial/accounting information more efficient. They are shown as they would apply to a manual system, but the same journals and ledgers can be generated in an EDP system. Such records may be simplified for a small company or greatly expanded for a larger, more sophisticated accounting system; the system should be designed to meet the needs of the company's managers and owners. Now let's continue with specific procedures that you may be asked to perform in the areas of bank reconciliations, petty cash, fixed asset control, and investment record-keeping.

Bank Reconciliation

The bank reconciliation is a comparison of the information contained in the bank's monthly statement with the company's own cash accounting rec-

Cash Receipts Journal

Sales Discount Taken (Debit)	Cash Sales (Credit)	Other Miscellaneous Receipts			
		Account		Amount	
		Title	Acct. No.	Debit	Credit
7					
	471				
		Marketable			
		Securities	105		2000
27					
		Bk. Loan	575		4500
		Payable			
26					
60	471				6500
Col. 6	Col. 7	Col. 8	Col. 9	Col. 10	Col. 11

Note: Column 3 = Column 5 + Column 7 + Column 11 − Column 6
9191 = 2280 + 471 + 6500 − 60

ords. A separate reconciliation should be prepared for each bank account. It should be prepared promptly upon receipt of the bank statement and canceled checks included with the statement. The canceled checks should be compared to the company's cash disbursements records to ensure that the checks have been made payable to the proper person or company (payee) and have been written for the proper amounts. The bank's list of deposits should be compared to the company's cash receipts records and the company's copies of the bank deposit slips to verify that all cash receipts have been properly deposited.

Because of timing differences between the company's recording of cash receipts and disbursements and those reported in the bank's statement, the ending cash balance in the company's records and the cash balance re-

Andrew Manufacturing Company

Cash Disbursements Journal			
Date	Check Number	Explanation/Payee/Invoice No.	Amount of Cash Paid (Credit)
12/12/92	7031	ABC Co.-No. C3704	1313
12/17/92	7032	R. W. Walp-rent	1100
12/20/92	7033	QRS Co.-No. 11078	728
12/21/92	7034	Bank Loan Interest	300
12/27/92	7035	Acton Water Dept.	152
12/30/92	7036	XYZ Co.-No. KBQ3	111
			3704
Col. 1	Col. 2	Col. 3	Col. 4

ported in the bank statement will usually differ. The sources of these differences are called *reconciling items*. The purpose of the bank reconciliation is to identify the reconciling items, and, by making the proper adjustments, to determine the correct cash balance.

Bank Reconciliation Procedures

1. Gather the current month's bank statement and canceled checks; the prior month's reconciliation; the checkbook or check register listing checks written during the period and the cash balance at month end; and the record of deposits or the company's copy of the month's deposit slips.
2. Trace all canceled checks and bank memorandums to the bank statement to ensure that there are no differences.
3. Put the canceled checks returned by the bank in numerical order.
4. Compare the canceled checks to the prior month's outstanding check list and the current month's listing of checks written by the company. Make a list of outstanding checks at the end of the current month.

Cash Disbursements Journal

Accounts Payable (Debit)		Purchase Discount Taken (Credit)	Other Miscellaneous Payments		
Subsidiary Ledger Reference No.	Amount		Account		Amount (Debit)
			Title	Acct. No.	
A 1002	1313	—			
			Rent	733	1100
			Expense		
Q 1772	750	22			
			Interest	602	300
			Expense		
			Water	939	152
			Expense		
X 0001	125	14			
	2188	36			1552
Col. 5	Col. 6	Col. 7	Col. 8	Col. 9	Col. 10

Note: Column 4 = Column 6 + Column 10 − Column 7
3704 = 2188 + 1552 − 36

5. List information from the bank memorandums for inclusion in the bank reconciliation.
6. Compare deposits per the bank statement with the company's copy of the deposit slips or other listing of cash receipts. Note differences for inclusion as deposits in transit.
7. Complete the bank reconciliation in a format used by your place of business.
8. Correct or adjust the company's records as needed. Notify the bank of any errors they have made.

Petty Cash Fund

Many companies maintain small amounts of cash on their premises to cover small disbursements when it is impractical to write a check or when cash is needed immediately. These petty cash funds may cover the purchase of office supplies, postage, coffee, and so on. Also known as an *imprest fund,* the

Petty Cash Voucher

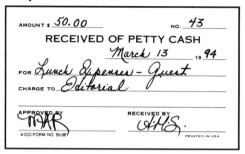

petty cash fund is normally established at an amount sufficient to cover two to four weeks of needs and is usually between $100.00 and $500.00. When the amount is determined, a check payable to Petty Cash is made out and cashed, and the cash is then placed in a locked box or drawer under the control of a custodian having sole responsibility for the fund. All expenditures from the petty cash fund should be made by the custodian, and adequate documentation should be maintained to support the payments. Often a petty cash voucher (purchased from any stationery store) is used for such documentation. The voucher shows the date, purpose of the expenditure, the department or account to be charged, the signature of the person receiving the cash, the signature of the person disbursing the funds, the amount disbursed, and a sequential voucher number. (This information may be maintained on a separate disbursement sheet rather than on petty cash vouchers, but that practice is less common.)

At any time, the amount of cash on hand plus the amount of disbursements noted on the petty cash vouchers should equal the established amount of the petty cash fund. When the cash in the fund is low, it should be replenished by writing a check to Petty Cash for the amount needed to restore the fund to its authorized amount. The check is cashed and the proceeds are placed in the petty cash box. The fund is now back at its original amount and is ready for use once again.

INVESTMENT TRANSACTIONS

Many organizations invest in stocks, bonds, and other vehicles to earn a return on excess funds. It is important for you to record properly all information related to these transactions not only for the company's financial records but also to comply with governmental agency requirements. When handling security transactions, you should maintain the following documents or files:

Andrew Manufacturing Company
Record of Security Transactions

Security _____

Exchange Listed on _____

Broker _____

No. of Shares	Date	Purchase/ Sale	Price/ Share	Broker's Commis.	Total Purchase Price Paid/Sales Price Rec'd

Cap. Gain or (Loss) on Sale		Bal.	
Short-term	Long-term	Shares Owned	Total Cost

1. A separate record should be kept for each security owned, and the records should be kept in alphabetical order. All investment activity should be posted as it occurs. (See the illustration, "Record of Security Transactions," on this page.)
2. An alphabetical list of all investments in securities owned should be compiled and updated on a weekly, biweekly, or monthly basis, depending on the volume of investment activity. (See the illustration, "List of Securities Owned," on page 352.)
3. A file of all brokers' trade advices should be kept. It is the basis for recording information in the individual security records. (A *trade advice* lists the purchase or sale of a specific investment including the trade date, settlement date, purchase/sales price, broker's commission, and security being purchased/sold.)
4. A file should be kept of monthly brokers' statements that are verified by tracing to the individual security records maintained by the company and noting agreement of month-end information.
5. A record of interest or dividend income received based on actual cash receipts and deposits into the cash account should be kept. (See the illustration, "Record of Interest and Dividend Income," on page 352.)
6. Security certificates should be kept in a locked vault with access limited to a very few people. Access to the securities should never be permitted to fewer than two authorized persons accompanying each other.

Andrew Manufacturing Company
List of Securities Owned
December 31, 1992

Number of Shares or Face Value	Security Name and Description	Total Cost	Current Market Value
Stocks:			
Bonds:			
Investment Funds:			
Other:			
Totals:		$	$

Andrew Manufacturing Company

Record of Interest and Dividend Income
Period Covered _____

Interest Income (grouped by security)

Security	Date Received	Amount	Annual Total

Dividend Income (grouped by security)

Security	Date Received	Amount Received	Annual Total
	qtr 1		
	qtr 2		
	qtr 3		
	qtr 4		
	qtr 1		
	qtr 2		
	qtr 3		
	qtr 4		

FIXED ASSETS RECORDS

Records of plant assets having a productive or service life beyond one year must be maintained to ensure the proper safeguarding of company-owned assets and to allocate properly the cost of the asset to the appropriate period the asset is benefiting (depreciation). A fixed asset record should be fully completed. (See the illustration on this page.)

The estimated life of a fixed asset is the period of time the asset is used in producing or selling other assets or services. This period of time varies by type of asset (i.e., buildings, equipment, furniture, or fixtures) but is usually standardized by company policy. Salvage value is that portion of the asset cost that is expected to be recovered at the end of the asset's productive life.

Allocating the cost of the asset over its service life (depreciation) can be done by many methods. Four of the more common methods are straight line, units of production, declining balance, and sum-of-years-digits:

1. When the straight line method is used, the cost of the asset minus the estimated salvage value is divided by the asset's productive life in years or months. This method allocates an equal share of the asset's cost to each accounting period.
2. The units of production method divides the cost of an asset after deducting estimated salvage value by the estimated units of product that the asset will produce over its service life. This process gives depreciation per unit of product. Depreciation for the period is determined by multiplying the units produced in a period by the unit depreciation.

Andrew Manufacturing Company
Fixed Assets Record

Asset Description _____
Purchase Date & Vendor _____
Purchase Price (including freight and installation costs)

Asset Location _____
Asset Identification Number _____
Estimated Life _____
Depreciation Method _____
Annual/Monthly Depreciation (if applicable)

Estimated Salvage Value _____
Disposition Date _____
Sales Price When Sold _____

Year	Original Cost	Depreciation Expense	Net Book Value	Sales Price	Gain or (Loss) Upon Disposition

3. Under the declining balance method, depreciation of up to twice the straight line rate, without considering salvage value, may be applied each year to the declining book value of a new plant asset having an estimated life of at least three years. If this method is followed and twice the straight line rate is used, the amount charged each year as depreciation expense is determined by (1) calculating a straight line depreciation rate (100% divided by the useful life in years) for the asset; (2) doubling this rate; and then (3) at the end of each year in the asset's life, applying the doubled rate to the asset's remaining book value.

4. Under the sum-of-years-digits method (SYD), the years in an asset's service life are added and their sum is used as the denominator of a series of fractions used in allocating total depreciation to the periods in the asset's service life. The numerators of the fractions are the years in the asset's life in their reverse order. For example, if the SYD method is used to depreciate an asset having a five -year life and a cost of $6,000.00, the following is used to calculate depreciation:

Number of years for the denominator = 1 + 2 + 3 + 4 + 5 = 15

Year	Annual Depreciation Calculation	Annual Depreciation Expense
1	5/15 × $6,000	$2,000
2	4/15 × $6,000	1,600
3	3/15 × $6,000	1,200
4	2/15 × $6,000	800
5	1/15 × $6,000	400
		$6,000

15

Business Law

LAW IN THE OFFICE ENVIRONMENT

A professional secretary in a law office will be exposed to the intricacies of the legal system and will be called on to understand the many peculiarities of legal form and style as well as some of the substantive framework of that system. While the secretary in a general business office will not have as great a need for an in-depth knowledge of law and the legal system, general knowledge of certain legal concepts will enable the secretary to deal more effectively with the legal issues that do arise in the business context. You may be called on to prepare documents intended to have legal effect, and the form chosen or the formalities followed in executing the documents may be critical. Familiarity with general principles of contract law, agency, and corporate law may assist you in dealing with various documents or issues that frequently arise in the business office. You also should be aware of a number of statutes and regulations generally applicable to the conduct of a business. While this chapter is not intended to address all of the issues of legal form and style or provide an exhaustive treatise on business law, it does explain a number of those areas of the law that frequently arise in a business office environment in order to give you an awareness of the legal implications of your work and to assist you in understanding the meaning and purpose of common legal documents, words, and regulations.

CONTRACTS

The law of contracts is basic to business law, as the negotiation, preparation, execution, and enforcement of contracts are the foundation for much of the conduct of business. In the office, an understanding of the elements of a valid contract and its legal formalities will aid you when you are called on to prepare a document or assist in its execution. It may also be helpful in connection with aspects of office management in matters ranging from ordering supplies and purchasing equipment to dealing with personnel functions.

General Principles

Stated simply, a *contract* is an agreement that is legally enforceable. It can be created by an oral promise or a written document, or it can be implied where the circumstances indicate. It is not always necessary that there be a formal, written agreement for a contract to exist. The factors necessary to create an enforceable agreement include *parties* who are competent to contract; an expression of the *terms* of the agreement; and *consideration* for the agreement. In addition, the object of the contract must not violate any public policy or statute.

There are two issues relevant in determining whether a party is competent to contract: whether the party has any legal disability and whether the party has the proper authority to enter into the particular contract in question. The issue of authority to enter into the particular contract depends on the circumstances of the situation. An agreement made by an individual who is legally competent will be binding on the individual. Agreements made by corporations or other business entities will be binding if they are executed by officers, agents, or employees who have been authorized to bind the company, either under rules of agency or by specific corporate action. You may want to refer to the section on Agency that appears later in this chapter for a fuller discussion of this issue.

There are no specific rules on the expression of the terms of the agreement, although this criterion is often expressed as a requirement that there must have been a "meeting of the minds" to create a binding contract. That is, there must be sufficient evidence that the parties had reached an agreement even though all of the terms and conditions are not clearly defined. Although the parties' failure to express adequately the terms of their agreement can result in a finding that no contract exists, more often a court will attempt to reconstruct what the parties intended at the time they entered into the contract. In certain instances, some of the terms of an agreement will be provided by statute if the parties have not expressed them. This is particularly true with regard to sales of goods under the Uniform Commercial Code, discussed in a later section of this chapter. It is generally more satisfactory, however, if the terms of the agreement are clearly expressed by the parties. Such a statement need not be extensive. An offer by a merchant of a certain product for a specified price and an acceptance of that offer by a customer by tendering payment or submitting a purchase order will be a sufficient expression of the terms of an agreement. More extensive provisions will be necessary in more complicated relationships.

Consideration for a contract most commonly consists of payment in exchange for services or goods or of a promise in exchange for another promise. Except in limited circumstances, if there is no consideration or if the consideration is regarded as inadequate, the contract will not be enforceable. The law considers that a promise not supported by consideration is a gift rather than a binding obligation and the courts will not compel a party effectively to make a gift. In spite of this rule, a contract "under seal" is considered enforceable without regard to consideration. Further, the courts will rarely look behind a statement in a contract that the parties consider the consideration to be adequate.

Formalities

A well-written agreement should follow certain rules of form, some of which relate to the elements described previously and some of which are simply good business practice. Many of the following suggestions relative to form can be varied to meet a particular situation or to suit an individual's style and are intended to serve as a general guide.

Introductory clauses. The agreement should begin with an introductory clause that describes the agreement and identifies the parties. Some circumstances require inclusion of the full address of each of the parties and, even where such information is not required, it is good practice to include the information. The introductory clause also provides an opportunity to assign a short descriptive term to each of the parties, such as "Buyer" and "Seller," as a means of easy reference throughout the agreement. The date of the agreement also should be stated, either in this introductory clause or in the testimonium clause described later. A common form of introductory clause is as follows:

> This Agreement is made this third day of February 1992 by and between Hemingway Incorporated, a Delaware corporation with a usual place of business in Boston, Massachusetts (hereinafter called the "Company"), and Peter F. Trombley, of 123 Park Street, Newton, Massachusetts (hereinafter called the "Consultant").

The manner of identifying a party will vary depending on the legal status of the party. An individual should be identified by his or her name and, usually, residence address. If the individual is in business as a sole proprietor and the agreement relates to the business, the business address should be used.

A corporation should be identified by its registered name, state of incorporation, and principal place of business. The name of the corporate officer who will be signing on behalf of the corporation should not appear in the introductory clause. The description of the corporation can be in the form indicated in the preceding example, or a more formal approach may be used:

> . . . Hemingway Incorporated, a corporation duly organized and validly existing under the General Corporation Law of the State of Delaware, and maintaining a usual place of business at 73 Tremont Street, Boston, Massachusetts . . .

For any number of reasons, a corporation may be organized under one name and actually conduct its business under an assumed name. If the information is available, it should be included as follows:

> . . . Hemingway Incorporated, a Delaware corporation doing business in California as Hemingway Business Forms, Inc., and maintaining a usual place of business at 1999 Wilshire Boulevard, Los Angeles, California . . .

Professional corporations should be identified by their corporate names in the same manner as business corporations.

General partnerships in most jurisdictions are not considered legal entities apart from the individual partners, and for purposes of bringing suit each of the general partners must be named. A general partnership usually conducts its business under a trade name, however, and may be referred to by such trade name for purposes of most agreements, especially where there are a large number of general partners. For example:

> . . . Thayer & Crispin, Attorneys-at-Law, a general partnership engaged in the practice of law . . .

It is also appropriate to identify each of the general partners:

> . . . Jean G. Thayer and Sandra Crispin, general partners engaged in the practice of law under the name of Thayer & Crispin . . .

Limited partnerships are in many respects more similar to corporations than they are to general partnerships. A limited partnership consists of one or more general partners who manage the business and can bind the partnership, and one or more limited partners who have no managerial authority. The partnership must adopt a name that must be registered, usually with the secretary of state. The limited partnership should be identified by its registered name, and the state of registration should be stated.

There are a number of different types of trusts, including general trusts, business trusts, and realty trusts. Generally, a trust does not have a separate legal identity and an agreement involving a trust should be made in the name of the trustee:

> . . . James P. Overmeyer, as trustee of the Adam Thomas Family Trust and not individually . . .

Similarly, where a contract is made by any other fiduciary, such as the guardian of a minor, the conservator of an incompetent, or the executor of a will, the fiduciary should be named as a party and clearly identified as acting in a fiduciary capacity.

Recitals. It is common practice to recite the background of an agreement, the relationship of the parties, or other facts that tend to clarify the basis for each party entering into the agreement. In addition, a recitation of the consideration for the agreement is often made, either as part of the preliminary recitals or in the body of the agreement (or both). Recitals generally take one of the following forms, the first of which is the more traditional:

WITNESSETH:

WHEREAS, Seller has developed and markets a software program relating to legal time and billing which has been adapted for use on the XYZ personal computer; and

WHEREAS, Buyer is a law firm which has need for a legal time and billing program for use on its XYZ personal computer and desires to acquire a license to use Seller's program;

NOW, THEREFORE, in consideration of the payment of the licensee fee by the Buyer to the Seller and of the mutual covenants and promises set forth herein, the parties agree as follows: . . .

or:

Recitals.

1. The Seller is in the business of manufacturing head-sets for use with tape recording equipment and has the capacity to produce in excess of 5,000 headsets per week.

2. The Buyer is in the business of marketing tape recording equipment to the general public and has need for head-sets which can be used with its equipment;

3. The Buyer desires to reserve the Seller's capacity to produce 5,000 headsets per week on the terms and conditions of this Agreement.

The Parties therefore agree as follows: . . .

Body. The body of the contract will contain all of the provisions relating to the actual terms of the agreement. There are no general rules as to form or style other than general rules applicable to all business documents, discussed elsewhere in this book.

Testimonium. The testimonium is the clause that appears at the end of the body of the contract and prior to the signatures of the parties. Such a clause, in its various forms, serves to affirm that the parties are aware that they are entering into an agreement and that they intend to be bound by the terms of the written document they are signing. Common forms of testimonium clauses follow:

> IN WITNESS WHEREOF, the parties have hereunto set their hands and seals to this Agreement the date and year first set out above.

> IN WITNESS WHEREOF, the parties have executed this Agreement in duplicate the 4th day of June 1992.

For business entities:

> IN WITNESS WHEREOF, the parties have caused this Agreement to be executed by their duly authorized officers on the 1st day of February 1993.

> The said Joseph P. Smith, as trustee of the Smithfield Realty Trust, and the said George A. Grey, as President of George A. Grey Associates, Inc., have signed this Agreement this 3rd day of April 1992.

Frequently, the testimonium clause will state that the parties have "set their hands and seals" or that the document is to have the effect of a "sealed" document. The concept of a sealed document derives from early common law, which provided that the presence of a seal eliminated the need to prove that there was consideration to support the contract. The effect of a seal and its necessity under current law depend on the circumstances and the applicable law of the jurisdiction. Most commonly, you will see an actual seal where a corporation is a party and the seal is used to prove corporate authority. Most jurisdictions provide by statute that a statement to the effect that a document is sealed is sufficient to give it the force of a sealed document, even if no seal is actually affixed.

Signatures. The agreement should be signed by a natural person who is a party or who is authorized to bind a party. The signatory's name should be typed below the signature line and, except where an individual is signing on his or her own behalf, the authority of the person who is signing should be indicated. An example of the proper form for execution of a document by a corporation is as follows:

Hemingway Incorporated

By _____
   James P. Jacobs, President

As a general rule, an agreement on behalf of the following entities should be signed by a person who fills one of the indicated positions:

Entity	Permissible Signatory
Corporation (including professional corporations)	Corporate Officer
General Partnerships	General Partner
Limited Partnerships	General Partner
Trusts	All Trustees, unless there is evidence of authority to act alone
Estates	Executor or Administrator

Frequently, one person is a party to a contract in more than one capacity and where this is the case the best practice is to have the person sign the document on separate lines for each capacity. At a minimum, the description under a single signature line should make it clear that the person is signing in more than one capacity.

Attestations. Although not always required, signatures are often attested by witnesses to the signing. This can be helpful if later there is some doubt as to who actually signed or the circumstances under which the document was signed. An attestation can simply be the signature of the witness under the word "witness" or an attestation clause can recite any information that is relevant, such as the following:

> Signed, sealed and delivered by the above-named Peter Gregory, in my presence, at Boston, Massachusetts, this 3rd day of June 1992.

Signatures of corporate officers are often attested by the corporate clerk or secretary to verify that the corporation has authorized the document to be signed. The attestation takes the following form and the corporate seal is embossed over the attestation:

Attest: [Corporate Seal]

_____

Clerk / Secretary

Acknowledgments. Some documents, most notably affidavits or documents dealing with real property, must be acknowledged before a public official such as a notary public or judicial officer qualified to administer oaths. An acknowledgment executed by a public official has the effect of verifying the facts stated in the acknowledgment, without the necessity to prove them by testimony. Frequently used forms of acknowledgment follow:

State of _____   December ___, 19___
County of _____

Then personally appeared the above-named James P. Jacobs and acknowledged the foregoing to be his free act and deed, before me,

_____
Notary Public

State of _____   December ___, 19___
County of _____

Then personally appeared the above named James P. Jacobs, Vice President and General Manager of Hemingway Incorporated, and acknowledged the foregoing instrument to be the free act and deed of the corporation, before me,

_____
Notary Public

State of _____
County of _____

On the ____day of _____, 19____, before me personally came James P. Jacobs, to me known, who, being by me duly sworn, did depose and say that he resides at _____; that he is the Vice President and General Manager of Hemingway Incorporated, the corporation described in and which executed the above instrument; that he knows the seal of said corporation; that the seal affixed to said instrument is such corporate seal; that it was so affixed by authorization of the board of directors; and that he signed his name thereto by like authorization.

_____
Public Official

The form of acknowledgment for an affidavit or other statement of facts should appear substantially as follows:

State of _____
County of _____

The undersigned, Lynn F. Green, known to me and known to be the person who executed the foregoing document, personally appeared before me this ____day of _____, 19____, and stated that the facts stated therein are true to the best of her knowledge and belief.

_____
Notary Public

If the affidavit includes a statement by the affiant that the statements contained therein are true to the best of his or her knowledge and belief, it is sufficient to add just the notary jurat at the end of the document after the signature of the party offering the statement. This should include a statement of the venue (state and county) and the language, "Subscribed and sworn to before me," a well as the notary's signature and seal.

AGENCY

The law of agency is concerned with a number of issues raised when an individual acts on behalf of another party. These issues should be of some concern to the secretary from at least two perspectives. On the one hand, contract law and business relationships raise a number of questions — such as who is able to bind a corporation contractually — which involve issues of agency. On the other hand, an employee is considered for many purposes to be an agent of the employer and, especially where he or she has administrative or managerial responsibilities, the secretary should be aware of the potential consequences of his or her actions as an agent of the employer.

Legal Principles

An *agent* is an individual authorized to act on behalf of another party. The party on whose behalf the agent acts is called the *principal.* Where a valid agency exists, the agent can bind the principal and the principal will be responsible for the acts of his or her agent which are within the scope of the agency or which occur in the course of the agent's fulfilling his or her duties as agent. In some forms of agency, the principal's liability to third parties for the acts of an agent may extend to acts not directly related to the agency, such as when an employee is involved in an automobile accident during the course of making a delivery for the employer, and to acts not expressly authorized by the principal, such as when a managerial employee refuses to hire an applicant because of the applicant's race.

The scope of authority of an agent depends on the terms of the agency. In some cases, the agent's authority is a legal consequence of the relationship of the parties. Hence, corporate officers are agents of the corporation, and general partners are agents of their fellow general partners and of the limited partners in a limited partnership. In each of these cases, the agent's authority to act for and bind the principal exists only to the extent that the agent is acting within his or her role as corporate officer or general partner, as the case may be. Unfortunately, it is not always clear whether the agent was acting within this role and that issue often leads to serious disputes. In other principal-agent relationships, the scope of the agent's authority is created by an express agreement and is, consequently, more clearly defined. For example, a homeowner may retain a real estate broker to find a buyer for his or her house at a certain price. The broker is the agent of the homeowner only for that limited purpose and clearly is not authorized to otherwise act for the homeowner.

Generally the agent is able to bind a principal contractually only to the extent that he or she acts within the scope of the agency. To some extent, third parties who deal with the agent do so at the risk that the agent is acting outside the scope of his or her agency. Where it is not clear from principles of agency that the agent is authorized to act as a consequence of his or her relationship to the principal, or where there is otherwise any question of authority, a third party will often require evidence of authority, such as a certificate signed and sealed by a corporate clerk certifying the adoption of a resolution by the board of directors that authorizes a specific corporate action or certifying that the officer signing an agreement is either generally or specifically authorized to do so.

There are some circumstances under which an agent can bind a principal even without express authority. The authority to do related acts may be implied from the express authority given to the agent, such as where an office manager's authority to hire a receptionist may imply the authority to fire the employee. In addition, an apparent agency may exist where the circumstances lead a third party reasonably to believe that the apparent agent has the authority to act for another person who could but who does not do anything to deny the agency. In some situations, a person will ratify the acts of another who purported to be his or her agent and thereby create an agency by ratification. In each of these cases, the determination of whether an agency exists depends on the particular facts.

The extent of the principal's liability for the acts of an agent which are not within the scope of the agency depends in large part on the degree of control the principal exercises over the agent. The strictest agency relationship is commonly referred to as a *master-servant relationship,* and exists where the principal exercises significant control over the conduct of the agent, such as by setting hours of work, providing tools or equipment, and supervising the work performed. It generally applies to employer-employee relationships. As a result of the high degree of control and close supervision, the employer is liable not only for authorized contractual commitments made by its employees on its behalf but also for accidents and personal injuries caused negligently or intentionally by them in the course of their employment. The employee need not be actually performing work for the employer at the time he or she causes personal injuries or similar damage; so long as there is a reasonable link between the activity and the employment, the employer may be liable. In other types of agency relationships where the principal exercises a lesser degree of control over the actual performance by the agent, such as those involving independent contractors, the scope of the principal's liability is correspondingly smaller. Even where the principal is liable to third parties for injuries caused by an agent, however, the agent is primarily liable to the injured party or, where the injured party recovers from the principal, the agent may be required to reimburse the principal.

Powers of Attorney

Many agencies are created by the use of powers of attorney. A power of attorney is a written document by which another person is specifically authorized to act for the person signing the document. Where a person is authorized to act for a definite and specified purpose, he or she is often referred to as an *attorney in fact* for such purpose. There is no particular form that must be used to create a power of attorney, although certain governmental entities — most notably the Internal Revenue Service — have issued printed forms which they require to be used in connection with matters brought before them. Any document intending to serve as a power of attorney should contain a clear statement of the powers and duties of the attorney in fact. In executing the power of attorney, the formalities required to effectively complete the act should be observed. For instance, if the attorney in fact is given the power to execute a deed, an act requiring an acknowledgment by an official, the power of attorney must be likewise acknowledged. It is always good practice to provide an attestation by witness even though it may not be legally required, as it may avoid questions later concerning the signature of the principal granting the power of attorney.

Execution of Documents

Whenever an agent is acting for a principal in the execution of a document, whether under a power of attorney or other agency, it is important that the fact of the agency be expressed. If it is unclear whether the agent is acting for himself or herself or for a principal, the agent may be personally liable on the contract. It is also possible that the principal will not be liable at all, which may be to the detriment of both the agent and the third party. A discussion of various forms of execution of contracts by agents on behalf of principals is contained earlier in this chapter and is applicable where the agent is acting under a power of attorney or any other agency relationship.

UNIFORM COMMERCIAL CODE

The Uniform Commercial Code (UCC), a collection of laws relating to commercial transactions, has been adopted in varying forms in most states. It is intended to provide for relatively consistent regulation of commercial transactions among the various jurisdictions. Our discussion focuses on two of the areas covered by the UCC, transactions involving sales of goods and secured transactions, as these are likely to be most relevant in the business environment.

Sales

Article 2 of the UCC applies to transactions involving sales of goods and has two basic functions. Most broadly, it establishes standards of fair dealing among buyers and sellers primarily by imposing an overriding obligation of good faith and commercial reasonableness in sales transactions. Article 2 also provides definitions of commonly used commercial terms that serve to clarify the expectations of the parties and standardize the usage of terms in the commercial world.

In addition to this general role, Article 2 has a more practical application. Although the law gives the parties wide freedom to set the terms of their agreement, it also recognizes that parties occasionally fail to provide for all contingencies. There are numerous situations where the UCC will come into play unless the parties otherwise agree. For instance, Article 2 contains rules for determining, in the absence of an express agreement, whether an offer has been made and accepted, where the goods are to be delivered, what warranties are given or implied, the buyer's right to inspect and reject goods, the seller's right to withhold shipment, and remedies for breach by either party. Frequently, the parties will intentionally omit a provision in a contract knowing that the UCC will govern or will specifically refer to the relevant section of Article 2 and incorporate its provisions into the agreement.

Security Interests

When your business finances the purchase of office equipment or similar items, or if the company takes out a loan for other purposes, the lender will usually require a security interest in the items financed or in the assets of the corporation. Article 9 of the UCC governs the creation of security interests and provides for a filing procedure by which such interests are perfected.

A security interest is created by the agreement of the parties. The agreement should be in writing and signed by the debtor. The parties are generally free to set the terms of the security agreement, although certain provisions of Article 9, primarily with respect to the rights of third parties, will override contradictory provisions in a written agreement. Generally, a security interest gives the secured party the right to repossess the collateral if payments are not made or if the debtor is otherwise in default and to receive the proceeds if the collateral is sold. If the security interest is perfected, as explained below, the secured party can repossess the collateral even if it has been sold or transferred to a third party.

A security interest is enforceable against third parties only when it has been perfected. Except in very limited circumstances, a security interest is perfected by filing a financing statement with the appropriate govern-

Uniform Commercial Code Financing Statement–UCC = 1

Uniform Commercial Code — FINANCING STATEMENT — Form UCC-1

IMPORTANT — Read Instructions on back before filling out form

This FINANCING STATEMENT is presented to a filing officer for filing pursuant to the Uniform Commercial Code.

4. ☐ Filed for record in the real estate records	5. ☐ Debtor is a Transmitting Utility	6. No. of Additional Sheets Presented:
1. Debtor(s) (Last Name First) and address(es) Gorham Enterprises One Park Place Arlington, MA 01000	2. Secured Party(ies) and address(es) Smith Leasing Co. 155 Wagner Road Arlington, MA 01000	3. For Filing Officer (Date, Time, Number, and Filing Office)

7. This financing statement covers the following types (or items) of property:

Xerox Copier, Model 1045, Serial No. XPF6666666

☐ Products of Collateral are also covered.

Whichever is Applicable (See Instruction Number 9)

Signature(s) of Debtor (Or Assignor)   Signature(s) of Secured Party (Or Assignee)

Filing Officer Copy — Alphabetical
STANDARD FORM — UNIFORM COMMERCIAL CODE — FORM UCC-1   Rev. Jan. 1980   *Forms may be purchased from Hobbs & Warren, Inc., Boston, Mass. 02101*

---

mental agency. The proper place of filing varies from state to state and may also depend on the type of collateral covered by the security agreement, so the statute in effect in the place where the collateral is located must be checked to assure proper filing.

Most states have adopted some version of a relatively standard financing statement which is called a Form UCC-1. There are some variations for different states and the requirements of your particular state should be checked. A completed UCC-1 relating to the purchase of office equipment appears above. The financing statement must be signed by the debtor, unless the security agreement signed by the debtor is filed with the financing statement. It is often necessary to file the financing statement with more than one office and a Form UCC-2 is designed for this purpose. It is a duplicate of the UCC-1, but has an extra sheet of carbon attached so that it can be placed over a UCC-1 and the form need only be typed once. There is also a form UCC-3 which may be used to continue, terminate, release, assign, or amend a previously filed UCC-1 financing statement.

REGULATION OF BUSINESS

Business enterprises are subject to a variety of statutes and regulations that may affect the conduct of the business generally or only specific aspects of its operation. There are statutes governing the creation of business corporations and providing rules for the basic structure and functioning of the corporation. The offering and issuance of securities is governed by another set of laws and regulations, and still other statutes regulate certain relationships between businesses. Some enterprises are subject to regulation because of the nature of their business. The most prominent examples of this specialized regulation are telephone and utility companies, insurance companies and, previously, the airline industry. Businesses dealing with consumers are generally subject to consumer protection statutes and companies involved in hazardous operations may be required by law to follow extraordinary safety precautions.

Every business with employees is also required to comply with a variety of laws and regulations relating to certain aspects of the employer-employee relationship, such as payment of wages, hours worked, discrimination, worker safety, and benefits for injured workers. It would be beyond the scope of this chapter to attempt to identify all of the regulatory statutes that may be of concern in the operation of many businesses. It will be useful, however, to identify two areas that are likely to be relevant in the daily operation of a general business office — corporate law and the employment relationship — and to discuss some of the general policies and specific statutes in these areas.

Corporate Law

Corporations exist only if created in accordance with state law. Every state has enacted a statute that sets forth the requirements for establishing the corporation and maintaining its corporate existence. General rules relating to corporate functions such as issuance of stock and the holding of annual stockholder meetings are also found in the statute. Often, much of the paperwork relating to the creation and continued existence of the corporation is done by the corporation's counsel. There are, however, certain forms and procedures that you may see in the course of your work, and we hope that the forthcoming general explanation will be of assistance to you in understanding these matters.

The charter document for a corporation is often called a *Certificate of Incorporation, Articles of Organization,* or something similar, and usually contains the following information: the name of the corporation and its purposes; the type and number of shares of corporate stock authorized; any stock restrictions or special rules for the governing of the corporation; and the names of the initial officers and directors of the company. The charter document must be filed with the proper state office, usually the secretary of state, and becomes effective upon approval. Amendments can be made by vote of the stockholders of the corporation and also must be filed and approved to become effective.

The corporate Bylaws are the rules by which the corporation conducts its internal affairs. The Bylaws, which must be consistent with state law, generally describe the relative functions and powers of the corporate officers, board of directors, and stockholders. Bylaws do not need to be filed and are effective upon adoption by the stockholders. They also can be amended by the stockholders, or in some instances by the board of directors.

A corporation is organized in three tiers. The stockholders own the stock, elect the board of directors, and must approve certain corporate actions such as authorization of additional stock, mergers, or sale of the corporate assets. The board of directors is responsible for overseeing the operation of the corporation at all levels and elects the corporate officers to handle the day-to-day affairs of the corporation. The officers, who generally include a president, one or more vice presidents, a treasurer, and a secretary or clerk, have such duties as are given them by the Bylaws or the board of directors. In a small company, the stockholders, directors, and officers are often comprised of a few individuals. Large corporations may have a very complex organization of officers and directors and usually a large number of stockholders not otherwise involved in the business.

Although the corporate structure is established pursuant to state law, one important aspect of the corporate operation — the sale of securities — is regulated under two federal securities statutes as well as securities statutes known as *Blue Sky laws* which are in effect in every sate. As a general rule, the securities statutes require that stock either be registered with a regulating authority or specifically be exempt from registration under the statute. Under the federal laws, stock that is not exempt must be registered with the Securities Exchange Commission (SEC) and each state has identified a state agency which enforces its Blue Sky law. Registration requires the preparation and filing of a statement and a prospectus that fully disclose pertinent facts about the history of the corporation, its financial and business affairs, and similar information. Once stock has been registered, the company must continually update the information that was provided in the statement filed upon initial registration. Properly registered stock may be publicly traded, which means that it may be offered for sale to the general public. All stock traded on the major stock exchanges or sold over the counter is registered stock.

The federal securities law and most of the state Blue Sky laws exempt private offerings or limited offerings from the registration requirement. Strict statutory requirements must be met to qualify for this exemption, but most small corporations whose stock is owned by a few individuals and which do not offer their stock for sale to outside investors qualify for this exemption. References to "public corporations" means those corporations which have registered their stock for sale to the general public. Private corporations with only a few stockholders actively involved in the corporate enterprise are often referred to as *closely held corporations.*

The Employment Relationship

The rights and obligations of employers and employees to one another are governed in part by the express agreement of the parties; in part by statutory regulation by federal, state, and local governments; and in part by the common law. Although the agreement of the employer and employee generally establishes the terms and conditions of the employment relationship, that agreement may intentionally or inadvertently fail to address many of the issues that arise during the course of employment. It may also include provisions that are unenforceable because they violate public policy or a specific statute.

Employment agreements. The agreement between the employer and the employee, like any contract, may be oral or written, simple or complex. It is important, from the perspective of both parties, that the agreement be as specific as possible with respect to the basic issues: What work is to be performed by the employee? Is there a formal performance review and evaluation? Is there a probationary period? What is the salary and when is it paid? Are there benefits such as medical and dental insurance, profit sharing or pension plans, and life insurance? Within the limits of certain regulatory statutes, these are all issues that are open for negotiation, and it is a good idea to raise them early. The oral and written agreement of the parties with respect to these and similar terms and conditions of employment constitute the employment contract. If the employer has written employee policies, these too will be considered as part of the employment contract. You should be aware that if you are interviewing or hiring new employees, you are considered an agent of your employer and what you say will be binding on the company.

In most instances, the relationship between the employer and employee is considered a contract "at-will." This means that it can be terminated by either party for almost any reason or for no reason. The agreement may require one or two weeks' notice, but generally no reason need be given to justify or explain the termination. Problems can arise upon termination by the employer, even in an at-will contract, when the reason for terminating is prohibited by law or public policy, such as when the employer terminates an employee in order to avoid paying a large commission that is about to become due.

Wages and hours. An employee cannot waive the protections established by the federal wage and hour laws. The National Fair Labor Standards Act, applicable to most employers having fifteen or more employees and engaged in interstate commerce, establishes minimum wages for regular and overtime work. The statute is enforced by the Wage and Hour Division of the Department of Labor. As a general rule, an employer must pay its employees not less than the minimum wage for the first forty hours of work per week. The employee must be compensated at one and one-half times his or her regular hourly rate for all hours worked in excess of forty hours for the week. In addition to the federal statute, there may be state and local laws that regulate the maximum number of hours a person can be required to work, whether work can be required on holidays or Sundays, under what conditions minors may work, and related issues.

Employment discrimination. A number of federal and state laws prohibit discrimination in employment. The federal laws include Title VII of the Civil Rights Act of 1964 (Title VII), which applies to most employers having at least fifteen employees and which makes it unlawful to base employment decisions on or to discriminate with respect to terms and conditions of employment because of an individual's race, color, religion, sex, or national origin; the Age Discrimination in Employment Act (ADEA), which prohibits most employers with twenty or more employees from discriminating against employees between the ages of forty and seventy; and the Equal Pay Act, which is part of the wage and hour law and which makes it illegal to pay unequal wages to men and women who do substantially equal work. In addition to these federal laws, many states have similar statutes prohibiting employment discrimination.

The federal Equal Employment Opportunity Commission (EEOC) monitors compliance with Title VII, ADEA, and the Equal Pay Act. Many states have local agencies or commissions responsible for enforcing the state discrimination statutes. The procedure established under most discrimination statutes requires the employee to file a claim with the proper agency within a relatively short time of the incident claimed to constitute discrimination. Generally, the agency then has the option to investigate, to attempt to conciliate, to bring a legal action on behalf of the claimant, or to authorize the individual to bring legal action. The filing of the claim within the period established by the applicable discrimination statute is almost always a prerequisite of later court action.

Some forms of employment discrimination are more obvious than others. It is important to note that a pattern or practice that tends to affect any of the identified classifications can constitute prohibited discrimination, even if there was no overt discrimination against an individual. Sexual harassment is a form of sex discrimination and exists where there are sexual advances, requests for sexual favors, and other verbal or physical conduct of a sexual nature. Sexual harassment is illegal if it affects the terms and conditions of an individual's employment or if it creates a hostile or negative working environment. Where a supervisory employee is responsible for a discriminatory decision, the employer will be liable. The employer also will be liable for discriminatory acts by employees who are not in supervisory positions if the employer is or should be aware of the conduct and does nothing to correct the situation. An employer guilty of employment discrimination may be required to hire or reinstate the affected individual, to pay back wages, and, in limited circumstances, to pay compensatory damages.

Workers' compensation. Workers' compensation laws have been enacted in every state. Although the statutes vary from state to state with respect to what kinds of employees are covered, how claims are administered, and what benefits are payable, they generally require that every employer maintain workers' compensation insurance to cover *compensable losses* of employees. Compensable losses can be very broadly defined as injuries from accidents or diseases resulting from an individual's employment.

Businesses are required to cover most employees by workers' compensation insurance, whether employed by a private business or by a public agency. A few statutes exempt businesses with fewer than three employees and some permit corporate officers, working partners, and owners of the business to be excluded from coverage. An employer can face significant penalties for failing to provide workers' compensation insurance, including fines, imprisonment, inability to raise defenses to a claim, personal liability of owners or corporate officers, and increased levels of compensation.

If an employee is injured on the job or suffers injury or disease resulting from his or her employment, the employee is entitled to receive compensation for lost wages, medical expenses, and rehabilitation costs. With few and limited exceptions, a worker's exclusive remedy against the employer for work-related injury is the recovery of workers' compensation benefits. This means that the employee cannot bring a personal injury suit against the employer, even if the employer was negligent or otherwise at fault for the injury. On the other hand, workers' compensation benefits are payable regardless of whether the employer was at fault. The theory underlying this system is that the employee is assured of a reasonable measure of compensation to be paid without delay, and the employer is relieved of the burden of defending personal injury suits in exchange for providing the insurance which pays the compensation benefits.

The amount of the benefits payable under workers' compensation is established by statute and depends primarily on the wage level of the injured employee, but also may involve other factors including the type of injury, whether the employee is totally or partially disabled, and whether the disability is temporary or permanent. There is usually a ceiling on the amount recoverable for a single injury. Workers' compensation insurance is available from private insurance companies and, in a few states, from a public fund. In addition, many states permit self-insurance by large corporations or groups of smaller businesses.

State workers' compensation statutes are governed in most states by a board or commission, and by the courts in a few states. The usual procedure is for an employee to file a claim with the employer and the employer to notify the insurance carrier. The administrative agency responsible for implementing the statute receives reports concerning claims and resolves disputes concerning the extent or duration of the injury and the amount of benefits payable.

Index